AF600127

Tamil Geographies

SUNY SERIES IN HINDU STUDIES

Wendy Doniger, *editor*

Tamil Geographies

Cultural Constructions of Space and Place in South India

Edited by
Martha Ann Selby
Indira Viswanathan Peterson

STATE UNIVERSITY OF NEW YORK PRESS

Published by
State University of New York Press, Albany

Printed in the United States of America

For information, address State University of New York Press,
www.sunypress.edu

Production by Kelli W. LeRoux
Marketing by Anne M. Valentine

Library of Congress Cataloging-in-Publication Data
Tamil geographies : cultural constructions of space and place in South India / edited by Martha Ann Selby, Indira Peterson.
p. cm. — (SUNY series in Hindu studies)
Includes bibliographical references and index.
ISBN 978-0-7914-7245-3 (hardcover : alk. paper)
1. Tamil (Indic people) 2. Tamil Nadu (India)—Civilization.
3. Social ecology—India—Tamil Nadu.
4. Tamil literature—Criticism and interpretation.
I. Selby, Martha Ann. II. Peterson, Indira Viswanathan, 1950–
DS432.T3T355 2007
305.89'481105482—dc22 2007010149

10 9 8 7 6 5 4 3 2 1

In memory of

A. K. Ramanujan (1929–1993)

Poet, Scholar, Friend

Contents

Acknowledgments

The editors would like to thank Nancy Ellegate of SUNY Press for her vision, guidance, efficiency, and infinite patience throughout the process of making this book, and to Wendy Doniger for graciously agreeing to include us in her series. Thanks are also due to Kelli W. LeRoux, senior production editor, for so ably guiding us through the last stages of the publishing process. We would also like to express our gratitude to our anonymous readers who made invaluable suggestions about organization, content, and the overall intellectual framing of the book, and to Paula Richman and to the late Norman Cutler for their encouragement and enthusiasm. These two generous scholars also gave us some very early and excellent advice on putting such a volume together. Norman's sudden death in early 2002 was a great blow to everyone in Tamil studies, and every single author represented in this volume has been deeply affected by the huge loss of an excellent scholar and a loyal, loving friend. We also mourn the loss of D. Dennis Hudson, extraordinary scholar, teacher, and advocate of Tamil studies. Dennis died after a long fight with cancer in December, 2006. We also thank every one of our versatile contributors for their hard work, superb writing, and good will from start to finish. We offer a vote of thanks to W. Roger Louis and the British Studies Seminar at the University of Texas at Austin for providing the funds for us to be able to generate the maps, graphics, and bibliography that accompany this volume, as well as our thanks to the person who toiled so hard to make them, Jarrod Whitaker.

Isabelle Clark-Decès' essay originally appeared under the title "Expel the Lover, Recover the Wife: Symbolic Analysis of a South Indian Exorcism" in *The Journal of the Royal Anthropological Institute* (N.S.) 3(2). Sections of it are included in her book, *Religion Against the Self: An Ethnography of Tamil Rituals* (New York: Oxford University Press, copyright 2000 by Isabelle Nabokov. Used by permission of Oxford University Press, Inc.). Both were published under the name of Isabelle Nabokov. The first few sections of Martha Ann Selby's essay appear in the third chapter of her book, *Grow Long, Blessed Night: Love*

Poems from Classical India (New York: Oxford University Press, copyright 2000 by Martha Ann Selby. Used by permission of Oxford University Press, Inc.). A slightly different version of Sara Dickey's contribution to this volume appears in *American Ethnologist* (27, 2: 462–489, May 2000. Reproduced by permission of the American Anthropological Association. Not for sale or further reproduction). A somewhat different version of Diane P. Mines's essay appeared as chapter 8 of her book *Fierce Gods: Inequality, Ritual, and the Politics of Dignity in a South Indian Village* (Bloomington: Indiana University Press, 2005. Used by permission). Sections of Susan Seizer's essay appear as excerpts in chapter 5 (pp. 202–231) of her book *Stigmas of the Tamil Stage: An Ethnography of Special Drama Artists in South India* (Copyright 2005, Duke University Press. All rights reserved. Used by permission of the publisher). We are most grateful to Oxford University Press, Indiana University Press, *American Ethnologist,* and Duke University Press for so kindly granting us permission to reprint these materials. We also wish to thank the Center for Asian Studies at the University of Texas at Austin and its director Kathryn Hansen for providing the funds for reprinting charges.

We would like to point out to our readers that some inconsistencies in our transliteration of Tamil and Sanskrit words remain. We have tried to be as consistent as possible, but some disciplinary differences as well as the diversity of subject matter have made some variations inevitable.

Finally, it gives us great pleasure to dedicate this volume to the memory of the late A. K. Ramanujan, whose brilliant translations and interpretations of classical Tamil poetry introduced a whole generation of scholars to the "interior landscapes" of Tamil literature and culture. We believe that he would have been pleased with the ways in which the essays in this volume build upon and resonate with his own work.

Martha Ann Selby
Austin, Texas

Indira Viswanathan Peterson
South Hadley, Massachusetts

Introduction

What the map cuts up, the story cuts across.
—*Michel de Certeau*

This volume is a collection of essays that examine various registers and modes of dialogue among people, land, and space in Tamil South India. The region we are concerned with is the area of peninsular South India roughly corresponding to the modern state of Tamilnadu.[1] Cultural constructions of place and space have been of central importance throughout the history of this region. Focusing on the notion of geography in its strictest sense, that is, on verbal descriptions of land and space and how these descriptions build and inform diverse social and aesthetic realities, each essay in this volume raises and addresses conceptual issues regarding Tamil geographies. The authors examine "texts" drawn from a range of time periods and a variety of sources in Tamil society and culture: imaginative literature, performances, historical events and narratives, religious rituals, and daily life in contemporary Tamilnadu. The essays offer fresh interpretations and methodological approaches.

The idea for this book grew out of conversations that took place among some of the authors, in the context of a panel on the topic of "Tamil Geographies" at the University of Wisconsin's Annual Conference on South Asia. Martha Ann Selby, the convener of the panel, had been intrigued by the ways in which the insights of her anthropologist friends working on Tamil culture resonated with her own interests and findings related to conceptions of space in Tamil literature. Key ideas regarding landscape that she had discerned in the constructions of aesthetic universes in classical Tamil poetics were reflected—transmuted, yes, but still recognizable in language and practice—in contemporary Tamil discourses about space and identity. The original participants in the Madison panel, Martha Ann Selby, Indira Viswanathan Peterson, Isabelle Clark-Decès, Diane P. Mines, and E. Valentine Daniel (the discussant), were amazed and delighted at how well the papers—on classical poetry, eighteenth-century drama, the narrative of a village temple ritual, and a ritual exorcism—deepened and informed each other. We decided to put together a volume of essays on Tamil geographies, with Selby and Peterson collaborating as editors. The scholars who joined our enterprise have enriched and widened its scope with their essays on the cosmographies of a medieval royal dynasty, the sacred geographies of an ancient city and a Śaiva religious poem, Tamil temple architecture, and the spatial discourses of the theatrical stage and the home in Tamilnadu today. Together, the essays explore the idea of an identifiably Tamil disposition or range of attitudes, a Tamil habitus (in Pierre Bourdieu's terminology) regarding space and place.

Tamil Geographies in the Context of the Scholarship on Space and Place

The authors of these essays are indebted in varying degrees to the writings of Pierre Bourdieu (1977) and Michel de Certeau (1984) on culture. We have also engaged with the recent surge of interest in the cultural discourses of space and place that has resulted in several volumes of essays on these subjects by anthropologists and cultural geographers. The social and cultural construction of place is the focus of *Senses of Place* (Feld and Basso, editors, 1996), a collection of essays from diverse disciplinary perspectives, and *Inventing Places: Studies in Cultural Geography* (Anderson and Gale, editors, 1992), essays by cultural geographers. The essayists in *Place/Culture/Representation* (Duncan and Ley, editors, 1993) are concerned with representations and discourses in the Western discipline of cultural geography, and European representations of the geographies of "others" in particular. The writings in *The Anthropology of Landscape: Perspectives on Place and Space* (Hirsch and O'Hanlon, editors, 1995) focus on the idea of landscape as the site of interaction between space and place. All of these recent collections have illumined space and place as socially and culturally constructed ideas. In the new scholarship, European ideologies of time and space have been set in juxtaposition with non-Western ones, and European "geographical" representations of the spatial environments of cultural others have been placed against indigenous understandings to challenge the claims to the objectivity of Enlightenment and colonialist geographical projects. Following the challenge of feminist and postmodern critiques, these essays have also broadened the field of cultural geography to include voices, perspectives, and subjects that had previously been excluded—female, non-elite, and non-exotic everyday spaces in the "modern" West itself—thus acknowledging geographical constructions as sites of contestations for power.[2]

The thematic and interdisciplinary range of our own volume, and its geographically specific focus, are intentional. We take our cue from Anderson and Gale, who suggest that "the cultural process by which people construct their understandings of the world is an inherently geographic concern. In the course of generating new meanings and decoding existing ones, people construct spaces, places, landscapes, regions, and environments. In short, they construct geographies" (*Inventing Places,* 1992, p. 4). By examining cosmology, space, landscape, environment, region, village, temple, the home and stage, in short, the entire range of geographical constructions in Tamil India, we hope to illumine the nature of these constructions in the context of broader, interrelated ideas of place and space. We approach verbal as well as other sorts of geographical constructions as *process,* hoping to give insight into how Tamils tell what Michel de Certeau has called "spatial stories"; how, through imaginative and expressive acts and performances, space becomes a "practiced place" in the Tamil region. We believe that the focus on a specific cultural region allows us to pursue the kind of "local" knowledge without which theory loses its edge. As Clifford Geertz puts it in his essay on the value of micro-studies of particular places and cultures, studying particular cultural geographies "is not a matter of reducing large things to small. . . . It is a matter of giving shape to things: exactness, force, intelligibility."[3]

The essays also interrogate univocal readings of Tamil geographies throughout history. We are interested in migrations, fissures, erasures, and displacements, as much as in dwellings and continuities, in margins and peripheries as well as in centers and centering, in exclusions and contestations as well as in affirmations, as these are manifested over time in the geographical discourses of the Tamil region. The thematic explorations reveal other sorts of dialogues at play within Tamil cultural discourses themselves, for instance, among older Tamil and transregional constructions of space. Among the conversations we wish to represent and generate in this book are those among humanists and anthropologists, with respect to the ideas of space and place. Returning to the question with which we began—"Is there a 'Tamil' grammar of space and place?"—we find that our essays test the limits of our diverse disciplinary approaches, and suggest that the answers to the questions are more complex than we might have imagined at the beginning of our enterprise.

The "Tamil" Region in Historical Perspective

The definition of regions and regionalism in India has been the subject of much discussion among anthropologists, sociologists and cultural geographers of South Asia.[4] While there is considerable evidence for the existence in the Indian subcontinent throughout the history of cultural regions conceived on a variety of bases, the most recent subdivision of the territories of the Indian nation-state after 1947 has been into "linguistic" states that are at the same time recognized as "cultural" regions with long histories. Marked by the dominance of the Dravidian language Tamil, with an ancient literature (dating back to the second century C.E. at the very least) and historical consciousness rooted in the region, the peninsular portion of South India has always tacitly been recognized as a distinct cultural region.[5] Late nineteenth- and early twentieth-century movements emphasizing perceived continuities with an older "Tamil" regional and language-based culture have played an important role in the construction of the modern linguistic state of Tamilnadu (Irschick, 1969; Ramaswamy, 1997, 1999).[6]

Classical Tamil literature is explicitly conscious about the close relationships among language, geographical territory, and culture. The first book of the *Tolkāppiyam,* the oldest extant grammar of Tamil language and poetry, is prefaced by an introductory verse that defines the geographical boundaries of the region in which the Tamil language and its grammar are operative; this is "the good world where Tamil is spoken (stretching from) northern Vēṅkaṭam to Kumari in the South."[7] Later texts offer variations of this formula.[8] The contours of the map of modern Tamilnadu are not widely divergent from this ancient "map," except for the splitting off of Cēranāṭu, the southwestern portion of the ancient region, into medieval and modern Kerala, with its own language (Malayalam) and distinct cultural identity.[9] When the Telugu-speaking state of Andhra Pradesh was carved out of the older Madras presidency in 1956, the Vēṅkaṭam hill (modern Tirupati), about one hundred miles north of Madras, the older northern boundary of the Tamil culture-area, was absorbed into Andhra Pradesh.

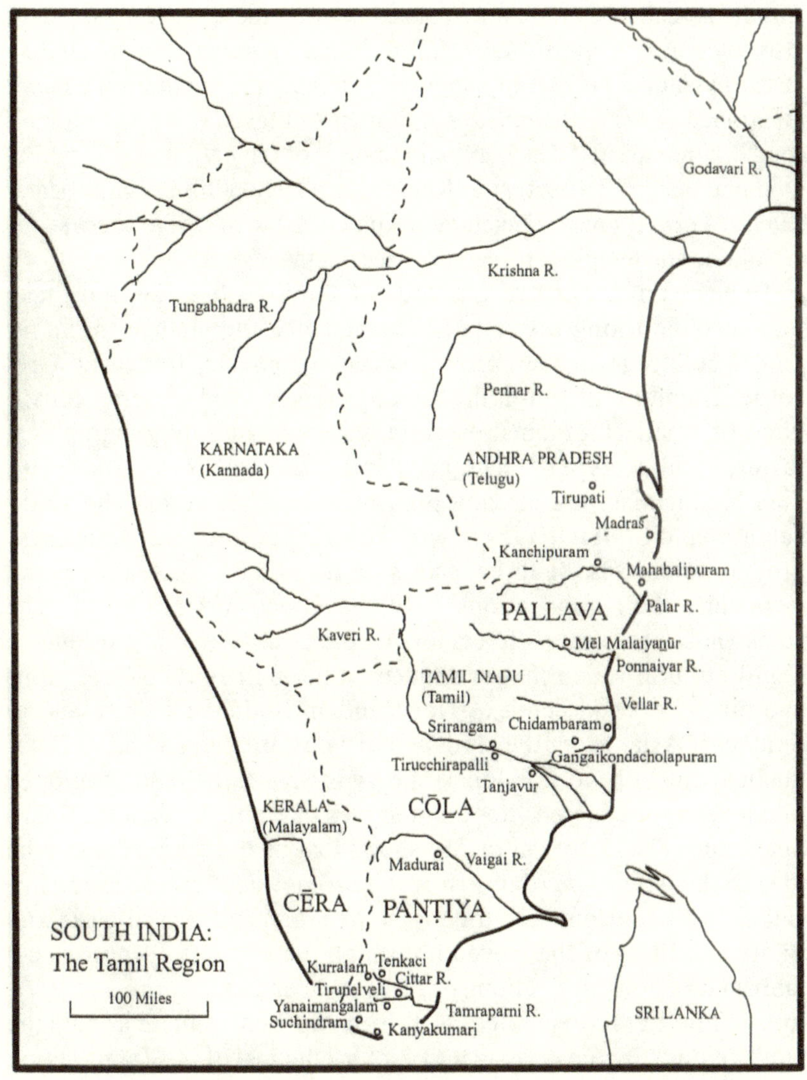

The modern state of Tamil Nadu (in 1969, the name "Madras" was changed to "the land of Tamil" or "the land of the Tamils")[10] covers the plains of the rivers Palar, Kaveri, Pennar, and Tamraparni, corresponding to the *nāṭu* and *maṇṭalam* territories of the Pallava, Cōḻa, and Pāṇṭiya rulers of the fifth through the sixteenth centuries. The region is bounded by the Western Ghats mountain ranges and Kerala (the old Cēra territory) in the west, the Coorg (Kudagu) hills in the northwest, and the so-called Coromandel coastal plain in the east. Kanyakumari, also known as Cape Comorin (Tamil *kumari muṉai*) on the Indian Ocean, identical at least in name with *kumari,* the southern boundary mentioned in the *Tolkāppiyam* and other old texts, mark the region's southern boundary.[11] The continuing power of the notion of a Tamil region bounded by Tirupati and 'Kumari' is reflected in *Vēṅkaṭam Mutal Kumari Varai* ("From Vēṅkaṭam to Kumari"), the title of a recent series of volumes on temples and sacred places in the region.[12]

To be complete, however, a study of Tamil geographies must take into account a long history of heterogeneity and change in the regional culture.[13] In the *caṅkam* corpus of poems, the earliest recorded literature in Tamil, the region is represented as being constituted of small chiefdoms, essentially demarcated by geographical features and ecotypes.[14] The gods and ritual practices of north Indian brahmanism are already present in this literature. The sixth-century epic *Cilappatikāram,* with its strongly Jaina religious background, celebrates the three realms (*nāṭu*) of the Cōḻa, Pāṇṭiya, and Cēra, and their connections with the Greco-Roman world. The somewhat later (seventh century) epic *Maṇimēkalai* presents a Tamil cultural space that is connected through Buddhist religious and other networks, both to North Indian Buddhist culture and to Southeast Asia. From the sixth century onward, the spread of brahmanical cults of the worship of the gods Śiva and Viṣṇu developed into a system of sacred sites and temples that transformed the Tamil landscape. The historical record shows that by the tenth century, the idea of the *maṇṭalam* (Sanskrit *maṇḍala*) political sphere as territorial unit was entrenched in peninsular South India. The Cōḻa and Pāṇṭiya polities of the eleventh through the sixteenth centuries established regional inflections of royal style and conceptions of territory. While Kerala separated itself from the Tamil sphere around the tenth century, by the seventeenth century the rest of the Tamil region came under the rule of Telugu Nayaks who migrated from the Vijayanagar empire in the Deccan. By the eighteenth century, this region included pockets of rule by rulers of varied linguistic and cultural allegiance, such as the Nawab of Arcot and the Marathas of Tanjore, as well as the European coastal settlements that preceded full-fledged British colonial rule. In various ways, our essays reflect on the role of change and the mix of cultural currents in the formation of Tamil geographical discourses.

Space, Place, and Person in Tamil Culture

The most significant studies of Tamil culture in the last thirty years have brought out the centrality of the geographical imagination in this culture. Exploring the world of the earliest Tamil poetic anthologies, A. K. Ramanujan (1967 and 1985) has shown that the aesthetic of *caṅkam* poetry is founded on a grammar of space.[15] According to the exposition of this aesthetic in the *Tolkāppiyam* (probably written in layers over a period ranging from the second century B.C.E. to perhaps as late as the fifth century C.E.), these poems are fundamentally classified into poems of *akam* ("inside"), with love as their subject matter, and poems of *puṟam* ("outside"), with war and public life as their subjects. As we shall see, *akam* and *puṟam* are not merely thematic divisions in ancient poetry but complex concepts that continue to pervade Tamil culture as contrastive pairs, encompassing such "interior/exterior" pairings as heart/body surface, kin/non-kin, and home/world. Both love and war poems are constructed from shared, basic poetic materials. These consist of *mutal* (the "first things"), that is, time (*poḻutu*) and place/type of land (*nilam*); *karu* ("native elements"), that is, the elements characteristically found in a particular type of place, including flora, fauna, and human populations; and *uri* (human feelings) appropriately set in *mutal* and *karu.* Although human feelings are the ultimate focus of these classical Tamil poems, they can be delineated *only in place,* specifically in one of the five "landscapes," (*tiṇais*) into which space is organized, and that correspond to the major ecotypes (*nilam*) of the Tamil region: hill, field, pasture, seashore, and wasteland.[16] The *Tolkāppiyam* and the *caṅkam* poems themselves offer nothing less than an early Tamil cosmology, in which space is perceived in terms of the contrasted categories of interiority and exteriority, as well as in terms of specific landscapes, with each of these categories and classes of "natural" space being precisely correlated with what would normally be perceived as aspects of culture: human beings, their feelings and actions, and their artifacts.

Place, in the specific sense of a particular location, has been identified as a fundamentally important category in Tamil culture. From at least the sixth century onward, in the Tamil regional setting, the worship of the brahmanical gods Śiva and Viṣṇu became cults of expressive devotion (*bhakti*) to these gods, in the form of particular personae, dwelling in specific places in the Tamil country.[17] The resulting proliferation of temples and sacred places (*pati, talam*) dedicated to these gods in the Tamil region has been termed a "sacred geography" (Spencer, 1970). Although the localization of deities and myths is by no means a peculiarly Tamil phenomenon, historians of religion have shown that orientation to place is fundamental to Tamil religion in ways that are not shared by Hindu and other religious traditions in other regions of India (e.g., Shulman, 1980). At the same time, while drawing on the spatial and aesthetic world of the *caṅkam* poems, *bhakti* and temple religion postulate very different brahmanical cosmographies in which gods, mortals, and others dwell in complex, ordered spatial worlds later systematically described in the cosmographical sections of the Sanskrit *purāṇas,* pan-Indian compendia of mythic and cosmological lore. In a widely accepted version of *purāṇic* geography, the earth (*bhūrloka*) consists of seven concentric island-continents (*dvīpa*), each surrounded by an ocean. Bhārata-varṣa (the modern South Asian subcontinent) is the southernmost region of Jambu-dvīpa ("Rose-apple Island"), which is the most central of the continents, and which has at its center the cosmic Mount Meru, itself the bearer of the celestial abode of the gods.[18] In his seminal work on peasant history in South India, Burton Stein has identified the territorial segmentation of society and culture—already present in the five landscape/culture types of the *caṅkam* poems—as a major distinguishing characteristic of the South Indian region (which he defines as including portions of the Telugu and Kannada-speaking areas, with the Kaveri basin of the Tamil region as the "core" region; Stein, 1980, pp. 54–56). Stein argues that this characteristic relates to the more intensely localized nature of interaction among social groups in South India than in other parts of the Indian subcontinent, exemplified, for instance, in the narrow territorial areas in which marriage and descent systems in South India operate, in comparison with their north Indian counterparts.[19] David Ludden, on the other hand, argues for a more balanced narrative of peasant history in the Tamil region, one in which the importance of social creativity and change stimulated by "widening spheres of social interaction" are given equal weight, without deemphasizing the particularities of the localizing disposition in Tamil culture (Ludden, 1985, pp. 3–18).

According to anthropologist E. Valentine Daniel, the relationships between a Tamil villager and the spaces and places he inhabits and the phenomena and persons he relates with—his body, his *ūr* ("home-village"), his sexual partner—are negotiated through an interaction of his own substance with that of the other, with the aim of maintaining or bringing about an equilibrium of substances (Daniel, 1984, pp. 1–12).

In this view, in Tamil culture, person and place interact with each other in organic ways. Both inhabited spaces (the house, the *ūr,* the *nāṭu*) and the persons who inhabit them, have porous, fluid boundaries (Daniel, 1984, chapters 2 and 3). In fact, Daniel argues that for Tamil villagers, unlike concepts such as *tēcam* (country) and *kirāmam* (village, settlement), *nāṭu* and *ūr,* a person's "home-land" and "home-village," are "person-centric terms that derive their meaning from the contextually shifting spatial orientation of the person" (Daniel, 1984, p. 70). One cannot help noticing the parallels between the home-village that is defined by its interactions with persons, the temples and sacred sites of Tamil *bhakti* religion, and the landscape-types of *caṅkam* poetry, with their designated populations.

A major insight that emerges in the above studies of Tamil culture is that, equally in classical Tamil poetry, medieval *bhakti* religion, and in spatial practices in a modern Tamil village, space and place are "person-centric" and inherently imbued with specific moral and aesthetic qualities. While Daud Ali, in his essay in this volume, rightly points out that this conception of space as an inherently "qualified" phenomenon is a pan-Indian one, the essays presented here, including Ali's own, illuminate specifically Tamil cultural inflections of the idea, especially in complex imaginings of space *as* place. In this connection we might mention a recent essay by Sumathi Ramaswamy on the ways in which late-nineteenth-century Tamil intellectuals deployed European theories of the "lost continent" of Lemuria to remap the Tamil region (*tamiḻakam*). The new maps made by the Tamil literati included geographical features which are mentioned in older Tamil literature, and are said to have been lost to the sea during the Lemurian catastrophes (these include the apocryphal Kumari river and mountain). Through this deployment of Lemuria, Ramaswamy argues, the Tamil mapmakers reclaimed lost cultural territory for the Tamil land, and cartographically converted Lemuria from "the paleo-*space* of the European imagination into the lived *place* of the Tamil imagination."[20]

While the essays in this volume build on the pioneering scholarship of Ramanujan, Daniel, and others, each essay explores new material or takes a new methodological stance toward familiar "texts." The original and important questions about Tamil geographies raised here should bring us considerably closer to describing a Tamil habitus of space and place. For example, the discussion of center-periphery cosmologies in several of the essays, in diverse historical, social, and disciplinary contexts, such as temple architecture and conceptualizations of political territory, allows us to explore the interactions between these and the older and, it seems, remarkably persistent, *akam/puṟam* pairing in Tamil culture over time and across milieux. As will be evident from the brief descriptions of the individual essays that follow, together the essays in this book give new insights into the relationships between verbal texts and the expressive practices through which space and place are constructed in the Tamil region, and make us look afresh at the ways in which space, place, person, and communities relate to one another in Tamil culture.

The Essays

Martha Ann Selby's essay, "Dialogues of Space, Desire, and Gender in Tamil *Caṅkam* Poetry," discusses the earliest theoretical formulations of the conventions that inform classical Tamil poetry and poetics. These conventions resurface in surprising and myriad ways in later Tamil literary texts and cultural practices. Her essay thus serves as an introduction to the other essays in the volume. Selby begins with a discussion of the aesthetic system developed in the oldest extant grammar and poetics in Tamil, the *Tolkāppiyam,* based on a language of space that is articulated in terms of the fluid complementarities of *akam* and *puṟam,* resonating with *tiṇai* landscapes (see above). Selby shows that the ultimate goal of *caṅkam* rhetoric as described in the *Tolkāppiyam* is the erasure, through poetic means, of what critic Georges Poulet has called the "sense of incompatibility between consciousness and objects of consciousness." She suggests that the language of the *caṅkam* poets arose from a desire for the erasure of the split between self and *tiṇai* (geographic/poetic "landscape"), foisting this desire outward onto the environment itself. Through close readings of poems from the two anthologies *Naṟṟiṇai* and *Kuṟuntokai,* Selby examines several ways in which the *caṅkam* poets reshaped their geophysical surroundings by literally "incorporating" them and transforming them into a system of language and poetic "gesture."

Norman J. Cutler's essay, "Four Spatial Realms in *Tirukkōvaiyār,*" provides an exploration of the reworking of classical Tamil literary convention within a medieval Śaiva devotional framework. *Tirukkōvaiyār,* composed by the ninth-century saint Māṇikkavācakar, is perhaps the finest example of a work from the *kōvai* genre, wherein the romantic elements of *akam* (expressed through the themes and conventions of love poems) mingle with heroic *puṟam* themes, here evoked in reference to the persona of the god Śiva, who is the hero of the poem. In this poem, interleaved with the classical dimensions of landscape delineated in the *Tolkāppiyam* are other sacred geographies, of Śiva's local residences in Tamilnadu and his "translocal" residence on Mount Kailāsa in the northern Himālaya mountain range. Cutler examines the ways in which these several geographies are configured in *Tirukkōvaiyār* and how they construct a specific poetic vision of sacred Śaiva reality in the Tamil context.

Indira Viswanathan Peterson explores the ways in which the *kuṟavañci,* an eighteenth-century Tamil dramatic genre, deploys discourses of landscape, continuing patterns from the classical and medieval literature, yet diverging from them in significant respects. Written by court poets for rulers of small "kingdoms," *kuṟavañci* plays glorify the patron-king, his town (*ūr*), and the god of the temple located in that town. However, the central characters in the *kuṟavañci* genre, the eponymous Kuṟavañci, a nomadic fortune-teller from the hills, and her birdcatcher husband, are marginal figures from the wilderness. Their activities are described in detail, in relation to the hill and field landscapes, and to the upper-class characters in the play, including the lovelorn lady whose fortune the Kuṟavañci tells. Peterson suggests that the genre's innovative treatment of older landscape conventions, and its focus on new and marginal social identities, embody an imaginative response to changing social relations and relations between person and land in Tamilnadu in an era of migrations and fragmented polities. This essay reminds us in a striking way of the uncanny talent that Tamil poets have for infusing the mundane world with profound poetic and symbolic significance.

In "Ruling in the Gaze of God: Thoughts on Kanchipuram's *Maṇḍala,*" D. Dennis Hudson discusses the symbolically potent threads that weave through *caṅkam* literature, Hindu, Buddhist, and Jaina religious narratives, temple architecture, and city planning. Poykai, an eighth-century poet, described the main temple complex at Kanchipuram as "a fortified and blooming flower that never closed," thereby building on an earlier poet's description of the city as an "open lotus blossom." Peeling away the many layers of development, urban growth, and modernity, Hudson employs the descriptions of the city found in old Tamil and Chinese texts as a lens through which discernment of the original city plan—a lotus-shaped *maṇḍala*—is made possible. He reflects on the many ways in which geographies are reflexive and found reciprocally mirrored in multivalent orderings of urban, cosmic, and ritual spaces.

Daud Ali defines geography as "an inquiry into the changing relations, both material and ideological, between humans and their physical environments" in his essay titled "Cosmos, Realm, and Property in Early Medieval South India." Linking the hierarchized ontologies found in early *purāṇic* texts with medieval geographies that are at once topographical and ideological, Ali examines the fascinating homologies created by kings between *purāṇic* ontology and royal conquest, and describes royal attempts to center polities in such a way that kings are not merely the centers of their own physical kingdoms, but are at the center of the whole of Bhārata-varṣa. Ali cites a specific case of such recentering and reorganization in a study of the imperial formation of the Cōḻa dynasty as its kings attempted to rearticulate their realms within the geographical construct of Bhārata-varṣa. Likening the mountain, temple, river, country, wasteland, court, city, and balcony of medieval literature to the *caṅkam tiṇai* system in that these places have "inherent and differential moral and aesthetic value," Ali challenges us to understand "place" in Cōḻa India as a construct that is fundamentally at odds with cartographic space.

Samuel K. Parker's essay, "Sanctum and *Gopuram* at Madurai: Aesthetics of *Akam* and *Puṟam* in Tamil Temple Architecture," proposes a "reading" of Hindu temples as architectural "texts." Parker's theoretically fresh and elegant argument that architecture is in itself a language that changes and evolves over time in much the same way in which linguistic usage changes over time through praxis serves to uncover the patterns of encoding that are metaphorically embodied in Tamil temples. Parker recognizes the "spatiotemporal aesthetics" set out in early *caṅkam* literature—the fluid complementarity of *akam* and *puṟam*—in the "spatiotemporal order of the later Dravidian temple style," even as it continues to develop in the present context. Working with A. K. Ramanujan's description of a *caṅkam* poem as expanding and contracting "in concentric circles, with the concrete physical particular at the center, getting more and more inclusive and abstract as we move outward," Parker demonstrates the spatial concentricity of Dravidian temples as "perpetually incomplete structures-in-process," with the intimate *akam* of the sanctum gradually opening outward to the public *puṟam* exteriors marked by the *gopurams*.

In "From Wasteland to Bus Stand: The Relocation of Demons in Tamilnadu," Isabelle Clark-Decès argues that Tamil women are "taught, even pressured, to frame their personal predicaments within the idiom of demonic possession"; that is, possession by *pēys,* who are generally thought to be spirits of humans who have met with an untimely end. Their deaths usually result from suicides due to unrequited love, and their attacks on young women are said to be motivated by love, lust, and an obsessive desire for intimacy. In her ethnographic study, Clark-Decès identifies specific landscapes in which these possessions occur, which are fallow, dry wastelands beyond the boundaries of settled areas. The landscapes of *pēy* possession are intimately tied to classical *caṅkam* constructions of wasteland or, more specifically, to the *tiṇai* called *pālai* (that of vast, desert wastes and abject hardship and separation) both spatially and temporally. Here, the romantic "separation" that occurs within *akam* poetry of the *pālai* type is brought about by the *pēy,* who catches "his girl" and forces her mental and physical separation from her community and from her husband. In her brilliant analysis of ritual discourses surrounding *pēy* possession, Clark-Decès uncovers what amounts to a "reinvention" of *pālai* conventions to suit the urban contexts of postmodernity: desolate, arid wastelands are reidentified as bus stands, railway tracks, or roads to movie theaters.

In her lyrical ethnographic essay, Diane P. Mines explores ways in which "movement makes space" in "Waiting for Veḷḷāḷakaṇṭaṉ: Narrative, Movement, and Making Place in a Tamil Village." Working with Michel de Certeau's assertion that "space is actuated by the ensemble of movements deployed within it," Mines describes some specific ways in which the residents of a village (*ūr*) in Tirunelvēli District define the *ūr* by the walks they take around and through it. She explains this "actuation of space" in terms of movement as narrative, as a form of "telling," arguing that different processional routes taken by different temple organizations "make" the village in multiple discursive ways. Since "each procession produces an alternative social and spatial reality in competition with other versions of that reality," Mines suggests that we cannot understand the *ūr* in terms of a fixed spatial entity, but that it must be understood as "a set of overlapping alternatives." Through her analysis of the story of Veḷḷāḷakaṇṭaṉ and the processions that honor him, Mines demonstrates how these multivalent "tellings" and enactments form part of "a current discourse on spatial and social relations" in the *ūr*.

Sara Dickey explores the *akam/puṟam* continuum in contemporary domestic boundary-making in her essay titled "Permeable Homes: Domestic Service, Household Space, and the Vulnerability of Class Boundaries in Urban South India." Domestic workers help to create and support their employers' class standing, but also introduce dangerous "outside" elements into a protected "inside" order. Domestic service "involves a mixing of spatial categories" which informs and "continually shapes daily behavior . . . molds . . . concepts of self and other, and affects . . . movements through space." Dickey deftly illustrates the fluidity of *akam* and *puṟam* in her meticulous discussion of domestic spaces; for instance, how particular parts of a home are more "*akam*" than others, or how something as seemingly public as a street is actually *akam* in certain contexts. In her interviews with middle and upper-class employers and with domestic workers, she analyzes concerns and fears about boundary and class transgressions, and what can be transported across boundaries by servants: they can bring in *puṟam* dirt, morals, and disease, and carry out *akam* property and secrets. Arguing that shifting *akam* and *puṟam* complementarities are central to constructions of class identity, Dickey clearly demonstrates that women householders are the primary producers and protectors of class status.

In the final essay of this collection, "Gender Plays: Socio-spatial Paradigms on the Tamil Popular Stage," Susan Seizer analyzes the use of stage space during performances of a popular theater genre known as "Special *Nāṭakam*" ("Special Drama"). Arguing that "the organization and use of stage space in Special Drama enables what is enacted on stage to speak directly to the dominant organization of Tamil social relations offstage," Seizer explores the gender dynamics of the comedic duet that typically opens plays of this genre. She finds dialogic ties with classical Tamil conventions, and juxtaposes these with "some of the more uncomfortable ambivalences" that structure contemporary gender relations. She particularly examines the lives of actresses, women who invert the typical Tamil ideal of "the chaste wife" due to the public nature of their livelihoods. As Seizer puts it, being constantly in the public limelight "threatens to expose the fragility of the culturally naturalized division of gendered spheres into home and world, as actresses move onto public stages to enact what are meant to be the most private of relations." In her detailed and refreshing analysis, Seizer offers us her intimate understanding of the Special Drama stage as gendered space; as a space that is, once again, "actuated" by human movement.

In sum, every essay addresses basic problems of boundaries and definitions of space, and how these are continually modified (and sometimes even radically violated) to redraw parameters and remake identities by superimposing and "grafting" new borders onto old. Although each essay draws on a different discipline and employs a different methodological approach, it is apparent from each one that lines between the "literary" and the "anthropological," for instance, are often blurred, and at times totally erased. While we have no pretensions or illusions of being comprehensive, it is our hope that this volume will serve well as an interdisciplinary introduction to Tamil culture. The essays clearly demonstrate the ways in which early aesthetic and linguistic paradigms have survived through the present moment as living, vital expressions through which contemporary boundaries are shaped and constructed—through poetic convention, temple construction, ritual experience, through concerns about maintaining differences between the "home" and the "world," and by an act as seemingly simple as taking a walk. They also illuminate the many ways in which, when confronted by new paradigms and experiences, Tamil individuals have continually modified and restructured classical paradigms through literary and metaphorical mapping, to reshape political, social, and religious identities. We hope that the volume will be of use to teachers of general courses on Asian and South Asian civilizations, and that it will also provide comparative material for use in courses on literature, anthropology, and religion. Even though the essays are, for the most part, grouped by "discipline," we strongly encourage our readers to read the book randomly, or to read the essays in tandem across academic disciplines. We would suggest, for instance, that our readers pair Norman J. Cutler's essay with Daud Ali's, Martha Ann Selby's with Isabelle Clark-Decès', Indira Viswanathan Peterson's with Diane P. Mines' or Susan Seizer's, or perhaps Samuel K. Parker's essay with Susan Seizer's, in order to experience the rich and endlessly generative nature of Tamil conceptions of space and place.

Notes

1. The idea of a 'Tamil' region is discussed more thoroughly below.
2. "Anthropologists are concerned less about place in broad philosophical and humanistic terms than about places as sites of power struggles or about displacement, as histories of annexation, absorption, and resistance." Feld and Basso, 1996, p. 5.
3. Geertz, "Afterword," in Feld and Basso, 1996, p. 262.
4. See, for instance, Crane, ed., 1967, a collection of papers on the issue of regions in South Asia, resulting from a symposium on the subject. See especially the essays by Cohn and De.
5. Note, however, that this region is also perceived as a subdivision of the larger regional division of "South India," distinguished from the North by geographical location (the Deccan plateau and the peninsula to the south) and the preponderance of Dravidian languages, all of which are related to Old Tamil, the only Dravidian language with an ancient literature. Cultural geographers and anthropologists cite

the Tamil region as an example of a well-defined region, one that is at once a linguistic, cultural, and historical region in the typological schema outlined in Cohn (in Crane, ed., 1967). For his history of medieval South Indian peasant society, Burton Stein (1980) proposes a South Indian cultural macro-region that includes the southern portions of territory now included in the states of Karnataka and Andhra Pradesh, whose respective Dravidian languages are Kannada and Telugu. On classical Tamil literature, see Hart, 1975 and Ramanujan, 1967 and 1985.

6. On the reorganization of the Indian states on the basis of language, see Wolpert, 2000, pp. 368–369.
7. "*Vaṭa vēṅkaṭan te̲nkumari āyiṭait tamiḻ kūṟum nallulakattu . . .*". Prefatory verses by Pa̲nampāra̲nār to *Tolkāppiyam, Eḻuttatikāram,* 1–2. For references in the *caṅkam* poems, see *Puṟanā̲nūṟu* 6 and 17.
8. E.g., *Cilappatikāram* VIII.1–2: "*Neṭiyō̲n ku̲nṟamum toṭiyōḷ pauvamum tamiḻ varampaṟutta taṇpu̲nal na̲nnāṭu.*" "The good Tamil land watered by cool rivers and bounded by Neṭiyō̲n (Viṣṇu's) hill (Vēṅkaṭam) and the Goddess's (*toṭiyōḷ*) sea."
9. For discussions of the geographical boundaries of the Tamil region, see De, especially p. 62ff.; Cohn (both in Crane, ed., 1967), and Stein, 1980.
10. See Ramaswamy, 1997, pp. 154–161 and *passim.*
11. Several nineteenth-century Tamil scholars hold that the *kumari* of the *Tolkāppiyam* refers not to Cape Comorin, but to either a mountain or a river of that name, referred to in some of the ancient texts, and which are said, according to legend, to have been submerged in the ocean in successive deluges. See *Tolkāppiyam, Eḻuttatikāram,* introduction by K. Subramaniya Pillai; Purnalingam Pillai, 1927; and Kanakasabhai, 1904.
12. Pāskarattoṇṭaimā̲n, 1967.
13. For an introduction to the history and culture of the Tamil region, see Nilakanta Sastri, 1955/1976 and 1964.
14. For the topographical and territorial divisions of the *caṅkam* poems, see Hart, 1975, and Marr, 1985.
15. The brief exposition of the theory of landscapes and poetic universes that follows draws from A. K. Ramanujan's "Afterword" in his *Poems of Love and War* (1985).
16. *Pālai,* "wasteland," is not a separate landscape-region, but a landscape-type into which any fertile landscape (e.g., mountain or forest) might be transformed. Actually, the texts speak of seven *tiṇais,* but only the five "middlemost" are appropriate for *akam* and *puṟam* poetry. For a detailed discussion of the *tiṇais* and their deployment in *caṅkam* poems, see Selby, this volume, and Ramanujan, 1967 and 1985.
17. On place in Tamil devotional (*bhakti*) religion, see Yocum, 1973, and Peterson, 1989. On the localizing character of Tamil temple myths, see Shulman, 1980.
18. For a detailed discussion of *purāṇic* cosmology, see the essay by Daud Ali in this volume, and Sircar, 1967. There are Buddhist and Jaina cosmographies, as well.
19. Cross-cousin marriage is the standard practice in many Tamil communities.
20. Ramaswamy, 1999, p. 69.

ONE

Dialogues of Space, Desire, and Gender in Tamil *Caṅkam* Poetry

Martha Ann Selby

In a marvelously unique and fluid blending of geography, metaphor, and imagination, space is the dimension in which all of the genius of *caṅkam* Tamil poetics develops. In this essay, I will discuss ways in which space operates as an organizing principle in Tamil poetics in general, and how familial and gender roles are represented in particular, in the rhetoric and imagery as first set out in the earliest extant work on Tamil grammar and poetics, the *Tolkāppiyam*. I will focus on specific sets of poems from four *caṅkam* anthologies, *Aiṅkuṟunūṟu, Naṟṟiṇai, Kuṟuntokai,* and *Puṟanāṉūṟu. Naṟṟiṇai* and *Kuṟuntokai* contain material that ranges in date from the first to the third centuries C.E. A plausible date for *Aiṅkuṟunūṟu* is the fourth century C.E. (Takahashi, 1995, p. 52), with *Puṟanāṉūṟu* possibly falling somewhat later, perhaps around the fifth century C.E. (Zvelebil, 1973, p. 43) Many of the poems that I have chosen for analysis are spoken by mothers primarily about their relationships with their daughters, and to a lesser extent with their sons. I will examine the ways in which the *caṅkam* poets have manipulated landscape imagery in their expressions of these dynamics, and will discuss the divisions and differences in *caṅkam* imagery as they pertain to and construct gender roles and identities.

The *caṅkam* anthologies were "rediscovered" by U. Vē. Cāminātaiyar (1855–1942) in the late nineteenth century, as he relates in his autobiography, *Eṉ Carittiram* ("My Story"). Cāminātaiyar's discovery of these texts did more than simply recover lost works of literature—it restored a sense of history and of ancient culture to the Tamils in the Dravidian south, spurring a movement of intellectual activity that is now referred to as the "Tamil renaissance." Drawing his inspiration from, among other things, an English-language biblical concordance, Cāminātaiyar edited the anthologies and wrote lucid commentaries on them. Taking his cue from parts of an old commentary on the *Puṟanāṉūṟu,* he adopted the notions of *tiṇai* ("context") and *tuṟai* ("theme"), which are, for all practical purposes, archetypal ideas that are unique to early Tamil aesthetic paradigms found in the *Tolkāppiyam.* Taking these two exclusively "Tamil" notions, Cāminātaiyar transformed them into critical tools. The very name of the *Tolkāppiyam* denotes its antiquity as well as its importance: *Tol-kāppiyam* simply means "the Old Text," though Tamil nationalist scholars offer a different derivation for the word *kāppiyam.* Refusing to accept *kāppiyam* as a Tamilized form of the Sanskrit word *kāvya* ("text," "poem," "work"), they derive it from the phrase *kāppu iyaṉṟatu,* "that which constitutes protection," the idea being that grammar is what protects language from deterioration.

There is still a great deal of controversy surrounding the date of this text. Both Kamil Zvelebil and the late Ku. Paramasivam have developed convincing but conflicting arguments. Zvelebil places the *Tolkāppiyam* in two periods, dividing the text into two strata, the *Ur-Tolkāppiyam* (containing the first two sections on phonology and syntax) and the *Poruḷatikāram,* which comprises the section on rhetoric, poetics, and usage. He places the composition of the *Ur*-text at around the second century B.C.E. and the *Poruḷatikāram* some seven centuries later (Zvelebil, 1973, pp. 131–149). Paramasivam (1980) has argued on linguistic and stylistic grounds that the *Tolkāppiyam* could only have been written by one author, and that its composition must have preceded the extant *caṅkam* anthologies. He places the entire text in the second century B.C.E., making it roughly contemporaneous with the composition of the earliest segments of the Sanskrit *Nāṭyaśāstra,* the earliest known work in Sanskrit on dramaturgy and, by extension, poetics. However, Takanobu Takahashi provides us with what I think are the most reasonable dates for the *Tolkāppiyam.* He puts forth a very sensible and concise discussion of the inconsistent linguistic and syntactic textures found in the *Poruḷatikāram* by working through the problems of organization, the arrangement of stanzas, interpolation, and the influence of Sanskrit. Takahashi divides the *Poruḷatikāram* into four discrete chronological layers with the earliest dating from the first through the third centuries C.E. and the later, more "Sanskritic" segments from the fourth through the sixth centuries C.E. (Takahashi, 1995, pp. 20–24)

Akam and Puṟam

The *Poruḷatikāram* of the *Tolkāppiyam* categorizes all love poetry under a heading called *akam*. *Akam* is half of the most basic genre division of *caṅkam* poetry. The other half is *puṟam,* and it comes as no surprise that these two words are antonyms. At their most basic levels of meaning, *akam* means "inner;" *puṟam* means "outer." By extension, *akam* comes to refer to a person's "inner life." More specifically, *akam* means "love" in all its textures and hues. *Puṟam* is all that is outside *akam*. In poetics, it refers to a person's "outer" or "public life" in the intersecting realms of politics and warfare. It must be kept in mind, however, that *akam* poems often refer to *puṟam* themes, and the *caṅkam* poets, who often composed verses in both genres, drew the techniques they applied to both from the same pool of poetic convention. In fact, to use the word genre at all is a bit misleading. I prefer to visualize *akam* and *puṟam* as two parallel systems with components that often intersect. These intersections blur, and at times, the poets even erase lines between these distinctions. Let us consider the following poem from *Kuṟuntokai:*

Kuṟuntokai 73

What her friend said:

You long only for his chest.
May you live long, Friend.
Don't be broken-hearted:

Like the ancient Kōcar warriors
who took an oath,
cut down King Naṉṉaṉ's[1]
fragrant mango tree
and overran his land,
all we need now is a little hard-hearted scheming.[2]

The above verse is spoken by the heroine's female friend. The heroine has already met with the man in secret, has engaged in intercourse with him, and is longing for another meeting and/or marriage.[3] The friend is telling the heroine to take heart, and by referring to an act of warfare (an event that would normally be described in a *puṟam* poem), suggests to the heroine that the man can be won over with a bit of bold, military-style strategy. According to N. Subrahmanian (1966), the Kōcars were Tulu warriors famous for their bravery, truthfulness, and for keeping to their sworn word (p. 334). U. Vē. Cāminātaiyar's commentary on this poem states that chieftains of ancient Tamilnadu had *kāvaṉmarams,* "protected trees," and that the rash act of cutting down such a tree was considered tantamount to a declaration of war. So, through these indices that are clearly *puṟam,* the lovesick heroine and her friend are going to make a pact and, as it were, "declare war" on the hero by metaphorically "cutting down *his* mango tree." Likewise, *puṟam* poems are often overflowing with themes and sentiments that one would normally expect to find in *akam* poetry or are spoken from within the frame of an *akam* context, as in the following elegy from the *Puṟanāṉūṟu:*

Puṟanāṉūṟu 113

To Pāri's Hill

The mead jars were opened.
Rams and bulls were slaughtered; cooked.
There were renderings, flesh, and rice
in endless supply
and multiplying your wealth
which you gave out as we wanted it,
you befriended us then.

Now, since Pāri has died,
we've sunk into a mire of sorrow.
We've worshipped you and praised you,
our eyes brimming with tears.

We'll go, famed Paṟampu Hill,[4]
and seek out men
who have rights to the scented black hair
of Pāri's daughters,
their wrists stacked with engraved bangles.

Here, the poet Kapilar, whose job it was to praise the chieftain Pāri, his patron, now can only praise what is left of Pāri—his hill and the memory of his generosity to the bards. At the end of the poem, Kapilar shifts his concern from elegy and praise, largely the business of *puṟam* poetry, to responsibilities that might seem more likely in an *akam* context: he must now see to it that Pāri's orphaned daughters[5] are suitably married.

There are definite structural parallels in the *Tolkāppiyam* itself that suggest that the relationship between *akam* and *puṟam* is to be thought of as interdependent, dialogic, and complementary rather than as oppositional. There are seven *puṟattiṇais* to match the seven *tiṇais* of *akam,* found listed in the *Puṟattiṇaiyiyal* of the *Poruḷatikāram*. The language of correspondence is highly regularized and logical, though the "logic" is not readily apparent until cross-genre comparisons are made among the texts of the actual poems. The *Puṟattiṇaiyiyal* constructs the correspondences thus: *veṭci tāṉ-ē kuṟiñciyatu puṟaṉ-ē, tumpai tāṉ-ē neytalatu puṟaṉ-ē, vākai tāṉ-ē pālaiyatu puṟaṉ-ē,* and so forth (literally, "*veṭci* is *kuṟiñci's* outside, *tumpai* is *neytal's* outside; *vākai* is *pālai's* outside," etc.). The *puṟattiṇais* often share the "primary elements" (the *mutaṟporuḷs*) of time and place, and also of "mood" (the *uripporuḷs*) with those of the *akattiṇais*. For example, *veṭci,* the *puṟam* context of the cattle raid, is situated as parallel to *kuṟiñci*. They share time (midnight) and place (the hill regions). They also share a mood that is clandestine. The stolen cows of *veṭci* are like the covert caresses of *kuṟiñci,* taken in secret under the covers of brush and darkness. Just as a cattle raid is a prelude to war, so are *kuṟiñci* encounters preludes to marriage.

Therefore, it would naturally follow that there are intertextual relationships between *akam* and *puṟam* poems. They seem to be especially present in *akam* poems composed on themes that have to do with absent or misbehaving lovers, and in *puṟam* poems of elegy and lament composed by bards whose patrons have either died or are no longer treating them well. The following two poems share the line *ācāku entai yāṇṭuḷaṉ kollō,* "our master who supports us—where is he now, I wonder?":

Kuṟuntokai 325

What she said:

When he said,
"I'll go, I'll go,"
I mistook it

for all his former mock departures
and I said, "Fine,
leave my side
and go away forever."

O Mother,
our master who supports us—
where is he now, I wonder?

The place between my breasts
has filled up with tears,
has become a deep pond
where a black-legged
white heron feeds.[6]

Puṟanāṉūṟu 235

Elegy for Atiyamāṉ Neṭumāṉ Añci[7]

If he had a little toddy, he gave it to us.
All gone.
If he had a lot of toddy,
we sang while he drank happily.
All gone.
If he had a little rice,
he portioned it out in many plates.
All gone.
If he had a lot of rice,
he portioned it out in many plates.
All gone.
He gave us all the meat along with bones.
All gone.
Wherever spears and arrows entered, he stood firm.
All gone.
He caressed my head that smelled of meat
with his hand which smelled of bitter orange.
All gone.

The spear that pierced his precious chest
pierced the tongues of poets

in their subtle search for pretty words,
dimmed the poor eyes of his suppliants,
ran through the palms of beggars;
bored holes in the wide alms bowls
of minstrels both famous and great.

Our master who supports us—
where is he now, I wonder?

Now, there isn't a single bard
or a single soul to give to them.
Like a big jalap blossom full of honey
that flowers in a cool shoal
and stays there without being worn,
there are a great many who die
without giving one thing to others.[8]

Despite the obvious references to warfare and the patron-poet relationship described in this beautiful verse, we cannot help noting the veiled eroticism in the two lines *naranta nāṟun taṉ-kaiyāl/pulavu nāṟum eṉ-ṟalai taivarum* ("With his hand that smelled of bitter orange/he caressed my head that smelled of meat"). This allusion is unclear, and Cāminātaiyar's commentary is silent, but it could also point to certain class markers that Añci is transgressing by stroking her meat-scented head with a hand that smells of more delicate things.

We cannot, therefore, treat these two systems as exclusive divisions, but rather as matrices that are in constant poetic dialogue. Each of these poems has shades of the other embedded in it; not only in the shared *verbatim* line, but in the complex emotional structures present in the mode of lamentation. There is little difference in the qualities of feeling in the act of mourning an absent lover or a dead king: each offers protection and support. Instead of being mutually exclusive, *akam* and *puṟam* are mutually defining, interlocked, and exist in a seamless continuum. According to Nacciṉārkkiṉiyar's fourteenth-century commentary on the *Tolkāppiyam,* "*akam* and *puṟam* are like the inner palm of the hand and its back."[9]

Both these poems display what Susan Cole (1985) describes as the ambivalence of an "absent presence," and exemplify the "paradox of embodied absence" (pp. 1–9). Both poems verbally construct their subjects as phantoms and ghosts, and this is what lends these poems their profound emotional acuity; their tragic power. Both poems are sung in a true tragic voice that is "located in a space where boundaries and identities are shifting, a liminal realm that does in fact constitute the world of tragedy" (Cole, 1985, p. 19). These poems visit the realm of the ampersand that links *akam* with *puṟam,* sexual longing with lamentation, and passion with death—those sad and immensely moving little frontiers of loss and absence. I would like to suggest that what we find in this interdependency between *akam* and *puṟam* is a phenomenon of "spatial doubling," as Cole would put it, a "superimposition of one world upon another" (ibid.), resulting in a poetics of violence and loss that is spatially fluid and drifting and which underscores the profoundly disruptive natures of physical longing and death, blending them into one in a single, blurred gesture of poetic symbolization.

An understandable reflex might be to interpret *akam* and *puṟam* as literary phenomena that construct space along gender lines, and this is true, to a certain extent. But these two "divisions" (I must reiterate here that I use that word with great caution) are not as exclusively "female" and "male" as one might think, though if one thinks along the lines of the human body in the poems and the various levels and limits of physical suffering, it is clear that women's bodies are destroyed in *akam* through the obliterating effects of passion and longing, and in *puṟam,* the male body undergoes death itself. It is worthwhile to note here that many Tamil words for love are ultimately derived from the two negative verbal roots, *il* and *al,* both of which negate existence, meaning roughly "not to be." This has perhaps inspired the popular etymology for *kāmam,* which, according to some, is derived from the Tamil root *kātu,* meaning "to slay, kill, or obliterate." It is also interesting and timely to note here that it is the character of the mother who moves with the most freedom between *akam* and *puṟam* realms, and I will discuss some of the roles of this character at the end of this essay. But first, I wish to explore the articulations of the various *tiṇais* as they are understood as evocative poetic and emotional spaces.

Tiṇai

Tiṇai is an extremely difficult word to translate neatly. The word "landscape" and the phrase "poetic situation" are currently the accepted and the most widely used definitions, but there is a problem with both. The problem is one of scope and boundary. *Tiṇai* is, in a very real sense, the artistic space circumscribed by the poets, along with everything contained therein. I tentatively choose the word "context" to translate *tiṇai,* but what must be understood is that this context is sweeping, and includes geographical space, time, and everything that grows, develops, and lives within that space and time, including emotion. In fact, the *Tolkāppiyam* stresses that emotion (or mood) is the only thing within a *tiṇai* that is actually fixed, a rather difficult concept to grasp, but crucial to the understanding of this system. *Akattiṇaiyiyal* verse 13 states: "The things that are not behavioral elements may overlap," meaning that everything except for the behavioral elements may. I would like to turn now to the *Tolkāppiyam* itself and examine the way in which the system of Tamil poetics is literally built "from the ground up."

The first chapter, or *iyal,* of the *Poruḷatikāram* is the *Akattiṇaiyiyal,* "The Chapter on Interior Contexts," describing the requirements for *akam* poetry, poems about one's "inner life." The first few verses of this chapter give the basis and set all limits for spatial dimensions and orientations, as well as corresponding fourth-dimensional aspects of time and season:

1. It is said that there are seven contexts that have been mentioned previously, beginning with *kaikkiḷai* (the context of "minor relationship," or one-sided love) and ending with *peruntiṇai* (ironically, the "major context"; that of mismatched love).
2. The middle five contexts, save for the middlemost (which is *pālai* in the traditional list, the context set in the wasteland), have the quality of being divided into lands attached to sounding waves.
3. When investigating poetic practices, these three are obvious in the following order: *mutaṟporuḷ*—the "primal" or "first elements," those of space and time; *karupporuḷ* or "germinal elements"—"regional features," the features that germinate and grow inside space and time as circumscribed by the *mutaṟporuḷ;* and the *uripporuḷ,* or "behavioral elements," those of mood, emotion, and so on.

In this discussion, I will only be concerned with the "middle five contexts," for which the author/s of the *Tolkāppiyam* go on to assign gods, types of people and their occupations, drums, plants, birds, and so on to each region. These "middle five" are considered the only ones that are truly proper for the aesthetic portrayal of love, though it is worth noting here that the five aesthetic categories are listed within parentheses of unaesthetic love. Below is a list of the regions and the *uripporuḷ* or "mood" that is associated with each one:

REGION	MOOD
1. *kuṟiñci*	*puṇartal,* "lovers' union"
2. *mullai*	*iruttal,* "patient waiting for the lover's return"
3. *pālai*	*pirital,* "separation"
4. *neytal*	*iraṅkal,* "lamenting the lover's absence"
5. *marutam*	*ūṭal,* "jealous quarreling"

It is best to think of Tamil *tiṇais* as occurring cyclically, rather than in a linear fashion, for I will demonstrate shortly that there are really no lines between *tiṇais* other than emotional ones. For instance, all the contexts out of these five are named after flowers that grow in the tracts of land associated with each one. *Pālai* also means wasteland, and although things do grow there inside the poems, they are generally scrubby, thorny plants, while the others are blooming, fragrant things such as jasmine and blue water lilies. A wasteland can appear anywhere, and it is significant that it is placed in the middle of the list. This middle placement gives it a central focus, as well as a kind of permeating aspect—it touches all the other contexts, making none of them safe from its desiccating, uncomfortable features. The primary shrubs of *pālai* are evergreen succulents, quite common to all of Tamilnadu even today, while the *kuṟiñci* flower is extremely rare. It grows only in cool mountain tracts and blooms only once in twelve years. *Kuṟiñci* has as its assigned season autumn and its assigned time is midnight; its land tracts are hills and mountains. Associations, therefore, are with rarity, comfort, and coolness, while the *pālai* context is both common and devoid of water. It has summer as one of its assigned seasons; high noon is its time.

If we take all of the above into account, the entire *tiṇai* scheme can be thought of as a system of physical and psychic "gestures." This gesturing, however, is not restricted to the human characters in the poems. At times, it seems that the overriding, constant emotional elements (the *uripporuḷs*) associated with each poetic context are actually responsible for animating everything within that context. Feelings belong not only to humans but are also transferred to the physical contexts of which they are a part. The very land itself is capable of showing signs of emotion, as are animals and birds. The following two poems illustrate this beautifully. The first poem is from the *caṅkam* anthology *Naṟṟiṇai* and is ascribed to Nallantuvaṉār; the second is from *Kuṟuntokai* and is ascribed to Iḷampūtaṉār. I have included condensed translations of the commentators' headnotes (these are modern in every case) in italics just above the text of each poem to provide the contexts that appear to have been long accepted by the Tamil literary establishment.

Naṟṟiṇai 88

What her girlfriend said:

Why are you confused
over old deeds we have done?

Live long, Friend,
and don't be sad.
We'll go.
We'll tell him,
and come back.
So get up
and look here.

Like that nectar from the sea
with its rows of waves,
the salt that faces rain,
I fear that you'll melt
and dissolve away.

Facing their man's cruelty to us,
their love for us is great
and they just can't bear it.
Friend,
those fruit-shedding hills of his
will weep waterfalls
of tears.

Kuṟuntokai 334

What her girlfriend said, quoting the heroine to make the hero understand her plight:

That man from the shores
with their spreading waters

where a big flock
of little gray-hooded crows
stays in a grove thick with flowers,
hating the cold
when a spray
cast up by waves
soaks their wet backs
to the skin:
If he leaves me,
my friend,
is there any thing
that we will lose,
other than my own sweet life?

Although at first glance, the first poem appears to be composed on the theme of separation, it is classified as a *kuriñci* verse by the modern commentator A. Nārāyaṇacāmi Aiyar (*Naṟṟiṇai Nāṉūṟu,* 1976, p. 152). This is yet another example of a *kuṟiñci* situation in which the initial sexual encounter has already taken place. The heroine is despondent, and her girlfriend speaks words of encouragement to her. The author has artfully manipulated the conventions of one of the landscapes of separation, *neytal,* to express the girlfriend's concern over the heroine's lovesickness. *Neytal,* the landscape of lamentation, builds its poetic language with seaside elements. Here, the girlfriend regards the heroine as a pile of salt left out in the rain to dissolve. As the poem ends, the girlfriend does not appeal to the man himself for mercy, but appeals to his land, the fertile, wet, hilly *kuṟiñci* tract, leaving the reader quite literally "in the right place" for the proper understanding of this poem.

The second example is a perfect illustration of a proper *neytal* poem. Cāminātaiyar's headnote infers an even wider gulf of separation between the hero and heroine than the actual poem itself might suggest. The poem is in the heroine's voice, but the girlfriend is actually repeating her very words to the hero to relate to him the heroine's pain and desperation. The initial line of the poem places the reader in the correct frame of reference, as it immediately identifies the man as a *neytal* hero. The poem then describes the heroine's discomfort by means of *uḷḷuṟai-yuvamam* ("comparison by means of a hidden meaning") by invoking the *karupporuḷs* of the *neytal* landscape: the cold, the spray; isolation in a marshy, seaside grove.

Context, Mood, and Body

As should already be evident from the poems I have cited, the poem is the place where environment and body meet. The "outside"—the *tiṇai*—is the picture of the "self," and the poem represents the play between a poet's "feelings and the world's responding reflection of them" (Skura, 1981, pp. 79–80). Further, the Tamil poem is an expression of the poet's recognition of the human body's discontinuity with its environment and perhaps it is also an expression of desire for continuity with it. What makes the *tiṇai* system a "poetics" is, in fact, a sort of "overdetermination." The composers of these poems foisted this desire outward upon environmental elements, and incorporated those elements into a multi-layered semiotics. In the poems, *tiṇai* becomes more than a "landscape" or poetic "gesture." It becomes an actual language—the constant repetition of *tiṇai* symbology gives it a "congruity," locking it into articulations of convention that are requisite for a full-blown rhetoric.

In many of the *caṅkam* poems, there is a successful unification of imagery with the speaker's (the hero's or heroine's) body, upon which there are overlappings, overlayings, and splicings of *tiṇai* elements. Let us return for a moment to the last stanza of *Kuṟuntokai* 325, translated in full above:

> The place between my breasts
> has filled up with tears,
> has become a deep pond
> where a black-legged
> white heron feeds.

The heroine of the poem hyperbolizes her tears by using two elements of the *neytal tiṇai,* that of the seashore, the "deep pond" and the "black-legged white heron." The poet, Naṉṉākaiyār, grafts these elements onto his heroine's chest, literally marking her body with two of the landscape features of the *neytal* context. The ponds of *neytal* are often salty, brackish places; the salt of the heroine's tears is in synecdochic correspondence with the salt of the seaside pond. The heron stands for the woman's lover; the fish upon which the heron is feeding represent her and also other women, a common convention in this context. In *Kuṟuntokai* 334, also cited above, the poet Iḷampūtaṉār uses an extended *uḷḷuṟaiyuvamam* in the indented stanza to evoke the heroine's physical discomfort. But perhaps the most striking example of the relationship between body and environment is *Kuṟuntokai* 290, composed by Kalporu Ciṟunuraiyār, who took his name from the image in the stunning simile around which he constructed this poem ("he who sang of a streak of foam dashed against stones"):

Kuṟuntokai 290

What she said:

These people who tell me
to bear my love:

Don't they know about love,
or are they that strong?

Since I can't see my lover,
my heart swells
with hidden sorrow
and like a flood in spate
turning to a streak of foam
as it's dashed against stones,

slowly,
slowly, I turn to nothing.

Here, the heroine complains to her friend about people who tell her to bear her love—according to Cāminataiyār's commentary, these people include anyone who "cannot understand the nature of desire" (*Kuṟuntokai,* 1983, p. 593), probably townsfolk and her own family members. Her lover is absent for some reason. The heroine is anxious for his return, and is probably exhibiting the physical signs of separation: it is likely that she has turned pale and appears disheveled and emaciated. Her people are worried and tell her to just be strong and endure the unendurable. The heroine speaks of the grief that surges thick in her heart, comparing herself to a swell of water that diminishes as it crashes against rocks. She is so overwhelmed by her longing that she fears that it will consume her; that she will simply stop being. The last line of the poem, *mella mellavillākutum-ē* ("slowly, slowly, I turn to nothing") reflects the repetitive (and slowly erosive) motion of the *neytal* waves.

The word *illākutum* is a fascinating juncture of two verbs that mean "not to be" (verbal root *il*) and "to be" or "to become" (verbal root *āku*). The elements of the *neytal* context figuratively swell up, consume, and nearly destroy the heroine as she grieves in her lover's absence.

There are also explicit relationships between the physical surroundings of *tiṇai* and the emotional and personal traits of the characters. Each *tiṇai* has its own "psychology," as it were, defined by the *urip-poruḷs* discussed above. To continue with *neytal* imagery, the overriding *uripporuḷ* of this *tiṇai* is *iraṅkal,* "lamenting the lover's absence." There is usually some sort of separation involved, joined with an overlay of impatience, restlessness, and suspicion. The "primary elements" (the *mutaṟporuḷs*) are the seacoast (for place), sunrise (for time), and for season, the *Tolkāppiyam* tells us that this can happen at any time of year. So, lamentation is seasonless. It is very interesting that sunrise is prescribed for the time of day—the poems often depict a woman waking in the morning and finding that her lover had not returned the previous night. The "germinal elements" (the *karupporuḷs*) are mostly things that shake and rustle—the branches of *neytal* trees are often described as "swaying" or "shaking." The lands are watery, salty marshes, and the animals that populate this *tiṇai* are mostly dangerous and predatory: herons, sharks, and crocodiles dominate the scene. Therefore, the general evocation of this context is one of unease. Nothing seems to be on solid ground, and everything is threatening, brackish, and uncomfortable. The following poem, composed by Veṇpūti, demonstrates one way in which a heroine has to bury her chastity and sorrow, depositing them together in a *neytal* marsh:

Kuṟuntokai 97

What she said (her lover not having returned for many days):

As for me,
I am here.

My virtue lies
with boundless grief
in a salt marsh.

He is in his town,

and our secret
has become gossip
in common places.

This poem serves as an excellent example of the ways in which a character can splice or graft his or her emotions onto the actual landscape. The heroine's grief in separation and her *nalaṉ* (her Goodness with a capital "G"; her virginity) are left to rot secretly in a fetid marsh, while her lover stays comfortably at home. She is bereft of him as well as her own chastity; she can grieve for neither publicly and resigns her feelings to the land, while the secret of their love has become grist for the local gossip mill.

It seems that readers of *caṅkam* poetry are required to have an ability to internalize a poetics that is based not wholly on emotion but on environment and the ability to attach significance to objects in the poems, decoding them, at times, in ways which smack of the unraveling of an extended allegory. Critic Georges Poulet (1980) has written that "the advantage of literature is that it frees one from the usual sense of incompatibility between consciousness and the objects of consciousness" (p. 43). It is the very erasure of this incompatibility that is the chief concern and ideal ultimate goal of Tamil poetics. Poulet writes of poetic language and the creation of an "interior universe"—*akam,* if you will—in which "external objects are replaced with a congeries of mental objects in close rapport with one's own consciousness" (ibid.). The Tamil *caṅkam* writers were obviously never quite free of that sense of incompatibility in their readings of reality: Tamil poetics developed from an acute and inescapable awareness of the incompatibility of the human body and its psychic trappings with the environment in which it moves, lives, and breathes. The language of the *caṅkam* poets arose from a desire for an erasure of the split between self and *tiṇai;* this desire was foisted outward onto the environment, which was then reshaped, literally "incorporated," and made part of their language.

The Problem of the Mother's Voice

An element common to all of the classical erotic anthologies of South Asia is that the characters who populate these poems seem to be drawn from a similar stock set. There are heroes and heroines, the woman's friend, the man's friend, "other women" (and, somewhat less frequently, "other men"), go-betweens, and parents. The Tamil and Prākrit poets also include the heroine's wet nurse or foster mother. The Tamil poets add itinerant musicians and dancers who act as messengers, and also have a fully developed sense of how parents fit in with the erotic lives of their children. I wish to turn now to the specific instance of the voice of the mother in *caṅkam* poetry as a unique female voice that speaks across the false "lines" of *akam* and *puṟam*. There are poems of separation in *Naṟṟiṇai,* for instance, that are spoken by mothers who are pining for their daughters who have eloped, "married down," or are living in a far-off place. These are still classified as "love poems," and, as far as I am able to tell, are unique to Tamil. An example from this anthology follows, poem 110.[10] The speaker is the heroine's mother:

I held in one hand
a pot of glowing gold
full of sweet milk,
white and tasty,
mixed with honey.
I ordered her to eat
and as I beat her,
raising a small rod
with a soft tip
wound round with cloth,
she toddled away,
her golden anklets clattering
with their fresh-water pearls inside.

That little prankster,
who ran under a canopy
so that the good, old nurses,
their hair gray and thinning,
would slow down and stop in their tracks,
where did she learn this knowledge,
these manners?

As her husband's family grows poor,
she doesn't think once
of the rich rice her father used to give
and more pliable
than fine black sand

under running water,
she eats when she can,
that little one
with such great strength.

Here is another parallel example, *Kuṟuntokai* 356. U. Vē. Cāminātaiyar identifies the speaker as the girl's foster-mother:

A man who wears a hero's anklet
keeps her safe as she hurries
through barren, dry lands
where the shade shrinks and dies.
At the bank of a scorched pool,
she sips at muddy, steaming water.
Where does she find the strength,
this girl, soft as a sprout,
with her tiny, curving bracelets?
    She had refused even to touch milk
    mixed with fine, puffed rice
    in a bowl clad in blushing gold
    that I'd held out for her,
    saying that it was too much.

In the first poem, the girl is fed milk and honey from a golden pot, and even though she is beaten when she refuses it, the rod her mother wields is padded with cloth to soften the blows. Both poems are *pālai* poems, the only context within *caṅkam* literature (aside from its parallel *tiṇai, vākai,* in *puṟam* poetry) in which we hear the mother's voice loud and clear.

The juxtaposition of these two wrenching verses, the first spoken by the mother and the second by the foster-mother according to the commentators, underscores a categorical problem: what does *tāy,* "mother," mean as a category of character? Cāminātaiyar uses two terms to separate what kind of mother he means. The biological mother is the *naṟṟāy,* literally the "true mother," and the foster-mother is the *cevilittāy*. In many poems, it is extremely difficult to tease these two characters apart, and, at times, it appears as if these two have been conflated into one. For the few *caṅkam* texts for which we have multiple commentaries, the commentators cannot agree at times on which character is speaking. One gets the feeling that perhaps the category of *tāy* designates the concept that "mother" is always plural; perhaps one entity expressing twin facets of a single self.

There are many instances, however, wherein the *cevilittāy* speaks and acts according to precise rules that are described in the *Tolkāppiyam*. There are contexts in which the *cevilittāy* sets out in search of the eloping couple and gives voice to her despair in such poems as the following, *Kuṟuntokai* 44:

> My feet have stumbled;
> my eyes have looked and looked
> and lost their light.
>
> There are more couples
> in this world
> than there are stars
> in the black and widening sky.

It is also the *cevilittāy's* role to comfort the bereft and grieving *naṟṟāy,* the girl's natural mother, and to say prayers for the eloping couple's comfort as they make their way across the *pālai* wastelands. *Kuṟuntokai* 378 serves as an exquisite example of this:

> Leaving us behind,
> our dark, simple girl crosses the desert
> with that young man, his spear long and flashing.
>
> Let cool rains fall today,
> on the sands overspreading
> their narrow path through the mountains
> under the shade of trees
> impenetrable by the rays of the sun.

This particular poem provides a fantastic insight into the ways in which *tiṇai* imagery is manipulated by the poets across what we might consider to be the standard semiotic boundaries of *caṅkam* convention. In the poem I just cited, the *cevilittāy,* in effect, wishes comfort and ease for the eloping pair, but not just in the physical sense of coolness and shade. Rain and coolness are part of the symbological scheme of *mullai,* the *tiṇai* of domestic happiness, of being settled in mind and in home as well as being physically comfortable. In fact, there is a subgenre of poetry that appears in the decads of *Aiṅkuṟunūṟu* in which the *cevilittāy* travels off to visit the young couple, and reports to the *naṟṟāy* what she has seen, all in terms of *mullai* symbolism. So, the *cevilittāy's* role differs from the role of the biological mother to the extent that her character straddles the boundaries of two *tiṇais,* and this is reflected in the symbological language in which she speaks. *Caṅkam* convention also tells us that the *cevilittāy* is often emotionally closer to the girl than her natural mother. The following unusual poem, *Aiṅkuṟunūṟu* 313, spells this out in perfect poetic detail:

What the mother said to the foster-mother:

This love for your daughter—
let it be destroyed.

Our beloved girl
has crossed over the wastes
through the place that traverses
both mountain and forest,
as grief addles our desolate hearts,
and with great pain and agony,
makes our life's breath leave us.

The line that is of most interest here is "through the place that traverses both mountain and forest"—that place is called *pālai. Pālai* does, in fact, represent an "in-between" place, a place only to be traversed and not dwelt in, a hostile region of hardship that rests between the two countries of *kuṟiñci,* love in union, and *mullai,* the *tiṇai* of domesticity, the eventual goal of a journey that is both a physical movement from one place to another, but also a shift in symbolic language from one semiotic register to another. In the taxonomy of the *Tolkāppiyam,* this is a movement from a love situation termed *kaḷavu,* "stolen" or "clandestine," into the mature love of *kaṟpu,* love that is "chaste." But the *naṟṟāy* never invokes *mullai* imagery in her speech. She is portrayed as being comforted by it, but we only hear her voice, it seems, in the harsh language of *pālaittiṇai*.

Aiṅkuṟunūṟu contains a decad of poems titled *makaṭpōkkiya vaḻittāy iraṅku pattu,* "the decad of the mother's lamentations at the elopement of her daughter." Translations of six of these poems follow below, all composed by the *caṅkam* master Ōtalāntaiyār:

#372

Going along with that bull of a man
who convinced her with promises
to persuade her heart,

> my daughter has crossed
> over many fertile hills
> as the gossip surges
> in this clamoring old town.

Has she thought of me at all, I wonder?

#373

May she be plagued with sorrow
each time she thinks of it,
the mother of that young man
with the strong bow of newly-cut bamboo,
who escorted my daughter
through the burning wastes

> where an old stag with forking antlers,
> escaping a tiger's pounce,
> bellows out to his doe,
> calling her back to him.

#374

Even though I've thought it through
many times, I've found no solace:

> Thinking that she is well-fated
> and protected by that bull of a man
> stronger than the God of Death,
> that girl with the hair
> that can't yet be tied in a knot
> has crossed over those tangled wastes
> unknown to even the monkeys.

#378

As we suffer in our loneliness
in the evening,
as a bat, endeavoring to go,
unfurls its wings
and flits skyward,
I refuse to grieve
for that girl who has gone.

But I will grieve
for this girl here,
her pair of lovely kohl-rimmed eyes
made to weep by the pain in her heart,
as she languishes alone
without her sweet-tongued companion.

#379

Uniting with that man
with the glinting, silver spear,
is going through the thickets
where a bull elephant roams
with its herd on the dewy hill

sweeter to her
than celebrating a good marriage,
along with all her loving friends,
I wonder?

#380

Somehow I have taken the name,
"The mother of that delicate girl
with the budding smile
and teeth white as pearls,
who went off with that man
down the long path through the wilds."

Her very own companions
have bestowed it upon me.

This is rightly called *iraṅkal,* or "lamentation," as the *naṟṟāy,* in turn, complains about the gossip her daughter's actions have caused, curses the young man's mother for having given birth to him, describes the utter foolishness of her daughter, who has gone traipsing off to wastelands that are so tangled that even monkeys stay out of them, and remarks on the name that her daughter's friends have given her. The particular placement of this decad in the overall scheme of the body of *Aiṅkuṟunūṟu* is also extremely interesting. It is followed by decads of poems that report to the *naṟṟāy* that her daughter has been seen and is about to return home. The *pālai* section of the text then ends, and is immediately followed by one hundred poems on *mullai,* beginning with a decad in which the *cevilittāy* comforts the mother with accounts of her visits to her daughter's new home and her apparent wedded bliss.

Let us not forget that we also hear the *naṟṟāy's* voice in the *puṟam* context of *vākai,* also the name of a flower, but usually translated as "victory." It is interesting within the context of gender roles and their construction in *caṅkam* imagery that this is the *puṟam* category that is analogous to *akam's pālai;* again, *vākai tāṉ-ē pālaiyatu puṟaṉ-ē,* "*vākai* is *pālai's* outside." The cursing of and grieving over the daughter is transformed into vain and bitter praise for the absent son in this parallel context. To paraphrase Colette, the *naṟṟāy* lets her loss shape all her spoken images, and allows her to gather the flowers and weave the garlands for her daughters and sons alike. The best known of the *vākai* poems are *Puṟanāṉūṟu* 86, composed by the female poet Kāvaṟpeṇṭu, and *Puṟanāṉūṟu* 312, composed by Poṉmuṭiyār:

Puṟanāṉūṟu 86

What a mother said:

Hanging on to the centerpost of my hut,
you ask,
"Your son, where is he?"

Wherever my son is,
I do not know.

Like a stony den void of a sleeping tiger
is this belly that bore him
and you can see him only on the battlefield.

Puṟanāṉūṟu 312

What a mother said:

To bear him and bring him up
    is my duty.
To make him honorable
    is his father's duty.
To provide him with well-honed spears
    is the blacksmith's duty.
To train him in good conduct
    is the king's duty.
To kill in a good fight with a bright sword,
to dismember bull elephants
and to come home again
    is the duty of my son.

Perhaps the most stunning parallels between the *tiṇai* divisions of *akam* and *puṟam* lie in the relationship between *neytal,* the *tiṇai* of jilted women who lament when their lovers leave them, and the *tiṇai* called *tumpai,* that of "battle frenzy" in *puṟam* situations. The salty pools of tears, the marshy, infirm land, and the female form emaciated and dying from love in the romantic contexts of *neytal* are transformed into the pools of blood and the gore-soaked battlefields of war. One is reminded, in fact, of the poems of the British war poet Ivor Gurney, as he tries to mask the red horrors of the battlefield with proud flowers:

You would not know him now . . .
    But still he died
Nobly, so cover him over
    With violets of pride
    Purple from Severn side.

Cover him, cover him soon!
    And with thick-set
Masses of memoried flowers—
    Hide that red wet
    Thing that I must somehow forget.[11]

I will conclude with this poem, not in the mother's voice, but describing a mother's behavior, upon hearing that her son had behaved like a coward. Like the purple Severn violets of Gurney's wrenching poem, the mother's grief is masked by her consuming, covering pride as it absorbs the gruesome realities of death. The poem is *Puṟanāṉūṟu* 278, composed by Kākkaipāṭiṉiyār Naceḷḷaiyār:

> The old woman had protruding veins,
> dry, thin shoulders;
> her waist a thorny twig.
>
> When some said,
> "Your son was afraid in battle
> and turned tail,"
>
> she said,
> "If he broke down in the throng,
> I'll slash these breasts which fed him,"
> and, angered, sword in hand,
> she picked the red field over,
> turning over fallen bodies.
>
> Seeing the place where her slain son lay,
> scattered in pieces,
> he pleased her more
> than on the day he was born.

Notes

1. Naṉṉaṉ is the name of any of a number of minor chieftains. See N. Subrahmanian, *Pre-Pallavan Tamil Index* (Madras: University of Madras, 1966), pp. 484–485.
2. This poem was composed by Paraṇar. The *tiṇai* is identified as *kuṟiñci,* "love in union."
3. This is one of the most common *kuṟiñci* situations. One general requirement of a *kuṟiñci* poem is that sexual intercourse should have taken place at least once.
4. It is likely that Paṟampu Hill, described in *Puṟanāṉūṟu* 109 as a naturally bountiful place, was a site of one of Pāri's victories. The word *paṟampu* means "beating" or "thrashing."
5. *Puṟanāṉūṟu* 112 is attributed to these very daughters.
6. This poem is by Naṉṉakaiyār, composed in the *tiṇai* called *neytal,* that of the seashore. The usual context in *neytal* is of a woman lamenting her lover's absence.

7. A famous chieftain of Takaṭūr.
8. This poem is Auvaiyār's work. Auvaiyār, whose name simply means "Granny," is *caṅkam's* most accomplished and prolific woman poet, and perhaps the most accomplished of *all* the *caṅkam* poets, male or female. She composed many poems in both *akam* and *puṟam*.
9. Nacciṉārkkiṉiyar, quoted in Zvelebil, 1973, p. 103.
10. This poem was composed by Pōtaṉar in *pālaittiṇai,* which denotes separation in its most extreme form.
11. These are the final two stanzas of Gurney's poem "To His Love," from *Poems of Ivor Gurney 1890–1937,* with an introduction by Edmund Blunden and bibliographical note by Leonard Clark (London: Chatto and Windus, 1973), p. 42.

TWO

Four Spatial Realms in *Tirukkōvaiyār*

Norman J. Cutler

Though included as part of the Tamil Śaiva devotional canonical corpus *Tirumuṟai, Tirukkōvaiyār* by the ninth-century saint Māṇikkavācakar stands apart from most *Tirumuṟai* poetry by virtue of its close links with the Tamil classical literary tradition.[1] This poem in 400 stanzas exemplifies a medieval genre called *kōvai,* which is usually viewed as a direct descendant of the classical *akam* poetic tradition, and, indeed, the stanzas of a *kōvai* poem employ many of the conventionalized elements of *akam* poetry.[2] However, every stanza of a *kōvai* also incorporates a reference to a historical or mythological hero—a king or a god—and in this respect *kōvai* poems are also affiliated with classical *puṟam* poetry. In *Tirukkōvaiyār,* the most celebrated of all *kōvai* poems, this hero is Śiva.

One of the most interesting effects of a *kōvai* verse is the particular way in which *akam* and *puṟam* elements are intertwined. In fact, it is probably fair to say that the aesthetic core of a *kōvai* verse is the juxtaposition of its *akam* and *puṟam* registers. In *Tirukkōvaiyār,* however, where the "hero of the composition" (*pāṭṭuṭaittalaivaṉ*) is Śiva, the juxtaposition of *akam* and *puṟam* is encompassed by a broader juxtaposition between the classical poetic tradition and Tamil Śaivism.[3] Consequently, this poem facilitates both aesthetically and religiously oriented responses, and indeed, these two possible avenues of interpretation are borne out, on the one hand, by the commentary attributed to Pērāciriyar[4] whose interpretation is couched in terms of classical Tamil poetics, and on the other by a theologically motivated allegorical interpretation of the text, which is circulated in the context of the Tamil Śaiva Siddhānta tradition.[5]

The interplay of *Tirukkōvaiyār's akam* and *puṟam* as well as its aesthetic and religious registers is realized in several ways. One is by incorporating references to several different spatial or geographical realms into the text's verses. These include the landscapes of classical *akam* poetry—mountains, seaside, pastoral land, cultivated land, and wasteland; Śiva's places of residence in the Tamil country, most prominently Tillai;[6] regions that belong to the realm of cosmological and mythological space that are documented in both Tamil and Sanskrit texts, such as Śiva's abode in Mount Kailāsa, the seven world-continents, and so on; and the interior space of the Śaiva devotee's heart and mind. In this essay I examine the variety of ways in which these four kinds of space are configured in *Tirukkōvaiyār's* verses, consider how they construct a poetic world in which several existential planes are interrelated, and attempt to recover the vision of the world that emerges from this inquiry. My discussion of these topics takes the form of a close reading of several exemplary verses included in Māṇikkavācakar's text.

Let us begin with a verse that is located relatively early in the sequence of incidents that constitute the narrative skeleton of the text.

> This man who would stand unmoved at the end of time
> when a murderous wind topples all seven worlds
> with their seven mountain-pillars,
> is deeply shaken by this slender-waisted girl
> with eyes deadly as poisoned darts.
>
> He wonders:
> Will she come to the cool field
> in the shadow of the vast grove sheltered by clouds
> on the mountain of Tillai's Lord?
>
> *Tirukkōvaiyār* 31

This verse is spoken by the *pāṅkaṉ,* the friend of the poem's "leading man" (*talaivaṉ*) who has recently met and fallen in love with the "leading lady" (*talaivi*). According to the conventions of classical *akam* poetry, the landscape appropriate to this stage in the story of the *talaivaṉ's* and the *talaivi's* relationship is the mountains, and Māṇikkavācakar retains this feature of the classical tradition.[7] The speaker observes that his friend is preoccupied with thoughts of his newly found love and anxiously anticipates his prearranged meeting with her in a field on the mountain slope. Thus far the poem could easily be taken to belong to one of the anthologies of classical poems. But unlike classical *akam* poems where mountain landscapes are strictly generic, here the mountain meeting place is Śiva's mountain, and thus Māṇikkavācakar gives a Śaiva cast to the classical poetic landscape. In this, as in many of *Tirukkōvaiyār's* verses, Śiva is spoken of as "Tillai's lord" (*tillaiyīcaṉ*). Tillai is one of Śiva's sacred places in the Tamil country, some would say the most important site in the sacred geography of Tamil Śaivism. It is also the setting for the culmination of Māṇikkavācakar's lifelong quest for union with Śiva, according to accounts of the poet's life found in traditional hagiographic literature.[8] In addition to the spatial registers of classical Tamil poetic landscape and the sacred geography of Tamil Śaivism, the verse also incorporates a third spatial register that is invoked in the speaker's hyperbolic description of his friend's uncharacteristic agitation. To underscore his point, the *pāṅkaṉ* declares that while his friend is not the kind to be shaken even by the cataclysmic spectacle of the end of a cosmic eon when the entire world self-destructs, paradoxically, a young girl has caused him to lose his composure. This declaration, obviously calculated for rhetorical effect, presupposes the reader's familiarity with Hindu cosmological notions regarding a universe composed of seven world-continents that are subject to a cyclic pattern of creation and destruction.

The image of the eon's end is also found in *Tirukkōvaiyār* 75, but in a different context:

> I'm hapless as people
> who live without the grace of Ambalam's lord,
>   the god who wears a lion's skin,
>   who stands unmoved at the end of time
>   when the heavens fold,
>   vast floods rise and cover the hills,
>   and solid earth caves in.
> This girl, slim as a vine,
> makes me ride a palm-leaf horse.

The above poem is spoken by the *talaivaṉ,* who threatens to resort to desperate measures to convince the *talaivi's* family, by raising the threat of public scandal, to permit him to marry the girl. It is a convention of *akam* poetry that in his desperation to realize a lasting union with the *talaivi,* the *talaivaṉ* will be carried by his friends through the village on a horse made from sharp palm leaves, while he holds aloft a picture of his lady love. In effect, he blackmails the *talaivi's* family into accepting him as the girl's husband. What gives this verse a specifically Śaiva coloring, and what distinguishes it from classical *akam* poems that draw upon the same convention, is the comparison between the *talaivaṉ's* plight and the state of people who are deprived of Śiva's grace. Here it is Śiva who is described as being unmoved by the world's dissolution, and the statement is meant to be taken at face value, not as a rhetorical flourish as in verse 31. Further, in verse 75, Śiva is referred to as Ambalam's lord (*ampalavaṉ*), Ambalam being the sanctum of Śiva's temple at Tillai/Chidambaram. Thus the verse incorporates both the cosmic spatial realm and the realm of Tamil sacred geography.

Like verse 31, verse 42 invokes three spatial realms, and is spoken by the *talaivi:*

> O blossoming vine,
> Grant me refuge here in this grove
> and spare me the suffering that plagues people
> who fail to pay homage to Ambalam's Lord
> who bounds past his enemies, mounted on his bull
> and is reverently worshiped by the god
> who crossed the whole world in three strides.

In classical and postclassical Tamil poetry, and indeed in other premodern Indian literatures, characters often express their feelings to plants, animals, or even to inanimate objects in their surroundings. The episode that contextualizes this verse occurs shortly after the first sexual union of the *talaivaṉ* and the *talaivi*. Both have been deeply affected by the experience, and here the *talaivi* demonstrates the quality of shyness or shame (*nāṇam*), a highly commendable female trait in the ethos of premodern Tamil poetry. Finding no place to hide, the *talaivi* asks a nearby vine to shelter her. Like verse 31, this verse includes references to a landscape associated with classical *akam* poetry (mountain grove), to a locale in the Tamil country that is sacred to Śiva (Ambalam), and to the cosmos at large (the whole world). The first of these three is incorporated into the poetic design in a fashion similar to verse 31: it provides the immediate setting for the *akam* narrative. The other two realms, however, fit into the overall designs of the two verses differently. Tillai is metonymically related to the *akam* landscape in verse 31: the grove where the *talaivaṉ* and the *talaivi* have agreed to meet is located on the mountain of Śiva, lord of Tillai. In verse 42 the reference to Ambalam is incorporated into a metaphor: the *talaivi's* shame causes her to suffer like people who fail to worship Śiva, lord of Ambalam.[9] (Note that the same metaphor is employed to highlight the *talaivaṉ's* suffering in verse 75.) In verse 31, the reference to the cosmos at large, as we have seen, is part of a hyperbolic description of the *talaivaṉ's* character, and in verse 75 a similar reference emphasizes that Śiva stands outside the vicissitudes of cyclic time. In verse 42, the reference to the whole world is again included for rhetorical effect, but in this instance as a not so subtle affirmation of Śiva's superiority to Viṣṇu.[10]

> O man from the mountainous land
> where flames rising from bamboo
> burning on the mountain slopes
> reach up to the sky
> and singe the trees of heaven,
>
> in the presence of this girl
> with eyebrows whose curves shame the bow,
> this girl beautiful as Tillai, home of the Lord
> whose three eyes burn bright as sun, moon, and fire,
> it is as if this stone-covered path were perfectly smooth.
>
> *Tirukkōvaiyār* 168

In order to keep their relationship secret, the *talaivaṉ* and the *talaivi,* with the help of their close friends, meet on the sly. Some *akam* poems describe how during the night the *talaivaṉ* braves the treacherous forest paths that separate his and his lady love's native villages, so he can meet with her secretly. In verse 168 the *talaivi's* friend (*tōḻi*) observes to the *talaivaṉ* that he is so entranced by his lady love that he barely notices the obstacles he must surmount in order to meet with her. Here the by now familiar reference to Tillai is incorporated into the verse as a metaphor for the *talaivi*—it is not uncommon in premodern Tamil poetry for the beauty of a woman to be compared to the splendor of a prosperous city. The realm of classical poetic landscape and the cosmological realm are interlinked in the friend's choice of words when addressing the *talaivaṉ* (mountain slopes/heaven). Further cementing the connection between the verse's classical conventions and its Śaiva registers, the description of flames (*tī*) that rise from burning bamboo near the *talaivaṉ's* mountain home are echoed on a far larger scale by the burning brightness of Śiva's eyes, compared here to the sun, the moon, and fire (*eri*).

In verse 337, as elsewhere, the fate of people who do not worship Śiva is compared to hardships people suffer due to other causes:

> O girl, beautiful as a flowering vine,
> What more can we say?
> Our lover must journey through the wilderness,
> burning hot as the hellish abode
> of people who fail to praise the glories of Tillai
> where the three great gods with the thirty-three others[11]
> praise the dance of Śiva,
>   chief of all gods.

At this point in the narrative, the *talaivaṉ* and the *talaivi* are married, but this does not mean that their trials and tribulations are finished. According to the conventions of *akam* poetry, after his marriage to his lady love, the *talaivaṉ* periodically leaves her to study, to serve the king, to make his fortune, or to live with his mistress. This verse is placed in the narrative segment devoted to the *talaivaṉ's* departure to acquire wealth. The *talaivi's* close friend injects a note of level-headed practicality, reminding the *talaivi* that the *talaivaṉ's* departure is inevitable. In order to seek opportunities to acquire wealth, he must endure the hardships of travel through inhospitable regions, compared here to hell (*narakam*), the destined dwelling place of people who neglect to worship Śiva. The verse sets up a dichotomy between hell, a realm associated with errant non-Śaivites, and Tillai, where even the gods worship Śiva.

> Gentle girl,
> before us rises Puliyūr city
> shining bright as the northern mountains—
> above its walls of gold
> flags flutter in the vast sea of sky,
> flashing bright as lightning.
> Like our King Śiva,
> its tall mansions wear the crescent moon as a crown
> and sport the sign of the trident.
> Like you,
> the swans there gracefully sway as they walk.
>
> *Tirukkōvaiyār* 222

In this verse, Puliyūr (yet another name for Tillai/Chidambaram) becomes the destination for the *talaivaṉ* and the *talaivi,* who have run off together. The verse implicitly establishes an equation between the premier Śaiva sacred place in the Tamil country and Mount Kailāsa, Śiva's abode in the Himālayas, a site that straddles the boundary between earthly and otherworldly realms. Through this equation, the sacred site in the Tamil land is placed on par with a locale that is universally recognized as Śiva's dwelling place. The verse further establishes a correspondence between Puliyūr and the god himself through a series of matching traits.[12]

The final verse I will consider in this small sampling of *Tirukkōvaiyār's* 400 verses introduces a fourth spatial realm, the devotee's heart and mind:

Did you go to study sweet Tamil verses
at the academy of Kūṭal,
high-walled city of the lord
  who dwells in my mind
  and in my heart,
  who stays at Tillai
  where flowing streams are held by dams,

or did you go to study music
where they play the seven tones?

My lord,
whatever has happened to your shoulders
great as mountains?

Tirukkōvaiyār 20

Like verse 31, this verse is spoken by the *talaivaṉ's* friend, and in both verses, the speaker comments that since meeting the *talaivi,* the *talaivaṉ* is not his usual self. The friend has noticed a change in the *talaivaṉ's* demeanor, and perhaps facetiously, he speculates on the cause. Besides the by now very familiar reference to Śiva's abode at Tillai, the verse contains a reference to Kūṭal, another name for Maturai, the residence of Śiva in his local manifestation as Cōmacuntaram with his consort Mīṉāṭci, and also the site of the legendary literary academy (*caṅkam*) patronized by the Pāṇṭiyaṉ kings. Most tellingly, the verse speaks of Śiva dwelling both at Tillai as well as in the speaker's own heart and mind.[13]

The preceding examples illustrate how several kinds of spatial and geographical references are incorporated into the verses of *Tirukkōvaiyār*. Let us now take a closer look at how some of these references function in the poetic design of the verses in which they are found. In broad terms, the structure of *Tirukkōvaiyār* is generated by mixing two registers that in other contexts often operate independently of one another: the conventions of classical *akam* poetry and Śaiva *bhakti*. There are several ways of viewing the status of the poem's Śaiva register in relation to its *akam* register. In some instances, the Śaiva elements in *Tirukkōvaiyār's* verses are melded with or function similarly to the "primary elements" (*mutaṟporuḷ*) or to the "germinal elements" (*karupporuḷ*) in classical *akam* poems (see Selby's essay in this volume). For instance, in verse 31 Śiva presides over the *akam* mountain landscape; in verse 222 the Śaiva sacred site of Puliyūr becomes the town that the *talaivan̲* and *talaivi* choose as their destination when they elope together; and in verse 20, the reference to Kūṭal (Maturai) is especially apt because it is both the traditional center of classical Tamil literary culture and a site sacred to Tamil Śaivites.

Another way to think about *Tirukkōvaiyār's* Śaiva register is as an injection of the *puṟam* side of classical Tamil poetics into the text's *akam* frame. Insofar as every verse of a *kōvai* poem incorporates one or more references to a "hero of the composition" (*pāṭṭuṭaittalaivan̲*), the mixture of *akam* and *puṟam* elements is built into the genre, but unlike many other *kōvai* poems where the "hero of the composition" is a human king, in *Tirukkōvaiyār* Śiva fills this role. Like the protagonists of *puṟam* poetry, the "hero of the composition" in a *kōvai* poem, especially if he is a king, is understood to be a historical figure who belongs to the real world and thus is named, whereas the *talaivan̲* of *akam* poetry (known as the *kiḷavittalaivan̲* to distinguish him from the *pāṭṭuṭaittalaivan̲*) and the other dramatis personae of the conventional *akam* narrative, inhabit the special interior landscape of the poetic world and are known only by their roles ("leading man," "leading lady," "friend," etc.). Not only is the "hero of the composition" in a *kōvai* a named historical figure: references to the "hero of the composition" in the verses of a *kōvai* may include details concerning his exploits in battle, acts of benevolence, and so on, such as one typically finds in *puṟam* poems. What sets *Tirukkōvaiyār* apart from other poems of this genre is the way Māṇikkavācakar deploys elements of Tamil Śaiva *bhakti* in the poem's *puṟam* register.

A third way to think about *akam* and Śaiva registers in *Tirukkōvaiyār* is as an analogue for the relationship established in *akam* poems between the drama of human relationships and scenes from nature that constitute a backdrop for this drama. In *akam* poems the relationship is highlighted by a poetic figure whereby elements of the natural backdrop are implicitly compared to and consequently augment the reader's perceptions of the humans who populate the *akam* world. In the parlance of classical Tamil poetics, this figure is called *uḷḷuṟaiyuvamam* ("comparison by means of a hidden meaning"). The distinctive features of this technique are the suppression of all explicit markers of comparison (the many Tamil equivalents of "like" and "as") and the coexistence of the terms being compared in a time/space continuum. As A. K. Ramanujan has observed, the relationship between the natural and human elements that are juxtaposed through this technique is both metaphoric and metonymic (1985, pp. 246–248). The poem suggests that its human protagonists resemble certain elements in the natural setting for their drama and at the same time, they themselves are coextensive with the natural realm.

In *Tirukkōvaiyār* only occasionally do the Śaiva elements of a verse relate to the drama of *talaivaṉ* and *talaivi* both metaphorically and metonymically in a manner comparable to a true *uḷḷuṟaiyuvamam*. More often, in a single verse the relationship is established either through metaphor or through metonym, not through both simultaneously. But by stepping back and contemplating the text as a whole, the reader is able to grasp that in Māṇikkavācakar's vision, humanity is like divinity. What is more, humanity and divinity cohabit a common universe.

Viewing the mixture of Śaiva and *akam* registers in *Tirukkōvaiyār* from these perspectives, we are better able to interpret the references to spatial realms in the poem in relation to the poem's overall design. What we find is that references to the four spatial realms discussed previously may be incorporated into the poetic structure of a verse in several ways and that there is no one-to-one correlation between spatial realms and poetic functions. To illustrate this point, let us examine the several references to the cosmological/mythological spatial realm found in the verses cited above. The reference to the end of time and the "seven worlds with their seven mountain-pillars" in verse 31 contributes to a description of the *talaivaṉ's* character, and thus it lies close to the poem's *akam* surface. Similarly, the reference to heaven in verse 168 contributes to a description of the landscape backdrop for the *akam* drama, as does the reference to hell in verse 337. In verse 75, the reference to the world's end contributes to a description of Śiva, the "hero of the composition" in *Tirukkōvaiyār* (in contrast to its function in verse 31). Further, in verse 75, the description of Śiva as the god who stands unmoved at the end of time, and so on in turn is incorporated into the *talaivaṉ's* metaphoric description of his plight ("I'm hapless as people who live without the grace of Śiva who stands unmoved at the end of time," etc.) The reference to "the whole world" in verse 42 fits into the verse's poetic structure in a similar manner, but here we find yet another structural layer. This reference, which alludes to Viṣṇu's dwarf incarnation Vāmana, is folded into Māṇikkavācakar's claim that Śiva is superior to Viṣṇu, and this claim, in turn, is incorporated into a metaphor for the *talaivi's* distress, likened to the suffering that plagues people who fail to pay homage to Śiva (who is worshiped by Viṣṇu who crossed the whole world in three strides).

In a similar manner, we could interrogate references to the other three spatial realms represented in the verses of *Tirukkōvaiyār,* and trace comparable patterns. But ultimately we must ask ourselves what we can learn from this exercise. Does it tell us something meaningful about Māṇikkavācakar's poetic vision and his vision of the world? To begin with, do the four spatial categories I have identified bear any resemblance to the categories that structure his perceptions and thought? Is some sort of metaphysical blueprint available that would enable us to answer this question? In Tamil Śaivism, there is a tradition that pegs the interpretation of *Tirukkōvaiyār* to the metaphysical categories of Śaiva Siddhānta, and some students of Tamil Śaivism find in Māṇikkavācakar's poetry a kind of presystematic exposition of the basic principles of Śaiva Siddhānta. According to the widely accepted reading of *Tirukkōvaiyār* based on Śaiva Siddhānta categories, the text is an allegory. According to this reading, the *talaivaṉ* in *Tirukkōvaiyār* represents *uyir,* the breath of life that animates the corporeal frame (*uṭal*) of a living being, and the *talaivi* represents *civam* or godhead. The other dramatis personae of the *akam* narrative are also assigned allegorized identities; most notably, the *talaivi's* close friend (*tōḻi*) represents God's grace (*aruḷ*) in the form of the "true guru" (*satguru*). Read as allegory, *Tirukkōvaiyār* thus becomes a saga of the vicissitudes of the quest of the life-breath and godhead to achieve union with one another. I am not sufficiently familiar with the finer points of this line of interpretation to specify precisely how the various spatial references discussed above would figure in this reading of the text. While I recognize the importance of this tradition of interpretation as an entry point into an intellectual climate that has held sway for at least half a millennium, I am not sure that this is the most interesting way to approach the text or indeed that Māṇikkavācakar composed the text as an allegory.

Other than Śaiva Siddhānta theology, the only other documented blueprints for interpreting *Tirukkōvaiyār* are two traditional commentaries on the text, one attributed to the renowned thirteenth-century commentator Pērāciriyar, and the other, possibly older commentary, by an anonymous author. Neither assigns allegorized identities to the characters of the *akam* narrative. In fact, the interpretive categories these commentators apply to *Tirukkōvaiyār* are lifted directly from the poetics of *akam* poetry, by and large. While compared to the Śaiva Siddhānta tradition, these commentaries seem closer in spirit to the manifest form of Māṇikkavācakar's text, they too are not fully satisfying. While the Siddhāntins' tradition of interpretation allows the text's Śaiva register to envelope and efface its *akam* register,[14] the other tradition does not adequately attend to the text's distinctively Śaiva features. It is Māṇikkavācakar's skillful and often ingenious blending of the two registers that makes *Tirukkōvaiyār* such an intriguing text.

In the absence of a documented tradition of interpretation that takes into account the delicately balanced orchestration of *Tirukkōvaiyār's* two registers, let us conclude by speculating a little on the significance of the four spatial realms discernible in the text in a manner that hopefully does justice to *Tirukkōvaiyār's* complexities. If we start from the premise that Māṇikkavācakar composed the poem primarily as an act of praise for Śiva, the spatial references in the text cumulatively reinforce the idea that Śiva pervades the entire world, or, more specifically, that he is present in the landscapes of the Tamil country, in the cosmos-at-large, in the sacred temple sites that represent a concentration of cosmic space on earth, and in the inner beings of living things. This is verified by complementary themes that appear in *Tiruvācakam,* a compendium of the other poems composed by Māṇikkavācakar. Generally better known to a larger, more diverse audience than *Tirukkōvaiyār,* the poems included in *Tiruvācakam* conform more closely in diction and rhetoric to commonly recognized models of *bhakti* poetry. Consider, for example, the following phrases taken from poems included in *Tiruvācakam:*

> You became the sky and the earth,
> wind and light, flesh and life-breath
> that which is
> and that which is not
>
> *Tiruccatakam* 15

our Father became man, woman
and one without gender,
sky, raging fire
and the End of all things

Tiruccatakam 29

I failed to see
that the seed of all being
resides in my own heart

Tiruccatakam 41

You are the earth and the heavens
and time
that comes and goes

Tiruccatakam 43

He's the king of the good Pāṇṭiya country

A<u>nn</u>aippattu 5

The lord of Northern Kōcamaṅkai
who's so hard to know
is fixed in my heart

A<u>nn</u>aippattu 6

The lord who rules his ardent devotees with love
and saves them from rebirth in this world
always resides in the southern land of Pāṇṭi

Tiruttacāṅkam 2

. . .our Father,
lord of Perunturai
who dwells in our mind

Tiruttacāṅkam 4

Employing a straightforward rhetoric, in *Tiruvācakam* Māṇikkavācakar expresses a vision of Śiva's ubiquity that in *Tirukkōvaiyār* is mediated by highly structured poetic conventions.

Is it then fair to say that *Tirukkōvaiyār* simply reiterates the themes Māṇikkavācakar develops in *Tiruvācakam,* but in fancier packaging? It may be useful to approach the relationship between Māṇikkavācakar's two works in terms of their performance contexts and their affiliations with other cultural domains. *Tiruvācakam* is closely affiliated with hagiography and the liturgy of temple worship, while *Tirukkōvaiyār* belongs to the realm of institutionalized literary study and performance. One appeals to a general audience, the other to a specialized one. As far as it goes, this is probably a fair evaluation of the relationship between the two texts, but it is also tempting to see in *Tirukkōvaiyār* a purpose that goes beyond simply producing a designer edition of *Tiruvācakam*. By choosing the *kōvai* form for this text, Māṇikkavācakar seems to be working toward a fusion of his brand of Śaivism with refined literary culture. This literary culture is not the exclusive preserve of any one religious sect, but adherents of various religious sects have sought to identify with it. During the centuries immediately prior to and following Māṇikkavācakar's time, the Jain community in particular was known to have cultivated Tamil through writing normative texts, grammars, texts on rhetoric and poetics, and literary texts (as well as commentaries on all).[15] If *Tirukkōvaiyār* can be seen as an effort by Māṇikkavācakar to claim Tamil literary culture for Śaivism, his would not be the only instance of such an effort.[16] In *Tiruvācakam* Māṇikkavācakar sings of Śiva as "king of the Pāṇṭiya country where cool Tamil thrives" (*Tiruvammāṉai* 10). *Tirukkōvaiyār* may be seen as a poem that embodies this theme, and effectively merges the interior landscape of *akam* poetry with a Tamil Śaiva geography and cosmology.

Notes

1. The edition I have used in my work on the text is Cōmacuntaraṉār, 1970.
2. For a detailed exposition of these conventions, see Martha Ann Selby's essay in this volume and also Ramanujan, 1985.
3. Employing the analytic perspective of semiotics, A. K. Ramanujan illuminates the relationship between the classical Tamil poetic tradition and *bhakti* in his "Afterword" to his *Hymns for the Drowning: Poems for Viṣṇu by Nammāḻvār* (Princeton: Princeton University Press, 1981).
4. The Tamil literary historian M. Arunachalam observes that the name Pērāciriyar ("great scholar") is associated with five different texts and it is unclear how many people these references correspond to. He mentions the generally held view that the thirteenth-century commentator on *Tolkāppiyam,* the authoritative manual on grammar, rhetoric, and poetics, and the author of the commentary on *Tirukkōvaiyār* are one and the same person. See Arunachalam, 1970, pp. 188–189.
5. The latter has been transmitted principally as an oral tradition. Many editions of the text, however, include a series of colophons, known collectively as *Tirukkōvaiyār uṇmai* ("the truth of *Tirukkōvaiyār*") that are intended to capture the

allegorical significance of each of *Tirukkōvaiyār's* 400 verses and each of the twenty-five sections into which these verses are grouped. The date and authorship of these colophons are unknown. The interpretation expressed succinctly in *Tirukkōvaiyār uṇmai* has been expanded by C. Taṇṭapāṇi Tēcikar (1965). The allegorized interpretation of *Tirukkōvaiyār* also informs Margaret Trawick's discussion of the text (1988).

6. The modern-day name for the place known as Tillai in the poetry of Māṇikkavācakar and his contemporaries is Chidambaram. In the Chidambaram temple, Śiva is enshrined as Nāṭarāja, "Lord of the Dance." Many of *Tirukkōvaiyār's* verses also mention Puliyūr, another name associated with the same site, and to Ampalam (Ambalam in Anglicized spelling), the sanctum santorum of this temple. Other Śaiva sacred places located in the Tamil country that are referred to in *Tirukkōvaiyār* include Kūṟṟālam, Paraṅkuṉṟam, Mūval, Kūṭal (= Maturai), Tiruveṇkāṭu, Pūvaṇam, Mūvalūr, Cuḷiyal, Ciṟkāḻi, and Iṅkōy.

7. The notion that the mountain landscape is the appropriate setting for poems that describe the union of lovers and other comparable notions regarding the coordination of poetic mood and landscape are found in the *Tolkāppiyam*. A good number of poems included in the Tamil *bhakti* corpus include descriptions of natural scenes that are reminiscent of those found in classical poems, but most *bhakti* poems generally do not preserve the classical correlation between landscape and mood such as one finds in *Tirukkōvaiyār*.

8. The traditional sectarian account of Māṇikkavācakar's life is found in a fifteenth-century (?) text titled *Tiruvātavūrar Purāṇam* by Kaṭavuḷ Māmuṉivar. Episodes from this story are also recounted in the "Old *Tiruviḷaiyāṭal Purāṇam*" of Perumpaṟṟappuliyūr Nampi (thirteenth century) and the better-known *Tiruviḷaiyāṭal Purāṇam* of Parañcōti Muṉivar (seventeenth century), both of which recount the sixty-four "sacred sports" of Śiva in the vicinity of Maturai. As one of a group of poet-saints known as "the four" (*nālvar*), Māṇikkavācakar is one of the most revered among the Tamil Śaiva saints (the other three being Campantar, Appar, and Cuntarar, authors of the poems known collectively as *Tēvāram*), but, unlike the others, his story is not included in the Tamil Śaiva hagiography par excellance, *Periya Purāṇam* by Cēkkiḻār (thirteenth century). There are various explanations for this, the most widely accepted being that Māṇikkavācakar lived later than Cuntarar, author of the poem that enumerates the names of the sixty-two Śaiva saints whose stories Cēkkiḻār tells in *Periya Purāṇam* (with the addition of Cuntarar himself).

9. For further discussion of metonym and metaphor as devices for integrating *Tirukkōvaiyār's akam* and Śaiva registers, see Cutler, 1987, pp. 87–88.

10. "The god who crossed the whole world in three strides" is, of course, Viṣṇu in his incarnation as the dwarf Vāmana.

11. The three great gods are generally understood to be Brahmā, Viṣṇu, and Śiva. From a Śaiva perspective, however, Rudra takes the place of Śiva in the trinity, and Śiva is placed above these three in the hierarchy of divine beings. The traditional number of Vedic gods is thirty-three.

12. Similarly, verse 16 of *Tiruvempāvai* (a constituent poem of *Tiruvācakam* by Māṇikkavācakar) and verse 4 of *Tiruppāvai,* its Vaiṣṇava twin by Āṇṭāḷ, establish a series of correspondences between a storm cloud and a divine being—Pārvatī in the former, and Kṛṣṇa in the latter.

13. A parallel concept is found in Śrīvaiṣṇavism where Viṣṇu is said to take five forms, one of which is known as the "in-dweller" (*antaryāmin*); that is, Viṣṇu as a presence within all living beings.
14. Śaiva Siddhānta distinguishes between "lesser pleasure" (*ciṟṟiṉpam*), the pleasure of sexual union, and "greater pleasure" (*pēriṉpam*), the blissful union between the life-breath (*uyir*) and godhead (*civam*). Śaiva Siddhāntins maintain that the ignorant view *Tirukkōvaiyār* as a poem about the former, while it is actually about the latter.
15. This is an area in which much scholarly work remains to be done. One of the relatively few available studies of this topic is Chakravarti, 1944 (1974).
16. K. Sivathamby writes of the legend of the Tamil *caṅkams,* which first appears in an eighth-century commentary as "the first attempt at a Śaivite history of Tamil literature" (1986, pp. 35–36).

THREE

The Drama of the Kuṟavañci Fortune-teller

Land, Landscape, and Social Relations in an Eighteenth-century Tamil Genre

Indira Viswanathan Peterson

This essay is an exploration of the innovative ways in which the Kuṟavañci ("Drama of the Kuṟavañci Fortune-teller"), a very productive eighteenth-century Tamil literary genre, deploys and extends discourses of landscape and place inherited from earlier genres. The landscape types (*tiṇai*) of classical Tamil poetry, though transformed in significant respects, are central to the themes of the Kuṟavañci drama. Equally important to the genre are constructions of place drawn from the postclassical literature of devotion (*bhakti*) and the cult of sacred places: the temple (*kōyil*), and the town or village (*ūr*), which becomes a sacred place (*talam, pati*) by virtue of the presence of the god and his temple. Praise of the god, and of the poet's patron, whose munificence makes both poems and temples possible, forms part of the Kuṟavañci's tapestry of constructions of space in relation to the natural and human worlds. The most innovative feature of the eighteenth-century genre, however, is its articulation of its spatial thematics through its central characters, the Kuṟavañci fortune-teller and her birdcatcher husband, wanderers associated with wilderness landscapes and livelihoods.

The Kuṟavañci is an opera-like genre, with a dramatic plot unfolding in a sequence of songs and intended to be enacted through dance. The stereotyped plot unfolds in three segments. Seeing the god of the local temple or the king riding in procession with his retinue, a highborn lady falls hopelessly in love with him. In the second segment, the Kuṟavañci or Kuṟatti, a wandering female of the Kuṟavar hill tribe and the eponymous principal character of the play, appears and offers to help the lovelorn woman.[1] After praising the god and the temple in the lady's town, the Kuṟatti names the hills with which her family is associated and the many places to which she has traveled. She describes the hill landscape and Kuṟavar ways of life, and uses Kuṟavar divinatory techniques to foretell the heroine's union with the hero. The lady handsomely rewards the Kuṟatti with gold and jewels. The third segment begins with a detailed description of the Kuṟatti's husband, the birdcatcher Ciṅkaṉ, trapping birds in the rice fields owned by the temple. While hunting, the birdcatcher suddenly realizes that his wife is missing. Maddened by desire, he leaves the birds, sets out to search for her, and finally meets her on the streets of the town. In the lively dialogue that follows, the fortune-teller wittily parries her jealous husband's questions about her activities, and the couple is reunited. The play ends with verses in praise of the god and the temple.

Although the Kuṟavañci drama depicts the love of an upper-class woman for a king or a god, the genre takes its name from the Kuṟatti fortune-teller. A significant portion of the play is devoted to the voices and activities of the Kuṟatti and Ciṅkaṉ. Mysterious outsiders, persons with marginal social identities, people of the hills, the Kuṟatti and Ciṅkaṉ are not "of the place" in the temple center. Yet the migrant couple's words and acts firmly connect them with the temple and the fields, place them within the boundaries of the town, and establish their relationship with the elites of the place. They are, in effect, the principal agents of the action in the play. In the remainder of this essay, I hope to show that the Kuṟavañci genre's representations of these dialogues between wilderness peoples and settled agrarian communities offer an imaginative commentary on changing relations among persons, land, and landscapes in an era of fragmented polities, increased migrations, and shifting social identities in the Tamil region.

Eighteenth-century Tamil Literary Genres

The Kuṟavañci is one of a number of Tamil genres that arose and flourished primarily between the late seventeenth and mid-nineteenth centuries, at least in partial response to major social, political, and economic changes that had been set in motion in the Tamil region. More than a hundred Kuṟavañcis are known to have been written during this period, and a large number of these are still available. From the sixteenth century onward, following the migration of the Vijayanagara Nayaka generals from the Telugu region in the north to the Tamil region, Telugu-speaking Vadugar ("northerner") peasants and warriors as well as members of the Tamil nonpeasant Maṟavar and Kaḷḷar castes rose to elite status in the Tamil area (Ludden 1985; Rao, Shulman, and Subrahmanyam, 1992). Migrating southwards in waves between the fifteenth and seventeenth centuries, they settled as owners of cultivated land and Pāḷaiyakkārar (English "Poligar") chiefs of estates and "little kingdoms," especially in the remote southern regions of Tirunelveli and Ramnad (Dirks, 1987; Ludden, 1985). By the eighteenth century, the actors in the political, economic, and cultural arenas in the Tamil region included the Telugu Nayakas of Madurai, the Western Indian Maratha rulers of Tanjavur (English "Tanjore"), the Muslim Nawab of Arcot, Mughal military officials, and European missionaries, traders, and colonial administrators. Each in its own way, the eighteenth-century genres, later classified as *pirapantam* ("sustained composition") or *ciṟṟilakkiyam* ("minor genre"), reflect this rich mix of cultural sensibilities and social agendas.

While in the seventeenth century the Telugu-speaking Nayakas of Tanjavur and Madurai had patronized works in their native Telugu and in Tamil (the local language), in the eighteenth century, literature flourished in these languages as well as in Sanskrit and Marathi in the court of the Maratha kings of Tanjavur, which remained the premier cultural center of the Tamil region until the late nineteenth century (Peterson, 1998). Patronage for the majority of the Tamil genres, however, came preeminently from the new provincial elites: the Maṟavar Cētupatis of Ramnad, the Kaḷḷar kings of Pudukkottai, the Maṟavar and Vadugar Pāḷaiyakkārar chiefs of the Tirunelveli region in the southern part of the peninsula, and lesser landowners and administrators all over the region. The Tamil works continued to be authored by *pulavar* poets who came from the high-ranking Vēḷāḷar agriculturalist caste groups and were trained in the traditional Tamil learning nourished at monasteries (*maṭam*) and temples (Zvelebil, 1973, 1974).

The new Tamil *pirapantam* genres blended many "folk" and popular elements of contemporary Tamil culture—including colloquial language and mixtures of languages—with more conventional courtly themes such as the praise of gods and kings. They also shared other important traits. First, like the Kuṟavañci, they tended to focus on representatives of particular social identities (*cāti,* "caste," from Sanskrit *jāti,* "birth"), portraying at the same time milieus composed of diverse linguistic communities and social strata. The *pirapantams* oscillated between a more conventional concern with particular sacred places, settled landscapes, and social groups, and a new interest in marginal identities and migrant populations. They had much in common with the genuine "folk" literary traditions that were developing at the same time. The principal characters of the three most popular *pirapantam* genres, the Kuṟavañci, Paḷḷu ("Field-laborer's Song"), and Noṇṭināṭakam ("The Cripple's Play"), are respectively a nomadic Kuṟavar couple, Paḷḷar agricultural laborers, and a Kaḷḷaṉ horse thief who travels the Tamil countryside.[2] Second, the most popular of the minor genres were musical-dramatic genres intended to be performed especially by the female Devadasi dancers who were maintained by local rulers to serve the temple and the court. Thematic connections with local temples as well as courts made them suitable for performance in either or both settings, and ensured their dissemination among diverse audiences.

In some ways, the representation of distinct social groups and their lives in the eighteenth century genres is the continuation of a long tradition in Tamil literature. The association of particular communities and occupations with particular natural landscapes is part of the *tiṇai* landscape system that forms the basis of the conceptual universe of ancient Tamil *caṅkam* poetry (Ramanujan, 1985; Selby, this volume). The Kuṟavar hill tribe (*kuṉṟakkuṟavar*) and other kinds of hunter and warrior tribes as well—Vēṭṭuvar, Eyiṉar, and Maṟavar—are part of the landscape system of the poems in the *caṅkam* anthologies and the narrative works of the later *caṅkam* period, such as Iḷaṅkōvaṭikaḷ's epic, *Cilappatikāram*. The conventions of the classical poems were taken over by later *bhakti* devotional poetry, hagiographical texts, and mythological narrative literature. The representation of communities in eighteenth-century Tamil literature carries forward many of these earlier currents and motivations, but this literature manifests a new sensibility as well. In contrast to the earlier literature, the eighteenth-century minor genres, especially those that focus directly on characters from low-class social groups, link and contrast these characters with high-class and elite figures. These genres also combine humor with idealization and respect in their depiction of the low-class characters. Both features reveal an interest on the part of poets and patrons in reexamining elite and lower-class social identities—in other words, in imaginatively representing eighteenth-century social relations. I have argued in this essay that the Kuṟavañci is one among several genres that allowed the new elites to articulate and legitimize their newly acquired positions as rulers and landowners through artistic representations of social relations.

Throughout the eighteenth century, the Maṟavar and Vaḍugar rulers of provincial kingdoms commissioned works in all the minor genres. The most important examples of the Paḷḷu (e.g., *Mukkūṭaṟpaḷḷu*), which related to labor relations in the agricultural economy, were produced in Tirunelveli, as were celebrated Noṇṭināṭakams (e.g., *Tiruccentūr Noṇṭināṭakam*) and Kuṟavañcis (*Kuṟṟālakkuṟavañci*). The new rulers in the peninsula had to establish their claims to land ownership and agriculture in contestation and collaboration with brahmans and Vēḷāḷar, older, entrenched landowning communities, particularly in the great temple centers where power was concentrated. They also needed to negotiate anew their relationship with tribes, lower castes, and marginal social groups, especially those from the mountains, forests, and wilderness areas that were vital to the political and economic well-being of their kingdoms. These themes were strikingly dramatized in the Kuṟavañci play through the intervention of Kuṟavar characters. Some of the earliest and best-known Kuṟavañcis—including some in Marathi and other languages—were also produced under the patronage of the Maratha court at Tanjavur. As "strangers" from a different linguistic-cultural region in India, and as rulers of the fertile Kaveri delta with its concentration of temples and agricultural resources, the Marathas of Tanjavur had to undertake their own negotiations with diverse constituencies. The Kuṟavañci was the preferred genre in Tanjavur, especially since it was ideally suited to the rich performance tradition that the Marathas had inherited from their Nayaka predecessors (Peterson, 1998). As we shall see, the Marathas were particularly intrigued by the play's nomadic central characters.

In the following sections, I will analyze the Kuṟavañci genre's representations of the discourses of landscape, place, and social relations that I have sketched above, especially through the characters of the Kuṟavañci and Ciṅkaṉ. In the Kuṟavañci drama, not only the structure of the play in three distinct segments but also the specific themes of the songs in each segment, and the sequence of these songs, are treated as fixed topics. The details of local mythology, history, geography, and personalities distinguish these dramas from each other, as do the variations achieved on the conventions themselves by individual poets.

My analysis will be focused on the *Kuṟṟālakkuṟavañci,* the most celebrated example of the fortune-teller play genre.

The Kuṟavañci Fortune-teller from the Hills

The *Kuṟṟālakkuṟavañci* ("The Kuṟavañci Drama of Kuṟṟālam") is the best known work of the Śaiva Vēḷāḷa poet Tirikūṭarācappa Kavirāyar (henceforth Rācappar), who authored several works dedicated to the ancient shrine of Śiva at Kuṟṟālam. A major pilgrimage center, Kuṟṟālam is situated on the Cittāṟu or Citrā River, in the western end of Tirunelveli, on the edge of the Western Ghats mountains and adjacent to the fertile rice-growing valley of the Tamraparni River. Rācappar composed the *Kuṟṟālakkuṟavañci* (henceforth *KK*) for his patron Ciṉṉaṇañcāttēvaṉ, the Maṟavar Pāḷaiyakkārar of Cokkampaṭṭi (also known as Kiḷuvai) *pāḷaiyappaṭṭu* in Tirunelveli. The play was performed for the first time at the Kuṟṟālam temple in 1718. A copperplate inscription of that year from the temple records the deed of a grant of irrigated agricultural land (*naṉcey*) to the poet and his family by Muttuvijayaranga Chokkanatha, the Nayaka king of Madurai, in whose presence the play was premiered (*KK,* Introduction, pp. 13–14).

Kuṟṟālanātar, the god Śiva as the Lord of Kuṟṟālam, is also the "lord" (*pāṭṭuṭaittalaivaṉ*) who captivates Vacantavalli, the highborn lady (*talaivi*) in the play. In the first part of the *KK,* Rācappar describes Kuṟṟālanātar's procession (*pavaṉi, ulā*) and its effect on the female spectators who line the streets. Without exception, the women fall in love with the god.[3] At this point, the lady Vacantavalli enters the street, playing ball. Seeing the god, she, too, falls hopelessly in love. Vacantavalli's girlfriends (*caki*) are unable to help the heroine, who pines for her lover.[4] Just as Vacantavalli completes the ancient rite of *kūṭal* (*KK,* song 48) in which a girl closes her eyes and draws a circle on the ground, believing that a completed circle (*kūṭal*) will indicate that her wish to be united with her lover will be fulfilled, the *malaikkuṟavañci,* the "Kuṟatti from the hills," enters the scene.

The poet describes the Kuṟatti in several "entrance songs" (*pāttirappiravēcadaru*), a type of song with which characters are announced in the play (song 48).[5] The Kuṟavañci of Tirikūṭam Hill "enters the street lined with mansions, carrying a fine basket and a divining rod, swinging her arms adorned with bracelets, singing the praise of Kuṟṟālam's gracious Lord" (song 48).[6] She comes "adorned with necklaces of coral and the crab's eye seed (*kuṉṟi*), a basket perched on her sari-draped hip, a divining rod (*māttiraikkōl*) in her right hand, speaking words of allure, with a bounce of her breasts, a flutter of her eyelashes, a coquettish gait." She is "capable of surpassing with her divination the omens told with drums, and every other kind of soothsaying." She has "wielded her divining rod like a royal scepter in the Aryan, Gurjara, and Koṅkaṇa countries," and has "planted a pillar of victory with Tamil in the lands of those who speak Kannada, Telugu, and Kaliṅga (Oriya)" (song 49). The Kuṟatti can "perform every kind of divination in an instant, divining past and present events, foretelling the future, reading signs on the body or the palm, in the eye and the word!" (song 49)

The Kuṟatti identifies herself as a soothsayer from the hills who specializes in telling fortunes for young women (song 52). Vacantavalli asks her to describe the splendor of her mountain home. In verses that have become popular songs known throughout Tamilnadu, the Kuṟavañci describes Tirikūṭam, the hill (*malai*) next to the town of Kuṟṟālam, a place famous for its waterfalls, on which she lives (song 54):

> There monkeys court their mates with fruit,
> apes beg for the fruit the female monkey lets fall.
> Hunters shoot arrows to propitiate the gods,
> flying Cittar adepts grow herbs of immortality.
> There the mist from the waterfall called "Honey"
> strikes the sky and comes down as rain,
> and the sun god's charioteer and horses
> slip in their tracks!
> Such is the hill from which I come,
> Kuṟṟālam's Tirikūṭam Hill,
> hill of the god whose hair is adorned
> by the young crescent moon!

On that hill, says the Kuṟatti, the local tribes dig for roots and tubers, extract honey from honeycombs, and dance, singing the hill's praise. There they pound roasted millet with elephant tusks, and great, sweet-smelling aloe and sandal trees grow in the forests that hunters clear for sowing millet. In the Kuṟatti's song, Kuṟṟālam's Tirikūṭam Hill is more glorious than the sacred Himālayan Mount Kailāsa and the mythic Golden Mountain Meru, situated at the center of the universe. It is also related to many other hills, through networks of kinship between the fortune-teller and others of her tribe. The Kuṟavañci's sister Celli lives on Kolli hill, while her brother-in-law has rights over Paḻaṉi. Her mother-in-law hails from Cāmimalai, and her *tōḻi* (girlfriend) comes from Vēḷvimalai in the Nāñcil country (bordering Kerala). The Kuṟatti ends her song of Tirikūṭam Hill with an account of the marriage customs of the Kuṟavar tribe and a reference to its association with the hill-god Murukaṉ, who is married to the Kuṟavar girl Vaḷḷi.

Next, Vacantavalli asks the Kuṟatti to describe the glories of the sacred town of Kuṟṟālam and the land (*nāṭu*) in which it is situated (song 55). The Kuṟatti obliges, singing five songs on these themes, including the praise of the Kuṟṟālam temple and the god who dwells there. The lady then asks the fortune-teller questions about her origins, her caste, and her professional qualifications. The Kuṟavañci declares that she has won countless rewards for her expertise as a soothsayer. Traveling all over the country, far beyond the Tamil region, she has told the fortunes of noblemen and women, not only in South Indian Cochin and Konku, but also in Makkā (Mecca), Maratha, Simhala (modern Sri Lanka), Kasi (Benares), and Bengal (song 62.1–3).[7]

The Kuṟatti shows Vacantavalli the beautiful necklace that Ciṉṉaṇañcāttēvaṉ, Rācappar's patron, gave her "in the illustrious Kollam (era) year 887 (1712 C.E.)," when "he covered with copper the tile roof of the *cittiracapai* hall (Sanskrit *citrasabhā,* 'hall of many colors or paintings') of the Kuṟṟālam temple." Already in 1272 C.E. (Kollam 444), her ancestors had predicted success for Ceṇpaka Pandiyan in constructing the temple at Teṉkāci (an old Pandiyan capital near Tirunelveli town), and in ancient times, Madurai city's Goddess Mīṉāṭci herself had approached the Kuṟatti's forebears for a divination regarding her marriage with Śiva![8] Kuṟavañci poets play delightful variations on these conventions of the Kuṟatti's impressive travels and her illustrious ancestors. For example, the soothsayer of the *Tañcai Veḷḷai Piḷḷaiyār Kuṟavañci* (*TVPK*), a late seventeenth-century proto-Kuṟavañci, traces her fortune-telling heritage back to her "grandmother's grandmother's grandmother's grandmother" (*pāṭṭikku-p-pāṭṭikku-p-pāṭṭikku-p-pāṭṭi*).

Before embarking on the ritual of soothsaying, the Kuṟatti asks Vacantavalli for "a little gruel, some betel leaf and areca nut to chew on, and a bit of the stuff from China (opium) that comes on the ship." Other Kuṟattis ask their clients for a little gruel for the babies that they are carrying in slings, or a little oil for their hair. Compared to the fortune-teller women's exaggerated claims about their wealthy patrons, these requests are modest indeed, and bespeak a marginal, poverty-stricken existence.

Reading auspicious omens, the soothsayer asks Vacantavalli to set up the sacred space and the implements for the ritual of soothsaying (songs 64–66). She reads the lady's palm, and predicts general good luck for her. Next, she invokes the local gods and goddesses in a long recitative set in *akaval* meter (that of *caṅkam* poems), which has ancient connections with augury and soothsayers.[9] Beginning with invocations to the "high gods" of the Āgamic temples in Kuṟṟālam and elsewhere, she calls on a large number of "fierce" gods and goddesses—unpredictable village deities, the guardian gods and goddesses of field and grove, forest and hill (such as Payiravar, Piṭāri, and Paṉṟi Māṭaṉ), asking them to help her divine the object of Vacantavalli's desire (song 72). The invocation continues with a long list of signs from which the Kuṟavañci must pick out the right one. Possessed by Jakkammā (a folk goddess of the Telugu region), the Kuṟatti identifies Śiva, Lord of Kuṟṟālam, as the object of Vacantavalli's love, and predicts the certainty of her union with her Lord. Vacantavalli sends the soothsayer off, having rewarded her with many golden ornaments studded with gems (songs 77–79).

The Identity of the Kuṟavañci Fortune-teller

The central segment of the Kuṟavañci, containing the fortune-telling episode, the high point of the drama, gives insights into the seventeenth- and eighteenth-century Tamil fascination with the fortune-teller, hill landscapes, and marginal livelihoods. It also demonstrates the genre's genius for synthesizing aesthetic and thematic elements of classical Tamil poetry with conventions of later origin, perhaps representing contemporary realities. The dialogue between Vacantavalli and the Kuṟatti is a dramatization of the curiosity as well as the stereotyping perceptions of the settled populations of the Tamil region regarding tribal peoples whom they call "Kuṟavar" in the seventeenth and eighteenth centuries. The depiction of a Kuṟatti fortune-teller telling a young woman's fortune made its first appearance in Tamil literature as a brief vignette in a seventeenth-century minor genre called "Kalampakam" ("mixed poem," an anthology of poetic themes), and became the focus of a separate short genre called "Kuṟam" ("The Kuṟatti's divination," also dating from the seventeenth century), of which very few examples are available.[10] Female fortune-tellers also appeared in Telugu literary works called Yakṣagāna, which arose in the Telugu region in the late Vijayanagar and Nayaka periods. "Kuramu" (Telugu), the dance of a Kuṟatti, had also become a part of the repertoire of late Nayaka and Maratha court dancers in Tanjavur (Peterson, 1998). But it is only in the 1700s, with the Tamil Kuṟavañci drama, that the Kuṟatti's fortune-telling plays a pivotal role in an elaborate dramatic plot focusing on the Kuṟavar people, presented as a dance-drama performed for large audiences.

The identity of the Kuṟatti as a woman of the mountain Kuṟavar tribe is based in part on the literary identity of the Kuṟavars of the *kuṟiñci* (hill) landscape, one of the five *tiṇais* of the classical poems. In the *caṅkam* corpus, the Kuṉṟakkuṟavar ("hill Kuṟavar") are one of the tribes who live in the *kuṟiñci* landscape, where they hunt and manage the produce of hill and forest. The classical *kuṟiñci* landscape is connected with dangerous and mysterious sacred powers. The hills are the abode of Murukaṉ (the god of the Kuṟavar) and the landscape of the clandestine sexual union of lovers, a situation that is itself a manifestation of the sacred (Hart, 1975). These older associations of the Kuṟavar with hills, Murukaṉ, the sacred, and sexual union are carried forward in the medieval myth of Murukaṉ's marriage to the hill-Kuṟavar girl (*kuṟa-makaḷ*) Vaḷḷi, and in the eighteenth-century Kuṟavañci drama. The Kuṟatti's description of tribal life on the hills is based mainly on older conventions about the occupations of the Kuṟavar in *caṅkam* poems and Murukaṉ myths: hill-Kuṟavar hunt, gather honey, clear forests, and grow millet, and Kuṟavar women chase birds away from fields of ripening millet.[11]

In her fortune-telling persona and techniques, the Kuṟatti in the Kuṟavañci play combines aspects of various diviner-figures and techniques of divination described in classical and medieval Tamil poetry. The wand or rod that the Kuṟatti carries appears to be derived from the rod of divination carried by the Akavaṉmakaḷ, the female oracle of a class of bards and drummers called Akavunar in the *caṅkam* poems.[12] The earlier literature depicts the hill Kuṟavar worshipping Murukaṉ in a religion that involves possession, dancing, and oracles.[13] In *caṅkam* poems the *kaṭṭuvicci* ("diviner," "shamaness"), a female diviner of Murukaṉ, gets possessed by the god, and divines future events by "reading" odd and even configurations of molucca beans (*kaḻaṅku*), or paddy (*nel*) in a winnowing fan.[14] The Kuṟatti of the eighteenth-century plays practices all the techniques of divination described in the classical poems. She gets possessed by a goddess and makes oracular utterances. She "reads" the meaning of her client's touching various parts of the body (*meykkuṟi pārttal*), and uses grains (usually *nel,* paddy) in a winnowing fan for divination (*neṟkuṟi pārttal*).

There remain, however, a number of elements in the description of the eighteenth-century Kuṟavañci drama's Kuṟatti that cannot be traced back to any earlier source. The typical Kuṟatti fortune-teller of the Kuṟavañci plays carries a basket and wears bead and seed necklaces, made especially of crab's-eye seed (Tamil *kuṉṟimaṇi;* Sanskrit *guñjā*). She carries a baby in a sling across her breasts. In many Kuṟavañci dramas, she sells beads and needles, and offers to tattoo her clients as well as to tell their fortunes, especially by reading their palms. Palm reading (*kaikkuṟi pārttal*), the quintessential technique of fortune-telling used by the Kuṟatti of the Kuṟavañci, is not included among the divination techniques of the *caṅkam* poems and the seventeenth-century genres. Likewise, the portrayal of the Kuṟatti as a nomad seems to be a late addition to the Kuṟatti fortune-teller's composite persona. Although we may find some echoes of the traveling Viṟali dancer and other female technicians of the sacred from the *caṅkam* poems in the Kuṟatti figure of the Kuṟavañci drama, the details of her wandering life and profession include new elements that correspond closely to the actual practice of particular nomadic communities in the Tamil region from the eighteenth century to the present. These elements will be examined below.[15]

In the Kuṟavañci, the fortune-teller has traveled far beyond the Tamil country, as far as Delhi, Gujarat, Mecca, and China. Although Rācappar presents his Kuṟatti as a triumphant representative of Tamil language and culture in foreign places, the fortune-tellers in other Kuṟavañci dramas are portrayed as women who have mastered many languages, and can speak to their clients in their own languages. In a number of fortune-teller plays, snatches of Telugu, Kannada, Marathi, and Hindi appear in the dialogue between the Kuṟatti and her client. The Kuṟatti in the *Carapēntira Pūpāla Kuṟavañci,* written in the early nineteenth century in honor of the Maratha king Serfoji II of Tanjavur, quotes from her conversations with her clients in Kannada, Hindi, Marathi, Tamil, and English (song 43). Finally, in her divination rites, after invoking the local gods, the Kuṟatti summons the Andhra goddesses Polerammā and Jakkammā, as well as Kollāpuriyammā (the goddess Mahālakṣmī of Kolhapur in Maharashtra), pointing to her community's association with these regions to the north of the peninsula. In the *KK* it is Jakkammā who possesses the Kuṟatti and directs her oracular utterance.

The newer details of the Kuṟatti's appearance as described in the Kuṟavañci have their visual counterparts in the life-sized sculpted images of female "folk" figures (these are identified by local guides as "Kuṟatti") at the Madurai Mīṉāṭci temple and in Śiva and Viṣṇu temples in Tirunelveli, most notably in Krishnapuram and Tirukkurungudi (Silpi, n.d.). Like the Kuṟavañci dramas, these sculptures date from the seventeenth and eighteenth centuries (Thomas, 1985). The non-classical elements of the Kuṟatti's descriptions of Kuṟavar occupations and ways of life match the portrayals of these occupations in eighteenth-century "Company" paintings from Tanjavur and Trichinopoly, commissioned from local artists by British patrons who collected albums of paintings recording the costumes and occupations of the peoples of South India (Archer, 1972, 1992). The same details also appear in the descriptions of "Kuṟavar" groups in nineteenth- and twentieth-century ethnographic accounts (Hatch, 1928; Malten, 1989; Thurston, 1909; Werth, 1996; Williams, 1912–13). The correspondences between the fortune-teller's descriptions and the ethnographic writing suggest that the Kuṟavar of the Kuṟavañci might well represent migrant peoples of the eighteenth century, with identities, occupations, and relations to the land that are considerably different from those of the "Kuṟavar" of the classical and medieval poems. In order to complete our understanding of these eighteenth-century identities, however, we must first consider Ciṅkaṉ, the birdcatching Kuṟavaṉ of the fortune-teller play, who offers an image of Kuṟavar life not found in Tamil literature prior to the appearance of the Kuṟavañci drama.

The Birdcatcher in the Paddy Fields

In the third segment of the *KK,* the scene changes from the courtly setting and the interior of Kuṟṟālam town to the rice fields surrounding Kuṟṟālam's temple. The segment begins with the arrival of Ciṅkaṉ or Kuḷuva-Ciṅkaṉ, a Kuṟavaṉ birdcatcher (the term *kuḷuvaṉ* appears to mean "birdcatcher"). The birdcatcher appears, announced thus in a song:

> Wearing a necklace of cockle shells,
> a heron feather bound in his hair,
> a tiger skin tied neatly
> into a sash around his waist,
> frightening tigers with his ferocity,
> a quiver slung over his shoulder,
> a curved bamboo staff in his hand,
> carrying various weapons and snares for birds,
> here comes Ciṅkaṉ, the famed Kuḷuvaṉ birdcatcher,
> Ciṅkaṉ, the Kuṟavaṉ of Kuṟṟālam's Tirikūṭam Hill! (*KK* 81)

Announcing himself, Ciṅkaṉ declares: "I am Ciṅkaṉ the birdcatcher! I set snares all day long. Springing like a lion, I catch birds in the sacred fields in the land of Tirikūṭam's Lord" (song 84). The birdcatcher goes about setting up snares and traps for birds in the paddy fields. Then Ciṅkaṉ's clownish assistant Nūvaṉ enters, carrying special traps and snares for different kinds of birds—for jungle fowl and red wag-tails, for quails and partridges, and special snares for water and shore birds, including herons and terns. In the songs that follow, Ciṅkaṉ and Nūvaṉ discuss the species of birds they expect to catch, and the specialized traps and snares that they will set up for their prey. At this point Nūvaṉ climbs up a tree and imitates birdcalls in order to attract the birds. The next sequence of songs weaves a complex tapestry of themes. Songs with descriptions of Kuṟṟālam temple's rich lands alternate with songs on the details of birdcatching, and others that delineate Ciṅkaṉ's passion for his wife, whom he misses so much that he cannot concentrate on his work. In his songs, Ciṅkaṉ calls his wife "Ciṅki," the feminine form of "Ciṅkaṉ."

Approaching the fields belonging to the temple, Ciṅkaṉ describes the many water birds that are feeding on the fish in each field canal and tank, at the same time naming each field and its owner and describing his contributions to the temple.

The birds are landing, sir, the birds are landing! (refrain)

In the *mēlvāram paṟṟu* fields of fertile Ceṅkuḷam,
In the Kāṭuveṭṭi field, and the field of the long *cuṇṭai* grove,
In the fine field of Kāṅkēyaṉ of Pēṭṭaikkuḷam,
In Srikrishnan *mēṭu* land, Muṉikkurukaṉ *pēri*, . . .
the birds are landing, sir! (*KK* 91.1, 3)[16]

The birds are feeding, sir, the birds are feeding!
Circling above every tank and field
Owned by Kuṟṟālam temple, the fields in Kulacēkarapaṭṭi,
Āyirapperi and Teṉkāci,
the birds are swooping down on *ayirai* and minnows and *tēḷi* fish,
the birds are feeding, sir! (*KK* 93.1, 2)

The birds are feeding, sir,
in the canals of the fields endowed for the morning worship rite
by pious Ciṉṉaṇañcēntiraṉ of Kiḷuvai (Cokkampaṭṭi),

hereditary servant of Kuṟṟālam's Lord
whom Brahmā and Viṣṇu praise,
the donor who built the wall around the temple,
who built an almshouse for feeding the poor,
built a bridge in Teṉkāci, and steps to the river as well,
he who is devoted to the service of the Lord's devotees. (*KK* 93.3)

In Taṭṭāṉkuḷam field, in Camphor Strip field,
watered by Lower New Pond in Kāṉāṅkuḷam,
in all the *tiruttu* fields of generous Piccai Piḷḷai
who wrote an *Antāti* poem for Kuṟṟālam,
younger brother of Cēṉai Cavaripperumāḷ,
Śaiva devotee, father of Kuṟṟālanātaṉ,
and of wealthy Vaittiyappaṉ of Marutūr,
commander of troops,
the birds are feeding, sir! (*KK* 93.4)

Ciṅkaṉ's list of Kuṟṟālam temple's paddy fields, tanks, and landowners, and his "history" of the temple and the relationship between the townsmen and the temple are richly detailed. The fact that these careful descriptions of land and temple relations (in no fewer than five long songs) are placed in the mouth of a forester and birdcatcher requires comment. Before turning to the details and implications of Ciṅkaṉ's praise-poem to Kuṟṟālam's fields, however, we need to see how the birdcatcher fits into the Kuṟavañci's plot, and how the play comes to closure.

While Ciṅkaṉ raves about Ciṅki's beauty, wit, and self-confidence, and especially her alluring physical charms, the birds fly away from the traps, but the passion-crazed birdcatcher pays no heed. He begs Nūvaṉ to find his Ciṅki for him, offering him in return magic spells, recipes for herbal medicine, potions for improving sexual performance, aphrodisiacs, and talismans for sexual potency, including a "jackal horn." Nūvaṉ tracks Ciṅki down in Kuṟṟālam town. After searching for Ciṅki in many towns, Ciṅkaṉ finally finds his wife on the main street in Kuṟṟālam town. A lively dialogue follows. Sick with lust and insane with jealousy, he at first accuses her of running off with a lover, but his anger turns to admiration when she tells him that she had only set off to tell fortunes "to women with flowers in their long hair" (song 125). The naive birdcatcher expresses puzzlement at the ornaments the Kuṟatti is wearing, and she explains the ornaments to him, one by one, in a clever and witty style.

You are wearing strange things, Ciṅki,
I am afraid to ask you what they are,
I'm afraid to ask!
No man ought to be afraid to say what he thinks!
    Speak up, don't be scared, Ciṅkā,
    tell me what's on your mind!
Why is a king cobra
coiled around your ankle, Ciṅki,
coiled around it?
    The anklet I got as my fee
    when I told a fortune in Salem country,
    That's what you see wrapped around my ankle, Ciṅkā!
(*KK* 125.3–6)

The dialogue ends with Ciṅkaṉ once again declaring his passion for her. Ciṅkaṉ and Ciṅki dance together. The play ends with the poet's invocation to the god, and a benedictory verse.

With the last segment, the Kuṟavañci drama, which began in the context of the town and temple, and moved through the hill landscape, the classical landscape of lovers' union, brings us to the agricultural landscape surrounding the temple and town. The focus of the segment alternates between the themes of birdcatching and cultivation. In Ciṅkaṉ's search for Ciṅki and in his sexual jealousy the Kuṟavañci drama draws upon the classical associations of the *marutam* (field) landscape with marital jealousy and quarrels. At the very end of the play, we return to the temple and town, and marital harmony is re-established, paralleling the union that has already been predicted for the lady and her lord. The genre's representations of the three landscapes can be fully understood only when we see the activities of the Kuṟatti and Ciṅkaṉ in relationship to each other, and the activities of the Kuṟavar couple in relation to the town, temple, and clients/patrons under whose auspices they have come to practice their occupations.

Land, Landowners, and the Temple in Eighteenth-century Tamilnadu: An Outsider's Perspective

The details of Ciṅkaṉ's description of the fields and irrigational tanks on which the birds land and feed serve as an exposition of the networks of cultivational rights and landownership by means of which the town of

Kuṟṟālam functioned as a social community in the early eighteenth century. The Kuṟavaṉ's description tallies remarkably well with the portrayal of the above relationships in recent scholarship on agrarian history in south India, especially in David Ludden's analysis of peasant history in Tirunelveli, the province in which Kuṟṟālam is located, and the region of Tamilnadu in which Kuṟavañci dramas proliferated under the patronage of Pāḷaiyakkārars such as Ciṉṉaṇañcāttēvaṉ in the eighteenth century.

Ciṅkaṉ uses a precisely nuanced agricultural vocabulary to name the various types of fields (*cey, paṟṟu, viḷaiyāṭṭam, nēri, pēri*) in which rice is cultivated in and near Kuṟṟālam. He also lists a large number of irrigational tanks (*kuḷam, ēri*) which attract the water birds that he can catch only in this kind of habitat. Throughout the Tamil region, a basic distinction is made between *naṉcey* (irrigated or "wet" land), and *puṉcey,* land which does not receive irrigation and therefore cannot support "wet zone" crops such as rice. David Ludden has shown that the construction of irrigational tanks is an important water-management strategy through which extensive rice cultivation has been made possible in the Tamraparni River valley in Tirunelveli since the fifteenth century. The cultivational land in this valley is "wet zone" land, containing the most fertile and well-irrigated soil in Tirunelveli, contrasting especially with the province's large black-soil tracts ("mixed zone"), and the wastelands (*taricu*) with which its "dry zone" areas abounded.

In his litany of the fields, Ciṅkaṉ praises not only Ciṉṉaṇañcāttēvaṉ, the poet's Pāḷaiyakkārar patron, but the landowners of Kuṟṟālam, as well. While the Pāḷaiyakkārar chief belongs to the Maṟavar caste, the names of the other men show their affiliation mainly with the high-ranking Vēḷāḷar "peasant" caste subgroups, and some high-ranking nonpeasant castes, as well. In addition to managing Ciṉṉaṇañcāttēvaṉ's interests in nearby Vaṭakarai and Teṉkāci (an old center of Pandiyan rule), bearing the offices of "minister, accountant, and manager," Piccai Piḷḷai, a Śaiva Vēḷāḷaṉ, also wrote an Antāti poem on Kuṟṟālam. The same Piccai Piḷḷai is the father of the wealthy Vaittiyanātaṉ, who bestowed several endowments and charities on the Kuṟṟālam temple. Ōmalūr Kiruṣṇaṉ is the "king of merchants," Rāmanāyakaṉ of Karuvai might hail from a Telugu caste group, and Caṭaittampirāṉ is a Śaiva Vēḷāḷar mendicant. Other landowners, also mainly from Vēḷāḷar castes, are praised in other verses throughout this section.

In praising the landowners, in addition to their wealth or learning, the birdcatcher speaks of the donations, endowments, and other charitable services they have provided for the Kuṟṟālam temple and to nearby temples as well. Ciṉṉaṇañcāttēvaṉ, who covered with copper the tiled roof constructed by an earlier Pandiyan king, gets the highest praise. Nevertheless, the Vēḷāḷars who serve under the Pāḷaiyakkārar have also given much to the temple, including portions of the crop (*vāram*) as *kaṭṭaḷai* fields (*paṟṟu, cey*), part of whose yield is donated to the temple, in exchange for temple honors that confer status.

The situation depicted in the Kuṟavañci neatly summarizes the social dynamics of land control David Ludden has described for the wet zone of Tirunelveli in the early eighteenth century: "In the wet zone, an institutionalized structure of shareholding embraced whole irrigated communities and pervaded village life" (1985, p. 167). After the breakup of the early medieval institutions of the *nāṭu* and other translocal assemblies that regulated agriculture, landownership, and commerce, and certainly by 1500, land rights were regulated at the level of the *ūr* (village or town). Upper-caste men in the *ūr* held *paṅku* shares in the cultivation of irrigated land, which made them owners of *kāṇi* (rights to land). Already in the sixth to the eighth centuries throughout the Tamil region, the temple, whose ritual structure based on Āgamic texts was controlled by Brahmans and Vēḷāḷar, had become the central agency for the distribution of power and status among kings and other elites (Ludden, 1985, map 10; Stein, 1980). Corresponding to the historical information we possess, the birdcatcher's songs in the Kuṟavañci depict land rights and control as being managed by *ūr* collectives, showing at the same time the centrality of the temple as a mediator in social transactions related to land, and in the bestowal of status on individuals in the town. During much of the eighteenth century, the period of the rise and popularity of the Kuṟavañci dramas, British colonial reorganizations of landholding and revenue systems had not yet displaced the older organizational patterns described above for the lands under Pāḷaiyakkārar rule.[17]

There is, however, one point on which the Kuṟavañci's account diverges from the historical record. Kuṟṟālam is an ancient Brahmadeya, a village/town gifted by the king to brahmans. The most important Brahmadeya centers in the Tamil region are found in river valleys where rice is cultivated, and the Kaveri River valley is the location for the oldest and densest concentration of such centers. In Stein's formulation (1980), these settlements participated in a Brahman-Vēḷāḷar alliance, a collaboration between Brahman and Vēḷāḷar cultivating groups, resulting in land control and rights to land resting primarily with these groups. Ludden's study of Tirunelveli shows the continuation of the

Brahman-Vēḷāḷar alliance in Tirunelveli temple centers of the wet zone well into the eighteenth century (1985, chapters 2, 3, and 4; maps 8–12). The Kuṟavaṉ birdcatcher's list, on the other hand, emphasizes the Vēḷāḷar landowners and their relation to the Kuṟṟālam temple, of course, under the leadership of a Maṟavar patron-king. The poetic narrative replaces images of Brahman-Vēḷāḷar domination in areas of high-yield rice cultivation with an idealized picture, a celebration, of the alliances that Tamil Vēḷāḷar cultivators had been making with Nayakas, Maṟavars, and other peasant groups of diverse backgrounds from the sixteenth century onward.

Ciṅkaṉ's livelihood is a symbiotic affair. Though he is a man of the wilderness, a hunter, *not* a cultivator, the birdcatcher earns part of his living on agricultural land. The *naṉcey* fields and tanks of Kuṟṟālam and surrounding wet-zone towns are the ideal habitat of the waterfowl he is expert in catching, and for whom he has developed so many specialized snares and techniques. Is the birdcatcher merely poaching, or is he indulged by the peasants because he helps them rid their rich crops of the birds who eat them, even as he bags the water birds who feed mainly on fish? The poet portrays the cultivators of Kuṟṟālam as benefiting from Ciṅkaṉ's activities, just as they benefit from the Kuṟatti's soothsaying. Why, by placing the praise of the temple, the god, and the landowners in the capacity of "patrons," does Rācappar make the Kuṟavaṉ a part of the eighteenth-century socioeconomic-cultural complex? Before investigating the Kuṟavañci drama's motives in this particular construction of the Kuṟavaṉ, we need to complete our enquiry into the identities of Ciṅkaṉ and the Kuṟatti in this genre.

From Hill People to Eighteenth-century Nomads: The Literary Transformation of the Kuṟavar Community

There are no models in classical and medieval literature for the vividly drawn character of the birdcatcher of the fortune-teller play. There is a single extant example of an eighteenth- or nineteenth-century genre with strong "folk" features, called *Kuḷuvanāṭakam* ("The Play of the Kuḷuvaṉ Birdcatcher"), a genre whose plot is essentially that of the third segment of the Kuṟavañci (*Ciṉṉamakipaṉ Kuḷuvanāṭakam*). It is possible that the *Kuḷuvanāṭakam* and the birdcatcher segment of the Kuṟavañci dramas arose from a shared antecedent in a seventeenth- or eighteenth-century folk dramatic genre focusing on a Kuḷuvaṉ birdcatcher (Muttuccaṇmukaṉ and Mōkaṉ, 1977, pp. 45–49). It seems as though the poets of the eighteenth-century Kuṟavañci forged a composite literary portrait of the Kuṟavar community by linking the fortune-telling Kuṟatti and the birdcatching Kuḷuvaṉ who originally appeared in diverse literary contexts. As we have seen, the occupations of both characters are organically connected, both with the play's plot and with the delineation of the temple-town around which the play unfolds. What are the contemporary elements that fed into this composite portrait?

In classical and medieval Tamil sources, the Kuṟavar tribes are hunter-gatherers, dwellers in forests and mountains, and millet growers. As we noted earlier, the wandering life of the eighteenth-century play's Kuṟatti fortune-teller is a new element, as are many of the details of her description of her tribe. The pairing of the Kuṟatti with Ciṅkaṉ completes the portrait of the Kuṟavar as a wandering tribe whose women earn a living by telling fortunes and whose men trap and sell birds, not only in the wilderness landscapes, but also in cultivated fields. While the hill-Kuṟavar of the older texts were always portrayed as part of the hill (*malai*) landscape, Ciṅkaṉ and Ciṅki practice their livelihoods in urban centers. As A. K. Ramanujan has pointed out, the Tamil poets have always been "literalists of the imagination" (1985, p. 250), fashioning the symbolic vocabulary of their poetry out of closely observed details of the objective world. In their construction of tribal characters, the eighteenth-century poets of the Kuṟavañci combined older literary conventions regarding the hill people with new stereotypes of migrant peoples who had emerged on the Tamil landscape from the sixteenth century onward. Indeed, there are remarkable correspondences among the eighteenth-century genre's descriptions of the Kuṟavar way of life and the portrayal of real-life groups called "Kuṟavar" in the eighteenth-century paintings mentioned earlier, the writings of nineteenth- and twentieth-century observers and ethnographers, and the usage of settled populations in modern Tamilnadu.

From the early eighteenth century onward, descriptions of wandering tribes locally called "Kuṟavar" are found in foreign accounts of South India, written by missionaries, travelers, British and other historians and administrators, and private diarists. We gather from these sources that several groups of these nomadic or seminomadic peoples migrated from north and western India to South India in tandem with Nayaka and Mughal military enterprise in the region.[18] Similar and related migrant groups have been circulating in India and far beyond for centuries, and the South Indian nomads may also have traveled back to the North. The Banjara, Lambadi, and Vagri (also known as Vagrivala or Pardhi), three major migrant communities spread throughout South India, speak some variety of a Western-Indian Indo-Aryan language related to Gujarati, Rajasthani, or Marathi, with an admixture of Hindi, Dakhni-Urdu, and Telugu or Tamil.[19] They are clearly related to groups in Maharashtra (Kaikadi, Pardhi), Gujarat, and elsewhere in the North. These wandering communities are described in detail in Edgar Thurston's compendium, *Castes and Tribes of Southern India,* published at the beginning of the twentieth century, and have been further investigated in recent ethnographic studies.[20] In Tamilnadu today, the Tamil word "Kuṟavar" is applied especially to the Korava and the Vagri, who specialize in fortune-telling, hunting, and birdcatching, and the ethnographic record confirms this situation for the nineteenth century as well.[21] It is reasonable to suppose that the Kuṟavañci's descriptions of Kuṟavar ways of life draw on the activities of these groups.

The activities of the Kuṟatti and Ciṅkaṉ closely resemble the ways of the Korava/Yerukala (Telugu *yeruku,* "prophecy") of Andhra and of so-called Narikkuṟavar ("Jackal Kuṟavar") or Kuruvikkārar ("Bird Seller") groups (these are really none other than the Vagri) we may encounter in towns and villages in Tamilnadu today, camping in small tents near bus and railway stations or on the sides of streets. Narikkuṟavar men peddle "jackal horns," birds, and stuffed small animals, forest produce, baskets, and aphrodisiacs. Narikkuṟavar women hawk beads and trinkets in baskets, tell fortunes (mainly by reading palms and getting possessed), and tattoo clients.

The following description in Thurston of Korava/Yerukala women is strikingly close to the depictions of the Kuṟatti's fortune-telling in the Kuṟavañci drama: "It is said that Korava women invoke the village goddesses when they are telling fortunes. They use a winnowing fan and grains of rice in doing this, and prophesy good or evil, according to the number of grains found on the fan (*Madras Census Report,* 1901). They carry a wicker tray in which cowry shells are imbedded in a mixture of cow dung and turmeric. The basket represents Kollapuriamma, and the cowries Poleramma. When telling fortunes, the Korava woman places on the basket the winnow, rice, betel leaves and areca nuts, and the wicker tray. Holding her client's hand over the winnow and moving it about, she commences to chant and name off sorts of deities. From time to time, she touches the hand of the person whose fortune is being told with the stick." The Kuṟavañci's mention of the Kuṟatti fortune-teller's ability to communicate with her clients in their own languages is amply supported by the ethnography of Yerukala and Vagri women fortune-tellers (Thurston, 1909, vol. 3, pp. 464–465).[22]

The Vagri/Narikkuṟavar specialize in birdcatching, fortune-telling, and hunting jackals and small animals. The term "Vagri" is derived from Sanskrit or Prākrit (Indo-Aryan) *vāgura,* net, snare, and is related to *vāgura, vāgurika,* "birdcatcher." As noted earlier, the local Tamil populations use the Tamil term "Kuruvikkarar" ("birdcatcher" or "bird seller") to refer to the birdcatching Vagris. It is also the Vagri who have earned the modern Tamil soubriquet "Narikkuṟavar" ("Jackal" Kuṟavar) by peddling the "horns" of jackals, which are really the sharpened skull bones of jackals covered with some fur, as fertility talismans. The name also relates to the Narikkuṟavar practice of eating the meat of jackals and other small wild animals. The descriptions of Ciṅkaṉ's birdcatching most closely fit the Vagri, who continue to live as professional bird-catchers and hunters of small animals, and pride themselves in their expertise with water birds. The snares, slings, and techniques the ethnographers describe as being used by Vagri birdcatchers match the ones described in Kuṟavañci dramas and Kuḷuvanāṭakams.[23] The convention of calling the Kuṟavaṉ and the Kuṟatti "Ciṅkaṉ" and "Ciṅki" is found for the first time in the Kuṟavañci drama, and remains confined to the genre. It seems that "Ciṅkaṉ" is a Tamilization of "Singh," a common surname among Rajasthanis and Marwaris and other Indo-Aryan-speaking communities of Western India, and also of men in the nomadic Vagri tribe. The appearance of this terminology in the Kuṟavañci play is another piece of evidence connecting the eighteenth-century drama's portrait of the Kuṟavar with "Narikkuṟavar" identities.

Apart from the details of Ciṅkaṉ and the Kuṟatti fortune-teller's occupations, the generalizations regarding "Kuṟavar" customs in the Kuṟavañci dramas are a mixture of factual detail and popular perceptions among settled populations regarding these intriguing nomads. Vagris and Yerukalas apparently do practice the custom of *couvade,* in which the Kuṟavaṉ takes medicine when his wife is confined for childbirth, a very common reference in Kuṟavañcis. But other of the statements made by the Kuṟavañci's fortune-tellers, such as "We (Kuṟavar women) sleep with our brothers-in-law" are simply inaccurate. A major difference between the Kuṟavañci and the ethnographic and popular accounts is that the former never mentions the dominant nineteenth- and twentieth-century stereotype of Kuṟavars as thieves.[24] It is not clear whether this stereotype did not exist in the eighteenth century, or whether it was omitted in the Kuṟavañci in order to sustain the play's positive image of the Kuṟavar. In sum, it appears that the Kuṟavañci poets selected from the lives of the wandering groups they knew just those details that would help create a portrait of the Kuṟavars as intriguing nomadic people, in command of mysterious powers and skills associated with their wilderness origins. The nomadic "Kuṟavar" groups easily lent themselves to such selective portrayal, for, while all of these groups have maintained identities distinct from the settled society around them, they have always adapted their "ways" to fit their local environments. The observation that H. Childers (1975, p. 248) makes about the Ghormati Banjaras seems to fit the Vagri, Korava/Yerukala, and other migrant groups as well: "In addition to peculiarities of dress and language, Ghormati think of themselves as sharing an integrated complex of religious, social, economic, and political characteristics which distinguish them from other populations. At the same time, these distinguishing characteristics are subject to manipulation in ways that facilitate the linking or articulation of their activities with whatever populations are in contact." What does the particular slant of the Kuṟavañci's portrait of "Kuṟavar" tell us about the relations between wilderness and settled landscapes and identities in eighteenth-century Tamilnadu?

In Praise of Wildness: Nomads, Birdcatchers, and Kings

Despite its insistence on the incorporation of the Kuṟavar couple into the agrarian landscape and the economy of the settlement, the Kuṟavañci drama makes it clear that the powerful fascination of the Kuṟatti and Ciṅkaṉ for the populations of the *ūr*—the patrons and audiences of the drama—depends in fact on their indisputable and essential "otherness." The fortune-telling Kuṟatti brings with her the mystery of the world traveler, the mystique of the mountain landscape and the hill people's way of life, and the powers and wisdom associated with these. At the heart of the birdcatcher's appeal are his own sexual drive, his command over the secrets of sexual potency, and his direct association with birds, animals, the forest, and hunting. The implications of these attributes for eighteenth-century Tamil understandings of land, landscape, and place need to be viewed in symbolic as well as social-historical terms. Together the Kuṟavar couple reminds the people of the town of the necessity of the wilderness as the ultimate source of the power and vitality of life in settled communities.

As we have seen, the continuous association of "Kuṟatti" soothsayer figures with hill landscapes, goddesses, and occult powers allows the Kuṟavañci to mold this figure very easily into a new plot that connects the hill with the field landscapes, and the nomads with the populations of the town. The *KK*'s undisputed position as the best of the Kuṟavañcis owes something to the especially vivid way in which the correspondences between real and imagined landscapes are realized in the setting of Kuṟṟālam. Kuṟṟālam is actually situated on the margins of the hills that are the habitat of the Kuṟavar tribes. By always focusing her praise of the *ūr* and its temple on the "Tirikūṭam Hill," the *KK*'s fortune-teller reminds us that, underlying the urban agricultural center, there is a primitive sacredness associated with the hills. Her songs articulate an experience that is vividly present for pilgrims to the Kuṟṟālam shrine in the juxtaposition of the temple and town with the great hill, the famed waterfalls, and the mountain landscape. Through her oracular gifts, the Kuṟatti becomes a conduit for channeling the sacred powers of nature goddesses and natural landscape into the lives of the people of the town.

We have also seen that the emergence of the Kuṟavar and other marginal figures in eighteenth-century Tamil literary genres had much to do with the upward social mobility and newly acquired elite status of caste groups that had formerly occupied marginal and "outsider" positions in the Tamil social hierarchy. The Kaḷḷar were known for earning their livelihood through systematic banditry; the Maṟavar began as fierce, marauding warriors (Dirks, 1987; Shulman, 1985, pp. 351ff.). Rulers from these very groups were the principal sponsors of the innovative eighteenth-century minor genres. The proliferation of such figures as the Kaḷḷaṉ horse thief of the Cripple's Play and the Kuṟavar of the Kuṟavañci in the *pirapantams* suggests the fascination of patrons and poets with marginal characters in these genres. It would seem that this fascination arose from the affinities and the sense of identification, however ambivalent, that elites of uncertain and marginal origins felt with various kinds of "outsiders."

What aspects of marginality do the figures of Ciṅkaṉ and the Kuṟatti contribute to the spectrum of "outsider" characters in the eighteenth-century genres? As David Shulman (1985) has shown, the portrayal of the king as the object of desire for courtesans and other female subjects in various medieval and Nayaka-period South Indian genres represents an affirmation of the king's role as a virile figure whose sexual energies underlie his role as the center of the vitality of his realm. In the Kuṟavañci drama, too, the king, or his divine counterpart, the god, is the object of the highborn heroine's desire. In this genre, however, the symbolic sources of the king's virility are also expressed in his identification with the persona of the lusty birdcatcher in search of his mate. The dialogue between Ciṅkaṉ and Ciṅki at the end of the play contrasts the birdcatcher's naiveté and crude sexuality with his wife's sophistication, wit, and self-control. Here, Ciṅkaṉ is bewildered by the ornaments that Ciṅki has earned as her reward, and mistakes them for wild beasts, birds, and insects. The Kuṟatti laughs at him and corrects his mistakes. The dialogue underscores what we have been told about the Kuṟavaṉ all through the birdcatcher portion of the play. Unlike the scheming Kaḷḷar horse thief of the *Noṇṭināṭakam,* Ciṅkaṉ is a naive wild man, a hunter who loses his catch because of his sexual passion, a true fertility figure. In these qualities, as much as in the aphrodisiacs he peddles, is the key to his appeal for kings and commoners in eighteenth-century Tamil society. This unique balance of "primitive" qualities—of wildness, vitality, and innocence—in the birdcatcher's persona distinguish him from Kaḷḷar horse thieves and other mock-heroic wild personae who inhabit the universe of Tamil *pirapantam* literature.

Such genres as the Cripple's Play portray the marginal figure in an ambiguous light. Although the Kaḷḷaṉ hero's escapades are the focus of the genre, he is crippled as a result of his misadventures, only to be cured in the end by the god whom he worships after repenting his deeds. Despite the attractiveness of their identification with wild landscapes and transgressive behavior, the Kaḷḷaṉ bandit and other low-caste heroes are also viewed as figures of disorder whom the king (and society) must subdue, especially because of their participation in the caste order. The low-caste heroes of true folk ballads, such as the hero Maturai Vīraṉ, pay for their transgressions of the caste order with their lives. The balance between identity and opposition in the relationship between king and marginal figure is a delicate one in the eighteenth-century genres. The Kuṟavaṉ of the Kuṟavañci, on the other hand, is finely contrasted with the other low-caste figures. As a nomad, he only fleetingly participates in the life of the settlement. As a true man of the wilderness, he does not really depend on agrarian society. As his rough and naive ways demonstrate, he has only the most tenuous ties with settled life. In fact, it is by *retaining* his identity as an outsider that he can relate to the kingdom and cultivated land. The Kuṟavaṉ's symbolic status in the Kuṟavañci as a person situated outside the caste order is an important expression of the positive and essential nature of his "outsider" identity.[25] Ciṅkaṉ thrives on his marginality, without compromising his transactions with the people of the *ūr*.

The Kuṟavar couple's nomadic identity must have been among the most attractive aspects of the Kuṟavañci for eighteenth-century patrons and audiences. The genre offers a fluid discourse of place, landscape, and social identity. Praisers of places and settled populations, the Kuṟatti and Kuṟavaṉ nevertheless retain their dedication to livelihoods that demand movement across landscapes. Indeed, their mysterious origins and associations with diverse "places," a key component of their identity, is also the key to their fascination for eighteenth-century populations. Of equal importance is the migrant quality of the Kuṟavar couple's identities, which allowed eighteenth-century patrons, poets, and audiences alike to share in an imaginative articulation of their own shifting identities and changing relations with places, landscapes, and "others" in the Tamil land.

It was easy for the Marathas of Tanjavur to discern in the Kuṟavar linguistic and ethnic connections with wandering nomads (Kaikāḍī) of their own western Indian homeland.[26] The enthusiastic response the genre evoked in the Maratha kings, from Shahji II in the early eighteenth century to Serfoji II in the early nineteenth, resulted in the creation of some of the best-known Kuṟavañcis, including several works in Marathi, and even in a combination of Marathi, Sanskrit, and Tamil.[27] It was also in the multicultural and multilingual atmosphere of the Maratha court in Tanjavur that the Tamil Christian poet Vedanayaka Sastri wrote the celebrated *Pettalēm (Bethlehem) Kuṟavañci* (1800) under the auspices of the German missionaries of the Danish Halle mission in Tranquebar (Peterson, 1999b). In the multilingual works of the Tanjavur Maratha court we may discern a resonance with another aspect of the cultural and spatial mobility embodied in the Kuṟavañci, especially in the polyglot persona of the Kuṟatti. It is also significant that both Vedanayaka Sastri and the European-educated King Serfoji II of Tanjavur incorporated accounts of modern European terrestrial geography in their innovative works *Bethlehem Kuṟavañci* and the Marathi *Devendra Koravañji* (Peterson, 1999a).

Eighteenth-century Tamil society's fascination with the wandering fortune-teller and the birdcatcher appears to be located in the oscillation between identification and otherness that is characteristic of the relations I have described above. On the one hand, mysterious identities, wilderness livelihoods, and nomadic habits define the Kuṟatti and Kuṟavaṉ as persons who are not fully included in the cultural system ordered by the temple-town-field complex and the culture of places. On the other hand, the shifting strategic location of selves vis-à-vis "others" in the fortune-teller play, reflected especially in the largely positive portrayal of the Kuṟatti and the birdcatcher, hints at a more flexible conception of selves and others than would be allowed by a merely exoticizing attitude toward marginality. The Kuṟavañci genre represents a flexible and creative eighteenth-century Tamil combination of geography, social history, and ethnography. The genre's fluid discourses of space, place, and identity are embedded in eighteenth-century realities and expressed in enduring metaphors of the relationship of human beings with the Tamil land and its real and imagined landscapes. At the same time, they enabled Tamils in the eighteenth century to encounter imaginatively an expanding world in terms of newer geographies.

Notes

The research conducted in connection with this essay was partially supported by National Endowment for the Humanities and American Council of Learned Societies/Social Science Research Council Fellowships. I gratefully acknowledge the generous support of these institutions.

1. In some Kuṟavañcis the heroine's girlfriend (*caki, tōḻi*) fetches the soothsayer, hoping that she will end the woman's suffering by predicting her union with her lover. While the Kuṟavar woman fortune-teller is usually called "Kuṟatti" in much of the literature, the Kuṟavañci drama preferentially uses the special form "Kuṟavañci." To minimize confusion, in this essay I will use the term "Kuṟatti" for the fortune-teller of the Kuṟavañci drama.
2. Matappuli, the Kaḷḷar hero of the *Tiruccentūr Noṇṭināṭakam,* travels from Tirupati on the northern edge of Tamilnadu to Tirucchendur on the southern coast of Tirunelveli, tracing the path of Vaḍugar migrations to the south.
3. Beginning his play with several songs of invocation to the gods and with praise of Kuṟṟālam, its temple, and the god who resides there, the poet devotes the thirty-eight songs that follow to the delineation of the theme of Śiva's procession and the lovesickness of the heroine Vacantavalli. The next forty songs focus on the soothsaying Kuṟatti, while songs 81–122 are devoted to Ciṅkaṉ's birdcatching, his search for his wife, and eventual reunion with her.
4. Vacantavalli's lovesickness is portrayed in terms of a sequence of conventional descriptions and tropes, such as the heroine's angry address to the moon and the breeze, whom she accuses of adding to her torment.
5. The *daru* is an important song form in the Kuṟavañci and several other eighteenth-century musical dramatic genres in Tamil and Telugu. See Peterson, 1998.
6. No translations of Kuṟavañci dramas have been published. All translations from the Kuṟavañci and other *pirapantam* genres in this paper are mine.
7. In song 62.2 the fortune-teller mentions important towns and cities in eighteenth-century Tamilnadu, including Tanjavur, Maṅkalappēṭṭai, Gingee, and the fort city of Trichy.

8. Teṉkāci is 5 km. east of Kuṟṟālam. The Malayalam Kollam era (Kollam 1 = 825 C.E.), prevalent in Kerala, was also used in adjacent Tirunelveli.
9. On these associations, see Kailasapathy, 1968, pp. 110–112 and Muilwijk, 1996.
10. See the *Miṉāṭciyammai Kuṟam* of the seventeenth-century poet Kumarakuruparar. On the differences among Kuṟavañci, Kuṟam, the Kalampakam vignettes, and a lost genre called Kuṟattippāṭṭu, see Mōkaṉ, 1985, and Muilwijk, 1996.
11. Examples include *Akanāṉūṟu* 308, *Aiṅkuṟūnūṟu* 251–260 and 281–290, and *Kuṟuntokai* 82. The trope of Kuṟavar women guarding millet fields is deployed as a pivotal device in the Murukaṉ-Vaḷḷi myth.
12. The Akavaṉmakaḷ's staff is called the *piṟappuṇarttuṅ kōl,* "the staff that reveals birth."
13. E.g., Nakkīrar's *Tirumurukāṟṟuppaṭai* 5 and 6, translated in Ramanujan, 1985, pp. 226–228 and 215–217.
14. E.g., *Kuṟuntokai* 23, *Akanāṉūṟu* 98. See Hart, 1979, p. 118 and 44–45. The Vaiṣṇava poet-saint Tirumaṅkai Āḻvār (eighth-ninth c.) describes a female diviner (Kaṭṭuvicci) in action (*Ciṟiya Tirumaṭal* 19–22). The Vēlaṉ, the shaman-priest of Murukaṉ, also practices divination using *kaḻaṅku* (molucca beans), e.g., *Aiṅkuṟunūṟu* 243 and 244.
15. On the Viṟali dancer see Kersenboom-Story, 1981, and Kailasapathy, 1968, pp. 105ff.
16. *Mēlvāram* is the "superior (*mēl*) portion of the crop, claimed by the landlord or by government, in contrast to the cultivator's share, *kuṭivāram*" (Ludden, 1985, Glossary, p. 264).
17. On the effects of the British East India Company's interventions, especially with the introduction of Thomas Munro's *ryotwari* system, see Ludden, 1985, chapters 4 and 6.
18. Thurston, 1909 and Childers, 1975. The Lambadi came to the South in several groups as commissaries to the Mughal and British armies, supplying salt and other necessities. Their numbers increased dramatically, and many settled in various parts of South India, primarily in Andhra and Mysore. Among the traditional commodities supplied to local populations by subgroups of the Lambadi Kuravas are salt and curry leaves. These Kuravas were named after what they sold: "Salt" (*uppu*) Kuṟavar" and "curry-leaf (*kaṟivēppilai*) Kuṟavar".
19. The Vagris speak Vagriboli, an Indo-Aryan language with a strong Western Indian (Gujarati/Rajasthani) cast to it (Srinivasa Varma, 1970). A fourth group, of uncertain regional origin, the Korava, called "Yerukala" in Telugu, are found mainly in the Telugu linguistic area (in what is now Andhra Pradesh), and speak a mixture of Telugu, Kannada, and Tamil, all Dravidian languages.
20. See "Korava," Thurston, 1909, volume 3; "Banjara" and "Kuruvikkaran," volume 4.
21. The migrant groups in Andhra and Mysore appear to be related to those in Tamilnadu, but no clear picture of their relationship has emerged from studying their similarities and differences.
22. The Banjara, Korava/Yerukala, Vagri, and Badhanyo offer blood sacrifice to particular goddesses, whose images they carry with them. Malten (1989) and Werth (1996) report that Vagri men practice divination in odd and even numbers when they worship the Goddess. Narikkuṟatti women usually dress in the western Indian gathered skirt and short blouse, and carry their infants in a sling across their

breasts. Some also wear the more common Tamil sari. The skirt costume is attested for the eighteenth century in Tanjore paintings of "Kuṟavar" couples. In seventeenth- and eighteenth-century temple sculptures and in the Kuṟavañci dramas, the Kuṟatti wears a sari. The paintings and sculpture as well as descriptions such as the one in the *TVPK* portray the Kuṟatti carrying her infant in a sling.

23. For descriptions, sketches, and photographs, see Hatch, 1928; Jagor, 1894; Malten, 1989; and Werth, 1996.
24. The identification of Kuṟavar groups as criminal tribes is the main thrust of the essays on these groups by Hatch (1928) and Williams (1912–13).
25. Theoretically, Kuṟavar are included among the lowest castes in the Left-Right division of caste groups. In practice, however, the status of nomadic Kuṟavar is treated in widely differing ways. "Kuruvikkarans are peripheral to Endavur and to the local Untouchable castes in every way. Their relations with the other Untouchable castes are intermittent and of little importance to the other Untouchables" (Moffatt, 1979, p. 144). But also see Werth's comments on the caste status of the Vagri (1996, pp. 67–75).
26. On the Kaikāḍiṇ fortune-teller in Marathi literature and the connection between Kaikāḍiṇs and Kuṟattis, see Dhere and Bhavalkar, 1975. In Serfoji's Marathi Kuṟavañci *Devendra Koravañji* (see below), the Kuṟatti and Kuṟavaṉ are called Buruḍ and Burḍiṇ.
27. The Marathi Kuṟavañcis include: *Śrī Korvanjhi* and *Pratāpa Rāma Korvañji* sponsored by Pratapasimha, and *Devendra Koravañji,* attributed to Serfoji II (1798–1832) himself. King Shahji II (1698–1715) patronized the multilingual *Mohini Vilāsa Kuravañji.* Shahji and Serfoji were the patrons of two of the best-known Tamil Kuṟavañci dramas, the *Tiyākēcar Kuṟavañci* and the *Carapēntira Pūpāla Kuṟavañci.*

FOUR

Ruling in the Gaze of God

Thoughts on Kanchipuram's *Maṇḍala*

D. Dennis Hudson

Kanchipuram was the ancient capital of the Pallava dynasty, which flourished between the fourth and ninth centuries C.E. Over 2300 years ago, someone laid it out between the Palar River and its tributary, the Vegavatī, and did so carefully. Later, as the Pallavas gained power and wealth, they expanded their city outward from its center in the form of a *maṇḍala:* a squared realm whose east-west axis crosses with its north-south axis to form a sacred center. Today, however, this *maṇḍala* is obscure. Gone are the palace at the center, the Buddhist *stūpa* and monasteries outside to the south, and the fortress wall with its gates and surrounding moat. The elephants that once paced Kanchi's thoroughfares in royal processions are now the chugging trucks and buses of modern commerce. Today, Kanchipuram is a relatively quiet town, famous for more than 100 temples, for classical literature, for the seat of one of five Śaṅkarāchāryas, for the goddess Kāmākṣī, and for heavy silk saris (C. R. Srinivasan, 1979, p. 6; K. R. Srinivasan, 1964, pp. 51–64, 67–71; Hudson, 1993a).

This essay is based on my research on the Vaikuṇṭha Perumāḷ Temple, built in Kanchipuram around 770 C.E. by the Bhāgavata emperor Nandivarman Pallavamalla (Hudson, forthcoming). This royal Viṣṇu-house and the city in which it stands share an ancient *maṇḍala* blueprint, and its role in this ancient city's design is the subject of this essay. I will examine buildings and texts in chronological order to elicit evidence for this *maṇḍala* and to explore its meanings. I will pay special attention to its east-west axis and secondarily to its north-south axis.

This blueprint governed the way humans and gods dwelled together in Kanchipuram. The directions their respective houses face, and the postures of the icons that embody gods in their houses, will be given careful attention as clues to their respective functions in this urban microcosm. I will briefly examine the prototype of this *maṇḍala* and of the *ācārya* ("teaching priest") in Veda, but my primary attention will be focused on the manner in which Veda has been "translated" for this particular place.

I argue that this "translation" occurred through the *Pāñcarātra Āgama,* a liturgical system (*śāstra*) that Bhāgavatas use for worship and theology, and through the stories of Kṛṣṇa in Books 10 and 11 of the *Bhāgavata Purāṇa*. *Āgama,* one might say, "translates" Veda's rituals in the way in which ancient legends (*itihāsa*) and stories (*purāṇa*) "translate" Veda's doctrines. "Hinduism," a term used to denote Veda-based religions, is more accurately expressed by the term *Vedāgama*.

The Bhāgavata religion teaches that the fullness of God was embodied as Vāsudeva Kṛṣṇa in the previous age. Its names for God are many, but important here are Nārāyaṇa, Vāsudeva, Viṣṇu, Kṛṣṇa, and the title *bhagavān*. They all refer to the Supreme Person (*parama-puruṣa*) who is One. The Bhāgavatas understand *bhagavān* to denote the "glorious excellences" (*bhagas*) that God possesses, and they use the Pāñcarātra concept of "formation" (*vyūha*) to explain how the One as "Master of Progeny" (*Prajāpati*) turns into everything while remaining One. A man or woman consecrated in this religion becomes the Bhagavān's possession or slave and is known as a Bhāgavata. The relation of slave to master is an important metaphor that runs throughout the religion's scriptures, notably the *Bhāgavata Purāṇa,* the *Mahābhārata,* and the *Bhagavad-gītā*.

Bhāgavatas also view themselves as part of the pan-Indian religious world and subsume other religions of Veda and Āgama within their framework, notably the Śaiva Āgama focused on God as Rudra Śiva. The Śaiva Āgama is also important to Kanchipuram. Other religions that do not share Veda—Buddhism and Jainism—are also important to Kanchipuram and, at the end of this essay, I will pay particular attention to Buddhist evidence for its *maṇḍala* design. For now, I will begin by investigating the earliest evidence at hand. My approach will include the usual data for the study of history, but I will add stories pointing to liturgies, which in turn point to people who act from a religious interest and sensibility. This approach reveals frequently overlooked dimensions to the usual data.

Four Ancient Icons

Kanchipuram, the "town of the *kāñci* tree" or of "the woman's waist-girdle," existed by the fourth century B.C.E. According to the archaeologist K. V. Raman, evidence shows continuous occupation at the site from at least 300 B.C.E. (Raman, n.d., pp. 61–72). He found remains from the Megalithic culture of South India in its central zone. Its most elevated portion is a mound holding the temples known as the Kāmakkōṭṭam, the Kumārakkōṭṭam, and the Ūrakam. It is possible that the goddess of the Kāmakkōṭṭam has resided in one or another form of her shrine on that center from the city's beginning and the city was built around her. Or, to put it from her perspective, she called the town into existence around her and placed Śiva's son Skanda in the Kumārakkōṭṭam nearby to gaze with her eastward. Their gaze falls on the Ūrakam temple.

The Ūrakam is now a small temple, but its icon is enormous. A nearly thirty-foot stucco image of unknown age depicts Vāmana (the "Dwarf"), an incarnation of Viṣṇu (the "Pervading Actor"; Raman, 1975, p. 5). Vāmana has just swelled up to take three enormous steps (*trivikrama*). Massive brick remains found near this temple may also have faced west toward the Goddess and Skanda. A similarly massive stucco image, also facing west, depicts the reclining Bhagavān. It is housed by the temple of Veḥkā, which originally stood outside the city walls southeast of its center. These four temples—the Kāmakkōṭṭam, the Kumārakkōṭṭam, the Ūrakam, and the Veḥkā—appear to be Kanchipuram's earliest cultic sites where rituals still take place, and their placement is our earliest evidence for the city's *maṇḍala*.

Kanchipuram in the *Perumpāṇāṟṟuppaṭai*

Three of these four temples appear explicitly, and one implicitly, in a Tamil poem about the city and its ruler dated to circa 190 C.E. (Zvelebil, 1992, p. 117 n.73). This means that the temples are pre-Pallava. The poem, *Perumpāṇāṟṟuppaṭai* ("A Bard's Long Praise of One Who Gives Generously," loosely translated) is one in a collection of "Ten Songs" (*Pattuppāṭṭu*) anthologized in the fourth or fifth century, at the end of the *caṅkam* period of classical Tamil literature.[1] In the poem, one bard tells another how to go to Kanchi (*Kacci*) to receive wealth from its king, who is famous for his generous gifts. He describes the sights he will see as he walks to its harbor and then inland to the capital. This wealthy kingdom, he says, extends northward to the Tirupati-Tirumalai hills where sages perform fire sacrifices.

The bard says that the ruler is "Kanchi's Owner" (*Kacciyōn̲*) in matrilineal descent from the "King of the Toṇṭai People" (*Toṇṭaiyōr marukan̲*). His title is "Man of the Waves" (*Tiraiyan̲*). He belongs to a family of the "Strong One" (*Uravōn̲*) in a lineage originating in the churning of an ocean (lines 29–37, 420, and 454). His description indicates a Bhāgavata identity:

> [He belongs to] the family of the "Strong One," in the lineage given by waves when the beautiful sea is churned to overflowing by him whose color is the three-fold sea, and whose chest bears Majesty's abode when he measures the broad Earth.[2]

This statement alludes to two well-known Bhāgavata stories that represent rituals important to kingship and are told at length in the *Bhāgavata Purāṇa*. The first is the churning of the milk ocean, which accounts for his lineage and the title "Man of the Waves." The second is the dwarf measuring the earth, which accounts for his family's identity with the "Strong One."

The Churning of the Milk Ocean

In the first story, the Bhagavān as Viṣṇu churns the Ocean of Milk to produce from it the royal emblems for the gods and the demons, and "majesty" (*śrī*) for himself (*Bhāgavata Purāṇa* 8.5–12). First, a deadly poison emerges and Śiva graciously swallows it until it is time for the world's destruction. When the "Goddess of Majesty" (*Śrī-devī*) emerges, she makes her home on Viṣṇu's chest, and he is now Śrīdhara, the "Bearer of Majesty." But when the elixir (*amṛta*) emerges that provides immortality for its owner, a continuous struggle begins between the gods and the demons for its possession. This story represents a ruler's consecration to *mantras* and to the ritualized life it requires (*sādhana*). The ocean is his consciousness, the milk is the *mantras* he receives, and the churning is his devout repetition each day before sunrise for the sake of immortality or prosperous longevity (*amṛta*). Thus, the King of the People of Toṇṭai is "born" as a Bhāgavata from the "churning of the milk ocean" during consecration and is thereby a "Man of the Waves."

The Dwarf Measures the Earth

In the second story, Viṣṇu as Śrīdhara takes on the form of Vāmana, a Brahmin dwarf, to resolve a serious problem for the universe. The demon ruler Bali has usurped Indra's place in the east, the gods have fled in disguise to earth, and the "true order" (*dharma*) of all things is in dangerous disruption. One day, Vāmana appears at one of the hundred horse sacrifices Bali sponsors to enhance his dominion, and Bali promises to give this little Brahmin anything he wants. Vāmana only wants land he can measure out with his own three steps. Bali thinks this too little to ask and reasons that it must be due to the Brahmin's youth and inexperience. But he gives it anyway, and instantly Vāmana swells to unimaginable proportions. In one step his foot encompasses the earth. In a second step his foot pierces through the heavens above, and his toe breaks through the highest boundary of space and time to allow the Ganges River to descend to earth. But he has no place for his third step. True to his promised gift, Bali offers his head for the foot of his third step. In response to this demon's devout faithfulness to truth in the face of his own deceit, Śrīdhara gives him a splendid realm in the dark water under the earth, and personally stands guard at his gate.

This famous version of the story of Vāmana "when he measures the broad Earth" is told at *Bhāgavata Purāṇa* 8.15–23, and represents the protective relationship of an *ācārya* to an inherently "impure" king. Like the demon Bali, this ruler is impure by birth, but true to his word. Like the little Brahmin, his *ācārya* is the pure Śrīdhara, but deceptive in appearance. Once the ruler has taken refuge in the *ācārya,* as Bali takes refuge in Vāmana, the *ācārya* uses *mantras* to defeat all threats to the ruler's possession of a long and prosperous life through Āgama rites called *prayoga*. In this way, the *ācārya* stands guard at the ruler's gate.

This story explains why Kacciyōṉ belongs to a family of Uravōṉ (the "Strong One") in a lineage produced by the churning of the milk ocean. Uravōṉ translates into Tamil Bali's Sanskrit name, which means "Powerful One." The family that provides Kanchi with its rulers resembles the demon Bali: they are inherently "impure" Śūdras according to Veda, but by means of Āgama they have taken refuge in Bali and now exist protected by him. They are Bhāgavatas and this king is as generous as Bali is.

The poet goes on to say that his family "blossoms" to protect the everlasting life of this world, and we may now assume that Bhāgavata *ācāryas* of the Pāñcarātra Āgama stand behind the clan. Their application of *prayoga* rites explains why, according to the poet, this King of the People of Toṇṭai is held in esteem by the Pāṇṭiya, Cēra, and Cōḻa rulers of the Dravidian south, just as they hold in esteem the right-whorling conch above other shells of the sea (lines 32–37). This analogy alludes to this king's success in battle, for the rare right-whorling conch allows the warrior to hold it easily in his right hand to sound it during battle.

Uravōṉ—the "Strong One"—also has another connotation. In the Pāñcarātra doctrine of formations (*vyūha*), the first formation God makes to bring all things into existence manifests the omniscience that is the ground of all being and its power. This formation is named Saṃkarṣaṇa—the "Plower"—and in iconography, he appears as a five-hooded snake (*nāga*). In the rites of consecration, Saṃkarṣaṇa operates through the *ācārya* to "give birth" to a Bhāgavata. A "birth" from Saṃkarṣaṇa represented as a *nāga* may therefore be understood as the "birth" of a *nāga*. The word *nāga* appears frequently in non-Tamil literature to denote people considered alien to Veda and classified ritually as servants (*śūdras*) and barbarians (*mlecchas*). But in some cases, *nāga* designates people who have been "cleansed" and "reborn" by God's *vyūha* as Saṃkarṣaṇa.[3] Classical *dharma,* for example, judged the Pallavas to be Śūdras, but we know that they were "cleaned up" and consecrated to the worship of Kṛṣṇa. One Pallava lineage claimed that the first Pallava was born from a *nāga* mother by means of the polluted Brahmin Aśvatthāman, and another claimed she was an *apsaras* (a "nymph"). The *nāga* memory may be accurate, for as we shall see below, Pallavas gained Kanchipuram's throne by marrying into the ruling "Nāga" family of Bhāgavatas.

Inscriptions beginning with Samudra Gupta in the fourth century proclaim Bhāgavata identities for three centuries of kings ruling in realms that stretch from the Gangetic plains through the Deccan plateau and into the Dravidian south. As in the Pallava case, some ruled much longer (Hudson 1994, pp. 113–140; McKnight, Jr., 1977, pp. 692–693; Narain 1983, pp. 34–38), and, as is the case of Tiraiyaṉ, some ruled much earlier. They all must have had *ācāryas* who employed the Pāñcarātra Āgama on their behalf, although the evidence is slight. But we do know, for example, that Samudra Gupta's son, Candra Gupta II (376–414), issued a coin with Viṣṇu's wheel as a person (*Cakra-puruṣa*) as taught in the Pāñcarātra *Ahirbudhnya-saṃhitā,* and this suggests *prayoga* rites. We also know that an Ānanda king of the fifth century believed that his *ācārya's* performance of the rite of the "Golden Womb" (*Hiraṇya-garbha*) would cleanse him of even the most heinous sin, just as the Pāñcarātra Āgama teaches (Narain, 1983, pp. 37, 46; Smith, 1975, p. 232). All of these rulers, in one way or another, may have employed a version of the *maṇḍala* that mapped the city "owned" by Tiraiyaṉ. But before we return to this poem and city, let us briefly consider the paradigmatic *maṇḍala* of which Kanchipuram is a variation: it reveals how an Āgamic "translation" reshapes a Vedic "original."

The *Maṇḍala* Paradigm

The paradigm for this *maṇḍala* appears in the new and full moon sacrifices as prescribed in the *Yajurveda's Śatapathabrāhmaṇa* (1.2.5) dated circa 800 B.C.E. This story explains the construction of the three fires used in the sacrifices. Prajāpati gives birth to gods and demons alike, who continually fight. Once, when demons have defeated gods, they decide to live in this world and begin to divide it up by measuring it from west to east. Gods, of course, want a share for their own subsistence, so they devise a method of deceit. They have Viṣṇu take the shape of the sacrifice in the form of a dwarf. With Viṣṇu as dwarf, they approach the demons and ask for a share. The demons grudgingly agree to give them as much as the little Viṣṇu can lie upon and no more. Pleased to have been given what is equal in size to the sacrifice, gods put Viṣṇu down with his head to the east and feet to the north. They enclose him on the south, west, and north sides with *mantras,* and on the east side they place a fire altar. The gods then "worship" and "toil" with this sacrificial form of Viṣṇu as dwarf and, as they do, the dwarf expands to cover the whole earth. The demons are pushed west and into the dark waters under earth.

The sacrificial dwarf, we later learn, takes over the world in three strides (*trivikrama*) by means of *mantras* in specific Vedic meters. With his first step he gains the earth, with his second the atmosphere, and with his third, the sky, where the sun's apex is the safe refuge that is Prajāpati, and its rays are the righteous who have departed (*Śatapatha-brāhmaṇa* 1.9.3.8–12). Viṣṇu's steps are ritually repeated by men imitating gods during sacrifices. When the *adhvaryu* priest of the *Yajurveda* has completed the new moon and full moon sacrifices, he replicates the three strides beginning at the southwest corner of the large altar. He steps eastward along its north side and makes each stride with his right foot in front as he recites the corresponding *mantra* (*Śatapatha-brāhmaṇa* 1.9.3.12, n.1). Similarly, when a man is made king in the *rājasya* sacrifice, he replicates the three strides after his unction, but within the confines of a tiger skin spread out in front of an altar for Mitrāvaruṇa. The tiger skin represents Indra's beauty when he drinks *soma,* and the king is now an "Indra." His three strides place this "Indra" in the realm of Prajāpati and now he is above everything else (*Śatapatha-brāhmaṇa* 5.3.5.3; 5.4.2.6).

To represent these three realms within the world they have taken, the gods establish a sacrificial arena and build a large altar on it along the east-west axis, which slopes toward the east and north. They cover it with a fertile soil, which they smooth from east to west. Then, for the safety of this "imperishable place of sacrifice," they lift up this "life-bestowing earth" by prayers and place it in the full moon by worship. If demons come back to take over the world, they can flee to the full moon to regain the sacrifice and use it against them. The full moon displays this place of sacrifice as black spots in the shape of a hare (*Śatapatha-brāhmaṇa* 11.1.5.3). The gods now build three smaller altars on this large altar. A circular altar on the west holds a fire for preparing food and represents the earth. A square altar on the east holds a fire for offering this prepared food and represents heaven above earth. A half-moon altar on the south holds a fire for offerings to the *rākṣasa* demons of destruction, and it represents the atmosphere between earth and heaven.

The eastern altar's four sides provide a *maṇḍala* to represent the meanings of the four sides of the larger altar on which it stands. The side facing east is the quarter of the gods, the side facing north is that of people, the side facing south is the quarter of deceased ancestors, and the side facing west is left as the quarter of the demons (*Śatapatha-brāhmaṇa* 1.2.5.17). Each quarter is ruled by a god. The full moon possessing the hare (*Śaśin*) rules the north as the source of human well-being. Indra rules the gods in the east. Yama rules the dead in the south. Varuṇa rules the demons in the west, and all of this together results in the paradigmatic *maṇḍala* ultimately derived from Viṣṇu's three strides.

There is, however, one more element. There is a priest called the *brahman,* who supervises the sacrifices using three fires (Ranade 1984). He sits south of the square eastern altar and faces north. In theory, he contains all of the Vedic collections (*saṃhitās*) in his memory, for he employs *mantras* of the *Atharvaveda* to correct mistakes made by the other priests, who employ *mantras* of the *Ṛg, Sāma,* and *Yajurvedas*. Because this *brahman* priest contains the whole Veda in his memory, he also contains the whole sacrifice, as does Viṣṇu in his dwarf form. This correspondence, I think, produces the *ācārya*—the "teaching priest"—of the *Pāñcarātra Āgama,* who, during ceremonies using a *maṇḍala,* embodies Viṣṇu. *Ācārya* and *maṇḍala* therefore belong together: where we find one, we will likely find the other.

Kanchipuram's *Maṇḍala*

Let us return to the *Perumpāṇāṟṟuppaṭai* and see how Āgama has applied this paradigmatic joining of *maṇḍala* with *ācārya* to this particular royal capital by circa 190 C.E. At the poem's beginning, the bard alludes to the Bhagavān's iconic forms in Kanchipuram and he describes them when his narrative reaches the city. When the traveler he has in mind comes from the port, he first encounters the "Bhagavān the color of the sea"; this is the long stucco icon reclining on the snake Saṃkarṣaṇa at Veḥkā outside Kanchi at the southeast corner (lines 373–375). Here, the Bhagavān faces westward, his head rests on his left hand, and his feet stretch northward in a reversal of *dharma's* "true order." The Tamil poet Pēyāḻvār later explained that this reversed orientation at the southeast corner means that the "Bhagavān at Veḥkā destroys evil deeds (*tī viṉaikaḷ*)" (*Mūṉṟāntiruvantāti* 76). By reclining south of the capital in the "wrong way" and facing west, he protects the city's residents from demons (*rākṣasas*) who enter from the south in the afternoon to prey on people polluted by evil deeds. He also protects them from demons (*asuras*) who emerge from the west at sunset to prey on people in the grip of lust. *Asuras* and *rākṣasas* converge at the inauspicious southwest corner of Goddess Niṟṛti ("Disintegration") where the south and west quarters meet.

The traveler then encounters the second icon, which stands inside the city. This is the huge stucco "on whose chest Śrīdevī dwells when he measures the broad earth." Vāmana stands in the Ūrakam temple and faces west toward the city's center as lord of "the City's Interior," which is the meaning of *ūr-akam*. The bard identifies him as Prajāpati, "the one with the tall form and black color," who earlier produced the four-faced Brahmā (and the world) from the lotus at his navel, the lotus whose pericarp Kanchi resembles (lines 402–405; see L. V. Gopalan, 1972, pp. 64–66). The city's *maṇḍala* is like an open lotus blossom, he says, but surrounded by a wall and a moat. It is ancient among places where people worship in many different ways, he also says, meaning that Buddhists, Jains, Ājīvakas, Śaivas, and Bhāgavatas have lived and worshiped there for a long time. Kacciyōṉ rules and protects them all "like the Five [Pāṇḍavas] who defeated the Hundred [Kauravas]" in the *Mahābhārata's* Great War (lines 405–420).

This simile alludes to another huge stucco icon, which depicts a sitting Kṛṣṇa. He faces east as an icon nearly twenty-five feet high in a temple west of the palace located in an ancient section of the city known as Pāṭakam. This Pāṭakam Kṛṣṇa is known as "the Pāṇḍavas' messenger" and represents Pāṇḍava victory over the Kauravas, which the poet has told us is the paradigm for this king's rule. When the King of the People of Toṇṭai sits in state at the center of this urban "lotus," faces east, and gives whatever people desire, his majesty gives him a brilliance like the sun rising from the "three-fold sea" (lines 438–454). But he sits there in imitation of Kṛṣṇa seated in the temple behind him, for he represents Kṛṣṇa to his subjects in the way a slave represents his master to others.[4] The bard has now cited all of the Bhagavān's iconic postures in Kanchipuram—he reclines, he stands, and he sits in huge images made of stucco.

Near the poem's end, the poet describes the lineage of Kanchi's king and praises his unlimited giving. His generosity is likened to Celvi's (the "Goddess of Transitory Wealth"), who dwells in the Kāmakkōṭṭam at the city's center:

> Celvi dances the *tuṇaṅkaiyam,* and an arrow of fine red gold comes from her womb to kill poisonous Fear in the expanse of white waves (lines 454–460, especially 457–459).

In later Tamil lore, the arrow that kills poisonous Fear (*kaṭuñcūr*) belongs to Śiva's son Skanda.[5] The arrow represents Skanda, Goddess Celvi is his mother, and her "womb" is the Kāmakkōṭṭam temple. She becomes famous as Kāmākṣī, "whose eyes (*akṣi*) of desire (*kāma*) fulfill desire." The milk ocean appears again as "white waves" (*veṇ-tirai*), but here it contains a demon of poisonous Fear that Skanda is born to remove. The poet thus implies a "rebirth" rite conducted at the Kāmakkōṭṭam to purify Kanchipuram's ruler (Tiraiyaṉ) and give him a consecration name, for he says this is a "great name" to call upon for gifts (lines 460–461). He does not reveal what the name is, but the context implies that it is a form of Skanda (see Mahalingam, 1969, pp. 1–24).

Kanchipuram in the Poem of Poykai

Elements in this poem—the milk ocean, Vāmana and Bali, five Pāṇḍavas and one hundred Kauravas, Kṛṣṇa, and Celvi—continued in Kanchipuram for centuries and appeared in the cave temples and rock carvings at the Māmallapuram port, as well as in the Emperor's "Viṣṇu-house" built by Pallavamalla. The poet Poykai (probably eighth century) expressed this continuity by continuing the bard's earlier theme of Kanchi as an open lotus blossom, noting the two west-facing temples of Ūrakam and Veḥkā. But he adds a third, the newly built Viṣṇu-house (*Viṇṇakaram*) that Pallavamalla completed around 770 C.E., which we know today as the Vaikuṇṭha Perumāḷ Temple. In a stanza he addresses to his own mind (*Mutaltiruvantāti* 77), Poykai begins with the icon standing on the Vēṅkaṭa mountain to the north, and then moves to the three west-facing icons in Kanchi, which he describes as a fortified and blooming flower that never closes. He calls Ūrakam's tall, standing stucco icon the "Power of the King" (*Kōval*) dwelling in a golden temple, and presumably means that this is the icon that embodies the power by which the Pallava king rules the lotus *maṇḍala* enclosed by a moat:

> Vēṅkaṭa, Viṇṇakaram, Veḥkā, and Kōval, the golden temple of the tall Power of the King, whose moat surrounds the flower that never closes—when you think of him in all four places standing, sitting, reclining, and striding, your sorrows vanish.[6]

The Bhagavān stands on the mountain Vēṅkaṭa, sits in the bottom sanctum of the Emperor's Viṣṇu-house (*Paramēccura-viṇṇakaram*), reclines outside the ancient city walls at Veḥkā, and strides in Ūrakam as Power of the King at the city's interior.

The East-West Axis

Although modern development obscures the city's *maṇḍala,* we discern it through these texts of the eighth century and earlier, and its most obvious axis runs east to west. In about 720 C.E., the emperor Rājasiṃha built for Śiva his Rājasiṃheśvara Temple (now the Kailāsanātha Temple) at the city's western limit. It faces east. About fifty years later, the emperor Pallavamalla built for Kṛṣṇa the Vaikuṇṭha Perumāḷ Temple at its eastern limit. It faces west. Between these divine places, one for Śiva and one for Kṛṣṇa, lay the city "lotus" with its east-facing temples Kāmakkōṭṭam, Kumārakkōṭṭam, and Pāṭakam, along with its west-facing Ūrakam, all at the ancient center. They constitute the portion of the city known today as "Big Kanchipuram." K. V. Raman (n.d., pp. 66–67) points out the significance of the orientation of these temples:

> They are all oriented towards the central hub, as it were, where probably the Pallava palace was situated. All the major temples in Big Kanchipuram look towards the central hub . . . even going against the normal conventions for temples to face east. Many of the temples seem to be line[d] as it were all along the four main thoroughfares forming the square plan.

In other words, all the major temples inside the city wall were built on the east-west axis to face the Goddess in the Kāmakkōṭṭam and the Pallava ruler in his palace. The four main thoroughfares constitute the "King's Road," a rectangular royal processional street running around the ancient squared center. It is used today for ordinary commerce, and every year for processions of the gods' movable icons during temple festivals.

To understand this ancient royal and cultic center better, let us look at the Ūrakam temple more closely (Hudson, 1992; L. V. Gopalan, 1972, pp. 63–65). It is no longer golden, and the building is small and undistinguished, but it still stands in the ancient central zone (*ūr-akam*) and houses the massive and powerful thirty-foot stucco sculpture that fills the entire sanctum wall, glistening from an applied mixture of oil that turns it black. It captures "the Lord who Measures the World" (*Ulakaḷanta Perumāḷ* in Tamil) in full stride. He faces directly westward, his two arms extend out to the sides at right angles, his left leg stretches at a right angle southward, and his right leg stretches diagonally down to the north, his foot on a human-like head resting on the floor, presumably Bali's. Light refracting from the black oil glimmers like drops of water on the folds and designs of his richly detailed royal costume flowing out in various directions.

As is usual in Āgama liturgies, small moveable icons of Viṣṇu, flanked by Śrīdevī and by Goddess Earth (*Bhūmidevī*), stand facing west on a small platform on the altar at the base of the stucco sculpture. They receive the offerings of worship. On the north side of the entrance hall, a similarly blackened icon (perhaps made of stucco) of a snake with five hoods and curving coils faces south. It resembles snake sculptures found at Buddhist *stūpas* elsewhere, and recalls the ancient remains found in the city, some of which may have been Buddhist (Hudson, 1995, pp. 151–190).

A Tamil poem by the poet Kalikaṉṟi (also known as Tirumaṅkai) reveals that the name "Ūrakam" has three referents in the eighth century. One is the macrocosmic universe that Vāmana measures out when he takes his three strides. Another is the microcosmic inner realm (*akam*) of the city (*ūr*) as having been measured out by Vāmana. And the third is Vāmana's body as the stucco icon. The walled city is a metonymic replica of the ordered universe within which it stands. Its ancient center suggests the large altar of the Vedic sacrifice and Vāmana standing in Ūrakam suggests the sacrificial fire burning in its square altar to the east. The area outside its walls and moat fall into the ritual category of disorder (*adharma*) where *rākṣasas* and *asuras* lurk. The reclining icon in Veḥkā facing west toward the dangerous southwest corner of disintegration suggests the southern Vedic altar used to ward off *rākṣasas*.

Inside the city, Vāmana in the Ūrakam temple faces west toward the Goddess temple and the nearby Pallava palace, but also toward Kṛṣṇa's Pāṭakam temple beyond them. Kṛṣṇa is a similarly glistening black stucco icon facing east to represent an important episode in the *Mahābhārata*. When Kṛṣṇa acts as "Messenger of the Pāṇḍavas" (*Pāṇḍava-dūta* or *Pāṇḍavatūtar*) to their enemy Duryodhana, he reveals his divine form as "King of the king of kings." Everyone but the deluded Duryodhana sees it. This twenty-five-foot-high stucco icon portrays his manifestation. Kṛṣṇa has two arms and a crown, his left leg is pendent and his right leg is drawn up onto the throne. His right arm bends up at the elbow in the ritual gesture of banishing fear, while his left arm extends outward, its open hand bent down in the gesture of giving boons. The rich folds on his lower garment envelop his legs to the ankles, spilling down to cover the throne. Like the Ūrakam icon, this icon's gleaming black surface receives a new ritual oiling each year during the "dark" month of Kārttikkai (November–December).

Because Kṛṣṇa faces east to reveal himself to Duryodhana, who nevertheless cannot see him, Duryodhana must be to the east and facing west. This imagined position places him in the now-missing Pallava palace and reveals an important meaning of this east-west axis. In the paradigmatic *maṇḍala,* gods ruled by Indra live to the east where the sun rises, and demons ruled by Varuṇa live to the west where the sun sets. The gods in the east thus face the demons in the west. The five Pāṇḍavas and the hundred Kauravas replicate these opponents in human terms. According to the *Mahābhārata,* the gods fathered the Pāṇḍavas, led by the eldest, Yudhiṣṭhira, and demons fathered the Kauravas, led by the eldest, Duryodhana. But when the Great War begins, the alignment of their armies reveals serious disorder. The semi-divine Pāṇḍavas are in the west facing east, and the semi-demonic Kauravas are in the east facing west. Like the demon king Bali, Duryodhana has taken over the throne and exiled the semi-divine Pāṇḍavas and their shared wife Draupadī. This is why Kṛṣṇa faces east when he takes a message from Yudhiṣṭhira to Duryodhana in hope of preventing a great slaughter of kinsmen, and Duryodhana faces west.

Duryodhana in this story represents Kanchi's ruler *before* his consecration as Kṛṣṇa's slave. Consecration as a Bhāgavata ruler, however, establishes the "true order" of the city now expressed by the east-west axis, and Kṛṣṇa's slave represents his master to his subjects. We might say he is like a small movable icon placed in front of the huge immovable stucco Kṛṣṇa behind him. To his subjects he is an "Indra" as a "walking Viṣṇu"; to himself he is merely an "Indra" as his master's slave. His throne faces eastward toward Vāmana, who faces westward. Caught between the open and unblinking eyes of these two icons, Kanchipuram's king rules in the gaze of God.

This huge icon of Vāmana represents the Bhagavān's protection of the king ruling in his gaze, and his protection points us to his *ācārya.* The king, who has little time for Āgama's elaborate *mantra* rites to obtain practical results (*prayoga*), may sponsor his *ācārya* to perform them on his behalf. The logic of this appears in the story of the paradigmatic *maṇḍala,* where Viṣṇu in the shape of the dwarf is the sacrifice and takes over everything; the *Bhāgavata-purāṇa* story of Bali applies his "takeover" to a specific ruler. In his impurity, a Śūdra king is analogous to a demon, and in his status, he is analogous to Bali. Just as Vāmana's protection of Bali in his realm is powerful, so is the *ācārya's* protection of his royal disciple, as we learn from a Pāñcarātra *saṃhitā:*

> *Mantras* properly employed can bring prosperity for oneself, which includes knowledge, wealth and vehicles, children and cattle, wives and servants, fame and victory, health and books, houses and position, and other such things. They can also bring suffering on others for one's own gain, including death, attack of diseases, expulsion from the country, prevention of victory, destruction of wealth or its appropriation by force, enmity, delusion, and bringing another under one's own control (adapted from *Parama-saṃhitā* 13.5–10).

Given his important role in the royal court, it is not surprising that the *ācārya* is a referent of the huge Ūrakam Vāmana. It is both amusing and astonishing to think that a small Brahmin man can embody the Bhagavān within whom he exists; and the poet Kalikaṉṟi played on the wonder of it to organize one of two poems he composed to record Pallavamalla's consecration in 753–754 (*Periya Tirumoḻi* 2.8; see Hudson, forthcoming). This consecration began in Attiyūr where the Bhagavān dwells as the Lord with Eight Arms. The Bhagavān's presence in the icon is unquestioned in the poem, but in this stanza, Pallavamalla's voice wonders about his presence in the *ācārya,* and the *ācārya* gives his answer:

> "Who compares to this Hero among heroes of burning vigor?" the skilled singers of Veda say as they worship, as do singers of fine Tamil when they worship. But is this man God? I don't understand. He's like the Brahmin who came to great Bali's sacrifice in a dwarf's form and stretched up to measure out the earth. "Who is this person?" I ask. "I am the one dwelling in the house of the Eight-Armed Lord," he says.

This east-west axis continues in other temples in the city, even in those situated to the north and south of the center. By 600 C.E., Śiva's Ekāmra temple stood to the northwest; its *Śivaliṅga* faces east even though the entrance to the temple was later built to face south (Toṇṭaimāṉ, 1964, p. 95). At that time, some distance southeast of the city walls on the north bank of the Vegavatī branch of the Palar River, stood the village called Attiyūr. It was named after the Bhagavān who stands facing west as an icon made of the *atti* or *udumbara* tree.[7] This temple later developed into the huge and popular pilgrimage temple of "The Lord as King Who Gives Boons" (*Varadarājasvāmi*). The "Resident of the House of the Eight-Armed One" (*Aṭṭapuyakarattāṉ* or *Aṣṭabhujasvāmi*) may also have appeared in Attiyūr by then; he, too, stands and faces west. Nearby is the much older Veḥkā temple (Raman, 1975, p. 4).[8] All these temples south of the city wall and moat have been enclosed by the expanding city and now constitute a portion known as "Little Kanchi" or "Viṣṇu Kanchi."

Bhāgavata and Pāñcarātra rites crucial to Pallava kingship apparently continued at Kanchipuram even when the emperors were devout Śaivas, and poets found the older stucco icons especially meaningful. Tirumaḻicai, for example, records the Bhagavān's three iconic postures at

Kanchipuram in his poem *Tiruccantaviruttam* (63–64), and says that the Bhagavān makes these same postures in his heart (*neñcu*), the center of his consciousness. The city's *maṇḍala* is now the macrocosm and the poet's heart the microcosm, and are both modes of the "city of *brahman*" taught in the *upaniṣads*.[9] When Pallavamalla (731–786) built his Viṣṇu-house inside the city walls, he pulled these three postures together into a single palace (*vimāna*) to replicate the "city of *brahman*" a third time: the Bhagavān sits in its bottom sanctum, reclines in its middle sanctum, and stands in its top sanctum. Now, the dynasty's capital, the poet's heart, and the emperor's Viṣṇu-house contain all three postures made by the Lord who Measures the Earth standing at Kanchi's ancient center.

Pallava Kings

According to a Pallava memory recorded in a grant of circa 835, the dynasty came to Kanchipuram from somewhere else (Hultzsch, 1984, pp. 501–517). A man named Kalabhartri began to move into the region and had a son named Cutapallava. His son, Vīrakuca, then took the hand of the daughter of "the king of hooded serpents" (*phaṇīndra*), which denotes a Nāga. With her, Vīrakuca received the "complete insignia" (*cihnam akhilam*), which presumably was of her father's Nāga lineage. They then had a son named Skandaśiṣya. He "seized" the Brahmin academy (*ghaṭikā*) from the king, whose name was Satyasena. Skandaśiṣya had a son named Kumāraviṣṇu and he "captured" the city of Kanchi (*Kāñcīnagara*). Kumāraviṣṇu's son, Buddhavarman, then fought the Cōḻas (Hultzsch, 1984, pp. 508, 510).

This statement appears to describe a Pallava takeover of Kanchipuram in three generations, but it may actually depict the careful manner in which Kanchipuram's "Nāga" clan of Bhāgavatas sustained its "purity" so that the *ghaṭikā* would continue to recognize it as qualified to provide kings for Toṇṭai's people. Vīrakuca's marriage into the ruling Nāga lineage gives the Pallavas the authority to rule eventually, but by means of a descendent that represents Nāga interests and status. Skandaśiṣya, his son by the Nāga princess, is now the *marukaṉ* of his mother's Nāga brothers; this means he is both qualified for cross-cousin marriage into the Nāga lineage and is the ideal husband for their daughters. We learn from Pallavamalla's unction that members of the Brahmin *ghaṭikā* perform, which explains why the *ghaṭikā* supports

Skandaśiṣya's male heir rather than the male heir of the ruling Nāga king named Satyasena. If the ruling Satyasena is Skandaśiṣya's mother's brother, a Nāga, and if Skandaśiṣya marries his Nāga daughter, then according to the custom of cross-cousin marriage, the Pallava Skandaśiṣya is preferred to the Nāga Satyasena, because Skandaśiṣya's male heir will combine in her person both Pallava and Nāga lineages. He will be the center of a coherent indigenous clan, some of whose members are "outsiders" who by now have become "insiders," a clan qualified to continue providing kings for Kanchipuram. The *ghaṭikā* therefore performs the unction (*abhiṣeka*) that gives Skandaśiṣya's heir, Kumāraviṣṇu, royal control of the city. Kumāraviṣṇu's firmly established rule of the city allows his son, Buddhavarman, to turn his attention to expanding the realm at the expense of the Cōḻas. Interestingly, his name suggests the Bhāgavata doctrine that the Bhagavān became Śākyamuni Buddha to lead impure demons or Śūdras away from practicing Vedic rites. The epigraphic statement of this doctrine first appears in an inscription in a seventh-century Pāñcarātra cave temple built by the Pallavas at their port, Māmallapuram.

Let us now consider two important rulers who help us to understand the city's east-west axis, its Bhāgavata rulers, and their *ācāryas*. One is the first Nandivarman and the other is the second Siṃhavarman.[10]

The First Nandivarman

The first Nandivarman ruled in Kanchipuram circa 490–520 (Mahalingam, 1977, pp. 5, 8). A land grant in the first year of his reign describes him as "the great king of *dharma* (*dharma-mahārāja*) of the Pallavas in the Bhāradvāja *gotra,* a supreme Bhāgavata (*parama-bhāgavata*) devoted to the foot of the *bappa bhaṭṭāraka.*"[11] In early Prākrit and Sanskrit inscriptions, Pallavas claim descent from the Brahmin Bhāradvāja, one of the seven seers during the seventh "Manu Term" (*manvantara*) in which we live. A ruler in the Bhāradvāja lineage who is Kṛṣṇa's slave is noteworthy for three reasons. First, Bhāradvāja connects him to the kings of the *Mahābhārata,* because Bhāradvāja fathered Droṇa, whose son was Aśvatthāman; the Pallavas elsewhere claim Aśvatthāman as the father of the first Pallava. Second, it connects him to Śiva as his lineage deity (*kuladeva*), because Śiva entered into Aśvatthāman as destroyer at the end of the Great War. Pallava royal insignia include Śiva's bull. Third, it evokes the huge seated Kṛṣṇa icon in the Pāṭakam temple.

The Pallavas claim descent from Aśvatthāman, a warrior Brahmin, who, with his father Droṇa, fought on the side of deluded Duryodhana. After the war, Aśvatthāman was banished into exile because he had slain Pāṇḍava forces immorally (*Bhāgavata-purāṇa* 1.7). While exiled, Aśvatthāman fathered the first Pallava, either with a Nāga woman or an *apsaras,* both females of sensual and deluded natures. Pallava descent from Aśvatthāman thus identifies them with Duryodhana's deluded demonic nature, but purified by consecrated submission to Kṛṣṇa. Unlike Duryodhana, they perceive Kṛṣṇa's true identity as God.

The status of the first Nandivarman as a "supreme Bhāgavata" illustrates early Pallava self-understanding, and his veneration of the *bappa bhaṭṭāraka* points to the royal *ācārya* as its source. According to the *Sātvata-saṃhitā* (21), the Bhāgavata is to venerate the *ācārya* from whom he receives his entire life.[12] *Bhaṭṭāraka* means "highly venerable" and was used especially by Buddhists to refer to deities and to spiritual teachers. *Bappa* or *vappa* appears to be a Prākrit word; judging from its use in other Pallava grants, it is synonymous with *pārppaṉ,* a Tamil word for a Brahmin.[13] This means that Nandivarman was devoted to the feet of his Brahmin *ācārya* as Buddhists were to the *bhikṣu ācārya*. *Ācāryas* in Pallava courts must have had an established presence throughout the centuries. A scholar of Āgama (*āgamika*) resided in the eighth-century court of Hiraṇyavarma somewhere outside of Kanchipuram, and in 753 his son Pallavamalla, now emperor in Kanchipuram, stated that his own ruling power had increased because he meditates on the feet of the *bappa bhaṭṭāraka* (Hultzsch, 1983, p. 350, line 78; p. 358).

The Second Siṃhavarman

With Siṃhavarman II (circa 535–580), our knowledge of the Pallavas becomes richer (Srinivasan, 1979, pp. 21–23). During a period that is not understood well, the "Kalabhras" disrupted the politics of the Pallavas, Cōḻas, and Pāṇṭiyas until the middle of the sixth century. The second Siṃhavarman restored the Pallava line in Kanchi. Inscriptions of this Siṃha lineage record its patronage of Jains and Śaivas; Siṃha's wife, for example, patronized Jains. Her husband Siṃha, however, appears to have been a Bhāgavata,[14] and their two sons, Siṃhaviṣṇu and Bhīma, definitely were, and were remembered during the eighth century as incarnations of Viṣṇu (S. Krishnaswamy Aiyangar cited by R. Gopalan,

1928, p. 231). Their eldest son Siṃhaviṣṇu (circa 560–580) was an enthusiastic Bhāgavata and produced the line of kings ruling in Kanchipuram until 731 (Foulkes, October 1879, p. 275, line 12).[15] His younger brother Bhīma left the capital to establish a kingdom somewhere else, possibly in Cambodia. Six generations later, Pallavamalla would come from Bhīma's dynastic line to renew Bhāgavata rule in the capital.

The same inscription that records Siṃhaviṣṇu and Bhīma's mother's dedication of a Jain temple describes Siṃhaviṣṇu's intellect as "purified by being washed in the waters of the different Āgamas." This suggests that he studied Jain, Buddhist, and other texts along with Bhāgavata scriptures. Such a curriculum, but set within a Buddhist framework, appears in the Tamil courtly poem *Maṇimēkalai* (27), which was probably composed in the sixth century and possibly in the Kanchi court (Hudson 1997). A breadth of religious learning in the Pallava family matched the complexity of its members' religious commitments (Mahalingam, 1969, p. 55). The literary learning of the lineage is further revealed by the decision of the Brahmin Sanskrit poet Bhāravi to marry and reside at Siṃhaviṣṇu's court, and by the Sanskrit plays written by Siṃha's son Mahendra. This king illustrates the fact that the Bhāgavata *dharma* and Pāñcarātra rites may continue at a court even when the king finds religious satisfaction elsewhere.

The First Mahendra

The first Mahendra had a long rule (circa 580–630) and chose a different direction for his religious patronage. At first he may have favored the Jains, but eventually he became an ardent patron of the Śaiva Āgama. His heirs continued that patronage down until Pallavamalla's ascension circa 731.[16] Mahendravarman was remarkable. He began feuds with the Chālukyas and the Pāṇṭiyas, which his Pallava heirs continued for a century and a half, and at the same time composed the earliest surviving Sanskrit and Prākrit farces for the theater, and originated rock-cut architecture among the Tamils (*Encyclopaedia of Indian Temple Architecture,* 1983, 1, 1: 23–25). His cave temples reveal a continuing interest in the east-west axis for sacred shrines. Four of them housed the *Trimūrti* (Brahmā, Śiva, Viṣṇu), giving Śiva the prominent place in the middle with Brahmā to his right and Viṣṇu to his left (Srinivasan, 1964, pp. 47–61). Three faced east and one faced south. The icons are now missing, but were either paintings or panels inserted into the shrines. They are among the earliest evidence of *Trimūrti* worship in India.[17]

The exceptional south-facing cave temple in this set of four introduces the north-south axis to which we will turn shortly. An explanation for it is found in two south-facing corner panels of the later Vaikuṇṭha Perumāḷ Temple. The southeast panel depicts the *Trimūrti* Brahmā, Viṣṇu, and Śiva incarnated as the three sons of the seer Atri and his wife Anasūyā named Candra, Dattātreya, and Durvāsas respectively. Viṣṇu as Dattātreya in the middle and facing south balances the panel at the southwest corner, which depicts Viṣṇu as the courtesan Mohinī ("She who Deludes"). She stands in the middle, faces south, and feeds *amṛta* to the gods in the east while the demons in the west look on. Both of these corner panels signify royal Bhāgavata concerns with demonic forces moving in from the south and west as night begins. Among other things, the panels refer to "twilight language" (*saṃdhyā-bhāṣā*) used by the royal *ācārya* during esoteric rites to generate "brilliant conquering power" (*tejas*) on behalf of the ruler against these demonic powers.

Returning to Mahendra's south-facing cave temple, Śiva placed in the middle between Brahmā and Viṣṇu may be a similar response to death by Śaivas. Śiva in the middle suggests his appearance as the seer Durvāsas, who is instrumental in the *Mahābhārata*. Durvāsas teaches Kuntī the *mantras* that allow her and Madrī to be impregnated by five gods to father the five Pāṇḍavas. Durvāsas is connected to three liturgical schools employing dangerous rites of death and passion, which in Kanchipuram were represented by *Maheśvaras* ("Great Rulers"). Mahendra repeatedly refers to Maheśvara ascetics in his play, *Mattavilāsa* (they include Śaiva Āgamikas, Pāśupatas, and Kāpālikas).[18] Devotion to Śiva continued with Mahendra's son, Narasiṃhavarman I Māmalla (630–668), who depicted the doctrine of Śiva's "five faces" (*pañca-mukha*) in a west-facing cave temple with one shrine devoted to each *mantra* "face": Īśāna, Tatpuruṣa, Aghora, Vāmadeva, and Sadyojāta.[19] This five-faced form of Śiva in a cave oriented to the west was the Śaiva version of the west-facing Bhāgavata temples inside the capital; the "*liṅga* of five faces" (*pañca-mukha-liṅga*) articulates the complete identity of Śiva as "Ever-Auspicious" (*Sadāśiva*). Mahendra also expressed his Śaiva commitment through six other cave temples, four of which have the sanctum facing east and the other two facing west (Srinivasan, 1964, pp. 61–64; 71–100).

Two other east-facing cave temples, however, reveal that Mahendra also continued his ancestors' patronage of the Bhāgavatas. One icon apparently had the "roaring" of a "dark cloud full of a thousand torrents," which may denote Kṛṣṇa or the Man-lion (*Narasiṃha;* Srinivasan, 1964, pp. 67–71). The other bears an inscription identifying it as "the house of the slayer of Mura (*Murāri*) named the Mahendra Viṣṇu-house" (Srinivasan, 1964, pp. 64–67). This icon appears to have been a painting that signified esoteric rites pertinent to royal rule.[20]

As the seventh century unfolded, rivalry in the royal court between Śaiva and Vaiṣṇava Āgamas intensified. Michael Lockwood (1982, pp. 19–55) argues that Śaiva modifications of Bhāgavata cave temples at Māmallapuram, made under the rule of Parameśvara I (672–700), document hostility between the two royal traditions. Bhāgavatas subsequently modified these Śaiva changes, perhaps during Pallavamalla's rule, revealing an Āgama competition that was long-standing.

The North-South Axis

The north-south axis denotes the human realm called Bhārata. As we recall from the *maṇḍala* paradigm, death comes to humans from the south and prosperous householder life is in the north. The Himālayas signify the route to Indra's heaven. This north-south pattern governs the story of the *Rāmāyaṇa,* which is about human well-being in Ayodhyā, an ideal kingdom in the north. In the story, Rāma, an ideal ruler, moves with his wife, Sītā, and his brother, Lakṣmaṇa, away from Ayodhyā, steadily southward. Eventually they become entangled with *rākṣasas* centered in the southernmost island kingdom of Laṅkā. Once Rāma and Lakṣmaṇa have defeated them and have rescued Sītā from *rākṣasa* capture, they immediately return to Ayodhyā in the north to rule perfectly for thousands of years. In the afternoon and evening of the south are *rākṣasas,* Yama, death, ancestors, purgatories, cremation grounds, funeral mounds, monasteries housing people "dead" to householder life, groves for monks, and shrines for esoteric rites to preserve *amṛta*—all leading to sunset and night on the west of Varuṇa. Directly opposite is the north side's "Brahmā's Hour" (*brahma-muhūrta*) of 4 to 6 A.M., where there are purification, purity, *japa* recitation of *mantras,* churning of *amṛta,* and awakening—all leading to sunrise and morning on the east of Indra. The north-south axis of the city's *maṇḍala* is about human life caught in the middle of the perennial struggle between gods and demons along the east-west axis. Pallava connections to Aśvatthāman's father, Droṇa, refer to this axis, too, but this is a Buddhist Droṇa. He appears in the story of Śākyamuni Buddha as told by Aśvaghoṣa, who explicitly likens him to the Droṇa of the *Mahābhārata* in his famous "Life of the Buddha" (*Buddhacarita*).

Aśvaghoṣa's *Buddhacarita*

In the last two chapters of his second-century Sanskrit "Life of the Buddha" (*Buddhacarita*), Aśvaghoṣa relates the way the tribe of Mallas ("Wrestlers") collects the Buddha's cremated bones as relics. A Brahmin named Droṇa, "the peer of Droṇa in knowledge," subsequently resolves a dangerous dispute over their possession by having the relics divided into eight parts and housed in eight funeral mounds (*stūpas*) in the capitals of the contending tribes. Later, the emperor Aśoka opens up these *stūpas* and, in one day, distributes the relics to be housed in 84,000 *stūpas* throughout India (*Buddhacarita* 27–28).[21] According to Aśvaghoṣa, these *stūpas* are equivalent to the body of the living Buddha (*Buddhacarita* 28.69). John Strong explains that the 84,000 *stūpas* match the 84,000 atoms in the Buddha's "body of form" (*rūpa-kāya*) and the 84,000 sections of the Buddha's "body of teaching" (*dharma-kāya*). This is why they have to be distributed evenly over India simultaneously (Strong, 1983, pp. 107–119). Thus spread out, the Buddha's physical and scriptural *stūpa* body not only makes him present in specific places, but also makes present Aśoka's authority as supreme emperor. The *stūpa* is thus an imperial symbol of "Dharma's King" (*dharma-rājika*), who is simultaneously the Buddha and Aśoka. When a *stūpa* stands at a ruler's capital, it means that the local king rules under the umbrella of both; and an "Aśoka *stūpa*" nearly one hundred feet tall stood south of Kanchipuram's wall and moat at least until the eighth century.

Pallava connection to Aśvaghoṣa's Droṇa and to the *Mahābhārata's* Droṇa was strengthened further by a claim that Aśoka was a Pallava ancestor.[22] Moreover, the Pallava clan that ruled Kanchi used the name Malla, which means "wrestler," and no doubt identified with the Mallas, who are the leading warrior tribe in the story of Śākyamuni Buddha. This may explain why the Malla clan of the Pallavas was the first to include the Buddha among the Bhagavān's incarnations in an inscription. It appears in a seventh-century cave temple at Māmallapuram, which depicts the four formations (*vyūhas*) of the *Pāñcarātra Āgama*.[23] A century later, on the second-floor sanctum of the Viṣṇu-house he built according to the *Pāñcarātra Āgama,* Pallavamalla prominently depicted Kṛṣṇa as a wrestler. He wrestles Cāṇūra in a scene placed just after one that refers to the Bhagavān Nārāyaṇa as "the pure Buddha who deluded the Daitya and Dānava" divisions of demons (*Bhāgavata-purāṇa* 10.40.22). This wrestler depiction is a double entendre, for while it illustrates Kṛṣṇa wrestling and conquering Cāṇūra, it illustrates the name of the emperor who built the temple, Pallavamalla, "Pallava Wrestler." The Pallava Wrestler was not Kṛṣṇa, of course, but Cāṇūra, because Kṛṣṇa had "conquered" Pallavamalla to make him a Bhāgavata.

All Buddhist structures and most Buddhist sculptures have disappeared from Kanchipuram. But if we examine the evidence that scholars have recently drawn together from a variety of Indian, Chinese, and Japanese sources, they reveal much about Buddhism in Kanchipuram during Pallava rule. Buddhists of the "Elders' Doctrine" (*Sthaviravāda* and *Theravāda*) appear to have made Kanchi their educational center from early on, and established themselves afterward in Sri Lanka, but in doctrine and liturgy all major Buddhist developments were represented there (Dutt, 1977, pp. 229–230).

The *Maṇimēkalai*

Two sources are pertinent to our discussion of the north-south axis. The first is the Tamil courtly poem *Maṇimēkalai,* dated to the sixth century C.E. As I have argued elsewhere (Hudson, 1997), the poet Cīttalai Cāttaṉār based it on the origin legend (*sthala-purāṇa*) of a Buddhist cultic site outside Kanchipuram's wall to the southwest. It reveals the presence of Esoteric or Tantric Buddhists in Kanchi, whom Mahendra's play *Mattavilāsa* indicates were patronized at the Pallava court. Although probably written circa 550, the *Maṇimēkalai* story relates legendary events during Kanchi's pre-Pallava period, when the Cōḻa king's younger brother ruled at the time the port of Pukār was destroyed. It appears to have been written for an elite and educated audience in Kanchi, because at the end of the story, the goddess of the ocean is enshrined in a newly built Buddhist temple in a grove southwest of Kanchi's wall named *Maṇi-pallavam,* in which *pallavam* alludes to the Pallavas. Moreover, *Maṇi-mēkalai* and *Maṇi-mekhalā,* the names of the heroine and of the goddess of the sea respectively, denote a "waist girdle (*mekhalā, mēkalai*) of jewels (*maṇi*)," and among the meanings of *kāñci* is "waist girdle." Kanchipuram, "Town of the Waist Girdle" or "Town of the *Kāñci* Tree," was the capital of a dynasty whose wealth came from commerce across the sea to the southeast. Their wealth depended, they believed, on the goddess Maṇimekhalā, whom Indra had placed in charge of that sea, the same goddess who had earlier destroyed the Cōḻa port of Pukār.

Cāttaṉār describes Kanchipuram in a way that matches what we know about it from other sources (*Maṇimēkalai* 28,165–245). He likens it to Indra's heavenly city of Amarāvatī, but now in decline due to famine. When his heroine, Maṇimēkalai, assumes a male form and flies to Kanchi, she first circumambulates its walls in veneration and then lands in its center at a Buddhist shrine built by the Pallava king. It houses an image of the Buddha's *bodhi* tree of enlightenment made of gold with emerald leaves. According to the "Legend of Aśoka" (*Aśokāvadāna*), the golden *bodhi* tree was like a *stūpa,* because it signified both the Buddha's body and the emperor Aśoka. The *bodhi* tree as the Buddha's body also appears in the story of king Duṭṭhagāmaṇi of Sri Lanka as told in the *Mahāvaṃśa*. When he built his *stūpa,* he placed a *bodhi* tree made of jewels, silver, and gold inside its relic chamber (*Mahāvaṃśa* 30.62–77).

This artificial *bodhi* tree has a range of further allusions, which, according to John Strong, include the *aśoka* tree, the virgin goddess who kicks it to make it blossom, and the Buddha's mother named "Great Māyā" (*Mahāmāyā;* Strong, 1983, pp. 127–130). In his account of the Buddha's life, Aśvaghoṣa plays with "Great Māyā" as meaning "creative and illusory power" when he tells of her conception of him; it was a conception "without defilement . . . just as knowledge united with mental concentration bears fruit" (*Buddhacarita* 1.3). Great Māyā as Śākyamuni Buddha's "virgin" mother appears to have been present in Kanchi through a series of goddess associations beginning with Tārā. Through her connection to the virgin goddess of the *aśoka* tree, goddess Tārā is a Buddhist way to identify the goddess Celvi or Kāmākṣī dwelling in the Kāmakkōṭṭam at Kanchi's ancient center who is connected to the *kāñci* tree. Presumably, the Buddhist shrine of the *bodhi* tree in the *Maṇimēkalai* stood near the Kāmakkōṭṭam.

According to Cāttaṉār, the *Maṇimēkalai's* heroine then walks southwest from Kanchi's center to a grove of trees earlier planted outside its walls by the king. Perhaps Cāttaṉār means that she goes to the large "monks' garden" (*saṅghārāma*), where a tall Aśoka *stūpa* stood, and where talented and learned men gathered, as the Chinese monk Hsuan Tsang would later report. Cāttaṉār calls the park the "Dharma Giving Grove." The king has it built under instructions from a goddess to replicate the island called Maṇipallavam, which lies southeast of India toward Java and is noted among Buddhists for esoteric powers. The king then has a lake dug in the park to replicate the island's lake called the "Cow's Mouth" (*Gomukhi*).

Still in her male guise, Maṇimēkalai adds to the king's construction. She has a pedestal built in the grove to support a *maṇḍala* that replicates the one on Maṇipallavam island. She has it built to hold the large begging bowl she earlier received on this island from the Cow's Mouth lake. The bowl, called Amṛta Surabhi, is the divine cow that pours forth *amṛta* that Bhāgavatas say was churned from the milk ocean; it appears from the lake every year on the Buddha's birthday near the summer solstice. Any offering placed in it multiplies to feed the hungry and is never exhausted (*Maṇimēkalai* 11.39–50). Maṇimēkalai also has a temple built to house icons of the goddess of Maṇipallavam island, named Dīpatilakā, and of Maṇimekhalā, the goddess of the ocean. Finally, Maṇimēkalai places the bowl at the center of the *maṇḍala* on the pedestal in the Maṇipallavam grove southwest of the city. Amṛta Surabhi pours forth prosperity and Kanchi's disastrous famine ends (*Maṇimēkalai* 28).

Hsuan Tsang

The second source for the north-south axis is the record kept by the Chinese Buddhist monk Hsuan Tsang. In 640 C.E. he reached "the Drāviḍa country" overland from what is now Andhra Pradesh. Narasiṃhavarma I Māmalla (circa 630–668) was reigning at the time. Hsuan Tsang describes his country and its capital this way (in Samuel Beal's translation):

> This country is about 6000 *li* in circuit; the capital of the country is called Kanchipura, and is about 30 *li* round . . . There are some hundred of *saṅghārāmas* and 10,000 priests. They all study the teaching of the Sthavira (Chang-tso-pu) school belonging to the Great Vehicle. There are some eighty Deva [god] temples, and many heretics called Nirgranthans. [Buddha] Tathāgata in olden days, when living in the world, frequented this country much; he preached the law here and converted men, and therefore Aśoka-rāja built *stūpas* over all the sacred spots where these traces exist. The city of Kanchipura is the native place of Dharmapāla Bodhisattva. He was the eldest son of a great minister of the country . . . To the south of the city not a great way is a large *saṅghārāma,* in which men of the same sort, renowned for talent and learning, assemble and stop. There is a *stūpa* about 100 feet high which was built by Aśoka-rāja. Here [Buddha] Tathāgata, dwelling in the old days, repeated the law and subdued the heretics, and converted both men and Devas in great number.[24]

If I understand Hsuan Tsang correctly, the realm he called "Drāviḍa" was about 1200 miles in circuit and contained about one hundred monasteries (*vihāra*) and 10,000 monks. Kanchipuram was about six miles in circuit presumably including the walled city and settlements beyond the moat, such as Attiyūr.[25] Samuel Beal interprets the monks as Sthaviras belonging to the "Great Vehicle" (*Mahāyāna*), and probably included followers of Sautranta, Yogācāra, and Vajrayāna. The eighty *deva* temples referred to those of the Śaiva and Vaiṣṇava Āgamas and perhaps included Jain temples of Indra, Brahmā, and *yakṣas*. By "heretical Nirgranthans" he probably means Jain and Ājīvaka ascetics (*śramaṇas*).[26]

The tall Aśoka *stūpa* Hsuan Tsang reported as standing south of the city in the vicinity of a monastery and park means that Buddhists understood Kanchipuram to be part of Buddhist sacred history, even that Śākyamuni Buddha had once visited there. He said that the monastery associated with this *stūpa* served as an intellectual center for the elite; indeed, it may have been the "Royal Monastery" Mahendra mentions in his play *Mattavilāsa*. The "Giving Dharma Grove" that Cāttaṉār in the *Maṇimēkalai* says is to the southwest may have referred to the same complex. Since the south is the direction of Yama, death, and *rākṣasas,* it is an appropriate place for a *stūpa,* even if this elaborate funeral mound is regarded as the Buddha's body. Śākyamuni Buddha himself had "died" to his own walled city and its householder life when he left in the middle of the night, cut his hair, exchanged clothes with a hunter, and walked south to defeat death (*Buddhacarita* 5–7).[27]

There is ample evidence for the cultic importance of the south in Kanchipuram, but why is there little for the north? I am not sure of the answer. Perhaps there are later temples that face north among the more than one hundred surviving in the city. Perhaps there are ruins to the north that have not been excavated. Perhaps the meaning of the north is not readily articulated through built forms. Or perhaps, as I think more likely, the walled city itself designates the north, the quarter of human life and prosperity ruled by the full moon bearing the figure of a hare (*śaśin*).

Conclusion

Let us end with the hare in the moon. As we know from the paradigmatic *maṇḍala,* the hare in the full moon depicts the imperishable place of Vedic sacrifice kept safely because humans and gods depend on it for life. For Buddhists, however, this hare signifies an astounding act of ritual giving (*dāna*). As Āryaśūra tells us in the *Jātakamālā* of circa 200–300 C.E., the Bodhisattva once lived as a hare with an otter, jackal, and ape (Āryaśūra, 1982, pp. 37–45). The day before the full moon arrives, the animals remember that on the next day, they are expected to feed a venerable guest before they eat. The hare vows to offer himself as food. Indra knows this, and at noon on the full moon day appears as a Brahmin who has lost his way and suffers from heat, thirst, and fatigue. To be hospitable, the otter brings him seven fish, the jackal brings a lizard and a cup of sour milk, and the ape brings ripe mangoes. The hare offers his own body. The Brahmin says he cannot kill living beings, but the hare asks him to rest and says he will find a way. Indra then creates a heap of burning coals and the hare sees it as the means to fulfill his vow. Rejoicing in his act of offering himself to another, he jumps into the blazing fire the way a great goose (*parama-haṃsa*) plunges into a lake blooming with lotuses. Indra then assumes his true shape, picks the hare's body out of the fire, and shows it to the gods to proclaim his astonishing deed. To glorify this extraordinary ritual giving of self for the sake of the world, Indra draws the form of the hare on the full moon. Thus the moon is known as "having the hare's body" (*śaśāṅka*).

The hare giving himself is not unlike great Bali giving his head as a resting place for Vāmana's foot as he takes his third stride. In both cases, the point of the story is not the power of ritual sacrifice to produce results, but the purity of intent. Yet, in both, purity of intent results in extraordinary results. Bali's simple gift of land to the Brahmin dwarf Vāmana, and his faithfulness to that gift in the face of Vāmana's deceit, followed then by the offer of his head in an act of taking refuge in the one who deceived him, results in his continuous protection by Vāmana in his own glorious kingdom. The Bodhisattva's simple gift to the lost Brahmin of his body as food ends in the hare's death, of course, but the purity of his intent produces yet another Bodhisattva body, which then allows him to continue his career of birth after birth until he enters "extinction" (*nirvāṇa*) as Śākyamuni Buddha.

These two stories about the hare in the moon represent the two ends of this north-south axis. The demon Bali rules as king in a prosperous realm worthy of the human quarter in the north, worthy of Kanchipuram itself. The hare eventually ends his long Bodhisattva career as the cremated Śākyamuni "ruling" as Buddha from an Aśokan *stūpa* in the south. The rulers of Kanchi, without exception as far as I know, personally opted for Bali's approach. For them, the northeast corner, where humans and gods meet at sunrise, was their comfort, and the southwest corner, where demonic *rākṣasas* and *asuras* meet at sunset, was their dread. They believed only the "imposter" ascetics of Buddhist, Jain, Ājīvaka, and Kāpālika orders could find comfort there; and to protect themselves and their reign from Nirṛti's disintegration, even when they personally were Śaivas, they sponsored Bhāgavata *ācāryas* to perform *prayoga* rites of the Pāñcarātra Āgama.

Notes

1. Nilakantha Sastri, 1958, p. 110. Translations of *Perumpāṇāṟṟuppaṭai* are from *Pattuppāṭṭu: Ten Tamil Idylls* (Chelliah, 1962, pp. 97–138) and from Raghunathan, 1978, pp. 69–95. Neither translation nor any uses of this poem by historians I have consulted pay attention to the poem's cultic dimensions.
2. *Perumpāṇāṟṟuppaṭai* 29–31. Here, I interpret *piṟaṅkatai* as "churned to overflowing" (*piṟaṅku-kaṭai*) rather than as "descendent" as cited in the *Tamil Lexicon* 1982, 5:2718, though the poet probably plays with both meanings. "Three-fold sea" can also mean "ancient waters" (*mūṉṉī*) and suggest the waters "churned" by the threefold consecration (*dīkṣā-traya*) of the *Sātvata-saṃhitā* (see Smith, 1975).
3. In South Asian lore, *nāgas* are cobra-beings who dwell in the dark watery realms upon which the earth floats. These realms are characterized by darkness (*tamas*), just as passion (*rajas*) characterizes earth and purity (*sattva*) the heavens.
4. See *Bhāgavata-purāṇa* 3.16.5. The Bhagavān's servants resemble him in appearance, but two of them have insulted the four Kumāra brothers. This prompts the Bhagavān to say, "When a servant does something wrong the world attributes it to the master, and the disrepute that one gets that way erodes one's good name, as leprosy erodes one's skin" (Tapasyananda's translation). Conversely, when the servant does something right, the world attributes it to his master.
5. The Kumārakkōṭṭam at the city's ancient center is said to have been the place where Kācciyappa Śivācārya composed the Tamil version of the Skanda story, the *Kantapurāṇam*.
6. Commentators interpret "Kōval" to refer to the temple of Kovalūr between Katpadi and Villupuram, where the icon is a mirror image of Trivikrama in Ūrakam: he faces east, holds the conch in his right hand, the wheel in his left, and his right leg stretches up to the sky (rather than the usual left). This east-facing icon may intentionally mirror the west-facing Trivikrama at Kanchi's Ūrakam; its reversed posture suggests *prayoga* rites for protection, as does the reclining icon at Veḥkā, which reverses the proper posture for sleep.

   In the context of Kanchi, however, Kōval appears to denote the thrice-striding Vāmana as Protector (*kō-val* literally means "king's power"). This "tall protector" (*nīḷ kōval*) appears to be the same as the "tall one" (*neṭiyōṉ*) in *Perumpāṇāṟṟuppaṭai* (line 402), which refers to the huge stucco icon in the Ūrakam temple in Kanchi (R. Gopalan, pp. 64–65). The Protector of the moat around Kanchi, "the flower that never closes," is likewise Vāmana as the triple strider (*Trivikrama*) in the temple "of the city's interior" (*ūr-akam*). The long and reclining stucco icon outside the moat at Veḥkā, then, is the Bhagavān in the city's exterior (*puṟam*) and probably depicts the "Slayer of Deluded Passion" (*Madhusūdana*).

Commentators have understood the sitting icon in "Viṇṇakaram" to refer to the transcendent realm of Vaikuṇṭha, but P. B. Annankaracharya (1928, p. 166) notes that it may be taken to refer to the Paramēccura-viṇṇakaram (Vaikuṇṭha Perumāḷ Temple) in Kanchipuram, as I do here. This means that the poet named Poykai was Pallavamalla's contemporary in the late eighth century.

7. According to Raman (1975, pp. 3–4), Attiyūr in the eighth century lay outside the walls of Kanchipuram to the southeast. Attiyūr today stands within the enlarged boundaries of the city and is called "Little Kanchi" and "Viṣṇu Kanchi." Five temples venerated by Āḻvārs stood outside the city walls in Attiyūr or near it in the eighth century. Of them, the icons of two stand facing east, the icons of two stand facing west, and the icon of one reclines facing west. See C. R. Srinivasan (1979, p. 256) and L. V. Gopalan (1972, pp. 59–63).
8. On page 44, Raman describes the standing icon as facing west, a correction of L. V. Gopalan's statement that it faces east (1972, p. 60).
9. See, for example, *Chāndogya Upaniṣad* 8.1–4 and *Kauśitaki Upaniṣad* 1 (*Upaniṣads,* 1998, pp. 273–277; 327–333).
10. The Sanskrit sources are discussed by C. R. Srinivasan, 1979, pp. 21–25.
11. Adapted from Foulkes, June 1879, pp. 167–173.
12. *Sātvata-saṃhitā* 21 describes continuing devotion to the *ācārya* after the devotee has received "Consecration to the Worship of an Icon" (*vibhava-dīkṣā*). For a summary, see Smith, 1975, pp. 530–531.
13. In 764–765, Pallavamalla gave a grant to one hundred and eight *bappa bhaṭṭāraka* in which *pārppar* in the Tamil portion corresponds to *bappa* in the Sanskrit portion. See Mahalingam, 1959, p. 145.
14. He has been identified with Ayaṭikaḷ Kāṭavarkōṉ, the Nāyaṉār devotee of Śiva (see Mahalingam, 1969, pp. 55, 139–155). Ayaṭikaḷ Kāṭavarkōṉ, translated as "King of the Khāṇḍava Forest," refers to Indra who protects this forest and is subdued by Kṛṣṇa in *Mahābhārata* 1.215 (*Mahābhārata,* 1973, pp. 415–417). This implies that he received unction as an "Indra of Men" (*Narendra*) and then Bhāgavata consecration.
15. For a Pallava genealogical tree, see C. R. Srinivasan, 1979, pp. 23–25. Here, I follow the dates given in *Encyclopaedia of Indian Temple Architecture* 1983, 1.1:22.
16. Cēkkiḻār, in his later Tamil *Periya-purāṇam,* attributed Mahendra's conversion to Appar and remembered him as intolerant thereafter (C. R. Srinivasan, 1979, pp. 28–29).
17. The south-facing cave temple is at Pallavaram and contains five shrines. It is now a Muslim tomb-shrine or *dargah* (K. R. Srinivasan, 1964, pp. 51–54).
18. The Kālāmukhas are a subset of the last, according to Dyczkowski, 1988, pp. 16–19).
19. Narasiṃha also gave Śiva greater prominence than Brahmā and Viṣṇu in a similar cave temple, in an arrangement that anticipates the later portrayal of the Bhagavān's four "formations" (*vyūhas*) in the Vaikuṇṭha Perumāḷ Temple (K. R. Srinivasan, 1964, pp. 100–107).
20. At *Bhāgavata-purāṇa* 10.59, Kṛṣṇa slays the demon Mura at Prāgjyotiṣapura in the northeast at the beginning of the episode in which he slaughters Earth's son

named Bhauma. Kṛṣṇa then takes the 16,000 women Bhauma had kept captive in Prāgjyotiṣapura to be his wives. He then captures the Pārijāta tree from Indra and takes it to Dvāraka on Garuḍa's back. The story is replete with esoteric meanings and encodes the doctrine of the Bhagavān's wheel, Sudarśana, which in the *Pāñcarātra Āgama* signifies the power of *mantra* rites, breaks through demonic bonds, slays the body's slayer, and bestows royal prosperity to refugees in Kṛṣṇa during the darkness of the Kali Yuga.

21. Aśvaghoṣa makes this Droṇa's connection to the "pot-born" Droṇa of the *Mahābhārata* explicit by having him house the pot of relics in his own *stūpa* (28.56).
22. A grant dated circa 753–754 claims Aśoka-varman as a Pallava ancestor (Hultzsch, 1983, 2:342–361).
23. See the "Ādivarāha" cave temple in K. R. Srinivasan, 1964, pp. 166–175, plates 53–56.
24. Samuel Beal quoted in C. R. Srinivasan, 1979, pp. 31–32. Watters (1961, 2:335) gives the year 640.
25. Following Watters (1961, 2:232), who uses about five *li* to the mile.
26. In addition to Digambara and Śvetāmbara *śramaṇas,* there were probably also *Yāpanīyas*. See Desai, 1957, pp. 163–174.
27. In *Buddhacarita* 7.39–41, hermits tell the Bodhisattva that the north where the Himālayas stand is the direction of the highest *dharma,* which leads to Indra's heaven, and that a wise man should never step towards the south. But in 7.48, when the Bodhisattva says he is not interested in heaven, but in release from death and rebirth, the hermits advise him to walk south toward the Vindhya mountains (7.54).

FIVE

Cosmos, Realm, and Property in Early Medieval South India

Daud Ali

According to our textbooks, history begins with the description of regions, environments, natural topography, and boundaries. Cartographic space, and more particularly the natural environment within geopolitical entities, is considered to be the template upon which history "moves." Upon it empires rise and fall, people and ideas spread, and humans construct their "identities." So conceived, geography would represent an inquiry into the changing relations, both material and ideological, between humans and their physical environments. How does one write a history of this relationship? One approach has been to document the various strategies that humans have developed for the transformations of nature for the subsistence and maintenance of their societies. Another, one that this volume hopes to explore, is to examine the ways in which humans represent their relationship to their environments. The study of spatial representations has in the main sought to explore the attitudes that human societies have held toward space—in our case, to trace the continuities and ruptures in the evolving spatial conceptions of South India or Tamilnadu. The three kingdoms of the *caṅkam,* the *nāṭu* locality, the region of Tamiḻakam, or the Dravidian nation become "cartographies" or "mappings" of the region of South India. The concern of this essay will be slightly different. Using a broadly structuralist method, I will conceptualize the simultaneity of three different sorts of spatial conceptions—cosmological, political, and proprietary—within the totality of a social formation.

Negatively, the argument here will suggest that medieval documents did not presuppose any concept of abstract or "cartographic" space that formed the underlying ground upon which political and historical entities were situated. This absence in part explains the absence or radical alterity of "maps" in early medieval India. This absence has often been understood as a failed rationality. This essay will treat what have often been called by geographers "cosmographic," "mythic," or "irreal" conceptions of space. In it, I will explore their operative principles and place these principles within the wider framework of social relationships. I will argue that principles of spatial organization in medieval India, which drew within their sphere material and immaterial elements, from the parts of the psyche to the stars in the sky, from the continents of the earth to the places of the village, were not posed or understood as autonomous and distinct from the principles of the social order, but were instead direct extensions of them. Ultimately, medieval Indian conceptions of space reveal a symmetry in the contours of society and nature, between the cosmos as an ensemble of places and as a hierarchy of lordships. It may perhaps sound banal to assert that ideologies of space are tied to social relationships, but I will suggest that *the way* ideas of space are tied to social relations in medieval India is quite different from the way we experience this relationship in modern societies.

The documents examined will be a group of eleventh-century inscriptions and the more expansive "cosmographic texts" that they presupposed. Though I will focus on one medieval South Indian kingdom, that of the Cōḻas of Tanjavur, I will not argue that the Cōḻas exhibit a consciously "regional" or Tamil conception of space. Even a brief perusal of the inscriptions of contemporary medieval dynasties elsewhere in the subcontinent reveals that the spatial conceptions we find in the Cōḻa inscriptions were widely shared by the ruling courts of the subcontinent. Moreover, though historians have placed the Cōḻas in a "regional" period of Indian history, they themselves never claim to be monarchs of South India. As we shall see, the very ascription of a "regional" political identity was avoided by dynasties with imperial ambitions.

I

In early India there were a number of concepts denoting "space"—we encounter Sanskrit terms such as *kṣetra, deśa, ākāśa, maṇḍala,* and *loka,* to name a few. Two problems arise in understanding these terms—

first, to locate them within their discursive contexts; and second, to provide a history of these contexts themselves. Studies of these terms by scholars of religions and art historians have generally placed them within an unwieldy, generic, and essentialized "Indian tradition," or universal human experience of space and divinity.[1] A cursory reading of Sanskrit texts such as the Vedas, *upaniṣads,* post-Vedic philosophical *sūtras,* and *purāṇas* reveals very different ideas regarding the structure of the cosmos. Furthermore, the relations between these various ideologies must be understood in discursive context. Vedic, Smārta, Buddhist, and Purāṇic conceptions of space, cosmos, and polity themselves existed in complex and asymmetrical relations with one another at any single point of time.

The inscriptions that come down to us from early medieval India have formed the major source for the historical reconstruction of the "regional" period of Indian history.[2] Unfortunately, these inscriptions emplot an ensemble of places almost entirely at odds with the geography of the modern world. This fact has been recognized by scholars by the anachronistic division of early medieval sources into "mythic" and "historical" dimensions. As this distinction is not recognized in the texts themselves, we will not begin with them, but instead explore the strategies of emplotment integral to this discourse as a whole.

The Cōḻas claim to have originated from the sun itself, and, through Manu, to have been born into the glorious clan of the Ikṣvākus, also known as the solar dynasty. These kings are said, at various times, to win, protect, embrace, and even seduce a feminized earth, "girdled by the oceans." Such references—to the descent of kings from the celestial bodies and to the earth's encirclement by the oceans—do not sketch out the modern geography of India or Asia but instead refer to the "rose-apple continent" (Jambudvīpa), at the southern quarter of which was situated the land of Bhāratavarṣa, with its numerous kings and peoples. The Cōḻas were not the only dynasty to count themselves among these inhabitants, for this geography was widely assumed by nearly all the dynasties of post-Gupta India. It had its origins in the late Vedic period but was greatly elaborated and systematized in the subsequent centuries that witnessed the emergence of cities and states, the proliferation of a reformed Vedic cult throughout the subcontinent, and the rise and spread of Buddhism, in what has been termed the early historical period.

How was this world laid out? Before turning to this problem, it is important to understand the nature of the accounts of geography in medieval India. Like modern atlases and gazetteers, medieval accounts of landscapes presupposed more fundamental assumptions about space, nature, and cosmos. Needless to say, these assumptions were radically different than those upon which modern cartography has been founded, which explains why we find no maps in early medieval India. These assumptions, which were tied to ontological assertions about the world, were not part of some generalized Indian worldview but rather parts of a specific group of conceptions that held sway at the courts of early medieval India, namely those associated with the various orders of Vaiṣṇavism and Śaivism. They are explicitly elaborated in the large compendiums called Purāṇas composed by Śaiva and Vaiṣṇava priestly adepts in the first centuries C.E. The Purāṇas marked a systematization of earlier, more inchoate cosmogonic and geographical notions (Sircar, 1967, pp. 9–69). They include not only long lists of mountains, rivers, and peoples who inhabit the world, but also purport to reveal the fundamental structure and composition of the cosmos.

The ontological assumptions of the Purāṇas are made most explicit in their narratives of creation. Purāṇic cosmology "begins" with the emanation or emission of the entire cosmos, both material and immaterial, from a single being, perceived by the Purāṇas as overlord of the cosmos. The process of creation itself proceeds through the continual evolution of the elements of existence into ever grosser and more differentiated forms from this original principle/author. Creation is continuous and successive. According to the *Viṣṇupurāṇa* (henceforth *VP*), Vāsudeva (Viṣṇu) forms the ultimate ground of the universe.[3] As the ground of all reality, Viṣṇu is infinite in both material and temporal expanse; it thus makes no sense to talk of a single beginning (creation) and end (destruction) of the universe. Instead, the Purāṇas speak of the expansion (*sarga*) and contraction (*pratisarga*) of the universe.[4] The universe continually evolves and devolves, expands and contracts, as part of the life and sport of the supreme lord Viṣṇu. Strictly speaking, then, both creation and destruction here are multiple and continuous. This applies not only in a larger sense—the eternality of Viṣṇu himself—but even within the instance of particular evolutions. The *VP* speaks of no less than nine creations (*sargas*) necessary to bring the world into existence.

How does the successive creation of the universe, through differentiation and expansion, occur? According to the *VP,* the supreme lord (Viṣṇu) in his most fundamental and unmodified existence evolved into four forms. *Puruṣa,* or pure spirit, was the first form (*rūpa*) of Vāsudeva. Spirit was followed by manifest and unmanifest matter (*vyaktāvyakta*), and finally by time (*kāla*). According to the *VP,* these four forms of Viṣṇu, in due proportions, are the causes of the production of the phenomena of the creation, preservation, and destruction of the universe (*VP* I.1.17). Creation proceeds when unevolved substance (*avyakta-prakṛti, pradhāna*) is approached by pure spirit (*puruṣa*) through the agency of time. This theory of creation, one emerging from the interaction of spirit with undifferentiated primordial substance was itself a reworking, found in most of the early Purāṇic literature, of the contemporaneously developing dualist philosophy known as Sāṃkhya, systematized sometime between the third and fifth centuries C.E. in the *Sāṃkhyakārikā*.[5] According to this theory, unmanifest "matter," primordial substance, was constituted by an equilibrium of three essential qualities (*guṇas*): goodness (*sattva*), energy (*rajas*), and inertia (*tamas*). As unmanifest matter is approached by pure spirit the equilibrium of these qualities is disturbed, resulting in a process of differentiation known as creation (*sarga*) or evolutionary transformation (*guṇapariṇāma*). In this process a number of components or principles (*tattvas*) successively differentiate themselves from the originary equilibratory state, beginning with the will (*buddhi* or *mahat*) and self-awareness (*ahaṃkāra*). From *ahaṃkāra* two sets of evolutes emerge simultaneously. The first is a group of eleven *vaikṛta* elements, which includes the synthesizing internal "organ" of the mind (*manas*), the five sense-capacities (*buddhendriyas*), and the five action-capacities (*karmendriyas*). The second group of components that emerge simultaneously from *ahaṃkāra* are the five subtler elements (*tanmātras*) that form the "objects" of the sense-capacities—sound, touch, form, taste, and smell.[6] The last *tattvas* to evolve are the five "gross" elements (*pañcabhūtāni*), which proceed from the *tanmātras,* and form what we would consider to be "material" substance proper—ether, wind, fire, water, and earth. Until this point the *VP* simply summarizes the detailed account of evolution elaborated by the adherents of Sāṃkhya. But hereafter, its account departs significantly from the Sāṃkhya scheme.

While the Purāṇas and later theist texts presuppose and retain the evolutionary scheme of Sāṃkhya, they advance crucial ontological and soteriological modifications to it. Whereas Sāṃkhya maintained that *puruṣa* and *prakṛti* (in both its unmanifest and manifest forms) were ontologically distinct from one another, the Purāṇic adepts, as Larson has noted, derive *prakṛti* and *puruṣa* from Īśvara, Śiva, Śivaliṅga, or some form of Viṣṇu (Larson, 1979, p. 289). In the case of the *VP,* as we have seen above, *puruṣa, avyakta,* and *vyakta-prakṛti* as well as time (*kāla*) are all considered to be forms of Viṣṇu Nārāyaṇa.

Throughout its recapitulation of the dualist evolutionism of Sāṃkhya, the *VP* emphatically asserts the unity of the basic evolutes as part of the more transcendent being of Viṣṇu. Śaiva Siddhāntins, on the other hand, held that Śiva remained distinct from the primordial constituents of the cosmos. This position, however, did not prevent the Śaiva Siddhāntins from developing an elaborate theory of Śiva's intimate agency in the emission, maintenance, and reabsorption of the universe—which, together with his two other functions of veiling and clarifying the structure of the universe to bonded souls, formed the five activities (*pañcakṛtya*) of Śiva so eloquently depicted during the Cōḷa period in the image of Śiva as "lord of dance" (*nṛtyarāja*).[7] Theist adepts on the whole, then, tended to place the realist evolution of Sāṃkhya within the larger frame of dualist or qualified-dualist theological ontologies.

Moreover, Sāṃkhya was not, strictly speaking, a cosmology. For Sāṃkhya, the evolution (*guṇapariṇāma*) of *prakṛti* gave rise to the apparently "material" aspects of the self and the world: the will, self-awareness, the mind, the senses, and finally the gross elements. The juxtaposition of the self (*puruṣa*) with unmanifest matter (*avyakta-prakṛti*) was placed within the frame of human spirit and the world that surrounded it—what one scholar has called a "science of the individual soul" (Larson, 1979, pp. 194–196). The Purāṇas, however, understand Sāṃkhya evolutionism as universal and cosmological. They also place this evolutionism within a larger agentive framework. This is done ontologically, as mentioned above, by making *puruṣa* and *prakṛti* forms of the divine lord Viṣṇu. Narratively, this is achieved by embedding the Sāṃkhya evolution of *tattvas* within a straightforward theistic account of creation. After the evolution so far described, the *VP* tells us that the various evolutes, from the *buddhi* to the gross elements, combined in the character of a massive unity, a cosmic egg. The egg, resting on the waters, was the natural abode of Viṣṇu in the form of Brahmā, the creator, and is known as the Brahmā-egg (*brahmāṇḍa*). The womb of the egg contained the continents, the seas and the mountains, the planets, the divisions of the discreet universe, gods, the demons, and mankind. Its shell was composed by the *bhūtādis, ahaṃkāra,* intelligence, and finally the unmanifest, which is itself pervaded by spirit—resembling a massive coconut.[8] This egg, then, was an inverted cosmological extension of the components of Sāṃkhya evolutionism, with the grosser parts located in its interior and subtler at its exterior. It is within this egg that Viṣṇu as Brahmā, the root of the universe, creates the world from his own being. Brahmā, located within this egg (itself born of the more rudimentary agency of Viṣṇu as *puruṣa, prakṛti,* and *kāla*) makes a number of further creations, including immovable things, animals, gods, and finally men, organized into their various estates.[9]

The cosmos contained within the egg of Brahmā was divided spatially into fourteen "worlds" or "spheres of activity" (*lokas*)—the most important of which were the earth (*bhūrloka*), the atmosphere (*bhuvarloka*), and the celestial sphere (*svarloka*).[10] The earth was further divided into seven island-continents (*dvīpas*) each of which was surrounded by an ocean. The most central of these continents was Jambudvīpa, which had at its center the great Mount Meru, atop of which was situated the city of Brahmā, which, encircled by a celestial river, was the residence of the gods. This continent was cut across by eight mountain ranges and four rivers that divided it naturally into nine drain basins, or *varṣas,* each possessing its own river and range of mountains. These nine regions were populated by various sorts of beings. The southernmost region of Jambudvīpa was Bhāratavarṣa, where the Purāṇic adepts located themselves, and which we can recognize as modern South Asia. The remaining eight regions of Jambudvīpa were inhabited by different types of celestial beings. Bhāratavarṣa, the realm of men, was, like the other regions of Jambudvīpa, defined by a mountain range and a river. But it was also divided into nine regions itself, each with its own mountain ranges and rivers and inhabited by numerous peoples and ruled by various hierarchies of kings. The Purāṇic accounts variously enumerated these regions and kingdoms.[11]

The entire cosmos, both spatially and temporally, was the expression or realization of a divine order anchored ontologically or soteriologically in the being of Lord Viṣṇu (or Śiva). Lordship was not concentrated in the being of Viṣṇu or Śiva alone, but extended, like the very being of these gods (either as an infusion or as an ontological sharing) throughout the cosmos. All worldly agencies were in fact conceived of as the capacities of greater and lesser lordships anchored in the agency of the supreme lord. Lordship belonged properly to the very ontological order of things; it was not an external adjunct to an already present cosmic structure. It *infused all relationships*. The question of lordship thus extended far beyond "the state" or "divine kingship." Relations of lordship and subjection formed the connecting links between all the various orders of gods, people, and things that constituted the cosmos. Perhaps the distinguishing characteristic of this great hierarchy of lordships that composed the cosmos was that of encompassment.[12] Lords were carefully *distinguished from* their inferiors, but at the same time *also included within themselves* these inferiors. This is absolutely clear in the theist accounts of creation like that narrated in the *VP,* where the universe is produced through successive emissions from a single source. That is, there was a hierarchical valuation emplotted in the unfolding of the cosmos.[13] More primary elements of the universe were ranked higher than its more derivative ones; less differentiated objects were prior and superior to more differentiated ones. They were closer to the source of emission and included within themselves the potentiality for further creation. Lower forms of existence were ontologically derived from, and thus mastered by, the forms "above" them. Thus, Viṣṇu as cosmic sovereign took ontological and agentive precedence over the four forms derived from himself—those of *puruṣa, pradhāna, prakṛti,* and *kāla*.

The structure of the cosmos revealed this hierarchy. The cosmos was ordered into gradations of more or less perfect beings, manifested spatially in a hierarchy of divisions and regions. If all the universe shared in the divine being of Viṣṇu, it did so unequally, falling naturally into an unbroken hierarchy in which each being was variously derived from, dependent on, and ontologically encompassed by that immediately "above" it. The important point here, to which we will return later, is that the cosmic hierarchy was not simply a chain of human and divine beings, but was part of the very structure of material reality. The cosmic hierarchy portrayed in the Purāṇic texts was not symbolic or metaphorical—it was literally a physical description of the universe. This hierarchy was enacted by creation (*sarga*), where narrative priority was inextricably linked with ontological encompassment and agentive mastery. The created cosmos was organized into successive stages on a continuum of increasingly "heavy" or "gross" elements of being. Thus, when speaking of the evolution of the material world, the *VP* narrates the emergence of the sensual faculties (hearing, touching, seeing, etc.) and the subtle elements (sound, touch, form, etc.) *before* the production of the gross elements (space, wind, fire, etc.) that arise from them.

The various stages of evolution were not replaced by their successive, grosser forms, but continued to exist as part of the cosmos. Beyond the terrestrial, atmospheric, and celestial spheres were a series of further worlds, each closer in proximity to Viṣṇu.[14] First was the sphere of saints, or *maharloka,* and beyond it *janaloka,* where the sons of Brahmā resided. Four times distant from this was *tapoloka,* the sphere of austerity, inhabited by deities called Vaibhrājas, and even further was *satyaloka,* the sphere of truth, whose inhabitants were immortal. These spheres, together with the seven lower realms and numerous hells, were surrounded by successive sheaths of water, fire, wind, and ether, which were in turn encompassed by the root of the subtle and gross elements (*bhūtādi*), and intellect (*mahat*). The entire egg was surrounded finally by unmanifest nature (*pradhāna*), the chief principle and the most subtle (*sūkṣma*) of substances (*VP* I.2.19), and within which resided spirit (*puruṣa*). The whole cosmos was finally encompassed by the energy of Viṣṇu, its most primary element. The structure of the cosmos from its center to its periphery represented an inverted hierarchy of being.

Bhāratavarṣa, however, remained the 'center' of this cosmos. According to the *VP,* the inhabitants of the eight other regions of Jambudvīpa experienced no sorrow, weariness, anxiety, hunger, or apprehension; their inhabitants were free from all pain and lived in constant enjoyment (*VP* II.1.25–26; II.2.51–52). Similarly, in other realms of existence, whether in the various worlds above or below the earth, beings lived lives of pure enjoyment or misery. The beings of these realms, however, had no *agentive* existence. They lived in these realms expending the fruits of actions previously performed in Bhāratavarṣa. According to the *VP,* only from Bhāratavarṣa could men pass into the conditions of animal existence or fall into hell. So, as conditions of being, heaven (*svarga*), emancipation (*mokṣa*), the middle states (*madhya*), and the lower realms (*anta*)—*all followed from existence in Bhāratavarṣa*. Bhāratavarṣa, then, had the unique title of "the land of acts" (*karma-bhūmi; VP* II.3.4–5; and especially II.3.22–26). The Purāṇic adepts considered Bhāratavarṣa, inhabited by humankind, as a privileged realm, a "center" that nevertheless occupied the midway point of an ascending cosmic hierarchy. Even the superior beings of the gods envied birth in Bhāratavarṣa, whence a direct path to Viṣṇu could be obtained (*VP* II.3.24–26). Purāṇic cosmology, like the lordship it expressed, was neither entirely otherworldly nor humanist—it placed this world both at the center of the universe and at the middle of the great hierarchy that composed that universe.[15]

Bhāratavarṣa, as we have mentioned, was considered to be the rain basin of the River Gaṅgā. The Gaṅgā had been brought down from its celestial course at Mount Kailāsa, the most preeminent mountain of the Himālaya range, which formed the northern border of Bhāratavarṣa. Bhāratavarṣa, as we have mentioned before, was divided into nine further regions by seven lesser mountain ranges and numerous rivers. This geography, as Ronald Inden has noted, was structured along the principles of homology, synecdoche, and metonymy (Inden, 1990, pp. 256–258).

So if Bhāratavarṣa as a whole formed the rain basin for the Gaṅgā and its tributaries, then each of its constituent regions was also bounded by mountains that were derived from the Himālayas (*kulaparvatas*) and drained by its own river or rivers that had as their ultimate source the Gaṅgā. That is, each region possessed geographical features that resembled those that constituted the other regions, all of which were ontologically anchored in their more primary forms—the Himālaya range with its Mount Kailāsa and the River Gaṅgā that flowed from it down onto fertile plains. In addition to the nine regions, the Purāṇas divided Bhāratavarṣa into five directions: north, south, east, west, and middle.

As may be expected, these regions were hierarchized, reflecting the ordering of lordships found among their inhabitants. In the earlier Purāṇic texts, the middle region (*madhyadeśa*), where the important polities of the Magadhas, Kośalas, Kurus, and Pāñcālas were situated, was considered the most preeminent (Sircar, 1967, pp. 71–73). Built into the topography of Bhāratavarṣa was a structure of political hierarchy—one that worked along the same principles of homology and encompassment that characterized the cosmos itself. The middle region and its inhabitants formed not only the superior center of this geography, but, through synecdoche, stood for the whole structure. The homologous structuring of this geography, however, allowed for a certain ambiguity, as Inden has argued. Any region, through the agency of its ruling lord, could conceivably be represented as the synecdochic center of the whole. In representing his domain in such a manner, a king simultaneously proclaimed himself as a universal sovereign, or *cakravartin*. Perhaps expectedly, such geographical claims involved political contestation. The imperial act that constituted this geographical "centering" and universal sovereignty, was a victorious military traversal of the four directions, known as a *digvijaya*. In performing a *digvijaya,* a king attempted to construct a political circle around himself, and thus to center the hierarchy of kingdoms that composed Bhāratavarṣa around his own realm.[16] And in doing so, he also attempted to gain for himself the "new middle" of the geography that complemented this hierarchy, a conquest that made him not simply the ruler of a region, but of the whole of Bhāratavarṣa, conceived of as "the earth."[17] He had to transform the homologues of the Gaṅgā and Kailāsa in his own realm into *topoi* less derivative of or identical to their paradigmatic forms. Such acts often required the simultaneous hierarchization and displacement of existing geographies, which reflected the established political order.

II

A number of medieval dynasties attempted such representations, including the Pallavas, Rāṣṭrakūṭas, and Cōḻas.[18] Here I examine the South Indian Cōḻa court's rearticulation of *topoi,* particularly rivers, in its attempt to constitute a new hierarchy of realms in Bhāratavarṣa. Though a fuller treatment of such a rearticulation would require the examination of claims made about mountains and mountain ranges,[19] the discourse around rivers sufficiently illustrates the agency afforded to royal courts by Purāṇic geography.

The Purāṇas name a number of rivers associated with the southern region of Bhāratavarṣa. Among these, the Kāverī, which had its origin in the Sahya mountains, lay within the domain of the Cōḻas with whom it was especially associated, and who themselves are mentioned as one of the polities or *janapadas* of the southern region according to the Purāṇic lists. These Purāṇic geographical claims are fully confirmed by the inscriptions of the Pallavas and Cōḻas themselves, which explicitly associate the Kāverī with the Cōḻa king. A seventh-century Pallava inscription on a pillar enclosing an *in situ* sculpture of Śiva Gaṅgādhara at the rock mountain of Trichy above the then-Cōḻa capital at Uṟaiyūr, claims that Gaṅgā, here denoted as "daughter of the mountain," being afraid that her lord Śiva, who was fond of rivers, would be lovestruck upon seeing the beautiful Kāverī, came to reside on the mountain, calling the Kāverī "beloved of the Pallava."[20] This explanation for the presence of Gaṅgā upon the rock-mountain of the Cōḻas aimed to establish the Kāverī as the "beloved of the Pallava," thereby signifying the Pallava conquest of the Cōḻas.[21] In doing so, however, the inscription implicitly relies on the homological principles of Purāṇic geography. This is achieved by inserting the Kāverī into the well-known Purāṇic story of competition and jealousy among Śiva's geographical consorts. In the Purāṇic account, Pārvatī harbors jealousy towards Gaṅgā because of her presence in Śiva's hair.[22] In this context, Gaṅgā takes on the role of the jealous Pārvatī while the place of the Gaṅgā is now assumed by the Kāverī. The rivalry between the Kāverī and the Gaṅgā for preeminence was a contest the Cōḻas would continue nearly four hundred years later.

Rising upon the ruins of the Pallava-Rāṣṭrakūṭa dynastic imperium, the Cōḻa kings Rājarāja (985–1040) and Rājendra (1012–1044) attempted to gain the paramount lordship of Bhāratavarṣa by the performance of two celebrated *digvijayas*. These *digvijayas* culminated in the production of an ensemble of *topoi* asserting the Cōḻa kingdom as the new middle region of Bhāratavarṣa. This centering entailed two objectives: first, the production and resignification of a series of places to create the realm of a world ruler (*cakravarti-kṣetra*); and second, an attempt to displace other already existing geographical imperiums. The first of these was achieved through an increasing association of the Kāverī with the Cōḻa family, who were themselves, according to their inscriptions, descended from the Solar Dynasty of the Purāṇas. The royal genealogies of the Cōḻas from the reign of Parāntaka Cōḻa (907–55) contain not only numerous references to the protection and adornment of the Kāverī by Cōḻa kings.[23] The Tiruvāḷaṅgaḍu plates claim that a Cōḻa king named Citradhanvan "reflected on how the river of the gods had been caused to descend to his own land as the maiden Kāverī" (my translation, *SII* 3 [1920], 395). The implication of this passage is significant. As the source of all the rivers of Bhāratavarṣa was the "river of the gods," the eulogist is able to equate Bhagīratha's winning of the Gaṅgā with Citradhanvan's acquisition of the Kāverī. The praise of the Cōḻa king's winning of the river of the gods in the form of the Kāverī also signaled a reordering of Bhāratavarṣa's realms.

This leads to the second point. In articulating the *topoi* of their own realm, the Cōḻas sought to displace those of others. Chief among these were the other rivers of the south such as the Godāvarī, the Krishnā, and the Tuṅgabhadrā, which, like the Kāverī, were all classed by the Purāṇas as rivers derived from the Sahya mountains. In the accounts of their military campaigns against their Chālukya rivals in the Deccan, the Cōḻas make a point of mentioning their numerous defeats of Chālukya armies on the banks of the Krishnā and the Tuṅgabhadrā.[24] Rājendra, according to his inscriptions, bathed in the Godāvarī during his *digvijaya,* repeating the act of an earlier king of the Solar Dynasty, Raghu, who during his *digvijaya* had bathed in the Kāverī and made the ocean suspicious of the river's chastity.[25] Implicit in these accounts is that bathing in the rivers of conquered kings had the effect of disarticulating the *topoi* of their royal realms. The most important act of the Cōḻas in this regard was undoubtedly the famous trip of Rājendra's armies to the banks of the Gaṅgā (Sastri, 1955, pp. 206–210; Spencer, 1983, pp. 42–45). According to his inscriptional eulogies after Rājendra conquered the Pāṇṭiyas in the south, the lord of the Kerala country in the west, and the Chālukya in the north, he retired to his capital, where he contemplated an even greater feat. The Tiruvāḷaṅgaḍu plates remark that Rājendra,

> Light of the solar race, laughed at Bhagīratha who had brought down the Gaṅgā to the earth from heaven with the power of his austerities, and desired himself to cleanse the earth, which he possessed, with the water of the Gaṅgā brought with the strength of his own arm (my translation, *SII* 3 [1920], 400).

As in the case of the king Citradhanvan, Rājendra's ambition rivals that of Bhagīratha. But the intention here is not simply to repeat Bhagīratha's act, but to appropriate and challenge an already existing order centered around the middle region and its kingdoms. Rājendra dispatched his general northward to "subdue the kings occupying the banks of that river" (*SII* 3 [1920], 400). The kings who were currently in possession and control of the banks of the Gaṅgā were in a sense its interlocutors, the spokesmen to the polities of Bhāratavarṣa, for the geography that placed that river as preeminent. A fuller account of this campaign[26] claims that Rājendra's army defeated various kingdoms en route—Oḍra, Dakṣiṇakosala ruled by the Somavaṃśi king Indraratha, and near the Gaṅgā the kingdoms of Daṇḍabhukti, Dakṣiṇarāḍhā, Vaṅgāla, and the Pāla king Mahīpāla based in Uttararāḍhā.[27] After these victories, the Cōḻa general had the waters of the Gaṅgā carried to Rājendra by the subjugated kings who occupied the banks of the river.[28] In the Cōḻa accounts these kings were made to recognize Rājendra's sovereignty through a surrender of their privileged *topos,* which they handed over to its new earthly possessor, thereby assuming a "tributary" role in a new imperial hierarchy. After conducting a further expedition to the kingdom of Srivijaya to complete his *digvijaya,* Rājendra returned to his residential city, which was renamed Gaṅgaikoṇḍacōḻapuram, "the city of the Cōḻa who conquered the Gaṅgā."[29] The Tiruvāḷaṅgaḍu plates claim that Rājendra further commemorated this act by establishing a "pillar of victory" (*jayastambha*) in his realm with the waters that had been transported from the Gaṅgā (*SII* 3 [1920], 400). This pillar, named Cōḻagaṅgam, or "Gaṅgā of the Cōḻas," was in actuality an artificial lake nearing five kilometers in length into which the waters of the Gaṅgā were poured, and which was filled through channels from the Vennār and Koḷḷiḍam Rivers, the latter of which was itself a branch of the Kāverī (Balasubrahmanyam, 1975, p. 234; Sastri, 1955, pp. 234–245). This mixing of the water of Kāverī and Gaṅgā reinforced the resignification of *topoi* that reflected the new political structuring of Bhāratavarṣa. In the Sanskrit eulogies of Vīrarājendra (1063–1070), the youngest of Rājendra's three sons, we find a description of an expedition southward in pursuit of a demon by an eponymous king Cōḻa from his northern home in Āryavarta. After describing his discovery of the Kāverī and the settlement of its banks with virtuous brahmins, the poet concludes by arguing that bathing in the Kāverī was more meritorious and efficacious than bathing in the Gaṅgā because it prolonged life along the Kāverī itself, which was more beautiful than the city of the gods (*Travancore Archaeological Series* 3 [1922–23], 146; *EI* 25 [1938–39), 261). The Cōḻas claimed this northern origin for the same reason that they went there to bring back the waters of the Gaṅgā—because Āryavarta formed the "middle region" of Bhāratavarṣa. Their claims to have settled in the south, their discovery and adornment of the Kāverī, and their conquest of the rivers of other kingdoms together formed parts of an attempt to "recenter" the realms of Bhāratavarṣa.

From the above discussion, it would seem that the spatial representation of a realm in medieval India was as an ensemble of *topoi* rather than as a set of boundaries. This is perhaps most clearly reflected in the role that territory played in the early medieval theories of polity. By the Gupta period, the intellectuals of the courts conceived of a kingdom as a vast body composed of "limbs" (*aṅgas*). The most widely accepted theory was known as *saptāṅga,* or seven-limbed—comprising a king, territory, ministers, army, treasury, fort, and ally.[30] The Cōḻa court reworked this theory into a ten-limbed (*tacāṅkam*) polity comprising king, territory, mountain, river, town, horse, elephant, flag, drum, and garland.[31] In both theories, the most central limb, both metonymic of the entire polity and its most fundamental element, was the king or lord. The *topoi* of a kingdom, the river, the mountain, and the city—all places in modern cartographic states that are finally emplotted on territory—are not enclosed in an embracing political space, but are enumerated in commensurate fashion *alongside* territory. Territory (*janapada*), for its part, was not conceived of in a solely spatial manner. Both the Sanskrit term *janapada* and the Tamil *nāṭu* denote a "land together with its inhabitants."[32] To articulate a realm, the king had to effect through policy a relation with each of the specified "limbs" of the kingdom. This included different elements, including territory itself. Consequently, the court chronicles of the Cōḻa dynasty begin not with the description of geography of Cōḻamaṇḍalam as the place upon which their events unfold, but instead with a genealogy of lords. The Cōḻa kings *acquire* territory, mountains, and rivers, along with the other limbs of polity through their own ingenuity and fortune.

III

The previous sections have shown that the ontological ordering of the cosmos was continuous with the hierarchy of *dvīpas, varṣas,* and the royal realms contained within them. From a modern social science perspective, it may be noted that the principles of society were indistinct from those of the cosmos. It might be assumed that social hierarchy in this world was thus "justified" by some recourse to the natural world. But such a proposition obscures the operation of these concepts, for these texts assert no strong distinction between society and nature in the first instance requiring recourse to "natural" law. The relation between these realms was in fact the reverse. The cosmos reflected the principles of the social order, but did not sanction them.[33] The Purāṇic cosmos embodied a hierarchy of perfection and value, rising from the grosser elements to increasingly subtler and lighter spheres of being and activity, culminating in the pure energy of Viṣṇu that enveloped the cosmic egg. Spatially, the hierarchy of the cosmos was derived from ontological *proximity* to Viṣṇu or Śiva, conceived as an ascending "chain of being," to borrow a phrase from Arthur Lovejoy.[34] Lordship referred to the capacity of agency that beings closer in proximity to god exerted over those "beneath" them, whose masteries were more derivative.

In this world, the relation between lordship and the distribution of objects and beings was not arbitrary. The physical structure of the Purāṇic cosmos was an expression of the ontological hierarchy that generated and sustained it. To use the words of Alexander Koyré, it was a world in which "the hierarchy of value determined the hierarchy of being" (Koyré, 1957, p. viii). The manifold relations of the Purāṇic cosmos, unlike those of the modern universe, were not governed by a set of laws that were conceived as purely "physical" in nature. There were no general physical laws that unified all the objects and places of the cosmos; that did not find their very being in divine lordship and hierarchy.

The spatial arrangement of the cosmos was an ensemble of more or less incommensurable "places" rather than coordinates on a homogenous and infinite continuum of space.[35] What is notably absent from this arrangement is the idea of an infinite "empty" space that contained particular locales or places. "There was no space that was not simultaneously a place" (Ferguson, 1990, p. 83). The universe was a vast hierarchy of "places" articulated through their ontological relation with a divine lord. The moral attributes of these places were tied inextricably to their position in the rising hierarchy of being. Like the *tiṇai* system of ancient Tamil poetry, in the medieval literature the mountain, temple, river, country, wasteland, court, city, and balcony were all places with inherent and differential moral and aesthetic value.

There were proponents in early India, as in Greece, of the idea that space and time were independent and foundational reals. The Nyāya-Vaiśeṣikas considered them to be ubiquitous and infinite elements that contained everything within themselves (Balslev, 1983, pp. 25–36; Mandal, 1968, pp. 116–125). But as Koyré has demonstrated in the case of Europe, the relation of these ideas to other conceptions of space was not one of dominance. The Vaiśeṣika conception of space and time did not form the foundation of a rationalist critique of cosmology, nor did it hold the same ideological hegemony as the modern scientific conception of infinite space. In medieval India the Purāṇic and theist conception of the cosmos held the dominant position, organizing the logic of land, kingdom, and cosmos. And in Purāṇic cosmology, space (*diś, ākāśa*) did not denote the infinite and homogenous empty space of the modern universe—an abstract space co-terminus with the universe itself. It merely formed one of the five gross elements (along with wind, fire, water, and earth) emitted from the subtle elements as a specific link in the chain of creation. That is, "space" had its own "place" in the cosmos. Space was an element of the larger ensemble of spaces, and not a fundamental aspect of all reality. The creation of the universe as the active agency of Viṣṇu does not occur *within* space and time, but rather space and time were emanations of a prior ontology, that of Viṣṇu himself. Viṣṇu emitted both time and place as a part of his creation. In fact, the whole cosmos was emitted from Viṣṇu's being. Time was measured by Viṣṇu's life through the days and nights of his being as Brahmā; for there was no time independent of his being. "Space" was merely the differentiation of the "material" form of Viṣṇu's nature; there existed no space *in which* Viṣṇu could be placed. The cosmos was literally emitted as an extension of his being.[36]

In Europe, the medieval cosmos of Christendom was gradually replaced by a universe no longer coherent through the principle of hierarchization and subordination, but unified only by the identity of its basic components and laws. The finite cosmos was destroyed and in its place appeared an infinite universe possessing the temporal and spatial attributes once possessed by God. Value and being, human society and the laws of the universe, were inextricably separated. This transformation was accomplished in part, according to Koyré, by the geometrization of space—the displacement of the Aristotelian conception of space as a differentiated set of innerworldly places—with the principles of Euclidean geometry that posited an infinite and homogenous extension—henceforward considered identical with the real space of the world (Koyré, 1957, p. viii). These debates in natural philosophy were accompanied by the development of new techniques in the measurement of cartographic space, which also worked to destroy older notions of the terrestrial distribution of peoples and continents.

The emergence of such transformations in India, mediated initially by the introduction of Islamic science into the subcontinent from the eleventh century, and more profoundly through the agency of colonial rule, is not the subject of this essay. A number of studies have now taken up the introduction of cartography in colonial India from the perspective of colonial rulership (Edney, 1997; Kalpagam, 1995). For the purposes of this essay, the somewhat superficial digression on the development of modern conceptions of space rehearsed above has sought only to underscore the historical specificity and theoretical insufficiency of the modern conception of "space" in understanding early Indian spatial understandings. It sought to draw attention to the different principles that underpinned spatial representation. The final section of this essay will demonstrate how the underlying principles that animated the Purāṇic cosmos, and that linked its physical constituents to the ensemble or realms that composed it into a great hierarchy of lordships, was also articulated through relations of property.

IV

The long copperplate inscriptions referred to in the second section of this essay were also concerned with a variety of lordships that we may today place under the category of property. The eulogies described above formed the preambles to written orders (*śāsana*) of the king, which were dispatched to particular places where they were read aloud to assemblies of lesser lords and notables. These decrees sanctioned the transfer of masteries and enjoyments in regard to property, particularly immovable property, or land. Typically, a king would donate revenue on land that he would otherwise enjoy as its protector to *brāhmaṇa* householders, temple establishments, or military leaders. Copperplate grants thus take some care in outlining the complex land rights and privileges enjoyed by various classes of people. In societies whose wealth was based largely on agriculture, the division of rights and privileges to land was a matter of utmost importance and for our purposes provides a useful perspective on the perception of spatial categories.

The nature of precolonial property in land has been a subject of considerable debate since the reform of tenures under colonial rule. In recent historiography, much of this debate has taken place over the applicability, both empirical and theoretical, of the "Asiatic" and "feudal" modes of production in understanding precolonial Indian society. The discussion below will not dwell at any length on the crucially important and still unresolved question of the exact nature of the medieval Indian social formation as a whole. The intention will be to explore basic parameters relevant for our topic; that is, the relationship of property to "cosmology."

It must first be recognized that in medieval India, property in land, as property-holding in general, should not be understood as a purely economic activity. Medieval notions of lordship did not recognize any separate domain of economy that functioned autonomously from its own operation and that was governed by its own immutable laws. The earliest Indian text on statecraft, the *Arthaśāstra,* defines *artha* (at 15.1.1–2) "as the livelihood of men; the earth with its men is thus *artha* and the science which is the means of attaining and protecting that earth is the science of *artha* (*arthaśāstra*)." In its most expansive meaning, *artha* was simply the livelihood of the king, which included within it the livelihood of those within his kingdom. The differential functions within the kingdom, the vast hierarchy of castes and *jātis* were thus at once political and economic in character. In the European context, Karl Marx recognized this as the *"directly political"* character of feudalism, where "the elements of civil life, for example property, or the family or the mode of labor were raised to the level of political life in the form of seignority, estates and corporations" (Marx, 1975, 3:165).

The problem here is partly categorical. While many modern historians have seen in caste a division of labor or a form of civil society functioning "under" the state, they have at the same time recognized the rather thin evidence for a state bureaucracy or imperial administration. It would be more accurate, however, to understand caste as the coalescence of modern economic and political categories, making caste ranks the constituents of polity, but constituents that at once implied differential domains of activity (*adhikāras*) that we would understand as economic. The different material lives of kings, temple priests, peasant proprietors, and agrarian laborers in medieval India flowed directly from the differential "political" rights enjoyed by these various estates, represented as the expression of their inherent qualities.[37]

The Cōḻa kingdom was composed of a highly complex pyramidal structure of lordships that included a highly differentiated composition of the *śūdra* estate. Land rights themselves, as they can be reconstructed from the inscriptions, were divided between the polarity expressed by the categories of right to cultivate (*kuṭikāṇi, kārāṇmai*), on the one hand, and a superior right over land enjoyed by either peasant proprietors (*veḷḷāmai*) or the more general right to have land cultivated (*miṭāṭci*) enjoyed by other classes as well, on the other, which could be seen as a type of ownership (*kāṇi*). The king, at the apex of the hierarchy of rights and privileges, had the right to appropriate the title to grant land (both settled and unsettled) and also to create superior rights over it, but could not do so in violation of the legal rights exercised by its *kāṇi* holder. Inscriptional records reveal a number of hierarchies below the king.[38] In terms of land ownership (*kāṇiyāḷar*), the ruling classes could be divided into *brāhmaṇas,* merchants, and property-owning *veḷḷālars,* who were often members of local assemblies (*nāṭus*) or *brāhmaṇa* villages (*brahmadeyas*). Large landowners retained higher control over *kāṇi* and a percentage of yields while alienating control over cultivation (*kārāṇmai*) and a percentage of yield to cultivators. Cultivators either directly oversaw labor or deputed this task to tenants, who controlled their own shares of produce and managed the landless groups that occupied the bottom of the Cōḻa hierarchy, collectively known as *paṟaiyars* (see Heitzman, 1997, p. 75). In another hierarchy below the king were underlords who functioned as the Cōḻa king's direct agents, possessing titles that indicated lordly rank as well as possession of land (*uṭaiyaṉ, nāyakaṉ, araiyaṉ*). Also below the king or his underlords were various kinds of eleemosynary villages such as *brahmadeyam, devadāna, paḷḷiccandam, śālābhogam, kāṇimuṟṟūṭṭu,* and *veṭṭāpperu*. In all these villages the tenurial pattern tended to be the same: tenants (*kārāḷa*), occupants (*kuṭi*), and agrarian laborers (*paṟaiya*) were placed one below the other in a descending scale of privilege.

From the vantage point of property relations regarding land, the hierarchy described above indicates that property was enjoyed neither entirely by the state as the theorists of the Asiatic mode of production had maintained, nor by discrete individuals as in the modern bourgeois sense.[39] Ownership of land was multiple and divided. Land could not be reduced to a "purely economic form" as an alienable commodity exchanged between individuals. While rights were to a certain degree alienable, the transfer of superior rights usually did not entail a displacement of encompassed rights. "Land" was often exchanged with laboring peasants attached to it (Heitzman, 1997, p. 68; Veluthat, 1993, p. 231). Land in this case was not, as property under capitalist conditions, treated as an object alienable between individuals through a free market. In the absence of such market-oriented social relations, property relations appeared not as the frictionless exchange of objects between individuals, but instead as rights flowing *directly* from class privilege, what Marx called a "direct relation of domination and servitude" (Marx, 1981, 3: 926). Property in land thus was nothing but the hierarchy of differential rights and privileges secured upon it from the direct producer to the king. Lords, tenants, occupants, and laborers could make simultaneous, albeit differential, claims upon a single plot of land. Royal land grants, the creation of superior rights in land by the king for the support of the ideological or military apparatus of polity, *placed the donees within an already existing structure of rights.* To understand such a grant in terms of simple individuated "ownership," whether in the form of the state or the landowner, would be, as Marc Bloch commented in the European context, "almost meaningless" (Bloch, 1982, 1:115).

In his speculation on precapitalist forms of property in the *Grundrisse,* Karl Marx suggested that in societies where land formed the basis of the economic order, the individual related to land as an extension of his own subjectivity, as his own "inorganic body," and not as a pure object of property in the modern sense; as a product of labor (Marx, 1973, p. 485). At the same time, this perception presupposed some form of membership in a community. If for the direct producer the earth was not a product but a presupposition of his labor, then his relation to the earth was at the same time always mediated through the occupation of the land by a community, in its more or less developed form. In the ancient Indian context, communitarian forms of property had already undergone a partial dissolution with the emergence of castes.[40]

Now if the individual perceives the land as an extension of his own social subjectivity, then land itself must have appeared fractured by the differential organization of castes. Though a kingdom was in part constituted by land together with its inhabitants, this land did not exist as a homogenous entity for the various estates that composed a polity. *Mayamata,* a Sanskrit architectural treatise composed during Cōḻa times, elaborates the various types of ground (*vastu*) appropriate for habitation. *Mayamata* names four types of *vastu:* the earth, buildings, conveyances, and seats

(*Maymata* 2.2; in Dagens, 1994, pp. 6–7). Of these, the earth of course was deemed most fundamental, but the fact that such various elements were included within the concept of *vastu* in the first instance, that a plot of land was only different in degree and not in kind from a lord's palanquin, reveals the hierarchy of places in medieval India as one that stretched across modern concepts of nature and society. And like the social order, nature revealed an inbuilt hierarchy. Dwelling sites built on earth, chosen after examination of color, odor, and flavor of the soil, location, and appearance, were "different for each class of men" (*varṇānāṃ viśeṣataḥ; Mayamata* 2.5). The text goes on to delineate the various types of dwelling sites (*vastubheda*) appropriate for *brāhmaṇas, kṣatriyas, vaiśyas,* and *śūdras*. When describing the type of soil suitable for the residence of *śūdras, Mayamata* notes that such a site, unlike those of other classes, is "abundant in riches and grain." The text goes on to say that while *brāhmaṇas* and kings are permitted to live in all four stipulated dwelling sites, *vaiśyas* and *śūdras* are limited to their own types of sites.[41] While this *śāstric* injunction would, no doubt, have been greatly complicated and differentiated in the case of the rights in land, its principle remains consistent with such an organization: differentiation of place and right, nested hierarchies within which were encompassed decreasing spheres of privilege and motion. This hierarchy may have been so seamless that direct producers appeared to their lords, along with other natural beings, as accessories to the earth, as an inorganic condition of production.[42]

The hierarchization and differentiation of place in Purāṇic cosmology is thus mirrored in the differential and "divided" character of property in land that we find in inscriptions. The great hierarchization of places in the cosmos, a hierarchization that provided the logic for emplotting the various estates of a polity, the *topoi* of lordship, and the scale of polities themselves into an imperial ordering through the ongoing reproduction of Purāṇic mountains and rivers by medieval kings, sustained a hierarchical social order that enabled, ultimately, the extraction of surplus from the direct producer through a hierarchical chain of rights and privileges manifested through superior claims upon *places as the instantiation of moral value and social being,* not the possession of property as an abstract and pure object, sanctioned by immutable laws of exchange. The physical structure of the Purāṇic cosmos was itself the projection of the ascending feudal hierarchy; it formed the ideal prototype of the social order. A nested structure of homologous, encompassing, and subordinate forms stretched effortlessly across the modern dichotomy between "man" and "nature." Within the theory of this hierarchy, every being and every thing found its place. The medieval Indian cosmos was in this sense without ideology. Representations of society had a *direct* relationship to the class hierarchies they sustained, rather than the inverted relation characteristic of ideology in bourgeois society.

Such is the prehistory of space. The ascending ensemble of medieval places has been irrevocably altered by the introduction of a new universe of abstraction. Land could only become private property "by the stripping away of all of its former political embellishments and admixtures, in short all those traditional accouterments that are denounced as uselessly and absurdly superfluous" (Marx, 1981, 3: 755). These accouterments sustained the inequality of estates, and were distinctions that had to be abolished for the emergence of capitalist class relations. Such a transformation required the destruction of the hierarchical cosmos centered around a divine lord. In the Indian context, the colonialist discourses that criticized the cosmological calculations of the Purāṇas as fantastic and rude were the same discourses that demanded a rule of property. The trigonometric survey and establishment of private property not only set themselves against the divided and overlapping nature of land rights of the late medieval social order, they also rendered the foundation of the Purāṇic universe, with its incalculable spheres and eons, null and void, relegating it to the world of myth and fancy from which it would gain new functions (such as national or regional heritage) wholly different from those it served at the time of its creation. Modernity has simultaneously naturalized the cosmos and produced a world of objects that may be emplotted by their location in abstract space and time—and possessed singularly by legal entities. This universe has an inversely ideological nature. In decrying the older world as an illusion, the architects of modern societies have masked new conditions of exploitation by means of a limitless universe completely free of human or divine value and appropriable through its objectness on the one hand, and a social world composed of abstract individuals whose needs dictate the use of these objects on the other. The cosmos revealed to us by medieval Indian sources had neither.

Notes

The author wishes to thank Sergio Targa for his thoughtful remarks on a draft of this chapter.

1. For the first trend, see the ahistorical treatment of various terms in Bäumer, 1992, 2:1–178; for the second, see selected essays in Vatsyayan, 1991.

2. I refer here to the theory, widely held among historians, that post-Gupta India saw an increasing regionalization of Indian polity.
3. Like many early medieval dynasties, the Cōḷa court witnessed a complex interlinking of Vaiṣṇava and Śaiva practices. The ultimate commitment of the Cōḷa kings, as reflected in their temples and royal preceptors, was to Śaiva Siddhānta. Many of their court poets, however, were Vaiṣṇava. Where relevant, I will point out philosophical differences between the philosophy of the *Viṣṇupurāṇa* and that of Śaiva Siddhānta.
4. These form two of the five distinguishing marks (*pañcalakaṣaṇa*) considered characteristic of the Purāṇas.
5. For a periodization and general estimation of the relationship between Sāṃkhya and Purāṇic philosophical notions, see Larson, 1979, pp. 284–291.
6. I use the term "capacities" and quotation marks around the term "object" because neither the *indriyas* nor the *tanmātras* are to be confused with the corporeal sense-organs and the actual material objects they perceive—these arise from combinations of the gross elements.
7. For a brief discussion of the five activities of Śiva (particularly emission and reabsorption) in the context of Śaiva philosophy, ritual, and iconography, see Davis, 1991, pp. 41–47.
8. For a complete description of the Brahmā egg, see *VP* II.7.22–43.
9. According to the *VP* (I.6–3), Brahmā creates the four estates from his own body, appropriating the earlier Vedic narratives of creation through the sacrifice of the body of *puruṣa*.
10. Beyond these three worlds were four higher spheres, and below seven lower regions (*pātālas*).
11. The most comprehensive attempts to correlate the Purāṇic geographies with the mountains, rivers, cities, and dynastic regions known from other textual and epigraphic sources are Ali, 1966, and Sircar, 1967, 1971.
12. In his attempt to avoid the dichotomy of a religiously inspired caste "society" on the one hand and a politically motivated yet powerless "state" on the other, Ronald Inden has argued, on the basis of medieval theist texts, that a highly nuanced theory of lordship stretched across the modern categories of state and society. See Inden, 1985a, pp. 159–179 and 1985b, pp. 53–73.
13. For a useful discussion of the principles of emission and absorption as valuative concepts in Śaiva Siddhānta, see Davis, 1991, pp. 41–47.
14. The account here follows *VP* II.7.3–29.
15. Similar paradoxes existed in medieval Christian thought, with its geocentric universe that posed man as both the privileged possessor of "freedom" and as simply a link in the divinely ordained chain of being.
16. This spatio-political centering is expressed in the texts on polity, beginning with the *Arthaśāstra,* as the circle of kings, or *rājamaṇḍala*.
17. Thus kings claiming imperial lordship in medieval India do not primarily entitle themselves as the rulers of particular regions; the idea of ruling a region implied partial lordship, and such appellations were reserved for subjugated kings and vassals.
18. For the Pallavas, see Lockwood, 1982; for the Rāṣṭrakūṭas, see Inden, 1990, pp. 224–262; for a fuller account of the Cōḷas, see Ali, 2000, pp. 207–212.

19. Important in this regard for the Cōḻas would be the understanding of the Bṛhadīśvara Temple at Tanjavur as *dakṣiṇameru,* or Meru of the South.
20. *South Indian Inscriptions* (henceforth *SII*) I (1890), pp. 29–30. For a retranslation of the inscription with analysis and corrections, see Lockwood, 1982, pp. 62–72. The above summary is based on Lockwood's translation, which differs considerably from its initial rendering by E. Hultzsch. According to Lockwood, the phrase "daughter of the mountain," which would usually refer to Pārvatī, must in this case refer to the Gaṅgā, since the relief sculpture depicts Śiva Gaṅgādhara.
21. The establishment of the shrine and its inscription undoubtedly followed the defeat of Cōḻa armies, whose enemy encampments are mentioned in it.
22. For a discussion of this story, see Doniger O'Flaherty, 1973, pp. 226–233.
23. The Anbil plates of Sundara-Cōḻa, for example, speak of a previous king Rājakesari Āditya I as having built a "row of large temples of Śiva, as it were, banners of his own victory . . . on the banks of the Kāverī from the Sahya mountain." *Epigraphia Indica* (henceforth *EI*) 15 (1919–20), p. 68. Cōḻa inscriptions refer to the construction of flood embankments around the river Kāverī by an ancient king Karikāla, known from earlier Tamil literature, although not in connection with the Kāverī. His association with the Kāverī first appears in the inscriptions of the Gaṅgas at the turn of the sixth century (*Mysore Archaeological Reports,* 1925) and of the Telugu-Coḍas, feudatories of the Pallavas, at the end of the eighth century. *EI* 11 (1911–12), p. 345.
24. Prominent here are the accounts of the battle of Koppam on the Krishnā in the inscriptions of Rājendra II, and the battle of Kūḍalasaṅgamam at the juncture of the Tuṅgā and the Bhadrā rivers in those of his brother Vīrarājendra. See Sastri, 1992, pp. 186–188.
25. *SII* 3 (1920), p. 400; cf. *Raghuvaṃśa* IV.45. I have elsewhere taken up the erotic dimension of the relationship between the king and the feminized *topoi* of his realm.
26. This account is included in a Tamil inscription at Tirumalai in North Arcot: *EI* 9 (1907–1908), pp. 229–233. For reconstructions of the precise sequence of this campaign and its implications for the contemporary history of northeastern India, see Sastri, 1955, pp. 206–210, 229–234; and Majumdar, 1971, pp. 132–134.
27. It has been suggested by some scholars on the basis of inscriptions that Rājendra's campaign was undertaken in alliance with the Paramāra king Bhoja of Malwa and the Kalachuri king Gāṅgeyadeva. See Bhatia, 1970, pp. 76–78; Inden, 1990, p. 262; and Sastri, 1955, pp. 250–251.
28. *SII* 3 (1920), p. 400; cf. *Memoirs of the Archeological Survey of India,* no. 79 (1984), p. 74, which adds that this water was brought on the heads of enemy kings.
29. Rājendra ended his conquest of the quarters, like his father, with the construction of a large temple devoted to his own lord, Śiva, named appropriately, Gaṅgaikoṇḍacōḻeśvaram. On either side of the main *vimāna* of this temple were two subsidiary shrines named in inscriptions *vaṭakailāsam* and *teṅkailāsam,* Kailāsa of the north and south (of the main shrine). See Balasubrahmanyam, 1975, pp. 252–254. Rājendra similarly named two already existing subsidiary shrines at the Pañcanadīśvara Temple westward at Tiruvaiyāṟu (Balasubrahmanyam, 1963, pp. 39, 44–45). This iconic representation of mountains is similar to the Rāṣṭrakūṭa representation of the rivers Gaṅgā and Yamunā at their Kailāsanātha shrine (Inden, 1990, pp. 259).

30. The first elaboration of this theory is in the problematically dated *Arthaśāstra,* where they are called "elements" (*prakṛti*) of state. By the time of Kāmandaki's fifth-century *Nītisāra* (4.1), *prakṛti* is equated with *aṅga,* "limb." In Tamil the idea of a seven-limbed polity is found elaborated in Tiruvaḷḷuvar's *Tirukkuṟal.*
31. This elaboration, which draws on earlier ideas of polity that we find in *caṅkam* texts, is found in a number of panegyric poems and grammatical texts. See, for example, the eleventh-century grammar *Paṉṉiruppāṭṭiyal,* with commentary by K. R. Kovintarāca Mutaliyār (1963, v. 139–141).
32. The term *janapada* literally means the "place with its inhabitants." For a similar definition of *nāṭu,* see *Tirukkuṟal* 731.
33. Brian Smith (1994) has argued this point in his study of Vedic cosmology—that the entire cosmos was categorized along the same hierarchical principles as the social order itself in ancient India.
34. A hierarchy stretching "from the meagerest kinds of existents . . . through every possible grade up to the *ens perfectissimum.*" Lovejoy, 1966, p. 59.
35. Here I follow the distinction made by Harvie Ferguson, who draws on the work of Koyré and Pierre Duhem. See Ferguson, 1990, pp. 80–82.
36. The Purāṇic conception here is no doubt an appropriation of the earlier Vedic creation through the sacrifice of the cosmic man (*puruṣa*) from whose body emerge both the physical universe with its three *lokas* as well as the social order. See Sircar, 1967, p. 11.
37. For a useful discussion of this problem, see Targa, 1999, pp. 95–109.
38. The account here relies on Veluthat, 1993, pp. 231–232, and Heitzman, 1997, pp. 54–78, especially 68.
39. In countering the Asiatic mode of production thesis, Dharma Kumar errs in the opposite direction. See Kumar, 1985, pp. 340–366.
40. Castes, however, serve the equally important function of maintaining the existence of communitarian forms of property. That is, the privilege of individuals can only be asserted by virtue of their membership (by birth) to a community that claims them as its property. See Godelier, 1984, pp. 240–241.
41. *Mayamata* 2.15. This stipulation restricts the mobility of artisan and peasant classes.
42. In early medieval South India we come across references to land being given "with men" (*āḷaḍaṅka*): Veluthat, 1993, p. 231. For a review of the somewhat dispersed and fragmentary evidence for the subjection of the peasantry in early medieval times, see Yadava, 1974, pp. 18–28.

SIX

Sanctum and *Gopuram* at Madurai

Aesthetics of Akam *and* Puṟam *in Tamil Temple Architecture*

Samuel K. Parker

Nāgara/Drāviḍa

Would anyone be impressed by the claim that the Hindu temples of Tamilnadu are dramatically different from their North Indian counterparts? I doubt it. The contrast is sharp enough that they could even be described in structuralist terms as formal inversions of each other. The North Indian temple visually builds toward a soaring, singular peak, explicitly marking the location of a central axis (Fig. 1). The Tamil temple visually builds toward soaring multiple gateways marking the peripheral reach of powers implicitly located at the heart of the temple complex (Fig. 2). However valid this contrast may be, as a structuralist insight it is inadequate. These temple styles are not opposites of each other. They are better understood as two distinct dialects of a South Asian architectural language, each saying something complex about space, time, human beings, and their relation to subtle powers. I refer to them as metaphorical dialects of the same language rather than separate languages because a North Indian accustomed to northern idioms would surely be able to adequately read most of the structure and imagery of a southern temple, but would also recognize profound differences in accent and usage.

Figure 6.1 Kandarya Mahadeva temple. Khajuraho. Circa tenth–eleventh century.

The temples illustrated in Figures 1 and 2 are typical representatives of two major indigenous categories: *Nāgara* and *Drāviḍa*. Following an ancient distinction used in the *śilpa-śāstras,*[1] contemporary Tamil temple architects and image makers[2] classify their own work as *Drāviḍa,* in explicit contrast to the *Nāgara* style of their North Indian counterparts. It is not my intention to reify this distinction with reference to essentialized North and South Indian "traditions." However, in shrinking from essentialism it would be equally indefensible to embrace a free semiotic play of pure, decentered difference. Difference is possible only in and through norms. Significance can only be imagined as "free" in the abstract; in any physically embodied instance, force and constraint are its necessary conditions (Tilley, 1990, pp. 243–255). Saying that significance is not absolutely centered by essence is not the same as saying it must be therefore absolutely decentered. The decentering moves of deconstruction do not invalidate the center per se, rather they show it to be historically contingent and constructed, much as Hindus have done in constructing temples at the center of the universe and ranking them (i.e., some centers are more

Figure 6.2 Minakshi temple. Madurai.

central than others). For all their reputation of tolerance, Hindus cannot, to their credit, be accused of inventing the oxymoron of an absolute relativism, which is an idea generated by simply inverting the old absolute certainties of Western intellectual history (if not pure objectivity, then pure subjectivity; if not absolutely invariant, then absolutely relative, and so forth). Derrida, a frequent target of antirelativist arguments, remarks, "I didn't say that there was no centre, that we could get along without the centre. I believe that the centre is a function, not a being—a reality, but a function. And this function is absolutely indispensable" (quoted in Tilley, 1990, p. 248).

The term "function" is ambiguous here. Is it used in a teleological or mathematical sense? Purpose or co-variance? This ambiguity is a useful one that requires norms, standards, or centers (grounds of function in the former sense) to be concretely embodied, and hence constrained by reciprocal constitution (i.e., function in the latter sense). It is along these lines that I wish to discuss a definitive aspect of Tamil culture, specifically as encoded in the *Drāviḍa* style of temple architecture, as a positive construct, and not as an essentialized stereotype or a unanimous belief system. For present purposes, I seek the critical reader's permission to be modestly concerned with the shape of a regionalized aesthetic praxis that can serve as an interpretive frame for long-term historical reconstructions of these categories.

It has been often and well established that the Hindu temple is a metaphorical cosmos and human body (e.g., Kramrisch, 1946, pp. 357–361). Here I propose to further flesh out that relation by examining ways that temples function in metonymic relations to bodies: as concrete objectifications of bodily actions and of the cosmological assumptions embedded in those acts. Because temples are the coarse material traces of human activity—or more exactly in this context, the remnants of the sacrifices of which the ritualized procedures of Tamil temple construction consists—they reveal in visible forms the organized qualities of the nonvisible forces that generated them.[3] For Hindu devotees these forms are routinely taken to reveal an ahistorical truth about reality itself; consequently, they may be understood as self-manifesting (*svayambhū*) in some sense. However, in the present context (which I take to be one of cross-cultural dialogue), they can alternatively be seen to encode contingent truth and historically constructed reality.[4] In the latter role they are complex semiotic formations, or architectural "texts" that may be metaphorically read and translated into English prose, with all the usual risks and benefits associated with literary readings and translations.

Unlike the soaring, vertical shape of the North Indian (or *Nāgara* style) *vimāna,* which is reminiscent of the outline of the *liṅga* it often contains, the *Drāviḍa* temple is identified by its builders as *kōyil,* a word that combines (among other connotations) much of the semantic range of the English words temple and palace. The "palace" sense of the word indicates that the building is a grand house (and, by implication, that the universe too is housing for the subtle life within it, and of which it is a coarse manifestation). The tower (*vimāṉam*) consists of horizontal "garlands" (*hāra*) made up of miniature buildings that are stacked one above the other in steps (*tala*) of diminishing size, thereby reiterating the cosmological/bodily "housing" theme of the whole in each one of its component parts (Fig. 3). The overall appearance suggests the horizontal layering of a stepped pyramid more than the vertical dynamic of the North Indian *vimāna*. However, the most obvious and spectacular distinguishing feature of the *Drāviḍa* temple is not the *vimāna,* but its proclivity to grow by the addition of increasingly vast and elaborate peripheral structures: concentric *prākāram* walls, each

Figure 6.3 *Vimāṉam* of Minakshi temple. Madurai. Circa seventeenth century.

more massive than the older one it encircles, enormous porches (*maṇḍapa* or *maṇṭapam*), some with as many as a thousand and one pillars, and most visible of all, immense and numerous gateways (*gopura* [Sanskrit] or *gopuram* [Tamil]) that sometimes rise two hundred feet and more in height.

The Pallavas built prototypical variants of the later *gopuram* in the eighth century; however, the two massive *gopurams* of the early eleventh-century Brihadisvara temple in Tanjavur represent the full-fledged emergence of the type. The *gopurams* of the Cōḻa temples at Tanjavur and Gangaikondacolapuram (circa 1030 C.E.) are nevertheless still smaller than the towering *vimāṉams* they open toward. By the twelfth century, temples built under Cōḻa patronage began to exhibit characteristics of the later development, as the *gopurams* increasingly came to soar above a smaller *vimāṉam,* now much more intimate in scale (Harle, 1963). From the eleventh/twelfth centuries onward, the *Drāviḍa* temple style developed through an increasing emphasis on the size and complexity of its peripheral structures. A typical example is illustrated here by an aerial view of the Madurai Minakshi temple (Fig. 2). Compared to the twelve major gateways visible in the photograph, the shrines of Sundareswara (Śiva) and Minakshi (Fig. 3) located at the core of the complex are relatively small. The gateways generally increase in size and complexity as they are built at increasing distances from the shrine. Barely visible in the upper third of the photograph is a huge hall (the *putu maṇṭapam*) constructed outside the eastern gateway. And just beyond that lies the colossal base of an unfinished gateway (Fig. 4), designed in the seventeenth century to accommodate a tower that, if ever completed, will rival the tallest ever built.[5]

Why did this highly distinctive temple form emerge and develop in South India? Some members of a previous generation of art historians have read the development of the later Dravidian temple as a sign of artistic degeneration (e.g., Goetz, 1959, pp. 195–196; Lee, 1982, pp. 216–217; Rowland, 1967, pp. 319–322). This view is implicitly based on a model of artistic "evolution" derived from an organic metaphor.[6] While this view may have a certain poetic or common-sense appeal, it cannot bear critical scrutiny. Natural processes of evolution are affected by biological and genetic modes of reproduction while buildings are social and cultural constructions; they belong to specific histories affected by human agency.

On a more positive note, Percy Brown attributes the development of the Dravidian temple complex to a combination of ritual and military functions (1956, p. 114). The concentric *prākāram* walls (the characteristic striped pattern marking two such walls can be seen in Fig. 2), provided excellent defensive barriers in times of attack, while the soaring towers offered a commanding view of the surrounding territory. However, Harle notes that as far as existing historical evidence goes, only Europeans and Muslims ever used South Indian temples for defensive purposes (to the horror of the local population; 1963, p. 5), making it unlikely that military functions had anything to do with the

Figure 6.4 Base of unfinished rajagopuram. Minakshi temple. Madurai. Circa seventeenth century.

logic of the design. The ritual function Brown refers to points in a more promising direction. George Michell similarly, and more precisely, attributes the style's development to a variety of ritual and community functions accommodated by the temple "such as civic meetings, education, dance and theatre" (1977, pp. 150–155).[7] Indeed, the temple *prākārams* and streets of cities like Madurai (Fig. 5) accommodate an elaborate festival calendar in which dramatic processions circumambulate the shrine(s) at varying distances from the center. The vehicles used in these processions are progressively more massive the further they travel from the center: the deity may ride in a small *capparam* (palanquin) inside the *cannitāṉam* (presence) or on an enormous chariot on routes leading further out through the city. *Vāhanas*[8] of intermediate size are typically used for ritual routes in between. This gradation suggests an underlying logic linked to the similarly graded scale of the gateways.

But if one accepts this line of explanation, it becomes all the more puzzling why the major expenditure of resources in this effort would be devoted to building massive gateways—the aesthetic sine qua non of

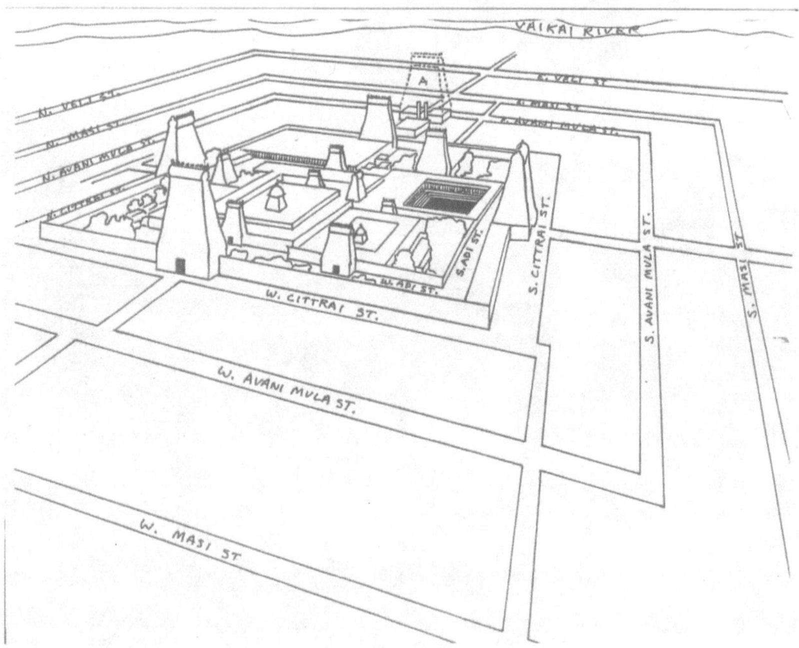

Figure 6.5 Layout of Madurai. A: Unfinished gateway.

this development—that serve no correspondingly important ritual or civic utility. Public meetings, education, theater, dance, and ritual processions do not depend on massive gateways in the same sense that they may require large *maṇṭapams,* processional corridors, and streets.

Harle endorses Kramrisch's explanation, which explains the phenomenon as the return to a primordial "hypaethral" shrine type. Ancient relief sculptures of such hypaethral shrines have been found on the remains of Buddhist monuments from Bharhut in the north (circa 100–80 B.C.E.) to Amaravati in the south (circa second to third centuries C.E.). They are believed to illustrate a type of shrine that once existed throughout the South Asian subcontinent prior to the codification of more elaborate Hindu temple styles known from archaeological remains and textual references dating from the Gupta period onward (Harle, 1963, p. 6; Kramrisch, 1946, pp. 203–204; K. R. Srinivasan, 1983, pp. 12–14).[9] Kramrisch's claim is better understood as a descriptive assertion than a theory, since it begs the questions how and why such a "return to type" might occur, and why it happened in this particular way in South India. But what most undermines her proposal is the visual testimony of the temples themselves. The massive gateways, concentric *prākārams,* and thousand-pillared halls of the later Dravidian temple are clearly not a *return* to any ancient model now known. The object of devotion is not really exposed to the sky, but is enclosed within a "womb house" (*karppa-k-kirukam* or *garbha-gṛha*). Even the tree of the site (*sthala-vṛkṣa*) is not invariably exposed to the sky in large temple complexes. For example, the blackened trunk of an ancient, long-dead *kaṭampa* tree, the *sthala-vṛkṣa* of the Madurai Minakshi temple, is located *inside* the goddess's *cannitāṉam,* a dark, roofed space. If the later Dravidian temple complex is to be distinctively characterized as a fenced or walled enclosure, and therefore "hypaethral," it would be better understood as an ongoing elaboration of type rather than a return.

Zimmer considers the elaboration of the Dravidian style in metaphysical terms, specifically as the symbolic link of eternity and time (Zimmer, 1955, p. 286). While this may be taken as a valid insight into an abstract semiotic potential of the form (or as a hidden truth, if one presupposes depth psychology's essentialist theory of meaning, as do Zimmer and his editor, Joseph Campbell), as a theory it works at such a high level of generality that it explains little or nothing in a concrete historical or cultural sense. Indeed, in this approach, culture and historical human agency tend to be implicitly displaced by the causal forces of an unconscious Human Mind.[10]

An ever-expanding temple complex also provides a framework for ongoing displays of devotion through acts of patronage (Parker, 1989, 1992), but continuous patronage per se does not explain the specific *gopuram* form, or the distinctive characteristics of later Dravidian temple complexes. More or less ongoing patronage patterns are also evident in the expansion of northern sites, such as Khajuraho and Bhubaneshwar (and even at important places of medieval Christian pilgrimage for that matter), but the Dravidian style did not emerge in those places.

Why the *Drāviḍa* temple developed as it did remains a puzzle that has not been adequately solved (Huntington, 1985, p. 532). Indeed the question has largely been on the shelf for several decades. Here I propose an argument consistent with an orientation suggested to me by the Jeeyar (a title used in Andhra Pradesh for the head of certain Vaiṣṇava religious orders) of Ahobila Matam, who was the South Indian holy man recognized as the driving force behind the construction of the huge *rājagopuram* at Srirangam in the 1980s. With a dramatic gesture of contempt, as if I was an idiot for asking about something as obvious as the purpose of a *gopuram,* he exclaimed that the *gopuram* is a *sign*! Just like the sign that you put in front of your house to let people know where you live. In semiotic language the sort of sign the Jeeyar is referring to may be classified as indexical. And however much it may be a sign of the lord's residence, the *Drāviḍa* temple style can also be read as an indexical sign of a culturally distinctive construction of time, space, and person in South India. The latter reading rests on several propositions. First, shared presuppositions about time and space are profoundly naturalized constructs. Second, like (and partially through) a native language they are internalized, reproduced, and modified from generation to generation more through everyday praxis; they are not usually verbalized in abstracted theoretical arguments or explicit acts of education (but on occasion they may be). Third, spatial gestures—both bodily and architectural—are instruments for the naturalization of space/time constructions. Architecture and the bodily gestures they articulate objectify socially generated paradigms of space/time as pragmatic, hard facts of everyday life. Fourth, this mode of pragmatic, mostly unspoken transmission facilitates a very slow, glacial rate of historical change: shared experiences of such elemental phenomena as time and space tend to exhibit characteristics of unforced, self-organizing, self-objectifying systems. Just as the words of a language may change far more rapidly and easily than word order, likewise physical architectural forms in South India have evidently changed much more readily than the sense of reality they encode. This helps explain why the spatiotemporal aesthetics of the earliest surviving Tamil literature can be rather precisely recognized in the spatiotemporal order of the later Dravidian temple style, even as it continues to develop in the late twentieth century. Were it not for the widespread acceptance of modernist myths of creation and innovation, this would be an unremarkable assertion. After all, even though the Tamil language has changed dramatically in the past century, it is still distinctively Tamil, with far more profound links with the Tamil of two thousand years ago than it has with, say, Chinese or Maori. Why should the spatiotemporal codes of Tamil temple architecture be radically otherwise?

Akam/Puṟam

The central aesthetic and spatiotemporal categories of ancient Tamil literature are *akam* and *puṟam;* roughly translated as "interior" and "exterior," respectively. The landscapes articulated within *akam* and *puṟam* categories each contain poetic "markers" or "signs" that indicate and evoke differing qualities of person and affect situated at specific spatiotemporal conjunctions (Hart, 1975; Ramanujan, 1967, 1985; Selby, this volume). But *akam* and *puṟam* are not sharply compartmentalized. The categories of *akam* poetry resonate throughout *puṟam* poetry, although not always following the neat, systematic correspondences suggested by the *Tolkāppiyam* (Ramanujan, 1985, pp. 251–257).

How can one justify invoking two-millennia-old Tamil poetics to interpret a development in Tamil temple architecture that has occurred within the past thousand years? If orthodoxy—represented in the explicit testimony of ancient writings—were taken to be the only acceptable form of evidence, the task would be impossible. *Akam* and *puṟam* are not salient categories in any of the *śāstras* dealing with sculpture or architecture. Nor do temple inscriptions provide a significant source of evidence. As literary devices *akam* and *puṟam* are highly unlikely to have had any direct impact on the development of the Dravidian temple style. But that does not mean that they do not share a more deeply naturalized source. Tamil temple architecture and the formalized categories of *akam* and *puṟam* can both be understood as objectifications of an underlying spatiotemporal doxa that has been both changed *and* perpetuated through the past two thousand years.

At the most superficial level, the lord's shrine may occasionally be identified as an *akam* in Tamilnadu, and contemporary Tamil temple builders do significantly connect the *puṟam* of *caṅkam* literature with the name of the temple's gateways through a creative Tamil etymology: *kō* (lord) and *puṟam* (exterior).[11] However, the *puram* of *gopuram* is spelled with a different "r" and seems to be derived from the Sanskrit word *pura*, "city" (Harle, 1963, pp. 1, 7). This Tamil etymology is significant, not so much as a true origin long obscured by the dominance of Sanskrit, but as a token of a much more widespread tendency for Tamil temple architects to appropriate and reinterpret imported Sanskrit signs when they are used in the reproduction and modification of local realities. Indeed, with the rise of regional and linguistic nationalisms in modern South India, that tendency may be more pronounced today than ever.[12]

However, the terms themselves do not lead us very far. More significant connections are to be made by juxtaposing the ordering principles informing *caṅkam* poetry and Tamil temple architecture. According to Ramanujan, each of the *caṅkam* poems is a "structure and a process" (1985, p. 265): "It is characteristic of this poetry and its poetics that the meanings seem to expand and contract in concentric circles, with the concrete physical particular at the center, getting more and more inclusive and abstract as we move outward" (p. 263). Similarly, Dravidian temples are best understood as perpetually incomplete structures-in-process, expanding and contracting in relation to concentric frames built around a particularized center (Parker, 1992, pp. 121–123).[13] "A temple, like a plant, must be able to 'grow'" (Dagens, 1984, p. 30). According to contemporary oral appeals to the authority of "*śāstra,*" the temple is supposed to be renovated and enlarged every twelve years[14] following the cycle of Guru (Jupiter), an "expansive" planet associated with wisdom, devotion, wellbeing, and progeny.[15] Although this schedule is probably never followed in practice, Tamil temples invariably oscillate between periods of decline and relative neglect followed by concentrated efforts toward renewal and expansion. The material remnants (*vastu* and *vāstu*) of these ritual (sacrificial) practices in Tamilnadu (Fig. 5) tend to display a concentric spatial structure similar to that of a *caṅkam* poem.

In "The Spatial Structure of Suchindram," Jan Peiper (1980) argues that the temple and surrounding town are an environment for generating what he usefully calls "haptic experience." This is a somatic and kinesthetic knowledge of space and place, known by physical movements in and around a structured environment (pp. 65, 69). Implicitly one's haptic experience of the city encodes a "culture-specific concept of space," and the urban rituals that the city is structured to accommodate enable personal, bodily experiences to be collectively stated and shared (p. 80). The town's spatial order is discursively understood by its inhabitants as "the body of the great goddess demarcated by the four Amma shrines around the town [which] is conceived as being 'pregnant' with the male Sthanumalaya temple within" (p. 70). The four protective shrines face outward, away from the center of town, while the guardians of the eight directions are located beneath the car street encircling the temple, thereby distinguishing the city's inner "body" from its outer "case" (p. 72). The aesthetic and somatic experiencing of urban spaces stressed in Peiper's account provides a useful perspective on the ways that human bodies and urban spaces can articulate each other, and in this culturally specific South Indian case, reciprocally map the spaces of one onto the other.

As a metaphorical human body, the public, exterior sheaths (*kośams* or *śarīrams*) of the Dravidian temple complex (and, by extension, the entire city or neighborhood it serves) display a range of systematic aesthetic contrasts with its intimate interior spaces. The gateways provide not cavernous interiors like a *maṇṭapam,* but vast *exteriors*. The comparatively small interior spaces they contain are passages designed to accommodate/prevent movement through them.[16] Their graded sizes primarily yield increasing *surface* areas to be covered with sculpture. These surfaces are aesthetically bright. If sufficient funds are available, the *gopuram* is painted with saturated polychrome; if not, an overall "light" color, white or an off-white, will be used; never a dark or dull color. The colors cooperate with the brilliant tropical sun to produce a radiant effect much appreciated by contemporary temple builders and their clients.[17] *Gopuram* sculpture vigorously exercises an aesthetic of exaggerations. It is theatrical in expression and often heroic in subject matter: fierce supernatural beasts (*yāḷis*), door guardians bearing weapons, fangs, bulging eyes, and bristling moustaches (*dvarapālas*), and broad-shouldered caryatids (*kōpurantāṅkis*) who seem to effortlessly lift each tier of the superstructure with a single hand. These standard characters are normally integrated into cult-specific iconographic schemes that celebrate the deity's manifold powers and mythological exploits, especially those involving the quelling of demons and the rescuing of devotees (Fig. 6). Heroic images and narratives such as these are similarly definitive of ancient *puṟam* poetry.

Besides gateways, huge halls (*maṇṭapams*) conventionally containing as many as a thousand pillars are also prominent manifestations of the tendency toward enormous scale in the peripheral structures of later *Drāviḍa* temples. Here too, the aesthetic properties of their sculpture routinely emphasize muscular themes of battle and heroism, appropriate to a *puṟam* context (Fig. 7).

Movement around and through the temple complex is ordered by ritual circumambulation (*pradakṣiṇa*). On festival occasions, devotees and festival icons (*utsava-mūrtis*) circumambulate the Madurai Minakshi temple on the city streets that surround it (Fig. 5). Within the temple complex itself, there are covered circumambulatory passages encircling the main shrines. Generally the further away from the center, the larger the festival and the vehicle used to transport the gods. Significantly, the *gopurams* are aligned, not with movements around the center, but with oscillating ritual movements, toward and away from it (Davis, 1991, pp. 60–74). According to Richard Davis,

> the movements of emission and reabsorption appear throughout daily worship, and all Śaiva ritual, as basic organizing principles. They order elements and actions within the ritual, and in so doing they

Figure 6.6 Detail of *gopuram* sculpture. Madurai. Minakshi temple.

bring this ritual order into accord with the fundamental order of the cosmos. As Śiva causes the constituents of the manifest world to be emitted and reabsorbed, the worshipper himself, acting as Śiva, causes the elements of the ritual domain to follow the same pattern of emission and reabsorption (1991, p. 47).

Figure 6.7 Detail of Tirumalai Nayak Mandapam. Madurai Minakshi temple.

The relation of sanctum to *gopuram* marks the interior/exterior axis of ritualized bodily motion. Once again the poetics of this architectural experiencing is anticipated in *caṅkam* literature: "The movement of *akam* poems is a crossing from outer to inner: from outer body to the heart within," while *puṟam* poems "tend to start inside a house (*akam*) and move, like the tiger [moving from his lair into the forest], out into the world (*puṟam*)" (Ramanujan, 1985, p. 265).

If the *gopuram* embodies the most exteriorized and public of the temple's spaces, the womb house (*garbha-gṛha*) lies at the other end of the continuum. It is the temple's most interiorized and intimate space. In contrast to the indiscriminate public mixing and pollution associated with the streets around the temple, the *garbha-gṛha* is densely framed by ritual restrictions (Fig. 8). Even though access to the *cannitāṉam* has been open to all Hindus regardless of caste for more than fifty years now, Tamil architects and sculptors still routinely justify the construction of new *gopurams* with reference to the former restrictions: people who are not allowed to have the lord's *darśan* (sight) inside the temple can take *darśan* of his or her image on the *gopuram.*[18]

In dramatic contrast to the bright and bustling aesthetics of the *gopuram,* the *garbha-gṛha* is designed as a dark, intimate environment conducive to experiencing the flavors of love and devotion (Fig. 9). The imagery the devotee sees there normally emphasizes male and female intimacy.[19] Even if the god and goddess of the temple occupy separate shrines, the temple complex as a whole celebrates their union. At a Śiva temple the main icon will be a *liṅga/yoni* that serves as (among other things) an explicitly sexual sign of creative power. If it is a Viṣṇu temple, a goddess temple, or the shrine of a *parivāra-devatā* (a "family member" such as Gaṇapati or Murukaṉ), the erotic connotations may be more indirectly expressed in the sensuous beauty or playfulness of the icon. "The meanings of *akam,* 'interior, heart, household,' are all embodied here," Ramanujan writes, with intended reference to a *caṅkam* poem, yet with equal applicability to the interior of a Tamil temple (1985, p. 233).

The iconographic program of Srirangam's new *rājagopuram* significantly articulates architectural space with gender in a quite novel way. All of the images on the exterior of the tower are male, anchored by a centralized icon of Raṅganātha. In contrast, all the images on the interior face of the tower are female, encircling the icon of Tāyār or Raṅganāyaki, Viṣṇu's local bride (Parker, 1992, p. 120). The architect assures me that this scheme is unique and unprecedented, yet what is noteworthy about this innovation is how it is both new and old at the same time. The implicit spatial proportions, female : male : interior : exterior, is as logical for an architecture that identifies its ultimate interior as a "womb house" and marks exteriors with armed masculine door guardians, as it is for an even more ancient classification of poems about love and war.

Figure 6.8 Entrance to Minakshi's presence (*caṉṉitāṉam*). Photography is prohibited inside.

Person, Space, and Human Flourishing

A striking feature of ancient *caṅkam* poetics is its metonymic bias.[20] The precise characteristics of the personae of the poems and their emotional experiences are signified by their juxtaposition with qualities of the landscape and time of day or season. Daniel observes that persons and places

Figure 6.9 A small sanctum for Viṣṇu in the Minakshi temple complex that is not subject to a taboo on photography.

are similarly linked in the conventions of everyday Tamil life. A person's subtle and coarse mental and bodily characteristics are formed by living on the soil of one's native place (*conta ūr*), eating the food grown in it, drinking the water of its wells and absorbing its mentality (*putti*) and qualitative characteristics (*kuṇam*). The qualities and physical leavings of its inhabitants in turn reciprocally condition the place, specifically represented by its soil (Daniel, 1984). Members of local descent groups act as though their well-being derives from cultivating and maintaining relations of substantive compatibility with the specific qualities of an *ūr;* a compatibility that is not, as the English term suggests, a state, but a moving equilibrium, a perpetual becoming, fueled by fervent devotion (*bhakti*) and effected by ongoing efforts (*saṃskāras; karmas*). Among these efforts, temple rituals—construction, maintenance, renovation, and expansion—must be recognized as prominent vehicles.

Just as every person is the same and different from every other, so too are temples and the specific places they represent. Significant places in the Tamil landscape are commonly identified with named goddesses (Pūmātēvi or Bhūdevī). The soil of the site is her body, through which she nurtures her children. Her discursive reification is further objectified through the construction of a temple; however, it is the site (*talam, sthala, sthāna*) that is the figurative and literal ground of the temple's significance. The built structure is not a fetish but a self-objectifying outgrowth (*svayambhū*) and sign (*liṅga*) of the site itself, acting in concert with its (her) people. The *talapurāṇam* (story of the site) routinely provides the local temple with semiotic distinction: its syntagmatic uniqueness emerges only in relation to its paradigmatic universality. For instance, at Madurai, the icon of Nataraja appears with his right leg raised, in contrast to the standard icon of Nataraja at Chidambaram where it is the left leg that is raised. This material distinction marks both Madurai and Chidambaram as special places; geographical centers of two ancient competing landscapes/powers: Pāṇṭiya-nāṭu and Cōḻa-nāṭu. Popular oral versions of the *talapurāṇam* of the Minakshi temple celebrate the difference in exactly those terms: a Pāṇṭiya king skilled in all of the sixty-four arts except dancing sought dance instruction from the Cōḻa king. The Pāṇṭiyaṉ wondered if Śiva was not discomforted by always supporting himself on his right leg and begged him to take rest by alternating legs. As a sign of special favor to the considerate Pāṇṭiya king, Śiva graciously agreed to perform his cosmic dance with his right foot raised in Madurai. Why is this story still endlessly repeated to visitors of the Minakshi temple today? The old distinctions of Cōḻa country and Pāṇṭiya country still resonate in contemporary Tamil identities and the lesson, if it must be spelled out, is that while the lord Śiva may be everywhere, his manifestation at the heart of Pāṇṭiya country is specific, particularly gracious, and potent. Furthermore, the appropriation and recontextualization of Nataraja at Madurai spatially and ideologically locates him as a peripheral and subordinated aspect of Sundareswara, the local form of Śiva.

Similarly, while every *Drāviḍa* temple is like every other in its general characteristics, the rituals of calculating proportions (*āyati*) and the subsequent planning of formal details ensure that no two temples will ever be *exactly* alike. No cookie-cutter methodologies are ever deployed in image making or temple construction. In fact, I often heard references to a popular taboo—allegedly a "violation of *śāstra*"—that prohibits the direct copying of any existing temple or image. Instead, each object is supposed to be generated anew, out of the *sthapati's* knowledge. This convention is commonly explained with reference to the idea that every icon and temple must be custom made to effect a complex set of auspicious relations among a specific patron (*yajamāna,* or sacrificing patron), deity, community, place, and time. It also ensures that the object will be generated out of a subtle source, the incarnated knowledge of the *sthapati,* rather than a coarse one, located in already existing physical objects.

Temples organize the landscape into qualitatively distinct locations, not by constructing sharply defined boundaries, but by embellishing centers of power that unfold, lotus-like, in all directions. The grandeur of their outward reach and inward pull, the latter marked by their qualities of visual attraction, takes form through the development of peripheral structures oriented toward the cardinal points. This understanding provides an ethnohistorical ground for the growth of a temple. Depending on her (i.e., the site's) power, as indexed by the prosperity, population growth, and success of the people she supports, her self-objectifying signs expand or contract in space, alongside those of whichever relatively more universalized Sanskritic god to whom she may be married (she is, after all, his *śakti,* or power).

Accordingly, through its construction, maintenance, and protection, the temple serves as an instrument in the constitution of authority, honor, and social order in Tamilnadu (see Appadurai, 1981; Dirks, 1987, pp. 285–305; Inden, 1990, pp. 213–262). In former centuries the social, political, and territorial expansion of the Pāṇṭiyas and Nayaks was indexed by the growth of the Madurai Minakshi temple. As their dominance and prosperity increased, so too did the architectural signs of the goddess's power. When their successes waned, so too did the growth and maintenance of the temple. When the Nayaks finally drove the Pāṇṭiyas out of Madurai in the fifteenth century, they adopted the local goddess of Tenkaci (the "Southern Kāśī," or Benares), their place of retreat, as a source of renewed power. They called her Ulakammaṉ, mother of the world, and represented her just as they had Minakshi, with an icon bearing a parrot on her shoulder.

Minakshi herself is honored at Tenkaci in a small separate shrine to the left of the main deities. This location spatially and ideologically subordinates her to Ulakammaṉ, placing her in the outer orbit of the now more universalized power erupting from the soil of Tenkaci. While physically smaller, the Pāṇṭiya temple at Tenkaci is even more ambitious and cosmologically totalizing in its iconographic scheme than the Madurai temple. The vast extent of Ulakammaṉ's territorial reach is not only indicated by her name, but by her marriage to the "Universal Lord" (Viśvanātha), the supreme form of Śiva worshipped along the Ganges River at Benaras. As their physical resources for grand temple construction declined, the Pāṇṭiyas apparently found it difficult to complete the gigantic *rājagopuram* begun by Parakrama Pāṇṭiyaṉ in the mid-fifteenth century. In an apparent plea to finish the tower after his lifetime, the sovereign had the following inscription carved into the massive stone base: "The temple at the fertile town of Tenkaci came into existence only by the will of providence; it is not actually my work. I, Parakrama Pandya, shall prostrate before the feet and serve those who extend and protect it" (Rao, 1910–13, p. 98). When this *gopuram* was being reconstructed in the late 1980s—the old superstructure had been ruined by a disastrous fire in the nineteenth century—popular rumor cited this inscription as a miraculous prediction indicating the benefits and prosperity to be expected upon the tower's completion. Politicians, scrambling to take credit for the construction (it was largely financed by the owner of a major Tamil newspaper), encouraged this conception with promises of local economic growth to be fueled by tourists and pilgrims flocking to wonder at the titanic structure.

As if to compensate for their waning ability to produce architectural signs of power, the use of linguistic hyperbole in Pāṇṭiyaṉ inscriptions increased throughout the seventeenth and early eighteenth centuries. Among the later Pāṇṭiyaṉ inscriptions at Tenkaci are some of the most wildly exalted royal references ever composed (Rao, 1910–13, pp. 98–103).

Even in the absence of royal patronage, many Tamils behave as though specific places in the landscape are both causes and effects of their inhabitants' well-being. Contemporary patronage patterns, marked by the renovation and multiplication of ever larger and grander structures, especially *gopurams,* implicitly operate through the presupposition that when the goddess's body (place/temple) is robust and growing, the people who are nurtured by her will also flourish, and vice versa. If "I" am not separate from my native place (*conta ūr*), then its flourishing is my flourishing, and vice versa. The temple is a focal point, and a kind of literal machine (*yantra*) through which the inhabitants of a place can transact with it and thereby actuate moral debits and credits and cultivate relations of compatibility, devotion, and concern. If the "children" of the place show a proper sense of devotion and obedience to the mother, she will respond with nurture and parental warmheartedness. Correspondingly, her displeasure may have a contrary effect.

The temple is also metaphor. Just as the body is a kind of "house" for the person, so too is the house a kind of body (Daniel, 1984, pp. 105–62). As a palatial house, the temple is an extraordinary body, displaying perfected proportions and, like an auspicious woman bearing a divine child in her womb, it is clothed in ornaments and brilliant colors: commonsense signifiers of erotic forces of attraction, reproductive potential, and consequent growth and prosperity. Beauty, according to many Tamil temple builders, is characteristically identified with luminous qualities and richness of ornamentation, much in the same way a woman is made beautiful with shimmering jewelry, cosmetics, and a brilliant sari. And just as the husband is to blame if the wife is not lovely, so too *sthapatis* blame the stinginess of patrons (which nowadays mostly means the state government) for the aesthetic shortcomings of modern temples.

Inside/outside of the body is closely linked with the social construction of pure/impure relations in Tamilnadu: substances that enter into the interior space of the body are of far greater concern than those that merely engage its surfaces. Concerns with the impurity of substances that exit the body are balanced by proportional concerns with the purity of substances entering it (Beck, 1976). Temple ritual displays an analogous concern with the purity of the interior. Several Tamil temple builders explained to me that the sanctum is the temple's head, the *prākārams* (compound walls and circumambulatory passages) are its limbs, and the *gopurams* are feet. While *dharmaśāstras* differentiate the cosmic body vertically, identifying the head with the most subtle and pure (the Brahmans) and the feet with the most coarse and impure (the Śūdras), here the code is made horizontal, consistent with the aesthetic emphasis on the horizontal direction in the *Drāviḍa* style generally, as well as the relative importance Tamils place upon the place-as-goddess; the horizontal earth (Pūmātēvi or Bhūdevi).[21] The pollution generated by more or less uncontrolled mixing of life in the streets is metonymically and metaphorically identified with the *gopuram*/foot, while the purity of the sanctum/head is maintained by carefully regulated transactions. Thus, while aesthetically accommodating local Tamil conceptions, degrees of purity/impurity are built into the temple's spatial organization, accommodating a common Brahman conception of social hierarchy based on inner purity/exterior pollution.[22]

But the sanctum is not just "head"; it is, inconsistently, also "womb" (*karppam* or *garbha*). This seeming contradiction highlights the context-sensitivity of the temple's significance. In the latter designation the core of the temple is identified with female auspiciousness, which places another valorizing axis to the fore besides pure and impure (Raheja, 1988).

While relations of *akam* and *puṟam,* interior/exterior, appear to be emphasized in Tamil practices, early Indo-European sources in South Asia emphasize center/periphery relations. The two are by no means mutually exclusive and are easily articulated. Their differences are not of essential *kind,* but of aesthetic orientations and degrees of emphasis. However, the semiotic resources used by Tamil architects and sculptors to organize center/periphery relations tend to be widely identified more with North Indian sources than with *caṅkam* poetics. A rich body of signs is available in the visual language of Tamil architects to indicate a central axis in relation to its spatial envelopes: parasol, erect spine, mountain, tree trunk, scepter, erect phallus (*liṅgam*), flag pole (*dhvaja-stambha*), mace (*daṇḍam*), finial (*kalaśam*); spear (*vēl*). The most ancient references to many of these elements are not architectural or sculptural, but written references in Vedic literature. The earliest surviving monuments that are directly ancestral to this visual language include the Aśokan pillars, which generally belong to the family of Vedic imagery: *skaṃbha* (pillar), *yūpa* (sacrificial post), *sthūṇa* (ritual stake), *Indra-dhvaja* (a battle standard), *Indra-kīla* (a ritual peg), and the churning stick, later associated with the mythological narrative of the churning of the ocean of milk (Irwin, 1976, p. 740). These Vedic images of centrality suggest an abstracted, and hence *portable* spatial order—one that can be constructed anywhere—suitable to a life of migration and conquest. In contrast, the literary poetics of *akam* and *puṟam* are grounded in specific, non-portable Tamil landscapes; homes *(akam)* and bodily extensions of the persons portrayed.

In turn, it is possible, to some extent, to interpret *Nāgara* temples through the distinction of *akam* and *puṟam*. They also display a systematic manipulation of formal contrasts between inner and outer. The emergence of a North Indian pattern of sacred sites suggests an orientation consistent with that of *caṅkam* aesthetic values, even if it may be impossible to prove the existence of a direct historical channel through which that might have happened. By the time the conventions of Hindu temple construction were taking shape in the North some fifteen hundred years ago, Dravidian and Indo-European dialectics were already ancient.

Nevertheless, the *degree* to which the interior/exterior dimension is emphasized in the South is unparalleled in North Indian temple architecture, and the overwhelming sign of this distinction is the dramatic development of the colossal *gopurams* (and other huge peripheral structures) that aesthetically mark the *Drāviḍa* style. The significance of the *gopuram* is impossible to recognize if abstracted from the whole, hence the generally unsatisfactory character of most previous attempts to explain it. The *gopuram* is a major component of a ritual order in which architectural forms encode a practical Tamil exegesis on the reality of time and space. By virtue of their contrasting sensory properties, bundles of articulated relations among the *garbha-gṛha* and monumental peripheral structures (interior/exterior, confined/vast, darkness/brightness, intimate/heroic, restricted/public, singularity/multiplicity, center/periphery, fixed/movable, enduring/ephemeral, and so on) serve to make a socially and culturally constructed space-time into an empirical fact of lived experience.

Conclusion: The No Thingness of "Tamil Culture"

The material traces of Tamil history point toward an implicit spatiotemporal habitus, a "history turned into nature" (Bourdieu, 1977, p. 78), and because it is experienced as simply natural, or self-organizing, it is resistant to rapid or forced modifications from within. But does this suggest that there is a distinct Tamil culture, or tradition, that has endured for the last two thousand years? No. Not if Tamil culture is conceived as a being; a collection of bounded essential properties that include a uniform, orthodox belief in the aesthetic principles of *akam* and *puṟam*. Clearly no such orthodoxy has survived into recent times. And it should be equally clear that any Tamil culture imagined along such lines would have to be seen as damaged goods; "contaminated" by ancient Indo-European culture and disintegrated by the corrosive solvents of European empire-building and global capitalism. On the other hand, maybe this conception is a needlessly weak, if not parochial, way of seeing "things," particularly if the "culture" we are talking about is not a "thing" in any case, but a function: alternatively imaginable as objectifications of self-regulating, self-organizing systems (however, replacing "culture" with "system" does little good if the latter is likewise reified).

Tacit and contested agreements, embedded within the codes constituting a distinctive and meaningful way of life in Tamilnadu, have dramatically changed over the past two millennia through everyday use. But it would be perverse to imagine that such ongoing changes were products of radical discontinuities. While they may be very different, modern temples and ancient ones, or contemporary Tamil and *caṅkam* Tamil, are also profoundly connected by situated human praxis. The abstract idea that change can somehow occur *ex nihilo,* beyond and outside history, is a peculiarity of a modernist myth of progress, articulating an imperial and empirical reality of great men, private property (discovery, conquest, invention, copyrights, and so on), and a correspondingly disjoined subject/object or owner/owned relationship, in which individualized personhood is juxtaposed with an objectified world. The reader should be clear that I am not commenting on Western intellectual history or the perspectives of trained scientists in this context. I refer to a common-sense, rationalized, secular universe presupposed by capitalist practices; a cosmology in which "nothing" is imagined as a binary inversion of "things," and where it can thus seem "rational," for instance, to arbitrarily believe that beings appear out of such a nothingness at conception and vanish into it again at death. As "things," both subject and object are configured against that presumed *nihil:* an ultimate scientific and statistical background of non-significance. It is within this popular mythic framework that we can recognize the alleged poisons of cultural relativism—ethical, aesthetic, and epistemological chaos, "subjectivist, half-baked, neo-Nietzschean theories" (Taylor, 1994, p. 70), or a hermeneutic "abyss," especially in Paul de Man's bastardized version of Derrida (Tilley, 1990, pp. 245–248)—the proposed antidotes to which (an ahistorical Human Nature or Mind) would be even harder to choke down than the supposed toxin (Geertz, 1984). If situated within the narrow horizons of *that* mythic frame, Tamil "culture" or "tradition" looks like either an essentialist concept worthy of the trash can, or an enduring "thing" that can only be perpetuated by artificial reinventions.

The continuity of the spatial/aesthetic values of *akam* and *puṟam* in the *Drāviḍa* temple styles of the early twenty-first century is utterly misrecognized if conceived as either the product of a phony, romantic reinvention of tradition, or of stagnation, hidebound conservatism, a failure of imagination, genius, or "creativity." It rests within other mythologies, other valorizing frames of emergent creativity and participatory modes of personhood neither abstracted from, nor independent of, the surrounding environment. It is a disciplined achievement, underwritten by methods distinguished by the unforced (nonviolent) unfolding of potentials, always already latent within the local, self-regulating, self-objectifying systems of coded relationships. Temple construction continues to serve as an effective strategy for constructing a center. Such physical centers provide anchors to spatial frames, such as the walls of the Minakshi temple and the streets of Madurai, which also serve as frames of reference. They place limits, thereby permitting significant distinctions to be made—they place a concrete and particularized "spin" on local lives and events, infusing what is immediate with values made relative to an Ultimate, embodied in the inner sanctum and its enveloping structures. And just as each delimitation of a frame automatically implies a metaposition outside it, ultimately suggesting an indefinite regress (or egress) of potential frames, so too does the practice of Tamil temple construction entail an indefinite pattern of expanding frames surrounding its center, each more grandiose than the one immediately preceding. It seems that succeeding generations of Tamils have stepped out of the architectural frames bequeathed by their ancestors to envelop them with a more powerful, more comprehensive complex of spatial gestures.

I would like to finish with a brief look at the broader implications and relevance of the arguments I have developed here. The concepts of "culture" and "tradition" are useful heuristic devices that have been profoundly compromised by their reification (Clifford, 1988, pp. 9–11), especially in Orientalist discourse (Inden, 1990). Yet in the same spirit it would also be erroneous to imagine that they are therefore compromised in essence, and must be tossed out like an idol that failed to deliver prayed-for goods. Tamil culture may be no-thing, but it can be an efficient way of indicating articulated bundles of coded practices that generate distinctive physical traces—the stuff of history—in the forms of architecture, speech, writing, dress, food, or everyday etiquette. Relations of space, time, and person are all embedded in the formal properties of these codes. They are used pragmatically to construct frames, values, meanings, and define a body of resources for making a poem, a temple, or sense to your neighbors. While they may sometimes be addressed explicitly, as in the case of the *śilpa-śāstras* or the *Tolkāppiyam,* more often they simply "go without saying" to the extent that they are already presupposed by the formal distinctions offered by the code itself.

These articulated codes can be understood to constitute something like a "symbol pool" (Cohn 1987) defined, much as Derrida suggests above, by constructed centers rather than by hard, naturalized boundaries. Like Tamil temples, these pools have changed and expanded over time, partly through adapting resources acquired from elsewhere. But also like the temple, they necessarily change in relation to a local background of habit, repetition, and continuity. South Indian centers have never been static, and yet they have been relatively enduring when compared to their peripheries. Without a continuous background of disciplined, self-organizing reproduction—in local conceptions, a Mother—it is more easily possible to imagine the course of historical change in Tamilnadu drifting toward a decentered, unbalanced, unsustainable order, driven by alternative value frames that celebrate, for instance, entrepreneurial risk, individualistic independence, fetishized novelty, forced change, and insatiable desires. There is ultimately nothing essential in Tamil culture, thus nothing that would prevent such value frames from taking hold, and traces of them do appear in limited, context-sensitive practices, such as in the marketing of commodities. Nevertheless, there are sacred centers similar to Madurai throughout Tamilnadu, enveloped by interrelated architectural, behavioral, and conceptual sheaths that pose formidable obstacles to their wholesale adoption.

Notes

All photos by Prithwish Neogy. (Collection of Samuel K. Parker)

1. The *vāstu-śāstras, śilpa-śāstras,* and *āgama-śāstras* are collections of received knowledge and authority bearing on temple construction. They typically present a three-fold classification of temples: *Nāgara* ("of the city") is conventionally used to refer to North Indian temple types, *Drāviḍa* is used to refer to the temple types of *Drāviḍadeśa* or South India, and *Vesara* ("mule") is ambiguously used to signify a mixture of categories. Kramrisch (1946, pp. 286–295) provides a summary of the textual uses of these categories in conceptual and geographic terms. Based on narrowly read textual evidence, Dagens argues that such uses are an "unjustifiable pseudogeographical" interpretation of the terminology (1984, p. 94), and yet the evidence of living practice indicates that the geographical basis of this classification is considered to be self-evident among specialists in the field. Tamil architects and sculptors routinely refer to all three, and yet none of my informants was ever able to cite a specific example of a *Vesara* temple. At best I was told that *Vesara* temples were made in Karnataka. And indeed, in Karnataka and Maharashtra there are many temple styles that are neither clearly *Nāgara* or *Drāviḍa*. Occasionally a *sthapati* would offer the observation that *Nāgara* means square, *Drāviḍa* means octagonal, and *Vesara* means circular. This three-fold classification of

geometric elements does occur in the written *śāstras* along with other analogously tripartite divisions, but in general *Vesara* seems to be an ill-defined category of little practical relevance to contemporary Tamil temple builders.

2. "Architect" here is used as an approximate English equivalent of the term *stapati* or *sthapati*. The semantic range of the latter term is culturally distinct and much broader in reference. "Image maker" is here used as a rough equivalent of the term *śilpi* or *ciṟpi*. See Parker (1989) for a detailed discussion of these terms.
3. Here I refer to temple construction itself as a mode of ritualized sacrifice conducted by architects and sculptors, yielding empowered physical remnants much in the same way that Brahman ritual yields sacred ash and blessed consumables. In his *Tamil Temple Myths,* David Shulman similarly reveals consistent sacrificial themes underlying typical temple origin stories. Literary, architectural, and sculptural practices can be seen to encode, in their respective media, an understanding of the temple as an objectification of sacrificial action.
4. Some of the senses of *svayambhū* can also encompass such historical contingencies.
5. The tallest such gateway in India, 237 feet in height, was completed at Srirangam in 1987 (see Parker, 1992).
6. Jouveau-Dubreuil explained the history of the Dravidian style in evolutionary terms without the negative judgments implied by some later writers. He described that history as "the path of natural evolution," made possible by the isolation of South India from foreign influences (1917, pp. 3–4). I suspect that few people today would grant that South India was really ever isolated from the rest of the world between the later centuries of Cōḻa dominance and the arrival of the Europeans. More importantly, however, it is necessary to acknowledge this history to be a product of *particular* human values, choices, and agency, and not just a vague force metaphorically imagined as "natural evolution."
7. Michell also endorses Brown's theory of the defensive functions of the *prākāram* walls (Michell, 1977, p. 150).
8. *Vāhanas* are vehicles. While chariots and palanquins are *vāhanas,* the term is typically used to refer to large teak sculptures of natural or imaginary creatures—horses, snakes, peacocks, *yāḷis,* and so on—associated with the mythology of the deity who rides on its back in the festival.
9. The term "hypaethral" usually refers to a type of Greek shrine that is open to the elements. Kramrisch uses it here to refer to simple shrines represented in ancient South Asian relief sculpture representing the object of devotion surrounded by a fence or a building that is open to the sky (to accommodate a growing tree, for instance).
10. This is an extreme and obvious example of some of the problematic metaphors and metaphyscial presuppositions built into Western imaginings of India generally. Inden (1990) critically explores this avenue in depth.
11. In the course of my fieldwork, several Tamil temple architects explained the term *gopuram* to me by way of the Tamil etymology. *Go* and *kō* are perceived as being interchangeable, since "g" and "k" are represented by a single letter in the Tamil alphabet. While scholars almost unanimously recognize the Tamil *gopuram* as derived from the Sanskrit *gopuram,* J. Filliozat (1959) accepts the *go-* part as the Tamil *kō-* or "lord," but is unable to account for the *–puram* except with reference to a Sanskrit origin.

12. The DMK party headquarters in Madras, for instance, rhetorically deploys an ancient *Drāviḍa* architectural idiom. Many of the Tamil temple architects and sculptors I interviewed were fervent DMK partisans because, as I was repeatedly reminded, the DMK is a strong supporter of traditional Dravidian art forms and encourages them to take pride in their distinctive Tamil heritage.
13. E. V. Daniel has documented a formal rule in Tamil house construction that he calls the "rule of incompletion" (1984, pp. 131–135). While Tamil temple architects invariably reject the notion that such a rule is overtly followed in temple construction, they generally will admit that the temple is designed to keep on growing so long as resources are available. Rich temples like the one at Tirupati have many ongoing architectural projects, while poor temples tend to disintegrate until one or more motivated patron(s) step forward to organize a renovation.
14. Popular opinion among living *sthapatis* about what the *śāstras* say is often (some might say usually) impossible to verify with reference to any known text. Written versions of the *śāstras* do prescribe that the *provisional* shrine built for use during temple renovation should not be used longer than twelve years (Dagens, 1984, p. 36; 1985, p. 341), but I know of no text that recommends that the temples themselves should be renovated every twelve years.
15. See, for example, B. V. Raman's popular primer on Hindu astrology *Astrology for Beginners* (1976, p. 6) for a characterization of Jupiter's qualities.
16. They also usually contain small stairways that lead to finials on the roof that require periodic reconsecration. Increasingly smaller replicas of the main passageway are located at the center of each story (*tala*). These allow some light into the stairway.
17. In response to questions about ugliness in temple architecture, *sthapatis* and *śilpis* commonly cited dull colors, dark stains, and various signs of weathering and decay.
18. Their standard argument is that *gopurams* serve as the primary objects of devotion for impure castes who are not allowed into the temple. Even though the law now permits access for Hindus of all castes, foreigners, Muslims, and Christians can still be legally excluded, and access to the sanctum itself is still denied to all but the priests.
19. Although it is usually a sexual intimacy, if the temple is dedicated to Kālī, Durgā, or another aspect of what Shulman calls the "black" side of the goddess, that male/female intimacy may be realized in signs of eroticized blood and death. It is the "golden" side of the goddess's eroticism and power that is realized in signs of birth, growth, and prosperity (Shulman, 1980).
20. As Daniel notes, metaphor and metonymy can be misleading terms in Tamil contexts. The boundaries between tropes and literal references are neither sharp nor consistent (1984, p. 107).
21. *Puruṣa* ("man," or more specifically, the primal code-man of the Vedas whose sacrifice transforms an original unity into differentiated structures) and *Vāstupuruṣa* ("man of the site") are commonly imagined as male, and represented in architectural practice in the form of abstract, underlying geometrical and proportional relationships. However, "Bhūdevī," and specifically the local, named goddess, constitutes the actual substance of the site, and of the temple too, which bears within it a *garbha-gṛha,* or "womb house," of the gods. Here I am stressing

the feminine side because I am making a point about the concrete aesthetics of the Dravidian temple, rather than the abstract, metrical structures imposed onto *prakṛti* (nature, substance) through the *puruṣa* concept.

22. But as Raheja (1988) has amply demonstrated, hierarchy based on a distinction of pure/impure (vs. raw power) is not the only, or even primary, dimension of South Asian social order, as it was argued by Dumont (1970). Depending on context, identities are valorized by alternative relations of mutuality and centrality (much as they do in the spatial and ritual organization of South Indian temples). Tamil temple construction generally operates in a manner quite similar to the North Indian village Jajmani system described by Raheja, except that it is a more temporary set of alignments that enable the Viśvakarmā artists to replicate their cherished self-constructions, especially vis-à-vis the *yajamāna,* as self-sufficient and whole (*viśva*).

SEVEN

From Wasteland to Bus Stand

The Relocation of Demons in Tamilnadu

Isabelle Clark-Decès

The propensity for women to predominate in spirit possession cults has been a continuing focus of anthropological discussion ever since I. M. Lewis (1971) offered a cross-cultural explanation of female participation in what he called "peripheral possession." Lewis argued that what was commonly considered a form of illness caused by amoral spirits afforded women and other marginal or subordinate individuals a safe outlet for protesting their "status deprivation" (1966, 1971, 1986).

Janice Boddy has pointed out that "this model and its assumptions guided a generation of scholarship" and was applied to many parts of the world (1994, p. 410). Following Lewis, some anthropologists have interpreted the propensity for new brides in North India to be afflicted with what is often labeled as "ghost-possession" (Freed and Freed, 1993) as calculated maneuvers to obtain redress within the Hindu patriarchal order (Freed and Freed, 1964; Harper, 1963; Kakar, 1982; but see Skultans, 1987). They propose, for instance, that exorcisms are perfect opportunities for Indian wives to resist, with little inhibition, their powerless role in their new families. This is possible because whatever outlandish rights the women demand during these curing rites can be imputed to their spirits. Christopher Fuller recently endorsed this argument: "It is clear . . . that women's possession episodes are also culturally tolerated opportunities to complain about female inferiority and subordination within Indian society" (1992, p. 233). And in her research on the Mukkuvars, a Catholic fishing people living in Kanyakumari District,

Kalpana Ram argues that demonic possession enables women to reinterpret "dominant" symbolic constructs of the female body and sexuality and "to challenge the daily discipline of living within the confines of respectable femininity" (1991, p. 93).

Based on exorcism rituals that I documented on twenty-four separate occasions in the South Arcot district of Tamilnadu in 1990–1991, this essay casts doubt on the widespread explanation that a major function of Hindu "ghosts"—known in Tamil as *pēys*—is to express women's dissatisfaction with husbands and in-laws or general cultural evaluations of female roles. That analysis may have the virtue of translating exotic beliefs and puzzling practices into terms that are accessible and even ethically pleasing to us. But my Tamil consultants never corroborated this, and it seems at variance from what comes to light through a closer analysis of the exorcism's symbols and ritual processes.

Nor does my research on Tamil exorcisms fall in line with the three alternative interpretations of female demonic possession that have stemmed from the ethnography of nearby Sri Lanka. The first, proposed by Bruce Kapferer, argues that "women . . . are subject to demonic attack as a function of their cultural typification, which places them in a special and significant relation to the demonic" (1991, p. 128). For example, Sinhalese women take part in polluting activities such as cooking, funerals, menstruation, and childbirth, which expose them to impure and potentially malevolent forces. They also attract demons because they are viewed and view themselves as sharing certain personality traits with them. Much like demons, women are more prone to "emotional disturbance and excess, attachment to persons and relationships born of this world, [and are seen] as being more engaged in the pursuit of worldly desires, and as being mentally weak" (1991, p. 140). And finally, to Kapferer the mediating position of women between the Sinhalese Buddhist poles of nature and culture makes them structurally "weak and vulnerable to disorder" (1991, p. 147).

At first blush, much of Kapferer's reasoning seems consonant with the explanations of my Tamil consultants. Both women and men agreed that women were more susceptible to being "caught" by demons because of an inherent weakness that was attributed to their ascribed impurity, as it was pointed out that women especially got "caught" by demons while menstruating (also see Bharati, 1993, p. 342; Caplan, 1989, p. 55, Mosse, 1986, p. 474). And it was also said that women were mentally and emotionally deficient and more susceptible to the fear (*payam*) that in South Asia strips the self of protection against malevolent powers (Caplan, 1989, p. 55; Kapferer, 1991, p. 71; Scott, 1991, p. 96; Trawick, 1990, p. 190).

But the argument that cultural representations of women predispose them to be possessed fails to explain why, at least in Tamilnadu, it is not women as a whole but predominantly new brides who are most at risk. Of all my cases of demonic possession, twenty involved women who had married within the past six years (also see Mosse, 1986, p. 473). Such statistics might be understood by invoking the Tamil belief that "the odour of sexual activity . . . [is] said to be particularly strong and attractive to demons in the period immediately after marriage" (Ram, 1991, p. 90). But these emic representations still would not explain why, in my sample of twenty young brides so afflicted, sixteen had run away from their husbands. It is true that here, too, Tamils have a ready-made interpretation. From their perspective, the spirits known as *pēys* indisputably cause the gravest psychic disorders, inducing their married victims to reject their spouses. But to formulate an explanation of why women do get possessed solely based on such beliefs runs the risk of making us blind to the social practices and ritual processes that actually enact this discourse. And when we link such representations and actions to the lives of the women in question, we discover a deeper layer of causes and agendas.

The second major researcher on demonic possession in Sri Lanka, Gananath Obeysekere, addresses precisely this question of the relationship between culture and individuals. His basic premise is that demons in any society belong to a particular class of cultural symbols that are invested with subjective significance in order to articulate psychological conflicts (1981). From his perspective, demonic possession is a culturally constituted idiom available to women for appropriately expressing and managing their personal problems (1970; 1977).

At least the argument has the merit of presenting culture as created and recreated through individual agency (Stirrat, 1992, p. 111). Yet my research on Tamil demonic possession does not suggest that the production of culture is such a wide-open, creative endeavor. As we will soon see, Tamil women are taught, even pressured, to frame their personal predicaments within the idiom of demonic possession.

Indeed, my research stands closer to that of R. L. Stirrat, the third major ethnographer of demonic possession in Sri Lanka. At Kudagama, a Sinhalese Catholic shrine that specializes in exorcism, he has noted that demonic possession is "primarily concerned with attempts to impose power over others, particularly young women" (1992, p. 112). This conclusion was based on the fact that the individuals who were defined as possessed often exhibited not merely symptoms of physiological illness but a "whole series of problems" that included "odd behaviour" and "irresponsible sexual attraction" (1992, pp. 112–113; 1977, p. 138). To Stirrat, the diagnosis of demonic possession and its subsequent exorcism allowed close relatives of the possessed person to reassert their authority within the domestic unit.

In what follows we will see how Tamil exorcist rituals force women to talk about their distress through metaphors and symbols that legitimize the control of those in authority. However, the field of power relations evoked by this ritual appears less broad than what Stirrat reports from Sri Lanka. For at the core of Tamil demonic possession is control over the women's marital sexuality. Here is a discourse that charges women with succumbing to disenchantment with conjugal life, surrendering to fantasies of extramarital intimacy, and hence jeopardizing their husbands' reproductivity. I will argue that it is the function of these Tamil exorcisms to force women to repudiate this behavior publicly and to recommit themselves to the cultural expectations of a "good wife" (*cumaṅkali*).

On *Pēys* and Their Environment

The term *pēy* is derived from the Sanskrit word *preta,* "departed." It refers to spirits of human beings who, from the actual moment of death until they are ritually enabled to join their ancestors in the other world ten or sixteen days later, remain in limbo, neither members of the society of the living nor that of the dead (Reiniche, 1975, p. 182; Blackburn, 1988, p. 217). But throughout Tamilnadu the word *pēy* usually characterizes the spirits of people who remain indefinitely in this liminal state because they met an "untimely" (*akāla-maraṇam*) death, the inauspicious (*turmaraṇam*) fate that prevented their transit into the hereafter (also see Caplan, 1989).[1] The German Lutheran missionary Bartholomaeus Ziegenbalg was not mistaken when he wrote in 1713 that "those men who die by their own hands" are particularly prone to become "evil spirits, called *Peygel*" (1984, p. 152). Of those demons I tape-recorded during exorcist rituals, one had been murdered, six spoke of bus or train collisions, but fifteen, the majority, told of hanging or drowning themselves. Equally interesting was the fact that virtually *all* of the suicides had suffered from what my field assistant referred to in English as "love failure." These *pēys* had apparently taken their own lives due to an unrequited passion or because relatives had opposed their marriage plans.

Stranded in this world, their limbo-like time on earth after death *remained* dominated by an unrelenting yearning to fulfill their frustrated desires for sexual intimacy. This appeared to be their driving obsession, and this was why they stalked and "caught" (*piṭi*) the living. *Pēys* do not seem to be compelled to possess people, as the missionary Robert Caldwell (1984) believed, because of their "hatred of the human race," nor as Lionel Caplan put it, out of "anger" (1989, p. 55). All my consultants, specialists, laypeople, and *the spirits themselves* were unanimous in their conviction that *pēys* were motivated by "love" (*aṉpu*) and "lust" (*ācai*),[2] an understanding that resonates with one of Wendy Doniger's key points about Hindu mythology in general. "The origin of evil," she writes, " is inextricably associated with the appearance of sexual desire" (1976, p. 212).

While twenty-two out of the twenty-four *pēys* I encountered were male, the reason for inactivity on the part of female untimely dead seemed patently obvious to my consultants: "They are too shy to catch people." Furthermore, I was told, women had the power of self-control; after death they behaved with the same degree of modesty that guided their conduct when they were alive.[3] Since the *pēys* were predominantly young males and known to be craving for intimacy, it could only be young women who stood out as their favored prey.

Symbols of sexual passion were also strongly suggested in my consultants' descriptions of the landscape in which the *pēys* carried out their attacks. When I heard that *pēys* continued to hover around the places of their deaths, I asked for topographical specifics and was told that these spirits had perished in inauspicious haunts, in a zone that people characterized as *taricu nilam* or the "wasteland" (also called *kāṭu,* "forest"). Rarely was this landscape given any more specific identification, for it was said that such "fallow" and "dry" land could be found anywhere, but definitively beyond the periphery of the settled community (also see Caplan, 1989, p. 55; Mosse, 1986, p. 471). Here one is reminded that in 1849 the Reverend Caldwell noted that the Nadars of Tinnevelly District believed that their *pēys* also occupied "uninhabited wastes" and "shady retreats" (1984, p. 163; also see Dumont, 1986, p. 341). The association of these spirits with wilderness perhaps clarifies why the term *pēy,* as Gustav Oppert discerned in 1893, can also be glossed as "wild or obnoxious plants" (1893, p. 559, in Caplan, 1989, p. 53).

Sometimes this forbidding territory was depicted with imagery symbolic of the demon's untimely death, such as pools of stagnant water where he had originally drowned, or a tamarind tree from whose spreading branches he hung himself. The hardy tamarind tree has natural and cultural properties that make it especially compatible with such an unseasonable landscape, for it seems to thrive even during severe droughts, and is classified in Tamil folk taxonomy as "sour" and "inauspicious."

So it was within *this* desolate landscape that virtually all my consultants imagined the *pēys* to launch their attacks on the living. They also concurred that the timing of their aggression was precisely at high noon when there is maximum heat and maximum light. That was when their victims were usually traveling "alone" outside their community; or as I heard more than once, "The girl gets *caught* on her way to the fields" (also see Dumont, 1986, p. 451).[4]

These spatial and temporal images invoked when speaking of *pēy* aggression appear to derive from Tamil aesthetic conventions of considerable antiquity. I refer to the middle of the five categories of landscape described in Tamil love (*akam*) poetry, compiled between the first and third centuries C. E. (Hart, 1979; Pillai and Ludden, 1976; Ramanujan, 1967). Named *pālai* after the ironwood tree characteristic of this arid country, this middle landscape was glossed as "wasteland." To evoke its barrenness, the classical Tamil poets used such phrases as "dried springs" and "stagnant water" (Ramanujan, 1967, p. 105). Even the key metaphor for this landscape, the *pālai,* a leafy tree with the same characteristics of the tamarind, was aptly chosen, for, as A. K. Ramanujan has pointed out, it was "unaffected by drought" (1967, p. 105). The poets also positioned this "wasteland" in a specific temporal setting: its climate was said to correspond to the peak of seasonal and daily heat, that is, during midsummer at high noon (Pillai and Ludden, 1976, p. 18).

These formulaic references to landscape functioned to intensify emotional descriptions, particularly to evoke a phase, or *uri,* in the development of love between a man and a woman (Cutler, 1987, p. 84, 91n; Hart, 1979, p. 5; Pillai and Ludden, 1976; Ramanujan, 1967, p. 105; Sopher, 1986, pp. 6–7). In the classificatory system of *akam* poetry, this *pālai* or "wasteland" landscape specifically evoked the time of their "separation" and, according to Ramanujan, connoted "the hardships of the lover away from his girl, but also the elopement of the couple, their hardships on the way and their separation from their parents" (1967, p. 106; also see Richman, 1988, pp. 62–78).

Transposed to the equivalent landscape of *pēy* aggression detailed by my consultants, commensurate meanings seem to prevail. When describing the typical scenario of a *pēy* attack, exorcists and laypeople alike overlaid it with seductive connotations and emphasized how gorgeous the victim was looking at the time. Thus the initial contact of demons with their prey was strongly visual and erotic: in broad daylight the *pēy* could clearly see the girl's beautiful skin daubed with turmeric paste and vermilion powder, her hair dressed with flowers.[5]

Once seduced by her allure, in a lonely place, the demon "touched" her. Startled, the woman grew "fearful," an emotional state that in South Asia, as noted above, has serious consequences, for it leaves the self open to malevolent forces. And so the demon was able to "catch" his girl and, according to my consultants, did so by "sitting" on her head, the locus of sanity, driving her half-crazy before "entering" her body through a lock of hair.

Much like the lovers in *akam* poetry, the demon-*pēy* then eloped with "his girl," forcing her to separate mentally and physically from her community, especially from her husband. For it is well understood that *pēys* not only sexually enjoy their victims but also prevent normal conjugal sexual relations, inciting wives to "kick" and "bite" their legitimate husbands to keep them at bay. And since a woman's liaison with a *pēy* is also said to make her barren, the husband is deprived not only of legitimate control over his wife's sexuality, but of her fertility as well. Thus if the couple is ever to resume a "normal" life again, it is absolutely necessary to conduct the ritual that "makes the spirit run away" (*pēy ōṭṭutal*).

How Shanti Got "Caught"

Here I must stress that in actual daily life, the production of a cultural symbol like the *pēy* is never as simple or straightforward as the above synthesis from dozens of ethnographic interviews might suggest. In fact, when we turn to the personal histories of women involved in Tamil demonic possession, we discover that the creation of such a symbol almost always depends on the specifics of family, marital tensions, and women's biographies. To illustrate how crucial these social and psychological dynamics are to the making of the *pēy,* I will relate the story of Shanti.

Shanti was a frail, high-caste Mutaliyār woman in her early twenties who grew up in a village near the town of Salem. When she was four years old, her father left home to start a new family with his second wife. The sole offspring from this first marriage, she was raised by her mother and paternal grandmother. At age seventeen, while attending the wedding of a relative, her soft, attractive looks caught the attention of a widower who was fifteen years her senior. Upon proposing marriage he met no opposition. As Shanti told me, "He did not ask much in terms of a dowry. My mother was poor. As for my father, he was relieved to give me away, for he was saving for the marriage of his two younger daughters."

After her wedding, Shanti moved to Madras where her husband worked as a government clerk. She described the misery that followed: "He would come home drunk, irritable, quarreling over any small thing. I cried every night. Tears would flow and there was no stopping them." Eight months later Shanti ran away. Back in her village she resumed her old job in a puffed-rice factory. But when her mother died six months later, Shanti's father sent her back to her husband in Madras, where life was little better than before. But she did make a few friends and began "to go to the movies." It was around then that she first experienced her mood swings. "One day I would be drowsy and could not bring myself to get up. Yet the next morning I would be giddy and restless." She rejected her husband's sexual overtures and soon they were no longer speaking. She became increasingly withdrawn, lost her appetite, and, most critically, she "lost interest in life." Alarmed by her physical deterioration and sullen disposition, her mother's younger sister took Shanti to a suburb of the city for a consultation with a diviner. His trance-diagnosis attributed Shanti's trouble to a *pēy*.

The sequence of events, which led to a determination that Shanti was possessed, was typical of all my other cases as well, and followed the pattern noted by Stirrat in Sri Lanka (1992, 1977). "First," as he writes, "there is some sort of abnormal behaviour" (1992, p. 104). In Tamilnadu the women also behaved in a way that struck their kin as being odd or inappropriate; they were withdrawn, apathetic, anemic, aggressive, incoherent, and barren (also see Dumont, 1986, p. 450), and, like Shanti, often refused to have sexual intercourse with their husbands and fled from their sight. Such behaviors immediately indexed to *pēys* precipitated what Stirrat calls "suspicions of possession" by close relatives, usually parents but also siblings, spouses, and in-laws (1992, p. 105).

At this point the women sometimes confirmed these suspicions, spontaneously entering a state of trance, "dancing" like demons, and even speaking from their perspective. But since few *pēys* were bold enough to entrance their victims, their influence was only expressed through the symptoms already cited (also see Stirrat, 1992, p. 101). The next step then was to seek out a diviner (either male or female) who generally verified that they were indeed under a demon's sway. Usually the women seemed to meet this explanation with passivity or resignation. Whether or not they fully understood the ramifications of this diagnosis, from that point on they were forced to think of their distress within the context of demonic possession.

Now their relatives began ceaselessly to conjecture how, when, and where their possession had to have taken place. But their joint construction of this scenario was not formulated in a vacuum; it drew on well-established collective representations. As David Mosse observed among Christian communities of Ramnad District, I noted how the basic plot of these retrospective accounts typically included the identification of "some pre-existing condition of vulnerability to demonic attack" and the "frightening incident" that resulted (1986, p. 473). For instance, people told me how a possession must have happened on such and such day when the woman was sent alone to fetch firewood outside the village. Or the attack was traced back to the week of her last heavy menstruation. Or it was said to have occurred on that day when she returned from the nearby town, with a "shaken" or "startled" expression on her face. Such hypotheses were then shared with neighbors who contributed their own details to the scenario.

As Stirrat also observed in Sri Lanka (1992), activities leading up to the exorcism ritual helped to enforce upon these women the reality of their possession. Many were prescribed to stay a minimum of ten days at the particular shrine where they would undergo the ritual (also see Mosse, 1986, p. 479). There they were made to fast and circumambulate the temple 108 times a day in order to "purify their bodies and heart." Some were whipped with freshly cut margosa leaves, a plant invested with the essence of the goddess, to ward off the *pēy*. Relatives accompanying them anxiously consulted exorcists who offered advice and additional information on the demons and the upcoming ritual. In short, from the moment a woman was diagnosed with possession she was "caught" in an encompassing discourse. In this process, then, her demon was constructed and the exorcism rite only furthered that objectification.

The Ritual of "Making the Demon Run Away" (*Pēy Oṭṭutal*)

To the best of my knowledge, the ritual that exorcises the untimely dead has received scant treatment in the ethnographic literature on South India.[6] The only general reference that I have uncovered is that of Caplan, who writes that in Tamilnadu "[t]here are several different types of Hindu specialists using a variety of ritual techniques to deal with possessory *peey*" (1989, p. 66). "Among the most common," he goes on, "is the 'god-dancer' (*samiadi*), a shaman-like figure who becomes a medium for the Goddess, who then drives out the *peey* either by appeasing it with a sacrifice or threatening it with her superior power, or both" (ibid., citing Moffat, 1979, pp. 241–242).

Those specialists who regularly embody and "dance" Hindu goddesses—deities such as Kālī and Aṅkāḷaparamēcuvari, who are known throughout South India to combat the forces of evil—are undoubtedly the prototypical exorcists in Tamilnadu. But here I will introduce another neglected category of healers, for in South Arcot District at least, troupes of male ritual musicians known as *pampaikkārar* are also empowered to drive demons out.[7]

The structure of their exorcist operations clearly differs from that of the mediums whom Caplan describes, for these musicians never "dance" the Goddess. Instead, they sing and beat percussive instruments in order to induce the possessed woman into a state of trance. Her "dance" (*āṭṭam*) then dissolves the normal boundaries that prevail between supernaturals and human beings, providing the musicians with direct verbal communication with her possessing demon.

All the exorcisms of this type that I recorded were invariably carried out on new moon days on the funeral grounds immediately adjacent to the Aṅkāḷaparamēcuvari temple in the South Arcot town of Mēlmalaiyaṉūr.[8] This site is where this goddess is said to have cured Lord Śiva of his madness on the same lunar juncture. Much like the Mahanubhav temple studied by V. Skultans in the state of Maharashtra, this divine precedent for a therapy of madness has turned the Malaiyaṉūr temple into a "healing centre . . . for spiritual afflictions, in particular, those which give rise to mental illness" (1987, p. 663). Since this is the identical disorder that besets the women "caught" by *pēys,* this highly popular shrine is especially well suited for the performance of exorcisms.

Whenever they are contracted to expel possessing *pēys,* the Mēlmalaiyaṉūr musicians hold a preliminary invocation at the entrance of the Aṅkāḷaparamēcuvari temple that seeks to notify or, more exactly, "to warn" (*ecciri*) the demon of what is coming. They alert the targeted *pēy* to "meet" them later in the day on the temple funeral ground. Usually the *pēy* then immediately responds to the drumbeats by "dancing" his willingness to cooperate; speaking through his victim's mouth, he promises to show up on condition that he is given a "life" (*uyir*) or a sacrifice. At the conclusion of this "warning," the woman usually drops in a faint on the ground. Then the musicians have her relatives purchase offerings that *pēys* are known to relish—puffed rice, cigars, arrack, toddy, bread, cooked rice, dried fish, and the chicken to be sacrificed.

At the appointed place and time, the actual exorcism begins with a delimitation of the ritual confines. Drawing a circle on the ground, the musicians position the woman in the center, facing east. The idea is to "tie down" her possessing demon, for as one of these specialists emphasized, "once inside this circle the *pēy* cannot escape." With the family and onlookers standing watchfully behind them, the musicians split into two groups, framing the enclosure with the young woman inside.

After securing divine "protection" (*kāppu*) through a formulaic invocation to both the great Hindu gods and key deities of the local pantheon, the lead singer then throws all his vocal energy and talent into inducing the woman into a state of trance in order to debrief her demon. First and foremost, he must establish the exact identity of this unwelcome personality now lodged within a female body. For we must never forget that, as Obeysekere has documented in Sri Lanka, these spirits are "a known *category,* but they are not known beings" (1981, p. 115, emphasis in original). So the singer begins his real work by cajoling from the demon his name, gender, ancestral village, caste membership, age, marital status, number of children, and the ominous circumstances of what Tamils call the "bad death" that left him or her wandering this earth in a state of unfulfillment and yearning (also see Mosse, 1986, p. 479):

> "Whether you are king, minister, or governor (*turaicāmi*),"[9] he may sing, addressing the *pēy* directly and using a mockingly exaggerated tone of deference, "open your golden mouth and please speak up. Where did you catch her? Dance and tell me your name, we have removed the gag over your mouth. Please speak up!"

Often the musicians must play for many tiring hours before achieving contact with the *pēy*. No matter how many compliments, sermons, or threats they issued, I observed that spirits are in no hurry to speak or dance. Meanwhile, the women usually stand awkwardly, hands clasped and eyes downcast. These behaviors are striking in light of the fact that all those women had "danced" quickly and satisfactorily at the "warning" previously held in the temple. Perhaps this is because that moment had only formulaic value, for when the *pēys* revealed that they wanted "life," the demand required little psychological effort; that is what they invariably want. By contrast, now the *pēy* is expected to reveal its true and unique identity, a confession that entails a complex investment from the part of the "possessed" woman.

But at this point there is no going back. As Stirrat notes at Kudagama in Sri Lanka, "[o]nce defined as possessed . . . the subject has little alternative but to go through the rituals of the shrine" (1992, p. 106). For the woman who is brought to Mēlmalaiyaṉūr to be exorcised similarly is also "exposed to extreme forms of pressure" (Stirrat, 1992, p. 105; also see 1977, pp. 140–141); surrounded by the five musicians who closely monitor all her movements, she is incessantly and aggressively urged to dance and speak. To accelerate her entrancement, she is instructed to stare at a burning camphor flame. Lime juice is frequently squeezed around her face and upper body, for, as I was told, "The lime contains the essence of the goddess; it scares the *pēy* and makes it speak." As Mosse observed at a healing Christian shrine in Ramnad, if these procedures are of no avail, there is "an escalation of verbal abuse and physical violence directed at the *pēy*" (1986, p. 479).

Finally the woman may be subjected to outside pressure as well, for not infrequently the drums of the musicians will induce nearby devotees to "dance" the goddess. These dancers then wend toward the exorcist scene, asserting the divine authority of their embodied goddess over the demon by grabbing the woman by the hair, pulling her on the ground, and attempting to beat the *pēy* out of her body.

As the woman eventually begins to sway and roll her head from side to side, the musicians immediately close in and quicken their cadence. Her gyrations accelerate; her braid loosens so that her hair swings wildly in the air. Now that she is fully entranced, the singer may begin to interrogate her *pēy*. Here I will offer a sample from the ritual exchange that took place between Shanti's demon and the Mēlmalaiyaṉūr musicians in mid-July 1991.

> Halting the music, the singer addressed the spirit in everyday speech.
>
> "WHO ARE YOU?"
>
> "I don't know," answered the *pēy,* speaking through the mouth of Shanti. But the singer was relentless.

"WHO ARE YOU? Male or female?"

At "male," the *pēy* nodded timidly. But the musician insisted upon a verbal response.

"Male or female?" he repeated.

"Male."

"What is your name?"

When the spirit gave no reply, the musician seemed undiscouraged, but shifted to a more humorous register.

"At least you could say *something,* 'Donkey,' for instance!"

Laughter came from the gathering cluster of onlookers. As if setting aside that crucial identity question for the moment, the singer then ventured the second most common query even a foreigner to Tamilnadu hears regarding identity:

"What is your *ancestral home* (*conta ūr*)?"

"I am from Tiruppūr."

"Where is that?"

"Near Salem."

"And your caste?"

"Why do you care?"

"How old are you?"

"Twenty-two."

Suddenly, the singer threw the central question back at the spirit, as if trying to catch it unawares:

"What is your name?"

"I don't know. Please leave me alone!"

"WHAT IS YOUR NAME?"

"I don't know, I'm from Tiruppūr."

Again the musician confronted the spirit head on, only now trying a different line of questioning:

"How did you die?"

"I hanged myself."

"On what kind of tree?"

"A tamarind."

"Why did you hang yourself?"

"They did not want me to marry."

"So you died. But you must have had a name. What was it?"

"Yes, they gave me a name. But I don't know it."

"Come on, the people here will thrash you. Tell me your name and I'll arrange a proper funeral marriage (*karumātikkalyāṇam*)."

"Will you arrange for my marriage?"

"Yes, I promise."
"My name is Shankar."

To that critical question of his name, this spirit first pleaded ignorance, and this was not surprising. All *pēys* whose testimonies I recorded initially swore that they did not know who they were. But, as we just heard, biographical details and even the names do eventually emerge over the course of the incessant interrogation.

Yet after examining a number of my transcripts, it slowly dawned on me that the *pēys* seemed actually to be constructing their self-identity by patching together vital statistics from their victims' lives. In this case they shared similar ages (23/22), places of origin (two villages near the town of Salem), and almost identical names (Shanti/Shankar).[10] Upon close analysis of two dozen *pēy* testimonies, I was also struck by how often the existential predicament that led most *pēys* to commit suicide was strongly reminiscent of their victims' own lives. In the case at hand, we must recall that Shanti's family, much like that of her spirit, had failed to arrange her marriage. As she told me, her father did not want to pay for her dowry and so she had been hastily wed to the first suitor who made no financial demand. Other women, much like their *pēys,* had been prevented from marrying sweethearts or were mistreated by their spouses.

From one perspective, then, it would appear that the interrogation does offer women a language with which to talk about themselves. And since the *pēys* are encouraged to speak about their personal problems, the dialogue would seem to enable women to talk indirectly about their own distress. But it would be erroneous, I think, to see in this process either an unconscious expression of feminine protest or a therapy in any Western sense of freeing the self from past, lived experiences. It is true that this ritual seems an expression of the Western therapeutic proposition that recalling a traumatic autobiographical memory to an attentive, well-meaning audience can help people recover certain genuine aspects of their identity (Csordas, 1996). For I noticed that it was precisely when the *pēys* recaptured what must have been the most troubling stage of their lives (the cause of their suicide) and were offered a way out of their misery that the women seemed to complete their own identification with them. It was only then that the spirits (like Shankar) usually named themselves, and when women, like Shanti, could be said to have "found themselves" in their demons. But in this exorcist context women were not exactly free to exorcise their past through free associations. Instead the formulaic interrogation required them to articulate a sense of self mandated to be consistent with what is culturally known of the *pēys*. Since *pēys* are known to be predominantly male malcontents with loose libidos, women end up only able to speak of themselves through symbols of masculine, frustrated sexuality. Now we can understand why this process does not occur without a drawn-out trial: women are slow to "dance" because they are resisting taking on this personality of a sex-driven man.

Once the musician-exorcist has successfully elicited the *pēy's* name, it becomes vital to find out precisely where and when he caught his victim. At this point, the demons always contradicted the testimonies of my consultants. They always recalled that their attacks had actually occurred *not* in any of the traditional wasteland landscapes I have described, but in the heart of large urban centers. When I asked about this shift to modern sites for *pēy* malevolence, an exorcist replied that, to be sure, times had changed. "In the cities," he explained, " there are more crimes, more suicides, and therefore more *pēys*."

Nine such spirits whom I tape-recorded confirmed Caplan's observation that within a city like Madras the *pēys* concentrated "near trees and wells, cemeteries . . . and railway tracks" (1989, p. 55). But twelve others announced that they had indeed "caught" their victims on the road to movie theaters, by the public bus stand, or even *on* the bus. Yet these new landscapes for demonic attack still remained associated with anonymous, threatening zones, for they were always away from the security of home, family, and clear-cut gender domains, in places where male and female strangers brushed up against each other in dangerous proximity, where illicit passions might be kindled, and where threats to normative sexual conduct were intensified. And the demon's own testimonies still highlighted the familiar connotations of visibility, vulnerability, sexual availability, and even emotional compatibility with the *pēys,* suggested in the "natural" wastelands described earlier. In my experience, all *pēys* reported that despite the crowded city surroundings, their victims always stood out, as if suddenly seen with great clarity, with everything else out of focus. "She was special," the obsessed demons would say. "I saw no one but her."

This interrogation stage of the ritual concludes when the singer explores the problems the *pēy* has brought upon his victim. Often the demon then confesses that it is he who has caused confusion in her marital relationship and rendered her disinterested, aggressive, and childless. Now the singer asks the demon to depart, to leave his victim alone for good, and the *pēys* usually agree.[11] But since these spirits are notoriously untrustworthy, the lead singer must call upon cosmic beings, especially the goddess, to witness their oath. At this point the verbal exchanges are concluded, freeing the exorcist to complete his banishment of the *pēy* through a series of ritual techniques.

First he asks the demon to surrender the lock of his victim's hair "on" which he resides. Once the *pēy* offers "his" hair from the woman's head, the musicians tie it into a knot. In exchange for his compliance, the *pēy* now receives the "life" he was earlier promised, symbolized by the sacrifice of a chicken. Tearing off the bird's head, one musician shoves its bloody neck into the *pēy's* mouth. Almost immediately the *pēy* spits it out and screams for help.

Suddenly the mood of the gathering abruptly changes. Everything speeds up as the Tamil term for the exorcism, "making the *pēy* run away," becomes dramatically explicit. Placing a large round rock in the victim's hands, the musicians begin chasing her. Staggering under its weight, she zigzags toward a nearby tamarind tree, drops the stone, and two musicians catch her, dragging her to its trunk. Slicing off the same knot of hair that had earlier belonged to the *pēy,* they nail it to the wood (for a comparable description, see Mosse, 1986, p. 483). At this, the victim always falls unconscious. And a few minutes later, returning to her senses, she is pronounced free from her *pēy* at last.

Therapy for the "Madness" of Gods and Women

Here, I will suggest that the ritual described above enacts not merely the expulsion of the demon from this world but also his decapitation. I will also show why this beheading symbolically enacted through the sacrificial operations of exorcism is necessary if the woman is to resume a "normal" life. But before exploring this final sequence, and what it may say about the expressive dynamics at the heart of this ritual, we must look deeper into Tamil representations of demonic possession.

To explore this "inner" realm, I believe we must first reexamine the key symbol of this discourse, the *pēy* himself. These spirits, we recall, are construed as human beings prematurely robbed of their lives. Sometimes they met their fate by accident, but more often they brought it on themselves. Unwilling to accept emotional frustration, they took the ultimate step of self-destruction. Hence, *pēys* lack what Tamils call *rajōkuṇam,* that quality of fortitude that, my consultants insisted, was an absolute requirement for social life.

All indications suggest that these victims of *pēy* attacks are identified with the same escapist tendencies as their demonized doubles. Indeed, women who are "caught" are commonly said in Tamilnadu to be afflicted with a "weak or timorous disposition," *pūtakkuṇam* (literally "demonic nature"). Confronted with the same marital problems that frustrate the demons, they too do not "adjust," nor do they seem to find a way out of their emotional entrapment. Instead, much like the *pēys* who possess them, they succumb to disappointment and withdraw from social life, attested by the fact that many women run away from home and that some, like Shanti, told me that before the entanglement with their demon they had begun to "lose interest in life."

We have seen how my consultants spatially represented the defection of these women, always imagining them at the time of the demonic attack as walking alone and away from the normative landscape and its headquarters, the family home. We have also noticed how their escapade was said to lead them to a forbidden space that, whether filled with stagnant pools and tamarind trees or with bus stands and movie theaters, was unincorporated, undomesticated, and lacking the features essential for the establishment of social life.

But the Tamil evocation of female alienation does not leave it at that. Once estranged from their constitutive relationships, women appear seduced by this desolate reality that lies beyond the boundaries of everyday understanding. Although their absorption into this alien world is represented first and foremost as the consequence of the *pēy's* aggression, there can be no doubt that women are seen as setting themselves up for being "caught." We recall that they are always said on the day of the attack to be dressed in their best attire as if to lure the demon. Moreover, during exorcist dialogues the *pēys* often emphasize the visibility and sexual availability of their victims.

Such representations suggest that demonic possession is conceived as a domain of experience in which women free themselves from the ordinary controls that govern female sexual behavior. Unaccompanied by a male guardian, they venture beyond the village settlement to engage in an unrestrained intimacy that lies outside the boundary of the legitimate, supervised sexuality ruled by their husbands. That this "wild" behavior is a source of danger and disorder for the human order is also attested by the fact that, in contrast with life-giving, marital sexuality, this union remains unproductive.[12] It is in this sense that the possessed woman shares the fate of the mythic Tamil prostitute who, according to David Shulman, is also a "symbol of barren eroticism" (1980, p. 262).

In Tamil cultural history, such associations between a woman's demonic possession and her desire for forbidden sexuality seem to run very deep. According to George Hart, almost two millennia ago the *caṅkam* poets commonly used the experience of spirit possession as an idiom for speaking of "a girl's despondency at being in love with an unsuitable man" (1975, p. 23; see also Ramanujan, 1967, p. 78). These meanings still prevail, for the *pēy* in today's social landscape is considered the "unsuitable" suitor par excellence, a home-wrecker, a tortured malcontent, and a social pariah of the first order.

But I believe that what truly makes the *pēy* an ineligible partner who must be expelled at all cost is the fact that, unlike the lover of the *caṅkam* heroine who at least had his own ontological reality, this demon has no independent personality. Of course this is an interpretation that my informants would probably deny because for many of them demons are "real" beings who lurk beyond the human settlement. But I found hints that in Tamil culture these disembodied spirits have a more subjective than objective existence. We may recall that the demon has neither personal name nor any biography outside of his victim. It is in this sense that he is what Obeyesekere calls a "personal creation" (1981, p. 115), a being who only exists in the woman's head.

There is even a sense that the original demonic assault constituted an event that was not "real," for, as we have seen, women not infrequently are "caught" by *pēys* on their way to movie theaters. It is as if they were victimized not by the *pēy* but by their mimetic involvement in melodramatic films, whose appeal to South Indians, Sara Dickey argues, lies in their staging of "utopian" and "fantastical resolutions" of social and personal problems (1993, pp. 110–111). Moreover, the timing of the attack at high noon coincides with the hottest period of the day, a time when, according to B. S. Bharathi, the Tamil landscape "seems to have *kaanal,*" which he translates as "mirage" (1993, p. 345). It is perhaps because they are assumed to blur the boundaries between reality and fiction that in Tamil culture these women are derided as *aṟiyāta makkaḷ,* "ignorant ones," the very same epithet assigned to the *pēys*.

It is the function of these exorcist dialogues to clarify and publicize the fact that the woman has crossed the line. She is trapped in an alien world that, as its exterior symbolism suggests, is not just liminal and wild but dangerously severed from the realm of "normal" expectations, a zone of deluding, erotic fantasies. Thus, once the victim and her *pēy* have been fully resituated into this maddening landscape, the exorcist asks the spirit what troubles he has brought his girl. Since *pēys* invariably answer that they have caused "evil" (*pāvam*), their responses help to expose them for who they really are: lecherous outsiders who have visited life-threatening problems on their victims.

The rest of the treatment, then, consists of expelling the demon. As we have seen, at this point the actual procedures that truly cause "the *pēy* to run away" work less through linguistic operations than through sacrificial transactions and are charged with tremendous emotional intensity. This closing sequence of ritual actions I have just described appears to be long-standing, for in 1709, in what may be our earliest Western source on this ritual, the French missionary Jean-Jacques Tessier seems to have witnessed an identical enactment in Pondicherry, less than 100 kilometers from the Mēlmalaiyaṉūr temple where I documented many exorcist rituals almost three hundred years later (see Dharampal, 1982, pp. 131–132). Let me show how these sacrificial transactions appear to confirm the crucial meanings that I have just reviewed, and contribute to the entire ritual's raison d'être.

To understand this climactic episode we should start with the notion of giving "life" to the *pēy* in exchange for "his" hair, since it is actually the central premise of the exorcism. We should remember that at the preliminary invocation (or the "warning") the *pēy* agrees to meet the musicians on the funeral grounds on condition that he is granted the "life" that is missing from his disembodied existence.

In the Hindu culture of Sri Lanka, as Obeyesekere has demonstrated, hair is invested with unconscious potency, especially where sexual meanings are concerned. For Sinhalese female ascetics, he argues, matted hair represents "the god's *liṅkam,* the idealized penis, his *śakti,* the source of life and vitality" (1981, p. 34). It is tempting to infer that in the exorcist context the lock of hair stands for the lustful genitalia of the demon. No such equation was explicitly developed by my consultants, but there were suggestions during the ritual dialogue. The *pēy* was said to "enter" his victim through a hair lock. The lock was also treated as the metonymic identity of the spirit, for no sooner had *pēys* revealed their names than the exorcist demanded to know, "Is this your hair?," as if drawing an association between it and lustfulness. And, not surprisingly, when the musician tried to tie the lock in a knot, demons often protested with some anguish, "It hurts! It hurts!"

Yet in Hindu culture hair is also associated with opposite representations, specifically with the public discipline of sexuality. Women's hairdos change according to marital status, and hair is likewise a major symbol of self-abnegation, as devotees, male and female, offer their tonsure to tutelary deities. The capacity of this symbol to unify such widely different meanings as rampant lust, sexual control, and ascetic devotion perhaps explains its capacity, in this ritual context, to "convert the obligatory into the desirable," as Victor Turner has argued of "dominant" symbols in general (1967, p. 30). In our exorcist context, the lock of hair would seem to begin as the symbol of the *pēy's* wayward libido and point of erotic contact with his victim. By the ritual's end, however, the hair has become the token of the demon's voluntary sexual renunciation of his victim, and punctuates their point of separation.[13]

Now let us look at the symbolic value of the "life" or blood sacrifice that is given to the *pēy* in compensation for his submission. We should remember that no sooner are the demons offered the chicken sacrifice than they customarily call for "help!" (*apayam*), the word that formulaically concludes the verbal operations of *all* exorcisms. The reason *pēys* cry out, I was told, was because they feel "in danger and fear for their lives." As we now know, it was such an emotion of "fear" that also left their victims open to the original attack in the first place. The demons, then, appear to be "caught" by the same terror they induced in their victims, and their fright has the same consequences, for at that instant they have been rendered voiceless and passive.

Losing their personal identities, they also turn into inert matter—into the heavy round rock that, we recall, the musicians place in the young woman's hands. Now this was not my comparison; a musician described this stone the victim was made to carry as "the weight of the *pēy's* desire." But this "weight" (*pāram*) had changed location. While initially it was possessing the victim, or "on" her head through the lock of hair, now the *pēy* seemed to be in the victim's hands, in the rock, and under her own control. While it made some sense for the exorcism to climax with her finally dropping the rock, my questions regarding any deeper significance of this mystifying episode were met initially with vague answers.

But as I pestered one musician about this obscure sequence, he volunteered the charter myth of the Aṅkāḷaparamēcuvari temple in Mēlmalaiyaṉūr where I documented these rituals, a narrative that put the entire exorcism and my foregoing interpretation into a larger context. Since my narrator clearly drew some correspondence between myth and ritual, let me suggest how his story restates the plots enacted in the exorcism performance and illuminates their symbolic meanings.

His narrative was none other than a folk version of the well-known Sanskrit story of the god Śiva's brahmanicide.[14] In this South Arcot variant, it opened with the uniqueness of Śiva's personality, epitomized by his five heads. When Śiva endowed the god Brahmā with a fifth head, the identification between the two was so complete that Pārvatī, Śiva's wife, could no longer distinguish which one was her husband. Taking advantage of the situation, Brahmā quickly made a pass at her.

So Śiva resolved to cut off Brahmā's fifth head, but it grew back. Then the god Viṣṇu intervened, advising Śiva to decapitate Brahmā once more, but this time to hold the severed head in his hand. Śiva did as told but now he had one too many heads. For he had six heads, with his state of imbalance conveyed by the odd location of that extra one—in his right hand. And Śiva remained stuck to this head, effectively "possessed" *by* an additional identity.

At this point the mythic representation of Śiva's possession becomes identical to that of our demon's victim. For after this the god, too, was condemned to dwell alone, on the fringes of society, in a wasteland where liminality became his permanent condition as he wandered around stark naked. And, like the demon's victim, he was also stripped of all reason, and the story eventually has him going mad. Finally, the similarity between the two extends into the ritual as well. As Śiva is possessed by a head stuck to his hand, the victim of demonic possession holds the "weight" of the *pēy* in hers. And this rock is smooth, round, and just about the size of a human head.

In the myth, the goddess intervenes, throwing a lump of rice soaked in blood upon Brahmā's head. Unable to tolerate contact with this polluted offering, it tumbles from Śiva's hand; the goddess, in effect, beheads Brahmā. Nor is this the first time that a South Indian goddess triumphs over those who, like the god Brahmā, lust after her.[15]

In the South Arcot ritual I am describing here, the exorcism likewise opens with a blood offering, the chicken's crude decapitation. This offering is problematic for the *pēy,* who immediately cries for help. He has good reason for fear, since, as I see it, the sacrifice foretells his own beheading. The victim runs frantically and drops the stone, the symbolic head of the *pēy,* near the tamarind tree. With this act, she, much like the goddess, beheads her own impostor-husband. Now she is free of her demon at last.

In most Tamil myths that feature decapitation, the narratives usually conclude with the head's reattachment, only rarely to the original body.[16] In our ritual context my sense is that the demon's head was symbolically detached from his victim but reconnected by a nail to *another* body, to the body of the tamarind tree.

Since in Tamil sacred symbolism the piercing of flesh by metal objects is often invested with sexual and particularly marital connotations, I suspect that at this point the demon was actually being remarried to this tree (Hiltebeitel, 1991, pp. 197–198). This interpretation is not as far-fetched as it seems, for in South Indian rituals, trees are commonly married to one another, to human beings, or even to supernaturals (Beck, 1981; Biardeau, 1989).[17] Moreover, the botanical and cultural properties of the tamarind would seem to qualify it as a "natural" bride or sexual partner for a malevolent creature like a *pēy*. As Maneka Gandhi has written, its bark is "rough, almost black, covered with long cracks" (1989, p. 27); furthermore, in Tamil folk taxonomy the tamarind is classified as both "hot" and "female" (Beck, 1969, p. 569).

In the end, once the requisite "divorce" from his victim has been secured, the *pēy* has still managed to obtain what was missing from his previous disembodied existence; he does get both a "life" and a "bride." As for Shanti, the victim of that particular exorcism in mid-July 1991, she was returned to the domesticated environment of collective life and acceptable identity and was reunited with her husband. The musicians who talked to me later said that she was "happy" at last.[18]

Conclusion

I might agree that the Tamil ritual known as "making the *pēy* run away" is one response to a pervasive source of female distress. I might also concur that the linguistic operations of this exorcism do give women some opportunity to voice what had been hitherto muted—their feelings of loneliness, abandonment, and marital disappointment. But other than a general outlet for expressing alienation and transcending isolation, it is hard to say what is fully or finally liberating for women about Tamil exorcism. As we have seen, the healers I worked with seemed to be operating from a much broader cultural premise, namely, that the source of a woman's alienation is locked in her head, precisely in her antisocial and life-threatening fantasies of extramarital sexuality.[19] This was why the musicians first sought to identify the woman with a prime symbol of male eroticism. For in Tamil culture, the *pēy* represents the kind of unbridled sexual energy that almost always is associated with men rather than with women.

And that is also why their ritual transactions did not offer marriage therapy in any Western sense of "working things out" between the woman and her husband. Instead, the work of these practitioners, in league with the family, was closer to what Luc de Heusch calls, in reference to treatment of mental sickness among the Tsonga of Africa, "a psychoanalysis of expulsion" (1981, p. 177). Their goals were to remove the *pēy* forcibly from the woman's head and to make her face the fact that her husband *and not* the demon was her rightful lover. The musician's attempt to "make the *pēy* run away" and his decapitation of the demon symbolized these consequences. Better yet, he had the woman perform this last operation on herself.

So now we can better appreciate how the theory that exorcist rituals somehow empower women to protest their lot does little justice to the fuller female predicament in the Tamil world. Far from working toward their emancipation, the ritual I have described here puts women on a kind of trial. With demons on the stand and men on the bench, women are compelled to confess that they have succumbed to marital disappointments and erotic impulses that put them in peril of losing their sanity. And so these confessions by these "caught" women require that the demons are expelled and wives returned to reason—that is, to the safety and structure of the patriarchal family fold and the woman's proper role in it.

Notes

This essay was originally published as "Expel the Lover, Recover the Wife: Symbolic Analysis of a South Indian Exorcism" by Isabelle Nabokov (see Acknowledgments).

1. The term *pēy* may also refer to a class of malignant beings who have an entirely different ontological personality from the demons discussed in this essay. Rather than being the ghosts of ordinary humans, these *pēys* have proper names, clear-cut identities, and myths of origin that interleave with the careers and narratives of the great Hindu pantheon. These demons too may possess people but they gain articulation through a different mode of apparition, etiology, and moral ethos that this paper does not analyze.
2. In Madurai District, Louis Dumont also noted that relationships between *pēys* and victims were "very clearly stated to be . . . love relationship(s)" (1986, p. 450).
3. The predominance of male *pēys* in my sample appears to contradict the findings of David Mosse, who notes that "63% of the ghosts exorcised at the shrine of St. Anthony [in Ramnad District] were female" (1986, p. 469). However, his statistics do not clearly reflect the actual gender distribution of the untimely dead exorcised at that shrine, for his sample of spirits also includes minor deities (1986, p. 455).
4. In Sinhalese scholarship much has been said about what David Scott calls "the vulnerability to the possible consequences of 'being alone' (*taniyama*)" (1991, p. 96).

Ethnographers seem to argue over the specific connotations of this important concept, but essentially agree that, as Bruce Kapferer put it, being alone "is a precondition of demonic attack" (1991, p. 70; also see Obeysekere, 1969, p. 176).

5. Mosse also notes that "beautification . . . increases vulnerability to attack" (1986, p. 470). It is because widows lose the privilege to wear Tamil insignia of female beauty that they are not "caught" by the untimely dead.
6. In Coimbatore District, for example, W. T. Elmore's meager account of such a ritual was not based on firsthand observation (1984 [1913], pp. 51–53). From Madurai District, Dumont managed to record one exorcist ceremony, but offered little interpretation (1986, pp. 450–452). And in a joint publication with D. E. Pocock he made it clear that he placed minimal significance on "the occasional possession of persons by evil spirits or 'demons'" (1959, p. 56). From Karnataka, Edward Harper acknowledged that in order "to remove the woman's spirit," "many hours" are spent in "negotiations," but he neither elaborated on the ritual nor explored the nature of the possessing spirits (1963). In Chengelput District, Michael Moffat obtained from one healer his mode of handling *pēy* spirits, but he does not appear to have witnessed his consultant in action (1979, pp. 241–243), while from Madras, Lionel Caplan has described such exorcist rites, but only from a Christian (Pentecostal) perspective (1989, pp. 64–68). Kalpana Ram has documented rituals of possession and healing at a Catholic shrine in Kanyakumari District (1991, pp. 94–105). And Mosse has provided a full description of Catholic exorcism cults in Ramnad District (1986, pp. 478–487; 1994).
7. To the best of my knowledge, there is little historical or ethnographic documentation concerning this body of specialists (but see Thurston 1987 [1909], v. VI: 29; Masilamani-Meyer, 1986, p. 3; Reiniche, 1979, p. 243; Nabokov, 1995, pp. 193–197; 1996).
8. According to Eveline Masilamani-Meyer, this temple "was and still is . . . the centre of the Aṅkālammaṉ cult in Tamil Nadu" (1986, p. 71). See her detailed study of the myths and rituals associated with this goddess (1986).
9. This term was also used to address Europeans in colonial times.
10. The exception to this is the issue of caste. As Mosse points out, "Ghosts are of any caste except Brahman." However, as he notes, *pēys* tend to identify themselves as being members of communities that are "associated with the fringes of Tamil village society, or with the 'forest'" (1986, p. 469). Their low or marginal status might explain why some *pēys* (like Shankar) refuse to identify their caste.
11. At this point the singer may also ask the demon if there is anyone else there with him, for as Mosse points out, "multiple possession" is frequent (1986, p. 455). In such cases, the musicians interrogate each demon individually in the manner described above. Then they exorcise them all at the same time (on multiple possession in Sri Lanka, see Stirrat, 1977, p. 141).
12. That this behavior is particularly threatening to men is also attested by Ram's excellent description of "the practices of physical containment and discipline which help to create the sexually appropriate, gendered body among Mukkuvar women" (1991, pp. 48–51).
13. My discussion of this ritual sequence thus contradicts Ram's interpretation of the symbolism of unbound female hair in demonic possession. I agree with her when she writes that in that context women's loose hair signifies "disorder," "extreme

passion," "sexual passion," and more generally, disrespectable femininity (1991, pp. 88, 100–101). But I do not endorse her argument that possessed women "are deliberately using hair as a symbolic weapon" to break loose from the daily restraints imposed on the female body (1991, p. 101). For as we have seen, in Hindu exorcisms, at least, women are required to dance fast and loosen their hair. Moreover, the request that they surrender a lock of hair—which is then tied, cut, and removed—strongly suggests that these rites aim at curbing rather than freeing their sexuality.

14. For Sanskrit versions of this myth, see Wendy Doniger, 1973, p. 127. For the full transcript and commentary on the Tamil folk version I recorded, see Nabokov, 1995, pp. 228–234. For other Tamil folk variants, see Masilamani-Meyer, 1986, pp. 36–38, 176–183.
15. See, for instance, Alf Hiltebeitel's detailed analysis of the myths and rituals associated with the goddess Draupadī (1988, 1991).
16. This motif is highlighted in the well-known story of the goddess Reṇukā, also known as "Mariyamma<u>n</u>" (see Assayag, 1992; Beck, 1981; Biardeau, 1969; Trawick, 1984).
17. Brenda Beck, for instance, documented how during a village festival in Coimbatore District the goddess Mariyamma<u>n</u> was "married to a tree trunk" (1981, p. 91). Her informants state that this tree represented "the goddess's husband" (1981, p. 122).
18. But the musicians acknowledged that sometimes this *pēy,* or another one, may return, in which case they had to start all over again. My sense is that this ritual was most successful when the musicians linked up the "cured" woman with the goddess, in the same process of turning patient into initiate that has been documented by ethnographers in other parts of the world (for my discussion of this initiation, see Nabokov, 1995, pp. 237–243).
19. This must be understood in the light of broader Tamil symbolizations of the human body. According to Ram, "The head occupies a key place in the merging of medical and religious discourses. The head stores the heat generated by desire" (1991, p. 56; also see Beck, 1979).

EIGHT

Waiting for Veḷḷāḷkaṇṭaṉ

Narrative, Movement, and Making Place in a Tamil Village

Diane P. Mines

This essay is about how movement makes space. More specifically, it is about how a particular walk taken by a particular man makes, in a particular way, a village (*ūr*) called Yanaimangalam, in Tirunelveli District, Tamilnadu. One midnight in the summer of 1990, as in many summers previously and since, a man took in a god's power, as he also took on the god's name, and set out from the village cremation ground for a lone procession "around the village." His simple accompaniment was the sound of bells that dangled from his spear and his jester-style hat, and a torch-bearer who lit his way through the night fields. He walked a long and slow route along the periphery of the village. As he walked, two hours, three hours, six hours passed, and even as dawn broke, the hundreds of people who were gathered at the cremation ground to celebrate the festival of the fierce god Cuṭalaimāṭaṉ waited. Until he returned, the festival could not come to its proper conclusion. This essay is about how Veḷḷāḷakaṇṭaṉ's walk did more than enable the festival's conclusion. Veḷḷāḷakaṇṭaṉ's walk, the route he chose to take, and the actions he performed en route together articulated a discourse on village social and spatial relations.

To understand how a man's walking around the *ūr* is discourse, it will be useful to start out with something of an analogy: the relation between stories and their tellings. In an essay on the *Rāmāyaṇa,* A. K. Ramanujan reminds us that a single story may generate hundreds of tellings. He writes that "the story may be the same in two tellings, but the discourse may be vastly different. Even the structure and sequence of events may be the same, but the style, details, tone, and texture—and therefore the import—may be vastly different" (1991, p. 25). So, for example, the story of Rāma—his life, the sequence of events in his life—may be repeated three hundred times, yet each telling may be discursively different: one telling of the story may be told to question the local structure of gender relations while another telling of the same story may serve as discourse on Indian politics or on religious difference (Richman, 1991).

Like a story that can be told in many ways, so too can a village be represented in many ways and enter into multiple discourses: geographers map it, demographers count it, ethnographers write about it. Depending on who does the telling, the meaning of a place—its import and spatial dimensions—may be defined quite differently. But the people who live in a village define it, too. The terms and symbols of village discourses are likely to be quite different from those employed in the aforementioned academic "tellings," tellings that may be described as alien discourses that "colonize" space.[1]

One way residents of Yanaimangalam define the spatial area called *ūr* is not verbal or graphic but motile: they define it by walks they take around it, walks that are said to encircle (*ūraiccuṟṟivaru*) or go "by way of" (*ūr vaḻiyāka*) the *ūr*. "Space is actuated by the ensemble of movements deployed within it," writes de Certeau (1984, p. 117). Yanaimangalam's residents actuate the space of their *ūr* by an ensemble of temple processions they take around and through it.[2] This proves a rather disharmonious ensemble, however, for the different processions—organized by several different temple associations in Yanaimangalam—take different routes.[3] All of these processions—walkings of one village—are like multiple tellings of one story: they make the village discursively and they make it in different ways.

Let us, then, allow ourselves the indulgence of taking literally the etymology of "discourse": "To run, move, or travel over a space, region, etc." (*Oxford English Dictionary*). To the extent that one person's or group's processional route around the *ūr* may differ from another's—as may one teller's telling differ from another's—we may say that the *ūr* itself is actuated in a motile discourse, a debate in motion, where each procession produces an alternative social and spatial reality in competition with other versions of that reality.[4] "There are as many spaces as there are distinct spatial experiences," writes Merleau-Ponty (quoted in de Certeau, 1984, p. 188). While Yanaimangalam may "count" as just one village in census reports and geographical surveys, this essay suggests that the *ūr* is best understood as a set of overlapping alternatives, and that movement is among one of the defining practices through which these alternatives are constituted.

Movement as space-making activity is not a concept foreign to Indian ideas about action and creativity. From early Vedic hymns to contemporary ethnographic accounts of politics and ritual, movement is constitutive action. Vedic hymns praise the power of Viṣṇu's heroic strides as he takes three footsteps that create the spaces of earth, heaven, and the distinction (space) between the two (*Ṛg Veda* 1.154). A later *purāṇic* embellishment dramatizes the hymn, and tells a story about how Viṣṇu, born on earth as a dwarf, reclaims the earth as territory for human occupation by tricking the ruling demon, Bali. The dwarf asks the demon to grant him just that bit of space over which he can stride in three steps. The request amuses Bali and so he grants the dwarf his three dwarf-steps, upon which Viṣṇu reveals himself and, growing to immense proportions, takes three strides that span heaven and earth (Doniger, 1975, pp. 178–179). As Viṣṇu claims mythical overlordship of heaven and earth with footsteps, so too have historical South Asian kings—Muslim, Buddhist, and Hindu—effected and pronounced their conquests in royal processions. In Hindu kingship, the *dig-vijaya,* "the conquest of the quarters," was a procession that established its performer to be "overlord of the four directional regions" (Inden, 1990, p. 229). Many early South Asian maps, both Hindu and Muslim, are inscribed with the routes of movement, whether of pilgrimage, or those of commercial or military expansions across territory (see Gole, 1989 and Schwartzberg, 1992). In the *aśvamedha* or "horse sacrifice," a king asserted the range of his territorial control by releasing a horse to wander as far as it could during the course of the year, followed by (and perhaps coaxed along by) a band of warriors ready to defend the horse against those whose territory it traversed.[5] More localized movement, too, is productive action. Circumambulations clockwise unite brides and grooms, while counterclockwise movements separate the dead from the living and, more generally, the inauspicious from persons, objects, and spaces (D. Mines, 1995, pp. 123–147; Raheja, 1988, pp. 85–86; Sax, 1991, p. 141). Contemporary ethnography from different parts of South Asia iterates the creative impact of processions, as political groups define their constituencies and debate their control over space (e.g., Kumar 1989; M. Mines, 1994; Sax, 1991).

This essay proceeds in three steps. First, I will discuss in some depth the ontology of person and place in Tamilnadu, for a Tamil actor's capacity to constitute space through movement (and hence to "discourse") is predicated upon that actor's substantial identification with place. Second, in order to illustrate the proposition that processions are a kind of motile discourse, I detail both Veḷḷālakaṇṭaṉ's walk and another procession at odds with his. Both of these processions are said to go "around the *ūr*" yet the route of each is significantly different. Third, I move from movement back to stories and their tellings. The analogy I have drawn above between tellings and walkings proves to be more than analogue. Rather, processions around the village, on the one hand, and the tellings of stories about the gods in the village, on the other, prove to be parallel channels of discourse through which residents of Yanaimangalam remake and debate the social-spatial contours of the *ūr*.

An Ontology[6] of the *Ūr:* Gods, Place, and Person in Tamilnadu

In order to understand how Veḷḷāḷakaṇṭaṉ 's walk makes the village in terms of social-spatial reality, it is important first to understand how closely place, person, and divinity are identified in Tamil culture. Here, I will bring together three relations that make Veḷḷāḷakaṇṭaṉ 's walk into real creative activity; those between place and person, place and god, and god and person. What follows might be considered a preliminary attempt at a "topo-analysis," that is, a "systematic psychological study of the sites of our intimate lives" (Bachelard, 1969, p. 8). In Tamilnadu, the *ūr* counts predominantly among a Tamil's intimate places of life, and it is in part how people understand their being-in-place (being-in-the-*ūr*) that makes their movement real creative activity.

Place and Person

The identification of place and person in Tamil culture has been well documented.[7] In Yanaimangalam, daily conversations signal this identification. Residents see their fields, temples, and houses as bodies, with heads, feet, and volume. Cultivators refer to the yield of a field as its "body" (*mēṉi*). They point out how they will divide their field among their sons when the time comes: the oldest will receive the head and the youngest the feet. Houses, too, have heads and feet, and even mouths and anuses, wombs, birth, death, and feelings, as well (Daniel, 1984, pp. 115, 130, 152; Moore, 1990). Like a field, a house may also be subdivided among surviving sons, again, with the oldest receiving the better, higher "head" of the house, and the youngest the lesser, lower feet.

Places are mapped to human form. Perhaps those familiar with the "person" called Vāstu see even such ordinary divisions of property as a kind of creative sacrifice, an echo of Vedic myth, where creation proceeds by division of the original cosmic man, Puruṣa (e.g., *Ṛg Veda* 10.90).[8] Tamil houses and temples, like Indian temples more generally, are constructed on the earth-bound body of Vāstu, understood by some as the corpse of Puruṣa that had fallen face-down to earth as a leftover of the original sacrifice (Beck, 1976, pp. 226–227; Daniel, 1984, pp. 117–118; Michell, 1977, pp. 71–72; Moore, 1990, pp. 179–82).

Identifications between place and person go beyond metaphoric mappings. As early as the first century B.C.E., Tamil *caṅkam* poetry, especially that branch called *akam* (that of the "interior"), connected place and person metonymically, so that a "man's land is like the man himself" (Ramanujan, 1985, p. 232). In *akam* poetry, the most interior aspects of human existence—the emotions—are connected through a language of metonym with the landscape in which humans reside. Between two ends of a continuum defined by interior emotion, at one extreme, and the physical reality of the land outside, on the other, one might place in a hierarchy of inclusion the whole denotative range of the Tamil term *akam,* whose meanings include these: interior, heart, self, kin, house, family, place of activity, settlement, earth (Ramanujan, 1985, p. 262; *Tamil Lexicon; CRE-A Modern Tamil Dictionary*).

Here, etymology evokes reality, and ancient poetic convention evokes contemporary reality, for, as Trawick has shown, Tamils commonsensically take land, house, kin, family, self, and emotion to be inextricably bound, related not merely metaphorically, but literally and substantially. Like a house of cards, to lose one relation is to lose them all. Body, active kinship, and home adhere in the sharing of land and fall apart with the fragmentation of property (1991, p. 237): "The bond of affection and belonging between brothers is carried in the land and lost when the land is lost" (ibid., p. 238).

What connects a person and their *ūr,* whether their natal village or the place they happen to live, is more than a postal address. Substantial relations of identity between person and *ūr* are established through substantial transactions between the very soil of a place and the people who reside there. Persons and *ūrs* share substances; hence the character of the village and that of its residents, over time, mutually alter and fuse as substances are transacted between them: "[A] person absorbs the nature of the soil by eating the food grown in village fields and by drinking the water that springs from the soil into village wells . . . [conversely], persons affect the substance of the *ūr* simply through their residence in the *ūr* and also through the combination of their food and water leavings, their bodily wastes, cremated and buried bodies, and so forth, all of which mingle directly with the soil of the *ūr*" (Daniel, 1984, pp. 84–85).

Gods and Place

Gods are persons, too, and their relation to the land is made quite explicit in everyday talk in the village. The power (*cakti*) of gods is said to reside in the very earth of the *ūr*. This is true not only of the village goddesses, whose power and energy suffuse the soil of the whole *ūr*, such that the *ūr* can be considered a form of this divine person (Daniel, 1984, p. 99). It is also true for other divinities who reside in the village, including those fierce gods whose temporary images are formed of the earth itself.

That gods reside in the soil itself is illustrated nowhere more clearly than in the common practice of moving gods from place to place through a transfer of soil (*piṭimaṇ*), a practice widely reported for Tamilnadu (e.g., Daniel, 1984, pp. 95–101; Dirks, 1987, p. 221; see also Inglis, 1985). There are many reasons people may wish to transfer a god from one place to another. They may wish to find it a more suitable home, one further from or closer to human habitation. One family in Yanaimangalam moved a fierce god from their backyard out to the more distant cremation ground. That god had originally come from an entirely different village and had been relocated to their backyard in a handful of earth. In some cases, it is the god who directs a person or family to bring him to their home. In other cases, a family or lineage might move from one place to another, and wish to bring their gods with them. Whatever the reason, the procedure remains the same. They take a "handful of earth" (*piṭimaṇ*) from the god's shrine and relocate that earth in a new place to establish that god's power in that place. This movement is not so much a complete transfer as it is an extension of the god's name and power over space, for the original site retains the power as the new site also gains it.

The following conversation illustrates further how gods' powers are thought to be effective in the particular places they reside. I was speaking with a well-known ritual specialist in the village named Āṇṭimūppaṉār about an exorcism I had observed him perform at the cremation ground temple where he serves as the oracle (*cāmiyāṭi,* literally "god-dancer") for the god Muṇṭacāmi. During a festival, a woman had come running from one end of the temple to the other, stopping in front of Āṇṭimūppaṉār who was positioned in front of Muṇṭacāmi. She bore the signs of an inappropriate (or "unmatching," to borrow Marriott's term; see also Moreno, 1985) possession—an unwelcome attack from a god—and Āṇṭimūppaṉār (as Muṇṭacāmi) began the task of ousting the invader. Among the procedures he used was feeding the woman *vipūti,* a divinely charged, pure, and cooling ash. *Vipūti* is a type of *piracātam,* a substance left over from worshiping and feeding a god, which was touched, consumed, and thereby transformed by a god. I had asked Āṇṭimūppaṉār how it was that the ash had the power (*cakti*) to effect the exorcism, and he—both amused and appalled by my ignorance—shouted rather than spoke this exasperated reply:

"*Cakti*! That's the god's *cakti*! It has nothing to do with my *cakti* or the *vipūti*."

The *cāmiyāṭi* then explained that his ash feeding and smearing could make the woman's possession stop because, as he put it, "between the god and me there is a . . . a kind of . . . a connection (*cērkkai*) [he claps his hands together to illustrate]. He thinks and it reaches me. It isn't because of what *I* do that it stops . . . it's because of god's *cakti at this place*."

God and Person

Gods inhabit not only the earth. They inhabit persons. They inhabit entire lineages, and they inhabit the houses of lineage members. In fact, they inhabit the whole chain of interiors, all of the *akams:* person, kin group, house, and land. The third relation I wish to consider, that between god and person, completes a triadic set of relations in which god, land, and person are mutually implicated.

When I say that gods inhabit lineages and persons, I mean this quite literally. In Yanaimangalam, lineage (*kulam*) and *ūr* gods are linked metonymically with their human worshipers, and humans understand their relations to gods in this way. Gods are part of their devotees by inhabiting them. For our purposes, two kinds of relations between humans and gods are important. These are relations to lineage gods (*kulatēvaṅkaḷ*) and those to the village goddess (*ūramman̲*).

The metonymic contiguity between gods and persons is most dramatically exhibited in possession. Village goddesses, as well as most *kulam* or lineage gods, choose one or more persons with whom to form overpowering connections (*cērkkai*). These persons are officially recognized specialists called "god-dancers" (*cāmiyāṭikāḷ*), such as Āṇṭimūppan̲ār introduced above (see also Inglis, 1985 and Moreno, 1985). But the connection between god and lineage holds for every lineage member, not only for those specialists. Connections are originally made through contingent events such as those illustrated in the following story (first told to me by Mūkkan̲, the low-caste Dhobi or Washerman,[9] who serves as the *cāmiyāṭi* for the god Cuṭalaimāṭan̲, and retold by me here).

Mūkkan̲'s First Story

One day, about a hundred years ago, the story goes, a man of the relatively high Mūppan̲ār caste was out working in his field by the riverbank. He saw something floating down the river toward him. He fished it out, and found it was a banana *kan̲ṟu* (shoot). He planted it on the edge of his field.

Now, it just so happened that his field lay in the line of sight of a god named Cuṭalaimāṭan̲. Cuṭalaimāṭan̲ is the god of the cremation ground and he's not a very nice god: he attacks people who displease him, sometimes quite violently. So, people tend to avoid him, to tiptoe around him. But if your field lies right in the god's line of sight, there's not much you can do about it other than defer to the god and try to win him over.

The Mūppan̲ār farmer did just that. He tried to win over the god by making a vow to him. He promised the god that he would give him the first stalk of bananas that the tree produced, in return for the god's protecting the plant and field.

Well, a year passed and the banana plant flourished and produced a big stalk of bananas. The owner came out and cut the stalk and took it home, forgetting his vow to Cuṭalaimāṭan̲. He took one banana from the stalk, peeled it, and took a big bite. Immediately, he choked, spat out the banana, and could eat nothing from then on.

He soon realized that the fault was his for forgetting his vow, and so this higher-caste man went to see the much lower-caste Washerman to see what could be done. He went to the Washerman because the Washerman and his whole lineage were the special devotees of Cuṭalaimāṭaṉ. They took care of him and he took care of them. The Washerman was the one whose connection to the god was closest: the god regularly possessed him and communicated his needs through his human host. The solution that the Washerman and god offered was that the Mūppaṉār man and his whole lineage should adopt Cuṭalaimāṭaṉ's younger brother, Muṇṭacāmi, as their own special god. They should construct a shrine to Muṇṭacāmi, Cuṭalaimāṭaṉ's brother, opposite his own shrine, and worship there from now on, side by side with the Washerman (a much lower caste), as equals (though with the older brother—Washerman Cuṭalai—ranking above the younger!). So, to this day the Mūppaṉār and Dhobis are equals (with the otherwise lower-ranking Dhobi in fact first among equals) at that temple.

Body and Metonym

So, a chance event (a banana shoot floating down a river) leads to a vow made, and then a vow broken. A vow broken establishes a permanent relation between a low-ranking god and a high-ranking caste. This relation is not metaphoric, but metonymic. It is understood to be a bodily relation between god and lineage members. This Mūppaṉār lineage is forever more physically connected with their new god. The god eats what they eat, the god possesses them, the god fills them with energy and can also cause them illness if weak or displeased.

That gods and their devotee lineages and castes are contiguously linked is further illustrated by the case of a young woman named Pēcciyamma who started cooking for her husband before the two were married (cooking both literally and, likely, figuratively, as "cooking" for a man is a euphemism for sex). Her husband-to-be happened to be the man who regularly became possessed by his lineage's god. On the very day that the two were finally married, that god possessed the woman out of anger for her having fed him (with food fed to her husband) without being *of* his family. Her lack of contiguity with the god made her an inappropriate feeder of the god. But her contiguity, established upon marriage—an act that substantially joined her to her husband's lineage—opened the channel for the god to possess her, too.

This metonymic, bodily connection between god and lineage members (or village members, as the case may be) cannot be attenuated at will. Aruṇācalam Piḷḷai, an old man who acted as *cāmiyāṭi* for the village goddess, told me that when his older brother died, he knew that the goddess would choose to connect through him next, but he did not want the connection (it was too much work and too much strain). So, he avoided the temple, and during the festival bathed far upriver so as not to have to pass within visual range of her temple. But, as he put it, the goddess walked his legs to the temple against his will. He was "always already" an agent—willing or not—of the goddess.

This triad of relations—person bound to place, god bound to place, god bound to person—makes human actors into agents of the very place they occupy. Persons, gods, and land are linked inextricably such that an act by one involves the others, and human actors may be seen as always in part agents of an emplaced divinity. And as they walk "around the village" in powerful processions led by possessed *cāmiyāṭis,* humans reaffirm and recreate their identification with one another and with the territory, the land itself.

All Hindu South Indian villages contain multiple gods, linked variously to lineages and castes, in multiple places, with different lines of sight and different paths of action (see, e.g., Babb, 1975; Beck, 1972; Beteille, 1965; Dumont, 1986 [1957]; Fuller, 1987; Harper, 1959; Hiltebeitel, 1989; Reiniche, 1979). It is this multiplicity of powerful actors connected variously to places and communities in a village that makes processions into discursive action. When people, accompanied by gods, walk "around the *ūr*" during festivals, they are in fact making that *ūr,* defining its extension in space (*veḷi*), and its spatial distinctions (its interiors—*akams*—and exteriors—*puṟams*). Any one procession may alter, extend, contract, intersect, or bisect other paths and other walks by other agents. This is the village: a set of overlapping alternative spaces made in actions, including processions.

Walking and Making Yanaimangalam

In 1990, Yanaimangalam's population was 1783, divided into about 530 households. Most households supported themselves to some extent by rice agriculture. The population was further divided into five core residential areas separated by both name and intervening fields: the main village ("Big Yanaimangalam") and four smaller hamlets—populated

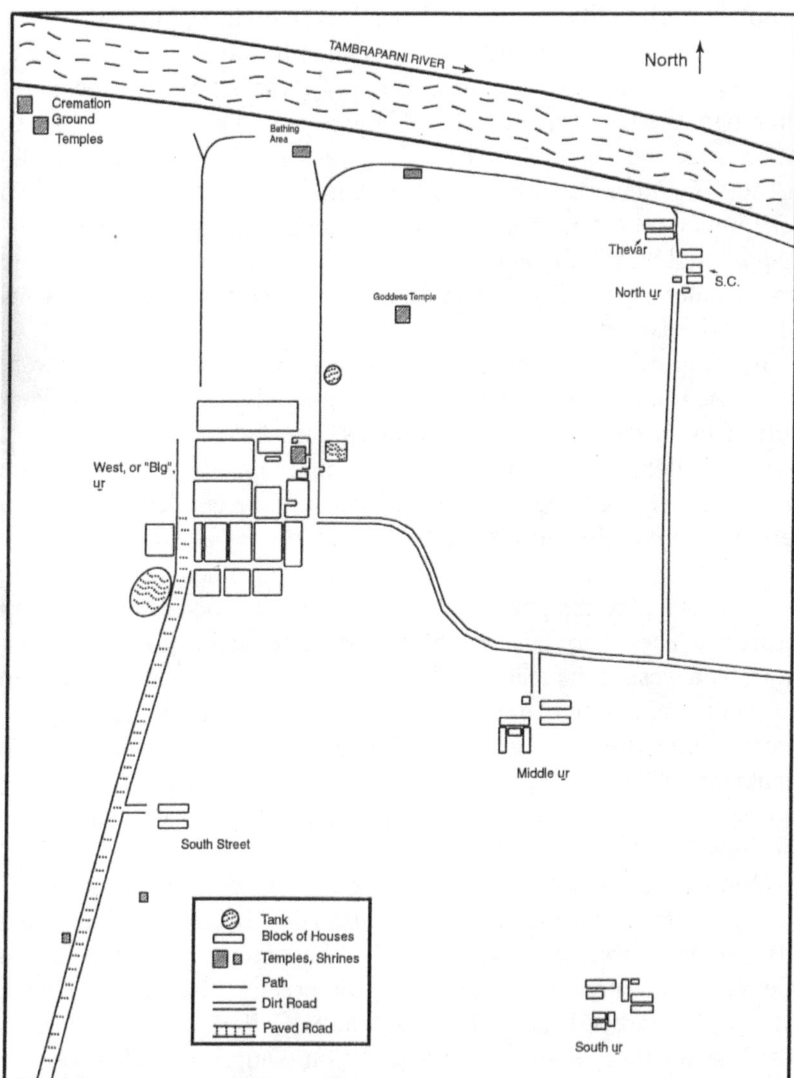

Figure 8.1 Sketch map of Yanaimangalam, showing all hamlets.

for the most part by Untouchable *jātis* ("castes") or relatively lower *jātis*—referred to as North, Middle, and South *Ūrs,* and South Street (see Fig. 1). (During the time of this research, so-called Untouchables preferred the relatively value-neutral S. C., "Scheduled Caste," designation, and for the remainder of this essay I will use that term as well.) Most residents check the "Hindu" box on the census surveys that come around occasionally. And they also call each other and themselves by a variety of *jāti* names and titles. The members of five of these *jātis* figure prominently in this essay. Three of these are Yanaimangalam's dominant or "big" (*periya*) *jātis:* Piḷḷaimār (also known as Veḷḷāḷar), Mūppaṉār, and Tēvarmār. These three *jātis* reside in the main settlement ("Big Yanaimangalam," as it is sometimes called). The other two *jātis* important for our purposes count among Yanaimangalam's "little" (*ciṉṉa*) and "low" (*tāḻnta*) *jātis:* the Dhobis (Washermen), who reside on the outer edge of Big Yanaimangalam, and the S. C. Paḷḷar residents of Middle Hamlet.

In addition to humans, numerous gods populate the village as well. To house some of them, one finds some thirty-five temples and shrines spread out among the residential areas, rice fields, and fallow land. Seven sit along the riverbank. Three of these thirty-five temples figure in the action discussed below. One is the village goddess (*ūrammaṉ*) temple, a red-and-white striped building that rises like some odd crop among the green of surrounding rice fields. The other two temples are both dedicated to the god Cuṭalaimāṭaṉ ("Fierce god of the cremation ground"). These two stand side by side at the cremation ground up river, north and west of the residential areas (see Fig. 1). While dedicated to Cuṭalaimāṭaṉ, these two temples also each contain an overlapping (almost identical) set of twenty other fierce gods and goddesses, a whole pantheon of fangs,[10] or, as the author of the 1917 District Manual describes, these temples are dedicated to "Sutalaimatan [sic] 'and his horrid crew'" (Pate, 1917, p. 107).

While the gods in the two temples are almost identical, the human associations that convene as patrons (*varikkāraṅkaḷ,* literally "tax payers") of the temples differ significantly. The larger and older of the two temples convenes an association comprising five *jātis:* Dhobi, Mūppaṉār, Barber, Illuttuppiḷḷai, and the S. C. Paḷḷar of Middle Hamlet. The smaller, newer temple association comprises exclusively the Tēvars of Yanaimangalam. Though these two temple associations convene different sets of village residents, they nevertheless cooperate with one another and celebrate their yearly festival together (albeit with some competition and contestation). Veḷḷāḷakaṇṭaṉ is one of the gods in the larger, older temple.

It was around midnight during the Cuṭalaimāṭaṉ festival in May 1990. Out at the temple, some of us had paid 50 paisa or so for a hot coffee-less decoction called "ginger coffee" (*cukkukkāppi*) to help us keep awake for this second consecutive night of the festival. Others had succumbed to sleep. Women jammed the corners and sides of the open-air temples, with children squeezed among the folds of their saris and babies swinging in cloth cradles hung above them from the temple's temporary *pantal* poles and beams. A few people dozed on the cremation mound itself (certainly the most unlikely place for a nap any other night of the year!). Many men had vanished into the thick gardens downriver to drink arrack, a country liquor. The ten or twelve policemen deployed for the festival were hanging out in their undershirts and khaki pants in a tent, their rifles leaning here, against wooden cots, and there, against canvas walls. It was peaceful, but hardly quiet. Generators chugged. And bullhorn loudspeakers blared taped music from the temple out into the still night air, as if to announce to the surrounding countryside that there was a festival under way somewhere nearby.

Asleep or awake, we were all waiting around for the finale of the three-day festival, when the gods would consume huge steaming mounds of meals called *paṭaippu* and when the human god-dancers (*cāmiyāṭikaḷ*) would consume blood from the dozens of goats (one of whom had butted me vigorously in the back of the leg earlier that night), roosters, and pigs that were tied to every available tree, post, and oxcart wheel in and around the two temples. The timing of this final event hinged not upon the conjunction of earth, and moon, sun, or stars, but rather upon the return of our "double-agent" (Steedly, 1994, p. 15) Veḷḷāḷakaṇṭaṉ—the god and his human god-dancer—from a guard or watch (*kāval*) circuit around the village. Veḷḷāḷakaṇṭaṉ (both man and god) is a Dhobi. Several hours previously, around midnight, Veḷḷāḷakaṇṭaṉ the god had connected with his god-dancer. Dressed in appliquéd shorts, a three-pronged hat—each prong weighed by a bell, court-jester style—and a thin spear, Veḷḷāḷakaṇṭaṉ had left the temple and set out across the dark fields, while those in the temple watched the flame torch accompanying him bob and then fade into the night.

Before he comes back, you the reader, too, must wait, because to understand how his walk—his guard circuit—makes the *ūr* in a particular way, we need—for contrast—another set of walks that make the *ūr* in a different way. This latter set of walks takes place every year at the festival for the village goddess, Yāṉaiyammaṉ, an event that occurs only a few weeks before Veḷḷāḷakaṇṭaṉ 's walk and the Cuṭalaimāṭaṉ festival.

Every year the dominant *jātis* in Yanaimangalam (the politically and economically powerful Piḷḷaimār, Mūppaṉār, and Tēvarmār) come together *as jātis* to fund and produce the village goddess festival. This festival overflows with the rhetoric of unity: it is said to be the festival of the "whole village" (*ūr pūrāvum*) and to benefit "everyone in the village." These village residents see themselves—as if trained structural-functionalists!—reproducing totalizing harmony and village unity.[11] This is how they talk about their village. Yet, this harmonious "whole village" is both contested and partial. Not everyone is allowed to pay the head-tax that funds the festival, and, consequently, not everyone has "rights" to temple shares, those coveted festival paraphernalia and leftovers that establish one's inclusion as well as rank in the community (Appadurai and Breckenridge, 1976; Dirks, 1987). Furthermore, the goddess temple processions that are said to encircle the "whole village" in fact assert a boundary that sharply demarcates space and excludes about 50% of the population of Yanaimangalam.

The goddess temple processions encircle specifically that residential part of the village in which the dominant village people live. Musicians, dancers possessed by the goddess, relatives of the dancers, and vow givers and their affines all walk around the village (*ūraiccuṟṟi*) and with their movement demarcate an interior space from an exterior one, an inside (*uḷḷē* or *akam*) from an outside (*veḷiyē* or *puṟam*), the livable *ūr* from the unlivable—but lived in—wasteland (*kāṭu*). They constitute interiors and exteriors not only by the paths they walk, but also by border-constituting actions they perform as they walk: they throw eggs, or sometimes pumpkins bloodied with turmeric and lime paste, as sacrifices (*bali*) to feed and appease maleficent beings who linger in the *kāṭu* outside and who want to but must not come inside the *ūr*.

The dominant village people thus define an *ūr* that includes themselves and excludes or peripheralizes others. Among those excluded and peripheralized in the village goddess temple practices, that is, among those who do not pay tax and whose houses are on the outside of the *ūr*—the *kāṭu* as defined by processions—are the Dhobis who live and work in Yanaimangalam.

Veḷḷāḷakaṇṭaṉ is, if you will recall, a Dhobi. The walk that he walks from the cremation ground temple, and the talk he talks as he walks, redefine the spatial dimensions of this dominant *ūr:* his walk includes those who are in other contexts excluded, and his talk—as well as a story Dhobis tell about him—centers those who are in other contexts relegated to the outsides and peripheries of the dominant *ūr's* livable space.

Take first his walk. When Veḷḷāḷakaṇṭaṉ leaves from the cremation ground festival after midnight, he begins a walk that pushes the *ūr* out to its widest perimeters. While the goddess temple processions encircle the dominant residential area and at best assert a metonymic inclusion of those who live outside the *ūr* that the processions constitute, Veḷḷāḷakaṇṭaṉ's route takes in everyone. His walk makes a space that encompasses all those within his purview and calls that space the *ūr*. His walk is called *ūr kāval* ("village watch") and it, too, is said to encircle the whole *ūr*.

Veḷḷāḷakaṇṭaṉ not only extends the *ūr* spatially to include literally "everyone" *in* it, he also shifts from the peripheralized position Dhobis occupy at the goddess festival as well as during other household life-cycle rituals where they act as servants and occupy peripheries (outside the temple, outside the house). Take the scene at the goddess temple on the night of his guard round, where his social and spatial position relative to other *ūrmakkaḷ*—the dominant "village people"—contrasts most sharply with the position he and his relatives take during the goddess temple festival. At this festival, Dhobis sit and wait on the periphery of the crowd, watch events from afar, and wait for the scraps they receive from the final distributions. When Veḷḷāḷakaṇṭaṉ arrives there on his walk, however, the small crowd waiting there—made up of all *jātis*—makes room for him as he moves up onto the steps of the goddess temple (which is locked for the night). He stands with his back to the goddess,[12] and the crowd circles around him, defers to him, and listens to his words. They take what words and *piracātam*—generally ash, *vipūti*—he gives them and then they go home.

Like two tellings of a story, these two walkings of the village may be said to be discursively related. Veḷḷāḷakaṇṭaṉ's walk refutes the *ūr* constituted by the first set of processions: he includes those previously excluded, and he centers himself, and his community, in places where he otherwise might occupy a periphery.

Perhaps the most surprising aspect of Veḷḷāḷakaṇṭaṉ's journey, however, is not the route he takes, the inclusive space he makes or the center he becomes, but rather the fact that he makes the journey at all. His walk is specifically a guard circuit, a watchman's round, a kind of walk called *ūr kāval,* but by all expectations and in all other contexts, *kāval* belongs to the Tēvars of the village. Tēvars are among the dominant *jātis* in Yanaimangalam and to this day they (sanctioned by the State of Tamilnadu, which has created government positions that village Tēvars have the right to fill) staunchly guard their right (*urimai*) to be the village watchmen (*kāvalkāraṅkaḷ*), and in the story I am about to relate, it was Veḷḷāḷakaṇṭaṉ's original attempts to perform *kāval* that led to his brutal murder at the hands of enraged Tēvars. As Veḷḷāḷakaṇṭaṉ walks his rounds, however, the Tēvars, too, wait and so participate in constituting a version of the village that refutes their own, in which they figure as dominant and central as well as the rightful village guardians.

I am moving from walks now to stories, but the story and the walk are not unrelated. This version of the Veḷḷāḷakaṇṭaṉ story was told to me by Mūkkaṉ, a Dhobi and a relative of Veḷḷāḷakaṇṭaṉ's. I quote him (in translation from a tape transcription) in the beginning and end, but summarize the middle with my own retelling.

Mūkkaṉ's Second Story

In the beginning, this *ūr* belonged to the Ukkaraṅkōṭṭai king—this place (*iṭam*) was his. When the Raja of Ukkaraṅkōṭṭai ruled over this village, he would come on a trip once every six months to see how things were. One day when he came, the Dhobi and his wife were in this house. They had just one daughter, Matippiḷḷai. She was very beautiful. When the Maharaja came into the village, all the people went and saw him. When the Maharaja came round on his horse, Matippiḷḷai too went and looked.

[D: This very house, you mean?]

Yes! When the Maharaja came passing by this very house, Matippiḷḷai was made pregnant by his gaze (*pārvai*).

The story continues. Matippiḷḷai had a son and he grew up into a strong youth who couldn't wash clothes to save his life but who excelled in the arts of war. One day he went hunting with the Tēvars of the village. The Tēvars cheated him of his fair share of the game and insulted him, calling him a bastard who didn't even know his own father. Veḷḷāḷakaṇṭaṉ—that was the Dhobi boy's name—forced his mother to tell him the name of his father (for it had been kept secret). She relented and he went to visit the king who offered him rights to the income generated from the fields around Yanaimangalam. But Veḷḷāḷakaṇṭaṉ didn't want wealth. He wanted to have what the Tēvars had rights to and what no Dhobi boy could ever have, namely, he wanted to be the village guardian. The king resisted because the Tēvars already had that right, but the son persisted and got what he wanted, all properly inscribed on a copper plate.

He returned to Yanaimangalam and performed *kāval* duty. The Tēvars were enraged. They called in all their allies. One thousand of them descended on Veḷḷāḷakaṇṭaṉ when he was alone in the fields.

Veḷḷāḷakaṇṭaṉ immediately killed 999 of them, of course, but the last one sneaked up on him from behind (a dirty trick!) and slew him, spilling his intestines. Veḷḷāḷakaṇṭaṉ died.

Now I end with Mūkkaṉ's version of the end:

> All the village people of Middle Hamlet came out. They put him on a plank, lifted him, and brought him to the eastern side of Yanaimangalam, put him down near the irrigation channel [just behind the Dhobi's house, still in the fields but closer], burned his body, then scooped up his remains and put them into the channel.
>
> As soon as they put his ashes in the channel, he became a god at that very place (*iṭam*). There he would frighten and threaten passersby. He changed into a cruel god. His mind wasn't like a god's but he was comparable (in power) to a god. We decided that we couldn't keep him here by the channel, and took him near the big temple and put up a place for him there. We took him out to the big Cuṭalaimāṭacāmi temple on the Tambraparni River, thinking that there should be a guardian god in front of that temple. We decided that once a year when we give a festival to our god Cuṭalaimāṭaṉ, we would also give a festival for him. So, to this day our twelve families come together to give a festival for Veḷḷāḷakaṇṭaṉ. That's the end.

In a rather straightforward way, the above story authorizes Veḷḷāḷakaṇṭaṉ's temple practices. It gives Veḷḷāḷakaṇṭaṉ and his descendents (who include the god-dancer, the storyteller, and those twelve families who worship at the shrine) the king-granted right (*urimai*)—not to mention the bio-moral capacity—to perform *kāval* in Yanaimangalam. The story connects Mūkkaṉ's lineage as well as S. C. Middle Hamlet residents to the god and to the places from which his power emanates.

It is Mūkkaṉ's *telling* of the story that makes the connection between the past event and his own family's current temple practices. Mūkkaṉ told the story in some ways as historical narrative, in the past tense as an event that happened to third persons ("hes," "shes," and "theys") no longer present. Yet at the same time, through his use of indexical (deictic) references to places, persons, and relations—to the wider context in which the story was told—he pragmatically linked present realities to the past he narrated: he placed the story in Yanaimangalam and in his own family compound using phrases like "in this same house," "those Tēvars," "that field over there," "that irrigation ditch," and by using gestures to indicate particular places. At the end of the story, Mūkkaṉ lifted the past into the present when he suddenly shifted from "they" to "we": "we decided," "we took," and now "we give." When that "we" breaks in, it dramatically shifts the temporal frame from an objective "past" that involved objective others to a subjective "present" continuous with "our" actions here and now.

Mūkkaṉ's creative use of indexicals not only connects him, his house, and his family to Veḷḷāḷakaṇṭaṉ's past and present (so that the story temporally overtakes the telling, as Genette [1980, p. 221] might put it). It is also what makes the story into discourse, first, by telling the story in the here and now, and second, through the more directed use of pragmatic, indexical signs (pronouns, deictics, gestures) that tellers everywhere use to make their stories part of a discursive present.

As Benveniste pointed out, the kind of first-person "presence" that first-person pronouns like "we" announce makes for *discourse,* makes for "inter-subjective communication" in the here and now (1971, p. 219; see also Genette, 1980, pp. 28–30). Ramanujan (1991, p. 25) also analogizes that the difference between a story and discourse is the same as the difference between a sentence (that says something) and a speech act (that, as Austin showed us, *does* something). The story tells us something, and the telling of it *does* something. The story's *tellings* are, along with Veḷḷāḷakaṇṭaṉ's walk, then, part of a current discourse on spatial and social relations in the village. That is, while the Veḷḷāḷakaṇṭaṉ *story* is a kind of history of past events that authorize Veḷḷāḷakaṇṭaṉ 's present agency, its *telling* is discourse about present circumstances, relations, persons, and events.

That residents of Yanaimangalam understand their tellings of past events to be potentially productive acts in the present is nowhere more evident than in the two tellings—or rather the difference between the two tellings—of the Veḷḷāḷakaṇṭaṉ story that Piccaiyyā, a young S. C. leader of Middle Hamlet, told me on the verandah of his house. In both tellings, he highlighted the role that members of his *jāti,* the Paḷḷars, played in retrieving Veḷḷāḷakaṇṭaṉ from his embattled fields and carrying him to the irrigation stream where he died. It was they who cremated him, threw his ashes in the stream, and who thus brought him to the place where he became a god on the spot. They were the first to see him as a god. Piccaiyyā's two tellings were set apart, however, by elements of context. He launched into the first telling angrily and spontaneously after narrating to me an incident in which a group of Tēvars, including their headman and some local police, had recently expelled Middle Hamlet residents from the goddess temple. As he told the

Veḷḷāḷakaṇṭaṉ story, he named *jātis—those* Tēvars, the Dhobis, we Paḷḷars—and gestured toward the Tēvar street with an angry wave of the arm when he mentioned them in the story, thus making connections between living Tēvars "over there" and past ruthless actors in the story.

The second telling, a few days later, was one I staged: I brought out my tape recorder and asked Piccaiyyā to repeat the story he had already told me. He agreed to tell the story again, but he told it differently. He omitted all references to *jāti,* and when I urged him to provide *jāti* names, he claimed he did not know what he had so vehemently asserted only a few days previously. In the second telling, he narrated that Veḷḷāḷakaṇṭaṉ was out hunting (and maybe guarding, he added, with some unscholarly prompting by me) and "many people" (*niraiya-pēr*) came and attacked him and killed him. My assistant pushed him a little, asking "*Who* is it who did that?" and Piccaiyyā replied, "I couldn't say which *jāti* . . . the bosses who *were* in charge of protection," using the past tense.

Piccaiyyā was well aware that his telling of the story was creative and potentially consequential discourse about present social relations and not a mere recitation of an objective history of events. One of the consequences he feared was the possibility of violence, for residents of Middle Hamlet saw the Tēvars, who were allied with the local police, as a physical as well as an economic threat (see D. Mines, 2002). When Piccaiyyā saw that I was trying to preserve his telling, that I could repeat it, that others could hear him tell it outside the context of his telling, he "hid" (J. Scott, 1990) the presence of the story he had voiced to me previously, keeping it in the anonymous third person and stowing it firmly in the past tense.

We have moved temporarily away from Veḷḷāḷakaṇṭaṉ's walk. To conclude, let us return to it briefly. I have shown that the story and the walk are not unrelated: the story authorizes the walk. The walk Veḷḷāḷakaṇṭaṉ takes is, however, more like the *tellings* of the story than it is like the story itself. The walk, like the tellings, is about present relations and realities. In fact, Veḷḷāḷakaṇṭaṉ's actions at the festival do not follow the story line at all. He does not reenact the story or repeat its history. Rather, he makes a different story as he walks it discursively into the present through movement and speech. Veḷḷāḷakaṇṭaṉ speaks for himself. He centers himself as a present first-person, an interlocutor in dialogue with persons and in motion across the territory. Veḷḷāḷakaṇṭaṉ speaks for himself as he crosses the present terrains of the village on processions and talks to those he meets. This time the Tēvars do not spill his guts. They wait along with everyone else.

Because Veḷḷāḷakaṇṭaṉ is a walking and talking "double agent" (an agent of god and of his *jāti* or lineage), his actions, like those of any agent, effect real outcomes. Among the outcomes Veḷḷāḷakaṇṭaṉ effects are the ontological expansion of the space called *ūr* to include those otherwise excluded. He also, as I indicated, reconfigures dominant social orderings of center and periphery. As Veḷḷāḷakaṇṭaṉ makes his guard round, he makes it possible for his community, his kinsmen, and for Middle Hamlet residents as well, to refigure their relation to dominant village *jātis,* and especially to the Tēvars.

Veḷḷāḷakaṇṭaṉ's walk is heroic. Like the steps Viṣṇu takes to open a field for others to act, to wage battle (de Certeau, 1984, p. 124), so does Veḷḷāḷakaṇṭaṉ's lonely night walk open and create a space for the activities—including discourses—of others. And it also gives these others, not only Dhobis but in this case the Middle Hamlet S. C. too, a place *in* an *ūr* of his—and their—own making.

Residents of Yanaimangalam debate and contest their village through a politics of movement. The kind of refigurings that Veḷḷāḷakaṇṭaṉ's walks effect are not at all uncommon in and around the temples to fierce gods in Yanaimangalam and, I would predict, elsewhere. In several fierce-god temples in Yanaimangalam, the dominant social orderings instantiated in the goddess temple are redefined and often undermined (see D. Mines, 1995). A thorough analysis of fierce-god temple rituals in Yanaimangalam complicates the common understanding of the social place of these fierce gods in South India. In many studies of the area, fierce gods are considered to reflect and parallel the position of their allegedly low-caste worshipers. That is, fierce gods are often thought to belong to "low castes" and, like them, to rank low in a rather static village pantheon (see, e.g., Babb, 1975, pp. 237–246; Dumont, 1986 [1957]; Fuller, 1987). My research shows that, on the contrary, these temples often include dominant, high *jātis* among their temple association members and shows also that what authorizes definitions of social orderings that take place in fierce-god temples is not political and economic dominance, nor is it essential, static *jāti* character or rank, but rather events inscribed in narratives like the Veḷḷāḷakaṇṭaṉ story, and made real in practices like telling stories and taking walks. These practices constitute the village itself as a highly contested spatial unit.

Notes

1. Mapping the village, counting it, and even the seemingly innocent chore of describing it, are actions that set about "knowing" the village and, as de Certeau puts it, they thereby "colonize space." Or, as Daniel puts it, such accounts are about "seeing" as opposed to "being," epistemology as opposed to ontology (1996, pp. 56–59). For other works that discuss the power of such knowledge or spatial—consonant with ideational—colonization see, for example, Appadurai, 1993; Carter, 1987; Cohn, 1987; Foucault, 1980, pp. 70–75; Sen, n.d.
2. The *ūr,* here, is contrasted to the village defined as a revenue unit. In the latter case, boundaries are fixed. In the former, boundaries are fluid (Daniel, 1984, p. 61ff.).
3. Not all of these thirty-five temples celebrate regular festivals, and not all of them have processions that presume to "encircle the whole village." Smaller processions nonetheless mark out the territory of the temple association, and thus are part of the set of organized processions that constitute the spatial dimensions of the *ūr* (see, e.g., D. Mines, 1995).
4. The idea that the village may be heterogeneously constituted through action is one in keeping with recent work on Indian social organization more generally, which moves away from unified and totalizing structures toward flexible, multiple, and shifting realities that stress how Indians themselves understand their world to be pragmatically constituted in action. See, for example, Appadurai, 1986, 1992; Daniel, 1996; Inden, 1990; Marriott ,1990 [1989]; Peabody, 1991; Raheja, 1988; Raheja and Gold, 1994; Richman, 1991.
5. Others have written of the power of processions to claim and contest territory, both historically and in contemporary South Asia (Inglis, 1985; M. Mines, 1994; Peabody, 1991; Sax, 1991).
6. I use the term "ontology" in order to express that I intend to outline how Tamils understand their relation to the *ūr* as one of shared existence or being. Ontology may be contrasted to epistemology, which works to know "from above" (Daniel, 1996, pp. 43–49). I take the distinction originally from Bachelard's discussion of spatial imagery in poetry (1969 [1958]).
7. E.g. Beck, 1976; Daniel, 1984; Moore, 1990; Ramanujan, 1967, 1985; Trawick, 1991. Sax confirms come of the same principles operating in parts of North India (1991, pp. 71–77).
8. For a folk variant of this creation myth, see Daniel, 1984, pp. 3–5.
9. Mūkkaṉ and others of the Washerman caste prefer the neutral name "Dhobi" to the Tamil Vaṇṇāṉ, which has negative connotations.
10. Doniger (1980, p. 91) distinguishes between "breast" and "tooth" goddesses. Fierce gods, too, have teeth. And they bite.
11. Indeed, there are examples of structural-functional analyses along these lines (Beck, 1972; Good, 1985; Srinivas, 1952).
12. Standing with one's back to a god declares one's capacity to channel the god's power and to possibly speak for the god. It is a claim to power that is not made lightly, given gods' capacities to severely harm, kill, and sink the ships of those who cross or block their line of sight (see, e.g., Hanchett, 1988, p. 159; D. Scott, 1994, pp. 40–47).

NINE

Permeable Homes

Domestic Service, Household Space, and the Vulnerability of Class Boundaries in Urban South India

Sara Dickey

Domestic service can feel like a mixed blessing to middle- and upper-class Indian women. Employing domestic workers helps them to support their family's class standing by maintaining a properly clean and ordered home, and by enabling them to pursue other status-producing activities and/or their own employment. The presence of servants also serves in and of itself as a crucial sign of class achievement. On the other hand, servants' entrance into employers' homes marks the introduction of a dangerous outside into an orderly and protected inside. Employers feel that servants threaten their families and, in particular, their class status. The movement of servants from their own homes into and between employers' households actually has a number of effects—including the distribution of information, labor, and material and cultural capital, as well as the creation of social networks across classes and neighborhoods—many of which are viewed neutrally or positively by employers as well as social analysts. Yet when I spoke with employers in the South Indian city of Madurai, their most consistent and compelling comments on servants' movements had to do with the dangers posed to their households by servants' entrances and exits.

Employers feel they must vigilantly protect their families and homes against the lower-class dangers that could destroy the order so carefully produced as a sign of their class standing. Servants represent the dirt, disease, and "rubbish" (Chakrabarty, 1991) of a disorderly outside world that, as we will see, employers commonly associate with the lower class and that pointedly contrast with the ideal cleanliness, order, and hygiene of their own homes. Slippage in the other direction is also a great risk; both symbolic and material capital must be prevented from escaping the house through gossip and theft. Employers' accounts project an image of a household whose perimeters need to be carefully and constantly ramified against the disorderly mixing of categories (cf. Douglas, 1966) that servants' entrances and exits entail. The household and its members communicate an image to spectators—from neighbors, to co-workers, to fellow guests at weddings, to the community at large—who interpret the symbolic markers of class produced in the home.

The threat that domestic workers pose derives from the juxtaposition of spatial and emotional intimacy with class distance. Anxieties about this conflict appear repeatedly in middle- and upper-class women's worries about the permeability of household boundaries, and in their attempts to control servants' actions both inside and outside the employer's home. Unraveling the construction of this threat reveals critical aspects of the class "system" in urban South India, its maintenance and vulnerabilities, and furthers an understanding of "how the domestic, even when ideologically separated from other aspects of human life, is inextricably bound to and mutually constitutive of broader political and economic structures" (Moran, 1992, pp. 98–99). In order to provide a clearer understanding of the nature of class in South India, I examine conceptions of inside and outside space, the boundary transgressions entailed in domestic service, and middle- and upper-class women's responses to these transgressions.

Although most of my work on domestic service in Madurai attends to relationships among people in a variety of class positions (see, e.g., Dickey, 2000), in this essay I focus on employers—women who define themselves as members of the middle and upper classes—in order to scrutinize their perceptions of the class relations that are constructed within their homes. In examining these women's contributions to class relations by focusing on their homes, I do not mean to perpetuate a stereotype that restricts women's agency in class relations to the domestic sphere. Many of these women are active, for example, in volunteer and/or paid work that contributes directly and quite publicly to the economic and symbolic bases of their family's class standing. I do wish to argue, however, that rhetoric about class that appears to be focused solely on domestic interactions in fact reproduces class relations and ideologies more broadly, and that women's responsibilities in the home are a primary source of their contributions to these relations and ideologies. In this regard, I support Moran's definition of the "domestic" as "both the socially defined space associated with a residential group and the meaningful practices that take place there." As she points out, "domestic spaces are neither 'natural' nor divorced from other domains of human behavior" (1992, p. 98). Indeed, as I will demonstrate throughout this essay, no space is "natural," but is imbued continuously with symbolic meanings through daily practice (Bourdieu, 1977). I will discuss actions within space and the accounts that portray them in order to examine the ideologies of class that they reflect and produce. I find that employers' accounts expose the insecurity of class in urban South India, and the centrality of the middle- and upper-class home—and of women's roles in particular—in producing and protecting class boundaries.

I began to study domestic service interactions in Madurai in 1991–1992, in order to consider how people in different classes come to conceive of each other in opposed terms. Domestic service provides an ideal domain for this work for several reasons. First, it allows a focus on domestic realms and the roles of women. Second, it provides a setting where class is reproduced and challenged on a daily and intimate basis. Finally, domestic service interactions constitute the most intense, sustained contact with members of other classes that most of its participants encounter. Most critical for my research, the participants perceive themselves to be on different sides of class lines.

My work takes a relational approach to the question of domestic service and class. In order to learn about domestic service relations, I spoke with domestic workers and employers who differed in gender, religion, caste, age, socioeconomic status, and household size. This included formal interviews with twenty-seven servants and twenty-eight employers, and conversations with numerous others. I also spent large amounts of time in workers' and employers' homes, talking informally, observing, and sometimes joining in the household work. For ethical and methodological reasons, however, I avoided interviews with employers and servants present in the same households, since I was concerned about the potential for and perception of violations of confidentiality that speaking with employer-employee pairs would have created. Finally, in addition to carrying out domestic tasks myself when living in Madurai, I have also employed domestic workers during portions of my years there. My experiences as an employer and my long-standing friendships with domestic workers gave me shifting and conflicted alliances with both workers and employers. Both sides were as interested in my domestic arrangements as I was in theirs, and they identified (and sometimes criticized) the similarities and contrasts between our situations and sympathies.

Class, Caste, Gender, and Domestic Service

Before going on to examine employers' accounts and actions, I want to set the stage by talking about Madurai and the forms of hierarchy that appear most explicitly in domestic service, including class, caste, and gender. In downtown Madurai, where four concentric roads circle the large Hindu temple complex of the goddess Minakshi, houses are densely packed, separated by a maze of narrow lanes, and while some of their residents are wealthy, the city's most luxurious residences are located in relatively spacious areas across the river. The poorest slums are also outside of the city center, interspersed with wealthier neighborhoods as well as businesses and markets, and domestic workers rarely have to travel far to their places of employment.

Despite clear socioeconomic divisions in Indian society, class in India has until recently received little scholarly attention. In the past dozen years, scholars inside and outside of India have taken to task a long-standing academic emphasis on caste, pointing to other hierarchies that provide competing frames of reference to the purity-pollution scale underlying most models of caste (Appadurai, 1986; Dirks, 1987; Raheja, 1988; Ram, 1991). Class, which is more mutable than caste and derives more directly from both economic and social standing, has become one of the most potent idioms of identity, rank, and political power in contemporary India, particularly in urban areas (Dickey, 1993a, 1993b; Kapadia, 1995; Kumar, 1988). My contention is not that caste has become unimportant in shaping identities and interactions, but that class provides an additional and largely distinct hierarchy and source of identity. The past fifteen years have seen increased attention to class in research on South Asia, though few studies have focused on its symbolic dimensions, or on class in the towns and cities where one-quarter of Indians and over one-third of Tamilnadu residents live (Government of India, 1991, pp. 8–9).

Furthermore, little of this work on class in South Asia has attended to the precise forms that class takes (Dickey, 1993a; for exceptions, see Athreya et al., 1987; Brow, 1981; L. Caplan, 1987; Holmström, 1984; Washbrook, 1989). My primary interest lies in indigenous concepts of class and their symbolic manifestations. I rely on the major divisions that Madurai residents use. These are usually based on two- or three-part models of class structure, composed either of the poor and the rich in the first case, or of lower, middle, and upper classes in the second (cf. L. Caplan, 1987, p. 11). The two-part model is held most often by people who are poor, and the Tamil terms employed in it are usually *ēḻai makkaḷ* ("poor people") or *illātavarkaḷ* ("people who have nothing") versus *paṇakkārarkaḷ* ("rich people") or *periyavarkaḷ* ("big people"). The three-part model, which is invoked most frequently by wealthier people, includes the lower class or the mass, the middle class, and the upper class. Whereas the domestic workers I spoke with used Tamil terms and placed themselves at the bottom of the hierarchy, employers almost always used English terms and placed themselves in the middle or upper category. The English terms are emic categories for employers, and although employers will occasionally refer to *ēḻai makkaḷ* and *paṇakkārarkaḷ* in casual conversation, they almost always use English terms when discussing the class system per se, even when otherwise speaking in Tamil.[1] Moreover, the referents of these terms vary according to the speaker. Although the employers of my acquaintance always identified themselves as middle or upper class, few saw themselves as *paṇakkārarkaḷ,* a term they generally reserved for the wealthiest and most elite people of their acquaintance, and they generally argued that no one who was a waged or salaried worker could be considered part of the *paṇakkārarkaḷ*. Domestic workers, on the other hand, considered anyone with a certain amount of material ease to belong to the *paṇakkārarkaḷ;* this certainly included all their employers. The distinction between the middle and the upper middle class shifted similarly (and was harder to identify; the difference was often viewed as a matter of degree), but the distinction between those who were and were not poor was easier for people to identify.

In Madurai, people who are locally referred to as either *ēḻai makkaḷ* or "lower class" include skilled and unskilled laborers or low-level office workers (and their household members), who possess or control little in the way of land and other property and endure a general lack of economic security. Almost all have incomes at or near the Indian poverty line; many servants' families, who are some of the poorest residents of Madurai, subsist at such a level that a day without work means a day without food. Heston reports that 34% of the urban population in India is at or below the poverty level, which in 1988 was approximately Rs. 90 per person per month; in South India, 30% of the urban population lives in poverty according to these standards (1990, pp. 103, 106, 109). Levels of poverty are relative, and Heston points out that over 95% of Indians would be considered poor by U.S. standards (1990, p. 103). It should be noted that the Rs. 90 figure was determined for rural areas, and is even less adequate in urban areas where a higher percentage of commodities must be acquired with cash.

Those Madurai residents who are locally referred to by the poor as either *paṇakkārarkaḷ* or *periyavarkaḷ,* or by themselves as "middle" or "upper class," include merchants, shop owners, professionals (such as doctors or lawyers), teachers, and government officials, large landowners, and the members of their households. While there are some differences between those who identify themselves as middle and upper class in terms of lifestyle, values, and income (such as an increasing reliance on returns from property and/or investments for income, rather than on wages or salary), they also share significant attributes. These include a degree of financial ease, and a corresponding ability to purchase and display a variety of consumer goods. Other shared features include a relatively substantial education and a set of values communicated through school curricula, and an awareness and expectation of personal opportunities to be gained through education and employment. They also share a common view of the poor, whom they generally portray as dirty, irresponsible, and often morally misguided. While there were individual variations, I found essentially no differences in the ways that people of different income levels, occupations, and education depict their servants. Finally, domestic service itself provides one of the clearest markers of class distinctions. The ability to hire servants is a sign of having achieved middle- or upper-class status; poor people, on the other hand, may work as servants but cannot afford to employ them.

There are no meaningful statistical data available to indicate the size and boundaries of the middle and upper classes. They are certainly, however, a relatively small portion of Madurai's population. Those who could be considered to constitute a Marxian "bourgeoisie" are fewer yet. Washbrook points out that Tamilnadu, with its "small-scale market economy," possesses only a small and relatively weak bourgeoisie (1989, p. 259), while Caplan (who does find strong evidence of an urban "middle class") notes that in urban areas, "ownership of the means of production resides principally with the state or multinational corporations, so that the indigenous capitalist class is only a tiny, highly compact, and barely visible minority" (L. Caplan, 1987, pp. 13–14).

Madurai residents often speak of and judge one another in class-related terms.[2] As the discussion above suggests, they rely on both economic and symbolic markers in reading class standing. The local terms for different classes imply this: "poor/rich/big people" and "people who have nothing" invoke the confluence and even indistinguishability of economic and symbolic features—of poverty and possessions, and of wealth and a metaphorical size that indicates social power and importance, command over resources, and cultural and political sophistication. When people make class judgments, they identify differences in clothing, food, hygiene, manners, sophistication, education, intelligence, language, mutual support systems, and attitudes toward money and consumption.

In turn, class is determined by both economic and symbolic features (cf. Ortner, 1991). Thus, class standing derives from not only income, material assets, and occupation but also from education, consumption habits, fashion, and ways of speaking, among many other signs and sources (cf. Bourdieu, 1984). I follow Lionel Caplan in arguing that such a view

> takes us away from the static and sterile notion of class as an occupational or income category, or even a set of people standing in a particular relation to the means of production. It invites us, rather, to regard class as a cultural as well as an economic formation. This enables us to treat class struggle as being every bit as much about definitive meaning systems or appropriate religious views and observances as about material means, scarce jobs, or the control of property (1987, p. 14).

The economic and the symbolic interact in everyday aspects of class relations and identity. While honor, reputation, and rank are all somewhat independent of class in urban India, they are all aligned with it as well. They play a crucial role, for example, in establishing the social connections that allow people to find the best jobs and to attract customers and clients. Nor is their role entirely utilitarian; a reputation for honorable or disreputable behavior, for example, can by itself contribute to the judgments others make of an individual's class, separately from that person's (or his or her family's) financial status. What makes class a distinct form of hierarchy, and not just a variation on caste or a conjunction of independent status markers, is its basis in economic power, combined with the things that financial resources can produce—such as education, honor, and conspicuous consumption—that themselves become sources of economic power. The economic and symbolic features of class are interdependent, but neither is reducible to the other.

Caste remains another significant form of identity and hierarchy in Madurai. Caste, or *jāti* (literally "genus," a classificatory form applied to nonhuman as well as human beings), refers to the hereditary, endogamous, hierarchically ranked, and sometimes occupationally specific units to which all Hindus belongs (as do, to an arguable degree, Indian Muslims, Christians, Jains, Parsis, Sikhs, and everyone else). Caste is essential to individuals' identities in part because, as this definition suggests, it helps determine whom they can marry, where their place lies in a social and ritual hierarchy, and sometimes what work they do. It affects individuals in other basic ways as well; domestic rituals, founding myths, goals for education, and rules about gendered behavior often vary by caste. Among Hindus and some Christians, different castes are understood to possess differential amounts of pollution, an essence that can be passed between people through any actions that transmit inherent substances (e.g., by touch, sex, or food sharing); this pollution increases as position in the caste hierarchy decreases (Babb, 1975; Marriott, 1969; Marriott and Inden, 1977).

Caste is, however, only one feature of identity, and cannot be assumed to be the ultimate or most "encompassing" determinant of behavior (Appadurai, 1986; Parish, 1996), as some analysts have suggested (primarily Dumont, 1970). Despite the attention that caste has been paid by many observers, it is cited less frequently by residents than many other principles of association. When Madurai residents talk about "people like us," they are much more likely to be identifying themselves with a socioeconomic category (e.g., "poor people" or "the upper class") or by gender.

While caste can be important in determining social behavior in rural South India (where divisions are especially rigid between the very lowest "untouchable" castes and other Hindus), it is less so in the cities, at least on the surface of social relations. While caste considerations are also present in the city, they are frequently submerged. Most people have absorbed the government denunciation of caste discrimination to the extent that they know they are supposed to believe that caste is not socially significant. Moreover, the crowding and anonymity of city life make adherence to strict rules of hierarchy impossible in public settings. Members of lower castes are aware—sometimes militantly so—of their legal rights to equality. All of these factors make it difficult for residents of urban caste-integrated neighborhoods to practice open discrimination, or to give caste any marked importance in public. Nonetheless, while the importance of caste is attenuated and modified in today's urban areas, it has neither disappeared nor become irrelevant. It is particularly visible in schooling and government employment, where quotas or "reservations" are allotted to castes officially recognized as targets of historical discrimination. As we will see, it also appears especially in the domestic arena, where caste concerns may now be voiced in the idiom of class.

One form of identity that receives constant and explicit attention is gender. Gender roles and expectations vary by religion, caste, class, and region, but they are always highly significant in determining identity and the interactions of daily life. For our purposes, the most significant gender norm to note is that, regardless of whether women hold paid employment, the care of the home and the nurture of family members is women's responsibility. This includes food preparation and serving, cleaning, laundry, and childcare (including overseeing children's education), all of which are subsumed under the term "housework" (the Tamil term *viṭṭu-vēlai* is a literal equivalent of the English word). In a culture in which extended family ties hold tremendous importance and carry frequent and significant obligations, women also have primary responsibility in most families for kin work (Di Leonardo, 1987), for keeping the broad network of relatives involved in each other's lives and their mutual obligations observed. Among Hindus, and to some extent Christians, women are also usually the major practitioners of domestic religious worship. Men, on the other hand, should be the primary earners in the family, and the male head of household bears formal authority over family members and household decisions. They too are often heavily involved in their children's lives; men take great pride in their children, often play with the younger ones, and are greatly concerned with later educational decisions, though they are usually much less involved with the daily details of education and nurture than their wives.

Marriage is virtually universal, and almost all marriages are arranged by parents. Strictures against premarital sexual activity are very strong for women, much less so for men. Modesty and chastity form the dominant cultural ideal for women of all religions, castes, and classes. Because avoiding public display is a key sign of modesty, women ideally should not go outside the home more than necessary. Actual behavior varies widely. In Madurai, the women whose movements are most restricted are generally Muslims or conservative high-caste Hindus. It is very rare, however, for a woman to be completely secluded in the home, and women in South India are generally much freer to move about than women of similar caste and class in North India. Staying in the home is in any case impossible for most poor women, whose families would often go without food if they did not earn money. Although some home-based employment is available to poor women (e.g., tying flower garlands or making foods that are then collected by middlemen and sold to dealers), it tends to be less lucrative, more tedious, and less independent than work found outside of the house.

This brings us back to the realm of domestic service—in which poor women leave their homes to work in the households of wealthier women—and the role of gender and the economy in its construction. Because household work is labor-intensive, largely manual, and poorly paid, most middle- and upper-class households hire lower-class servants. Housework in Madurai is, as I have said, the domain of women. The alignment of women and domestic service must not be taken for granted, however, but should be understood as the result of specific economic and social forces (Hansen, 1990). Although many poor women cannot afford to remain at home as they should "properly" do, their work options are limited by a lack of education, perceived lack of physical strength, and/or the need to do protected (i.e., nonpublic) work (P. Caplan, 1985; Raju, 1993). Domestic labor satisfies these criteria, and is moreover eschewed by men and higher-class women due to low pay and stigma. By taking it on, poor women free themselves and their employers from certain gendered expectations—employers from the most onerous household tasks and themselves from the restrictions of staying at home—though each is a complicated freedom.

Domestic workers and their employers come from a variety of castes and religions. In my sample, just over one-quarter of employers are Brahmans, 22% each are other high castes (Chettiars, Pillais, and Nayars) and mid-level castes (Reddiars, Thevars, and Mudaliyars), just over one-quarter are of the ritually low-ranking Nadar caste, and one employer belongs to a scheduled ("Untouchable") caste whose name I did not learn. About 15% are Christian, and the rest Hindu. Of the domestic workers, about 15% are high-caste (Vaitthiyars and Pillais), a third are evenly divided among middle and lower castes (Thevars, Agamudiyars, and Nadars), and half belong to scheduled castes

(Chakkiliyars, Paraiyars, and Pallars). About one-quarter are Christian, one woman is Muslim, and the remainder are Hindu. This sample is representative in terms of the range of castes and religions of Madurai employers and domestic workers (except for the absence of Muslims among employers); it is not precisely representative of their distribution.

Some employers hold paid jobs, and many carry out some other kind of formal responsibilities outside the home, such as charitable, social service, or religious work. Most domestic workers provide the primary economic support of their families (although their husbands may earn more money than they do). Today, most domestic service in Madurai is part-time, which means that servants may put in a full day's labor, but in multiple homes, often at a single task—such as washing pots, dusting and scrubbing, doing laundry, or cleaning latrines. Other domestic workers do most or all of these tasks, along with cooking, in a single home. Part-time workers labor anywhere from 2 to 10 hours per day (the women I knew typically worked 4 to 8 hours, usually in two or three homes), the length depending on their own household responsibilities, current availability of jobs, their family's need for income, and (when married) their husband's attitude toward their work outside their home. For those who work full-time in a single home, domestic service fills most of their days from morning until evening, with a couple of hours of rest in the afternoon.

Whether working part- or full-time, it is now fairly rare for servants to live in the homes of their employers. Wealthy families have also become less likely to employ large retinues of servants. This is a notable change, and has taken place over the past several decades. In many ways it represents increased independence for workers, who are now less vulnerable to demands for long or irregular working hours, have greater power to negotiate wages and tasks, and have greater control over their own family lives than when they were dependents of a wealthy patriarch. At the same time the change can mean greater insecurity, since employers no longer feel as much obligation to provide financial assistance with such needs as education or medicine or life-cycle rituals, or to provide continued care in lean times. Nor, however, as both employers and employees argue, are their relations like those of factory workers and bosses; both sides feel some informal obligations to one another, much more than in a formally contractual relationship, and "affection" remains a quality cultivated in the other by workers and employers alike.[3] All the domestic service participants I spoke with saw advantages in this state, since the ambiguity and personalization allow them to try to work the relationship in their favor. This is an important point, and leads to an equally significant corollary: in Madurai the negotiation of power in domestic service is such that neither side typically sees itself entering the relationship with predetermined control.

Inside and Outside Space

Domestic service is distinct from many other forms of employment, as are the relations developed within it, because it takes place in and focuses on the employer's home. Literature about domestic service in numerous cultures suggests that similar tensions appear widely because of the combination of an intimacy based on the worker's closeness to the family and a distance based on class and other hierarchies that are reproduced through the work and that must be maintained in the home. Domestic service thus involves the mixing of a variety of categories that might otherwise be kept separate—including class, race, ethnicity, nationality, and gender, depending on the particulars of local hierarchies and economies.

In Madurai, it also involves a mixing of spatial categories that generally remain segregated. These categories, those of inside (*uḷḷē*) and outside (*veḷiyē*), form an enduring and gendered spatial polarity. The contrast between them molds urban residents' concepts of self and other, and affects their movements through space. The concepts of inside and outside are aligned with a number of parallel contrasts, including family/not family, like/different, close/distant, affection/distance, safe/unsafe, protected/unprotected, clean/dirty, and private/public. I explore all of these contrasts in greater depth below. Here, I set out the general parameters of the categories of inside and outside, and explain their relevance to the organization of domestic space.

First, the center of the inside, and the space most closely associated with it, is the home. This is an association that appears to be both enduring and widespread in South Asia. Masselos notes that in nineteenth-century Bombay, the center of what he calls "accustomed" space—that part of the city most known and familiar, demarcated by both space and time—was "the place of habitation—the home, room, chawl, apartment—and its immediate environs. Even when an individual did not live in a dwelling but on the pavement, a sense of residence was established around a hearth, cooking spot, or other regular eating place" (1991, p. 40). Chatterjee examines the contrast that appeared between the home (*ghar*) and the outside world (*bahir*) in nineteenth- and twentieth-century nationalist rhetoric in Bengal. The home was identified with the spiritual, the pure, and the authentic, while the outside world was portrayed as an external material sphere constructed and dominated by the colonial ruler. This dichotomy was also a gendered division: as Chatterjee contends, "the home represents one's inner spiritual self, one's true identity . . . and woman is its representation" (1993, p. 121). The purity of the home includes spiritual, cultural, and physical elements, and women are not only to be protected from the outside, they are themselves the protectors of the home and all it represents. In contemporary India, Chakrabarty argues that the conception of the house as "an inside produced by symbolic enclosure for the purpose of protection" is "an instance of a theme general to South Asia," in which the inside is sharply distinguished from an "outside which can . . . be rubbished" (1991, p. 22). It is, as we will see, this "rubbish" that threatens the home that middle- and upper-class women are struggling to protect.

This distinction between the safe, pure, ordered space of the inside and the dangerous, contaminated, disordered space of the outside appears to hold true for contemporary Tamils. Based on his work in a village in central Tamilnadu, Daniel notes that houses are homologous to persons (1984, pp. 109, 114, 115), like whom they have essential substances that must be kept in proper balance—i.e., protected from improper additions or deletions of substances—and therefore their boundaries must be safeguarded. Person and home are also linked in the concept of *akam,* a category that refers to the "interior, heart, household" and is distinguished from *puṟam,* or the "exterior, outer parts of the body, yard outside the house, public" (Ramanujan, 1985, p. 233), in a system of Tamil poetics that finds its fullest elaboration in classical poetry but that remains, as Ramanujan has argued, "crucial to Tamil culture" (p. 235). And, in an especially compelling example, Seizer (2000) points out that even stage actresses—women who must move through and perform in highly outside spaces—work diligently to construct inside spaces on the road in order to see and project themselves as proper women.

Second, the perimeters of the inside and outside are relative, shifting, and fluid. Daniel argues that like the *ūr* ("village") or *nāṭu* ("land" or "country"), the *vīṭu,* or "home,"

> is defined person-centrically. What a given person refers to as his *vīṭu* changes according to what structure is contextually relevant to him at any given time. Thus, to a speaker, *vīṭu* can mean the external structure of a house, the particular residential unit of his nuclear family

> in a house inhabited by a joint family, a particular room in the house inhabited by a joint family, or a particular room in the house (1984, p. 108).

As Daniel suggests, the same is true of spaces outside the home. Other areas that are defined as relatively inside or safe, familiar space at one particular time can change over the course of a day (between daylight and darkness, for example), or over the course of longer periods. Streets can become less public and more inside or outside during times of religious tension, for example, when people who venture into neighborhoods in which their religious identity makes them outsiders become vulnerable to attack (Masselos, 1991).

Third, as the last example suggests, it is worth emphasizing that the outside and the inside do not entirely correspond to Euro-American notions of public and private. Thus some streets are only partially public spaces in India. In certain cases, especially in rural areas, only certain castes are allowed to walk on particular streets; even in the cities, many streets are tiny lanes on which outsiders are closely watched and may feel unwelcome, especially if the lane or neighborhood is segregated by religion or caste. In these cases, streets can be inside spaces, but, as I have suggested, their definition as inside or outside—safe or unsafe, protected or unprotected—may vary with time. Finally, public and private spaces can be mixed, and arenas that in many industrialized countries are kept separate (such as family and commerce) can be combined in taken-for-granted ways. Urban spaces often have multiple functions: a marketplace can be "a sleeping place and even a customary thoroughfare" as well as a worksite (Masselos, 1991, p. 40); a home can be a workshop or site of commerce as well as the family's gathering place.

All of this suggests that the concepts of inside and outside are crucial cultural distinctions. Since, as I discuss below, employers identify servants with the outside, this distinction helps to illuminate employers' fears about servants' encroachment on the inside space of employers' homes. It is also important to note that, given the relativity of these two categories, there are gradations of space within each category as well. Thus in the home, some spaces are more unadulteratedly inside than others. Another way of putting this is that the outside is less allowable in some domestic areas than others. Consequently, the concepts of inside and outside help to explain spatial organization inside the home itself, and restrictions placed on servants' and other outsiders' movements within the home. Before looking more closely at employers' reactions to servants' boundary crossings, we need to know more about the organization of domestic space.

The primary principles that determine the spatial organization of households are concerns about purity and privacy, both of which are closely allied with notions of inside and outside. These principles are followed across classes, castes, regions, and other divisions in India with remarkable regularity, but the elaborateness with which they are played out depends on two general tendencies. First, the higher the *caste* of the household, the greater the concern for purity, which determines the placement of certain areas and the persons who have access to them. Second, the higher the *class* of the household, the greater the number of rooms in a house, and of rooms with single functions, and often the greater elaboration of outdoor space as well.[4] Traditionally, in Hindu and Christian homes, the purest spaces are placed farthest from the entrance. These include the cooking, food storage, and *pūjā* (worship) spaces. Each of these areas can be a separate room in the houses of the wealthy, or a delineated space within a single room in smaller houses. Another principle simultaneously in operation in contemporary larger homes is the placement of the family's most private areas, especially bedrooms, at the furthest reaches of the house. (Note that both of these principles require that access be increasingly restricted to people most immediately connected with the family.) The most elaborately constructed households today are built on the dual and often overlapping continua of purity and privacy, with spaces occurring in more or less this order:[5]

Street
Gate
Yard (a pavement and/or garden space between the street and the verandah)
Verandah/doorway area
Door
Living room
Eating area
Kitchen and storeroom
Pūjā room (in Hindu and Christian homes)
Bedroom(s)

Latrine and bathing area (this can be inside or outside the house)
Backyard, stables, roof
Servant housing

Here, the gate is the most stable marker of inside/outside and family/nonfamily space, though as always these categories are relative and shifting, and operate on a continuum rather than as a clear dichotomy. Areas closest to the inside/outside boundaries serve as transitional, liminal spaces that normally moderate the entrance of the outside into the inside, and vice versa. (Note that those spaces I have listed below the line do not follow exactly along the continuum; lying beyond the house [either behind or above], they are more secluded than the front space, but much less private or pure [with certain exceptions, such as areas where holy plants are grown on rooftops] than internal areas of the house.) Of course in many houses some of these areas are absent, or combined in single homes, but the same principles are followed with notable regularity. My friend Viji, for example, had married into a wealthy family, and lived in a very elaborate house within a walled complex. The first floor of her home was entered through a foyer opening onto a living room, beyond which was the dining room and then the kitchen, a *pūjā* room, and a locked storeroom. Upstairs was a television room, which led to two bedrooms and two bathrooms. On the other hand, most servants' home space (like that of other poor residents in Madurai) consists only of a doorway area and one enclosed room. Sonia, a servant who is a friend of Viji's cook, lives in a house that is part of a "line," a row of single-room houses that share adjoining mud walls and a long thatched roof. Each house has a low doorway, which is often used for casual socializing. Inside the doorway, Sonia's home has a wood hearth for cooking in the back right-hand corner, the furthest spot from the entrance, and pictures of deities hang along the back wall. Mats rolled in a corner are used for the family to sleep on. There is a latrine behind the houses that is shared by all the residents of the line.

Both these houses are constructed on the same principles. In each case, the purest areas (those for cooking and worship) are as far from the entrance as possible (and well apart from polluted areas such as bathrooms), and food is eaten well inside the home; similarly, the storeroom in Viji's home is well set off, though in Sonia's home there are rarely any foodstuffs to store. Nor in single-room homes can there be separate rooms for sleeping—the interior of the house remains more associated with the family than is the exterior, but privacy in general is less of an operant principle. Still, in both cases, there are clear distinctions between spaces that are protected from outside people and pollution, and those that are more open to the outside.

Space and Domestic Service

The home is, not surprisingly, a frequent focus in middle- and upper-class women's discussions of domestic service. Concerns about the mixing of inside and outside spaces appear frequently in their comments. These concerns do not mention these spatial categories directly, but are couched in terms of fears and anxieties about servants' passage into and out of the home. Despite these fears, employers understand that domestic service is necessary to ensure the status and continuation of those homes, and that once servants have been allowed to enter and exit, the only means to minimize the danger of their crossings is to control their movements while they are inside the household. Employers' comments about these movements reveal their understandings of the permeability of household boundaries, their own roles in shoring them up in order to protect class perimeters as well, and the ways in which the domestic realm becomes identified with class (as well as with caste and family).

What dangers are posed by domestic service? Servants themselves represent a dangerous mixing of inside and outside. They transgress household boundaries, which are conceived of both physically and symbolically, by bringing the outside in and by taking back to the outside what properly belongs inside. Servants are feared both for what they can bring into and what they can take out of the home: they may transport in dirt, disorder, and disease, and contaminate children with lower-class habits and language (cf. Bourdieu 1984); they may remove valued belongings and information through theft and gossip. All of these dangers were raised repeatedly by employers, and here I examine excerpts from their accounts about domestic service to illustrate the construction of these threats.[6]

Employers' fears about the breaching of household boundaries come up in a variety of contexts, but they are most likely to surface when employers discuss what to look for in a servant. For example, Usha, a fairly affluent Brahman, spoke about the qualities that would be important if she ever had to replace her servant Tharini, a young Thevar woman whom Usha thought highly of.[7] "First, I think," she said,

> the cleanliness. This girl is very clean. She has her bath every day and she comes with nice flowers in her hair, a new sari . . . she changes [her clothing]. That's very important. And Fridays and all she takes her hair bath like all of us do, she's like that. So she's very clean. And of course . . . she's very honest. That will be the first thing

> I'll see. I wouldn't even ask whether she'll do her work properly, but I could again wash it myself and check the [cooking] vessels and I don't bother about the house much. Cleanliness and honesty will be the first. Then the work. [Sara: Then the work.] Definitely.
>
> Sara: What kinds of things would make you fire a servant?
>
> Usha: Maybe if she is too talkative or too inquisitive. Talks something out of turn or listens to me and butts into the conversation. That would really . . . into a family affair maybe. Then that would really irk me a bit. [Sara: Yes.] And if she steals, of course, definitely. And then I wouldn't even think twice before firing her. I don't/I'm not scared of doing the house job myself. I mean, I make sure that she knows nobody is indispensable. So the moment they get that into their head that they are indispensable, they start doing all this. But when you show them that you can do it yourself, then they are not going to, right?

Usha's narrative introduces us to the topics that appear most frequently in employer accounts. The first point to take from her responses is the attribute cited as *least* important in a domestic worker: the quality of the work she does. Although both employers and workers define domestic service in terms of household tasks, the "work" turns out to be the least of the concerns that either side reports. I will return to this point below.

Another point to note is the qualities that worry this employer: dirtiness; dishonesty; inappropriate involvement in family conversations, disrespect and subsequent gossip; and theft. Note how each of these topics appears in Usha's account. First, Tharini is clean not only because she bathes her body and hair regularly—a habit expected of Brahmans, but not necessarily of lower-caste or lower-class people—but also because she presents herself well, with flowers and a neat and clean sari. Neatness, which includes combed hair and attire that is neatly draped and not too badly worn, is frequently cited as an attribute of cleanliness. Being clean also appears to correspond with doing work cleanly, all of which keeps the employer's family clean and, as we will see, healthy. (The Tamil term for cleanness, *cuttam,* also suggests neatness and, when applied to carrying out any kind of work, perfection.)[8] Second, although it is not elaborated here, honesty is mentioned as the most important quality in a servant, one whose lack cannot be overcome as unacceptable work can be. The third issue raised is excessive talking—as they themselves often related to me, servants are not supposed to have a voice in or otherwise insert themselves into the employer's home. Nor, although this is only implied here (it came up directly in our conversation later), are servants supposed to listen to family conversations, because in addition to implying an improper level of intimacy with the family, this gives them access to information that they can spread outside the household. Finally, also notable is the assumption that even the ideal servant must be prevented from thinking too highly of herself. In the Indian English idiom of hierarchy, she must be prevented from being given too much "place." This idiom is suggestive, implying that servants who are allowed the markers of high status will take up more space than they deserve. (The phrase is almost identical in Tamil: *iṭam koṭukka* means literally "to give place." Note that this reverses the sense of place in the parallel American English phrase, "to put/keep her in her place.")

Although Brahmans are often thought of as the caste group most attentive to cleanliness because of their concerns with maintaining inherent purity, in fact all the employers I spoke with—not Brahmans alone—were concerned about cleanliness and neatness. One of the strongest statements about dirt and domestic service came from Lakshmi and her mother-in-law Mrs. Chinnanadar, women who belong to the Nadar caste, a ritually low-ranking caste group that wields significant socioeconomic power in Madurai due to the wealth and education of many of its members. They sat with Mrs. Chinnanadar's teenaged daughter Priyanthi, and talked about what they looked for in a servant. Lakshmi began, "They should be clean first. Valli [one of their current servants, a girl in her early teens] and all, she's very, she doesn't have a bath and in fact you don't feel like letting the children play with her. That's what the doctor also says strictly. Infection, you know, like." Mrs. Chinnanadar said in Tamil, "Yes, it comes only through the servant. Her nails are full of filth [*aḻukku*]." Lakshmi added, "And they don't have bath. Usually I don't let them cut onions and all [i.e., foods in general]. I do it." Her mother-in-law continued, "The doctors say that the servants are the source of all these diseases." "T.B. and all that, you know. Dust," Lakshmi concluded.

Notice the formulation here: because servants are dirty and do not practice proper hygiene, they act as a vehicle to transport dirt and infection into the middle-class home and threaten its clean but vulnerable members, especially the children, whose bodies as well as minds are at risk. Servants' dirtiness threatens to disrupt the order of cleanliness by injecting itself directly into it. Cleanliness is a crucial marker of the privileged home, and its contemporary importance is connected to a colonial British and now elite Indian discourse of public health and hygiene. Concerns about dirt and disease also, and relatedly, often appear to be "rationalized" forms of pollution concerns. I have frequently heard high-caste Hindus say that their scriptures' injunctions about purity and pollution have been vindicated by "science" and its revelation of germs and the processes of disease transmission. Note how these concerns have been taken on by upper-class lower-caste members, including Mrs. Chinnanadar and Lakshmi, who would themselves be regarded as being polluted by some members of higher castes.

Lack of cleanliness also poses another risk. As my friend Viji said, employers must make sure that servants are clean "so that when they do the work also it will be clean . . . if you have a guest in the house . . . there's a particular picture you want to keep of your house, and after doing everything [to present that image], there might be this person who's all dirty all over and not had bath and, you know, smelling, and that won't be nice." Servants communicate the prestige of the household they work in, and those who are badly dressed or groomed reflect badly on those who employ them, in the eyes of a watchful community. Thus the cleanliness of all those in the household is crucial to the images that middle- and upper-class people want to project of proper selves and homes.

Another dangerous import is the practices of lower-class culture. In particular, these include language, taste, and manners. The employers' children, who have not yet been fully socialized into the cultural practices of their own class, are especially susceptible. Madurai employers are often worried about letting their children spend too much time with servants or servants' children, anxious that their own offspring may pick up "bad habits." A number of employers I spoke with talked about their servants' children as dirty and unsuitable playmates for their own children. Viji, for example, gave up a prestigious job as a government administrator in order to spend more time with her five-year-old son Prakash, after the boy's teacher warned Viji that Prakash's English was slipping. Viji blamed the deterioration in his English on the amount of time her son spent with Nalini, the cook. Even though Nalini is a member of the highly ranked Pillai caste (a higher caste than Viji's) and is financially better off than most servants, nonetheless her lack of education, inability to speak English, and lower-class manners meant she had a detrimental influence on the young boy's acquisition of the practices associated with his class.

If servants are dangerous hosts of dirt, disease, and lower-class culture, from which children and other family members must be protected, they are equally dangerous as purveyors of protected items taken from inside the household to the outside world. Theft and gossip, both of which involve transporting family valuables to the outside, are two of the main causes for letting servants go. Saraswati, a Brahman woman, told me, "Work can be taught. Honesty is the first thing" to look for in a servant. Lying and stealing posed the biggest threats to her household, and were ineradicable qualities where they appeared. Most employers assume that servants will steal if they are not closely watched. After telling me how she tests new servants by leaving money out, a Nadar housewife named Manjula explained that she does this "because if they're of a mind to steal, first [they take] money, then clothes and saris. Most of the servants take a sari, nice sari, that they take. So if it's a new servant and we are careful from the beginning, we can find out. Within one month or two months, we, we can easily [tell]." Similarly, other employers watched for small thievery, and even when they were sure it was not occurring, they kept wardrobes and storerooms locked against servants. Almost all could tell horror stories about expensive jewelry and clothing, money, supplies of grain, or even cars that had been secreted away by carefully cunning servants; these stories could be said to comprise a genre of conversation in wealthier Madurai households.

Gossip also poses its dangers, since family information is closely guarded from outsiders. In the small and relatively fluid community of Madurai's upwardly mobile residents, family reputation is a key factor in securing prestige and honor. Prestige is one of the factors used to read class standing. Family honor also has the utilitarian function of attracting customers and clients for businesspeople and professionals and thus of ensuring financial success (Derné, 1994). One of the greatest threats to reputation is the information that servants pass on to other servants and the households they work in. As Usha said, describing how her husband waits until their servant has left for the day before he will talk about what happened in his office, "We never say anything in front of her so there is nothing she can spread." Mrs. Chinnanadar also stressed the importance of keeping servants at a distance from family information. She told me that when her daughter Priyanthi married, she would instruct her to keep her own servants from getting too close to the family. One of the methods she recommended was never to speak about family matters in front of the workers. "Even if we are talking on the phone," she told me in Tamil, "if we need to speak about anything [personal], she [the servant] goes away, we talk and she keeps on working [rather than listening]. Then, if there is any talk about family matters, money matters—all those things are kept inside only [*uḷḷē veccutāṉ ceyyuṟatu*]." Information belonging to the family stays inside—that is, inside the family (defined by its members) or inside the household (defined by space), and even inside the family member's mouth or heart, remaining unspoken when the servant is nearby.

Interestingly, many employers implicitly link stealing and gossip as parallel dangers, and some see gossip as an even greater threat to their families than theft. Rachel, a middle-class Catholic woman in her forties who belongs to a scheduled caste, told me that she and her sister had strongly suspected their long-time servant of stealing one of Rachel's daughter's anklets. Speaking in Tamil, she said, "We asked her, 'Did you see the anklet lying anywhere when you swept?' We asked her whether she saw the anklet when she swept the house. She said that she didn't see it, and went outside. I don't know if she had hidden it outside, but she brought the anklet when she came back in, saying that she had thrown it out along with the garbage." For most employers, as for Rachel, this act would have constituted compelling evidence of theft. Yet Rachel did not fire her servant; when I asked why, she answered, "We continue to keep her on. When she comes to work, she completes the work quickly, and then leaves." "All right," I prompted, and she continued, "It's true then, she won't go and complain in the neighboring house if we run out of idlis[9] and don't give her any . . . she won't talk about what happens here when she goes to other houses. She has good qualities like these. That's why we continue to keep her."

Finally, one form of mixing that is particularly intensely feared but rarely mentioned is sex between servants and household members. Sometimes these fears appear in restrictions around servants' movements in the house. A few employers clean the household's bedrooms themselves, for example, so that servants will not have to enter them. Bedrooms are private space in which the family is reproduced, and in which many of the valuables that display family status—such as gold jewelry and silk saris—are stored. When servants do enter bedrooms, their movements often cause significant anxiety. This is one reason that wardrobes are locked, and servants' honesty is tested: servants are too close to the core of the family when they enter such space. But while fears about theft are easy for employers to discuss, fears about sexual transgression are almost never mentioned by either employers or servants; the damage to families' and women's reputations that the mention of such possibilities can incur is so great that sexual liaisons and abuses are rarely discussed, even among close friends. Occasionally, however, they do appear in employers' accounts. My elderly Pillai friend Parvathi, herself a widow, joked that young widows should never be hired as servants because they would attend to the young men of the household instead of to their work—although, she added, they would do one job well: cleaning the men's laundry until it became "brilliant like glass."[10] Janaki, a Chettiar society matron, told me that servants are no longer loyal and hard-working because of the influence of movies, which "project very ordinary menial servants making love to their employers, [e.g.] a doctor. You know," she said, "subjects like that in box-office hits, with the songs and all that, have triggered off all sorts of thoughts in these people."

Whatever the source and whoever the initiator of such desire, employers fear it greatly, and the access that this desire gives servants to the center of the family is hardly to be contemplated. The threat of this particular mixing brings together all the other fears about servants that their presence entails, and, for all the silence surrounding it, it carries an unparalleled intensity. There is the "dirtiness" of sexual disease, and the pollution inherent in sexual fluids themselves. There is the threat of miscegenation—an unthinkable mixing—and of damage to the family's reputation. And there is perhaps the greatest threat of all, that of the servant undermining household power structures by using sex to gain control over men, and usurping the wife's role as the creator of family and the lover of her husband; this is the deepest invasion of the family.

Servants are crucial for maintaining class standing, yet all of these boundary crossings threaten that standing. It should by now be clear why the quality of work is stated to be the least of employers' concerns. First, as Parvathi, my old Pillai friend, wrote to me in Tamil, "Everyone decides to have a servant in order to get prestige from commanding someone else's work, not because they need a servant to help them with the work they are incapable of doing." Servants are straightforward signifiers of status, regardless of the quality of their work. Their presence tells visitors, passersby, and the wider community that this is a home of a certain quality. The order that servants produce in the home (as well as the order that employers impose on servants' bodies) displays values that communicate class standing to those who view the home and its members. Servants also enable employers to produce the labor-intensive work required to run a middle- or upper-class household, and allow employers the time necessary to engage in paid employment or status-producing activities of their own. But second, employing domestic workers introduces perils that may become more compelling concerns than is the quality of their labor. Clearly employers fear that, as Daniel contends, houses' substances "can be contaminated and changed by mixing with other substances (hence the concern with what kind of substance crosses the vulnerable thresholds—windows and doors—of the house and affects its own substance and that of its inhabitants)" (1984, p. 114). The inside of the home will remain safe and orderly only if the disorder of the outside is prevented from contaminating and, ultimately, dissolving it. Dissolution threatens both the inside space itself and the family honor that gossip can destroy. Thus it is not only the well-being of the household that is at stake but its existence, at least as a middle- or upper-class home.

Closeness and Distance: Controlling Servants in and through Space

What, then, do employers do? Their household work and status concerns generally require them to employ servants, so they cannot entirely seal the home from the dangers of the outside. Instead, they must control and contain them. The idioms that enact this control reveal a tension between closeness and distance, and between similarity and difference, in the attempts that are made to manage relationships with servants. Closeness and distance both echo and complicate the concepts of inside and outside. Employers use a variety of means to draw the servant closer and make her more similar, such as making her "one of the family," and simultaneously try to avoid bringing her too close, which could give her too much power, skew the hierarchy on which class privileges are based, and further threaten the distinctiveness that defines higher classes.

Employers often claim that they treat their servants as "one of the family," or even as "a daughter of the house." In most cases this means a certain consideration in giving the worker decent food (as opposed to providing stale food, or refusing to give food altogether), donating old but serviceable clothing to the servant and possibly her family members, and treating her with courtesy (such as by avoiding degrading language and honoring occasional requests for time off). Providing food and clothing (as well as soap, combs, and bathwater) may be represented as a kindness, but it also helps to reduce the more objectionable differences that employers see in their workers, such as dirtiness and shabbiness. (Some employers, however, complain that no matter how much they offer these advantages to their servants, the servants never adopt them. As Mrs. Chinnanadar said, "I'm telling [the servant], 'Okay, I'll give you soap here, you can bathe right here,'" but still the girl "never ever takes up the habit." Her daughter-in-law Lakshmi added, "You can't change them, that's what they are.") Treating servants well is also seen as a mechanism for creating affection (*an̲pu* or *piriyam*) in workers, and affection, it is believed, binds one person to another and will therefore make a servant more pliable, reliable, and trustworthy. This attempt is a reciprocal one, since workers believe that engendering affection in their employers will make them more generous, flexible, and amiable. In either case, it is seen to be in one's interest to pull the other closer by making her feel affection, while simultaneously maintaining one's own distance in order to avoid acquiring too much affection for or attachment to the other.

Distance is also a crucial factor in gaining control over servants. The more "outside" the servant, the more this distance must be maintained. A number of different rules of hierarchy and respect are called upon to establish the proper distance. These serve primarily to emphasize the class difference between worker and employer, but they also take into account a variety of other hierarchies, including caste, age, and gender, thus placing both parties in a matrix made up of the multiple hierarchies and identities of the moment.

Attempts to keep servants from gaining too much place are played out through several means, one of which is the rigidly maintained semiotics of power differences in the workplace. Employers, for example, address workers by their given names (unless the worker is much older, or unless a female employer of any age is speaking to a relatively old male worker), while workers must address employers and their family members more respectfully by using kin terms. Thus servants use "mother" or "older sister" to address female members of the household, depending on their age; and although the male head of household would usually be addressed by a term similar to "sir," other males would be called "older brother" or "younger brother." Using such forms of address among nonfamily members is frequent in Tamil society, and simultaneously indicates both politeness and kin-like affection. Employers also speak to servants with the informal verb forms reserved for intimates and inferiors, while servants must use the forms that denote distance and respect.

Power relations, and the distance they require, are also operationalized through control over workers' bodies and their access to and movements through space. Workers are expected to be clean and to dress neatly, as we have seen, but they must not wear clothing that is too similar to employers' in type, fabric, colors, or style of wearing; if they do, employers may become nervous about the reduction of class distance. Viji revealed this point when she told me that her servants had gained enough sophistication by working for her family that "they dress up to the standards of almost us, I mean they—of course they spend a lot on this stuff, but they—if you look at them outside you might not be able to figure out that they are people working for somebody as servants." Similarly her cook's friend Sonia told me that servants ought to be neat and clean, but added that if they dressed too nicely, they would be mocked for going about as if they were teachers or some other kind of respectable people.

Sameness in servants' bodies is resisted in other ways. Their bodies must be physically disciplined in the workplace, so that servants follow standard rules of deference in their stances—for example, looking down when appropriate, and sitting modestly, with genitals well covered and feet pointed away from others—and their movements through and use of household space must be restricted. Access to certain rooms is especially strictly controlled, based on the principles of purity and/or privacy described above. The epitome of this control is found in orthodox Brahman households, in which non-Brahman servants are never allowed to enter the kitchen, even to wash dishes or clean the floor. Instead, servants clean the dishes outside, then women of the family rewash them inside, and the kitchen floor is cleaned by a household member or a Brahman cook; in fact the kitchen door may be shut when a non-Brahman servant passes by in order to avoid the pollution possibly carried by her glance. In other households as well, servants stay out of the kitchen as much as possible and avoid entering a room that household members are eating in. Most are also forbidden to enter the storeroom (a prohibition that reflects fears about theft as well as pollution and dirt). In addition, as I have noted, access to the family's bedrooms is an especially sensitive issue in some households. The kitchen and bedroom, the rooms that represent respectively the most pure and most private ends of the spectra, are also the two rooms most central to the physical and emotional nurturing of the family; they must be protected from improper incursions.

Finally, servants' difference is also marked through rules about their use of space *within* each room. Status distinctions are reflected in use of furnishings, whether these be floor mats, chairs and sofas, or Western-style toilets. If servants are allowed to watch television with the family, they will sit on the floor while family members (at least high-status ones) sit on a sofa. Servants are almost never allowed to eat with the family; if they eat at their employers' households at all, they eat after the family, never at a table, and sometimes they must eat less desirable food and on separate plates. If they live at their employer's house, they will also sleep and bathe in separate areas, often in separate "servants' quarters" behind the main house.[11]

Employers are continuously negotiating these terms of distance and closeness, as are servants, trying to push the boundary in one direction or another through a constant process of manipulating all the markers I have noted—speech patterns, mutual terms of address, clothing, body stances, foods eaten and the time and place of meals, access to different parts of the household, use of household appliances and furniture, places for sleeping and bathing, and access to supplies.[12] From the employer's point of view, the servant must be both similar and different; employers must find the balance between transforming her into a less threatening member of the lower class, and preventing her from thereby gaining unacceptable power and becoming too much like the family. There is indeed a tension in finding this balance, as I learned by watching the employers I knew. Viji, who had unusually close and egalitarian relations with her household workers, worried that she gave the cook in particular too much place, and believed her lack of control was due to her intimacy with and dependence on this woman. Reflecting on the dangers of giving place and being bound by affection, she said, "Sometimes it worries me that, you know, you can make a person more like family, but also too much of family . . . I would like to keep some distance, but it's not been possible." She added, "But you know the fear of losing her is also there. I'm very attached to her and she is to me, but we've had our fights and . . . I cannot think of how I'm going to deal with it if she leaves." As Priya, a Nadar woman, said about a worker of whom she was very fond, "It's those you love most who can hurt you, right?"

As in all other ways, too much closeness makes employers vulnerable to their servants. Simultaneously, the difference constituted by servants' outsideness always remains, and the need to mitigate the distance of difference with the closeness of sameness presents an ongoing tension in employers' relations with their workers. In the seesaw balancing of their relationships with domestic workers, employers use spatial metaphors that correspond to inside and outside spheres. The closeness created by affection and the similarity produced by proper hygiene make a servant more like the family and a less dangerous crosser of boundaries; the differences of the outside and of the lower class that the servant carries into the house are then minimalized and made less threatening. But likeness also carries with it power and control—it is those most like employers who have access to their purest and most private places—and these must be guarded against by marking servants' essential differences, by resisting too much similarity in the person of servants, and by controlling their movements within the employer's home. If they are made reassuringly similar without being given too much place, the disorder of the outside can be safely incorporated into the order of the middle- and upper-class home.

Conclusions: Class and Domestic Space

Domestic workers are more mobile on average than are their employers, and enter both higher- and lower-class households. This means that they provide information, serve as links among households, and also cross symbolic boundaries. While their movements thus have a variety of social effects, it is the transgression of spatial boundaries that employers' accounts focus on, and my purpose in this essay has been to examine the reasons for employers' concerns with this transgression.

The asymmetrical movements in domestic service account in part for why domestic workers do not join their employers in raising fears about the mixing of inside and outside. It is not that the distinction between inside and outside is insignificant to domestic workers, or to the poor in general. Rather, while domestic workers regularly enter others' domestic spaces, they rarely face employers' entrances into their own. Furthermore, although they too are concerned with keeping inside spaces clean and protected, hygiene and orderliness are generally more elaborated concerns among higher classes. Concerns with purity are also greater among higher *castes,* who have a proportionately higher representation among the middle and upper classes. All told, crossing the threshold of employers' households does not create parallel anxieties for domestic workers. Since their own domestic space is not encroached upon in the same manner, they are usually less worried about order and purity than are their employers, and they would moreover be less likely to associate the wealthy with dirt and disease in the way their employers do the poor. Domestic workers have their own store of anxieties, but the fears they express most potently are different from their employers'; they have to do with gaining wages and feeding their families.

At the end of most any day, many domestic workers find themselves struggling to buy food that will feed their family one main meal, while their employers find themselves managing other kinds of family concerns. Workers' fears—about having insufficient resources to provide for their families' daily survival needs—are more likely to be realized, and thus more "real," than are employers' fears that their households and class standing will be dissolved. Yet employers do face threats to their class standing. Most significantly for this analysis, their anxieties are passionately voiced and deeply felt, and my intent is to consider what they tell us about the nature and experience of class for middle- and upper-class residents of Madurai. The domestic service accounts presented here reveal everyday aspects of the class system within which they are produced. Three related issues appear most clearly: the insecurity of class identity; the ambivalent overlapping of class and caste; and the connections among domestic space, gender, and class.

Employers' discussions of domestic service treat class as a salient form of hierarchy and identity that is distinguishable from caste. In doing so, they simultaneously expose both its difference from and its identification with caste. Employers' accounts and actions portray class as a contested category—more so, I contend, than ascribed categories of identity such as caste. Class is not a stable category; since it is mutable, it is always under threat. In the case of domestic service, the sign of its achievement can also be the agent of its dissolution. Employers' comments reveal a deep sense of vulnerability and insecurity about the solidity of class. On the one hand, their comments portray the home as a buttressed but porous container of the middle- and upper-class family and its values, and their attempts to control servants' appearances and actions demonstrate a concern with not only protecting themselves from difference but also maintaining that difference as a crucial reminder of their own class identity, as though if servants were to look and act like employers, employers would no longer "have" their class (cf. Tolen, 2000). Yet at the same time, employers speak at length about the immutability and inherent nature of class. The innateness of class-based characteristics suggests, in these moments, a similarity with caste. Employers also equate certain aspects of caste and class when they speak of their workers, and the poor in general, as dirty, disease-carrying, and polluted. Outsideness contributes to the congruence, since it carries many of the same traits that wealthier people ascribe to poorer people, and higher-caste people ascribe to the lower castes. This suggests in part, as M. S. A. Rao has argued, that class in India involves an "interpenetration of religious-ideological and politico-economic structures" (1989, p. 17). Yet because Madurai residents *do* distinguish between class and caste—as when they speak of a "poor Brahman" or "rich Nadar," or when wealthy lower-caste people apply the vocabulary of dirt and disease to their *class* inferiors rather than their *caste* inferiors—employers' partial elision of caste and class carries another implication. It acts, as much as anything else, as an assertion that servants cannot ever take on the essential characteristics of their employers. Thus, the anxiety about maintaining class is one of the strongest messages of domestic service interactions and accounts.

Although men may voice the same sentiment, I have heard women address this anxiety more often. If women feel it more deeply than men do (such a possibility requires further investigation), this may be a result of their specific roles in producing and maintaining the symbolic indicators of the family's class status. Men's primary contribution to class is generally financial input and occupational prestige, while women more often control the symbolic aspects of the domestic realm—the home and its appearance; the health of family members; the educational achievements, manners and other cultural practices of household members; as well as the physical reproduction of the family and the daily sustenance that allows its members to earn and to learn. The home is central to the construction of class identity and difference, and women hold primary responsibility for this.

For members of the middle and upper classes, not only does the home become the exemplar of what is ordered and pure, its spatial dimensions also become the tool for reinstating a difference that must continuously be maintained because it is assailable and, in the end, not simply innate. Within the household, maintaining a sense of distinction and difference requires keeping the inside and outside as separate as possible. Insideness and outsideness are spatial categories with strong class valences, and the dichotomy is central to middle- and upper-class constructions of class identity. People who are like the family enter the home more easily than outsiders. As I have noted, such similarity is marked in a number of ways, including kinship, caste, and friendship, as well as class. But the concepts of inside and outside are especially class-marked. People who are viewed by employers as lower-class both come from and stand for the outside. They are associated with dirt, rubbish, disease, rusticity, wildness, and other disorders and dangers. When they enter the middle- or upper-class home, as they must, these clean, ordered, and safe homes must be protected from absorbing what servants bring in—and from giving up the valuables that the homes hold. The home is portrayed by women as the central container of class values and of the people who hold them. Women are responsible for producing these values—in part, paradoxically, through the employment of servants—and of protecting them from external threats. Men as well as women act on the ideological principles that women reproduce by caring for their homes in this way.

Employers' accounts and actions reveal both the domestic sphere and women to be crucially linked to class identity and ideology and their production. Their perspective is notable given the frequent emphasis in class analysis and in daily Madurai rhetoric about men's roles in producing class. Here we see that because class values become associated with the order of the home, and because the family is identified with the house and household, protecting the home, the family, and class are one and the same. While keeping the home's boundaries firm is far from women's only role in the production of class, maintaining the home and family remains most women's primary responsibility. Likewise, it is their responsibility to protect their family's class status by shoring up the permeable boundaries of the household and controlling inside what they cannot control outside—the movements of intimate strangers.

Notes

1. Although there are Tamil terms that can be used to gloss "middle class," such as *naṭuttaravarkaḷ* or *naṭuttara kuṭumpam* ("middle people" or "middle family"), these were considered awkward usages when I carried out this research in 1991–1992. By the time I returned to do research in 1999–2000 and 2001, however, such terms were used occasionally by Tamil speakers in everyday speech, as was the more frequent term *naṭuttaramāṉavarkaḷ* ("people in the middle"), reflecting the growing consciousness of a middle-class identity (see Dickey, 2002).
2. Although people in Madurai do not often organize politically on the basis of class, they are highly aware of it, and I would concur with Béteille that insisting on class consciousness as a minimal feature of class threatens to "define classes out of existence" in India (1974, p. 52). It also prevents us from recognizing critical features of urban life that cannot be accounted for consistently by other forms of identity or hierarchy (see also Ortner, 1991, p. 170).
3. For a discussion of the meaning and significance of affection in domestic service, see Dickey, 2000.

4. I am much more familiar with Hindu and Christian families' homes than with Muslims', but the Muslim houses I have visited are built along similar lines, though among lower-class and orthodox Muslims the principles have to do more with protecting women and family honor than with maintaining essential purity; in the homes of the wealthy, less conservative Muslims that I know, class considerations predominate. In both cases, house layouts are similar to those that I describe in this section.
5. This pattern differs from the house style in which all rooms open off of a central courtyard, an architectural pattern that is much less prevalent in Madurai than in much of the rest of India (for a description of such houses, see, e.g., Wadley 1994, p. 13). For other discussions of household space, see Moore (1990) and Pramar (1987).
6. All accounts were in English unless otherwise noted.
7. I provide information about individuals' caste in part to highlight the distinction between caste and class.
8. The English words "clean" and "neat" are also used by Tamil speakers. Terms used for their opposites include *aḻukku* (dirt, filth), *aciṅkam* (muck, filth, ugliness), and *acuttam* (uncleanness).
9. Idlis are a steamed muffin-like food eaten in the mornings and evenings, made of ground rice and lentil batter.
10. Parvathi may have meant "brilliant like a mirror." The Tamil word *kaṇṇāṭi* is used for both glass and mirror (as well as for eyeglasses). Parvathi normally speaks in Tamil, but during this discussion she briefly switched into English—a language in which she is less comfortable—because her current servant had entered the room, and Parvathi did not want her to understand our conversation. In any event, the meaning of the phrase was clear: the men's clothing, and the men's clothing alone, had been brilliantly clean.
11. The housing provided for high-level Indian government employees often includes servants' quarters within the compounds. See Tolen (2000) for a discussion of the "knowledge transfers" that take place between employers' and servants' households in a Madras Railway Colony.
12. Servants' boundary negotiations involve putting forth a variety of their own symbolic claims (which are also intended to have material effects). Refusal to "take advantage" of the soap and used clothing that employers provide, as Mrs. Chinnanadar reported, is one method of resisting attempts to make over servants' bodies; similarly, sneaking food or more significant items out of the household is a way of refuting control over their movements, while the spreading of unflattering information outside is often aimed at fighting employers' claims to a higher moral standing. Like employers, servants can try out different forms of address (or posture, or furniture usage) both to communicate a particular stance of respect, deference, or intimacy, and to make symbolic bids for the respect or intimacy that they wish to claim in return. Servants may also support employers' efforts to separate them from the family's most significant belongings and intimate spaces—such as by requesting employers to lock wardrobes or storage rooms—in order to protect themselves should food or jewelry suddenly disappear.

TEN

Gender Plays

Socio-spatial Paradigms on the Tamil Popular Stage

Susan Seizer

In this essay I look at the geography of stage space in the popular Tamil theater genre known as *Special Drama*. My thesis is that consistent usage of stage space in Special Drama performances makes that stage a platform that resonates with the analogous relations between theatrical representation and real life. I focus here specifically on the use of stage space in the comedic duet that opens every night of Special Drama. This opening duet establishes spatial paradigms employed throughout an entire night of performance. Moreover, the comedy duet has a narrative structure that, curiously, fits so seamlessly into existing Tamil social and spatial paradigms that its very existence as a specific narrative tends to escape local notice. That is, the narrative structure of the comedy duet is so naturalized that it disappears. My ultimate aim, then, is to make visible the contours of the socio-spatial world that this enacted story otherwise assumes.

In this endeavor, I approach theatrical performance as a cultural system that is itself necessarily embedded in the cultural context in which it is staged and to which it speaks. My emphasis is on how a particular spatial organization establishes the particular local terms in which a resemblance between social reality and its theatrical representation may then exist. What intrigues me is how the organization and use of stage space in Special Drama enables what is enacted on stage to speak directly to dominant organizations of Tamil social relations offstage.

Specifically, every Special Drama scene staged is situated spatially in ways that index the more general gendered organization and use of space in everyday Tamil social life. I argue that the analogic relationships pertaining in special Drama between onstage and offstage socio-spatial paradigms provide the conditions of possibility for comedic flights of fantasy—such as those enacted in the comedy duet—that bear directly on the social reality of the Tamil sex/gender system. This play with gender relations on the Special Drama stage exists in dialogue with classical Tamil mythical models, while simultaneously enacting much that is never spoken aloud. Such stagings both capture and instantiate some of the more uncomfortable ambivalences structuring Tamil gender relations today.

During my ethnographic field research in Tamilnadu (1991–1993), I studied the lives and the social positions of the artists who make up the Special Drama acting community. A key focus of my subsequent work has been understanding how artists negotiate their stigmatized social position onstage and off. My interest in the actors' use of stage space is very much informed by an awareness that actors carry onto the stage with them a burden of social disrespect that they must somehow negotiate each time they present themselves to an audience. Borrowing the subtitle of Goffman's insightful study of stigma (1963), my analysis here might equally be characterized as "notes on the management of spoiled identity."

Three Stigmas

There are three highly interconnected dimensions to the stigma that pertains to stage actors in Tamilnadu. I introduce these dimensions here only briefly. Overall, the stigma on actors stems from a notion that their social relations are disorderly and, consequently, overly mobile; in short, actors are perceived as unsettled and are thus unsettling.

The first dimension of the problem inheres in acting itself, and in the very fact of mimetic fluidity: acting arguably necessarily involves illusion and not reality, and actors make a profession of offering "false" selves in place of the "true," raising the possibility that social and personal identities are mobile rather than fixed. The second stigmatized dimension involves perceptions of actors' behavior in the offstage world, where again their behavior is seen as overly fluid: actors frequently intermarry across established caste, class, religious, and ethnic boundaries, and are thus accused of not maintaining normal, orderly, sanctioned kin relations.

The third dimension concerns an India-wide stigma on actresses, who have long been the very definition of "bad" women. Unlike the chaste loyalty of the good wife who reveals herself to only one man, the actress's profession requires that she willingly expose herself to the gaze of many unfamiliar men. This blatant step into the limelight of "the public sphere" threatens to expose the fragility of the culturally naturalized division of gendered spheres into home and world, as actresses move onto public stages to enact what are meant to be the most private of relations. In their inescapable roles as public women, actresses are thought of as breaking a cardinal Tamil rule of female marital chasteness; the reputation of female performers as courtesans is now encoded into the Tamil language itself: several Tamil words whose etymological origins refer to actresses and dancers commonly mean "prostitute" (*kūttāṭi, tēvaṭiyāḷ, tāci*).

To understand the boundaries a woman oversteps by stepping onto a Tamil public stage, brazenly entering the gaze of male strangers, we must remember that the Tamil sex/gender system is structured primarily through a division of sex-segregated social spaces. Apart from the "home and the world" public sphere/private sphere distinctions so often noted throughout South Asia, in much of Tamilnadu sex segregation is meant to be observed even within these spheres, such that women and men eat separately in the home, ride on separate sides of the local bus, watch movies from different halves of the theater, and stand in different lines to pray to Hindu deities. Both common and scholarly self-representations of "Tamil culture" tend to invoke the strict social division of the sexes as a defining virtue, and questions of the deleterious effects of modernization on the strict maintenance of these foundational gendered binaries provide a staple of conversation and debate generally, as they do on the Tamil popular stage. On stage, an actor's ability to propound the importance of gender role maintenance and the social duties entailed therein—and to do so convincingly and creatively in both comedic and dramatic modes—is crucial to establishing his or her competence as a performer.[1] The successful female Special Drama performer thus lives a contradiction: she attains competence on stage by propounding a gendered morality that, by virtue of her profession as an actress, she has always already lost any chance of inhabiting offstage.

A Stigmatized Genre

In addition to these three stigmas on actors qua actors, there is also a very particular stigma attendant on the actors who perform in Special Drama, which is itself widely considered a "vulgar" genre. This dismissive attitude originated with middle-class critics in the early decades of the twentieth century, when Special Drama first appeared as a bastard child of the move to modernize Tamil drama. In the 1910s, 1920s, and 1930s, actors and actresses who were not well-disciplined enough, or so it is said, to make it in the drama companies of the day came away from these companies and worked freelance as independent artistes. Drama events utilizing such freelance actors were called "Special Dramas" (*Special Nāṭakam*) as the performers were hired "specially" for each show. The name stuck, and today every performer in Special Drama is an independent "artiste": there are no troupes, no companies, and no directors in Special Drama. Instead, each artist is contracted individually for every performance, and actors and actresses who may be previously unknown to each other meet, onstage, for any given performance, having traveled from their homes in different towns and cities across the state.

This organizational structure has an important entailment for actresses, as the practice of hiring independent artists for every role relies on each individual performers' willingness to travel. Such public mobility raises particular problems for Special Drama actresses, who are necessarily sensitive to the stigma that accompanies the reputation of actresses as "public women" who move out into the world beyond the bounds of proper, modest feminine behavior. In Tamilnadu, as throughout much of South Asia, the ideology of properly separate spheres for women and men—the home and the world, respectively—continues to exert a good deal of pressure, particularly on poor urban women who do not have access to the kinds of ideological loopholes middle-class women regularly deploy to circumvent such strictures on their movements outside the home.[2] For actresses, the fact that their profession requires their public mobility clearly feeds into the larger stigma on the acting community, noted above, of a propensity to overly mobile, dissolute, and disreputable relations.

Special Drama performers do not rehearse prior to performing; instead, what enables this unusual theatrical organization to work is its adherence to a shared repertory canon. Special Drama relies both on a set repertory of plays (overwhelmingly "mythologicals," the most popular of which is "Vaḷḷi's Wedding [*Vaḷḷi Tirumaṇam*]), and a set repertory of players' roles.[3] Such roles—Hero and Heroine, Buffoon and Dancer—are enacted within the context of a well-known repertory of scenes: these include a frolicsome Garden scene between the young Heroine and her *tōḻi,* or female companion; a melodramatic Forest scene between the Hero and Heroine as young lovers; and a broadly parodic Comedy scene that opens every Special Drama performance event, usually set on a public road between the Buffoon and Dancer. In this essay, I analyze the situated antics of this opening comedy scene, focusing on how this scene establishes patterns of spatial use on the Special Drama stage that carry over into all the succeeding dramatic scenes.

The dismissive, originally middle-class accusation of this genre's vulgarity, and the concomitant notion that Special Drama actors lack discipline, has since been adopted by Special Drama audiences and performers alike, none of whom are themselves middle-class people. Adopting this attitude, however, comprises a bid at social respectability, and the common dismissal of Special Drama in present times as vulgar partly hinges on a notion of comedy itself as spurious, corrupt, degraded, and lewd. Physical comedy in particular is a magnet that attracts a virtually Victorian censure of overly expressive, loose bodies (see Seizer, 1997). While its traffic in comedy is not the only reason for Special Drama's appraisal as a vulgar art—the other stigmas adhering to Special Drama actors, and particularly the disdain for the public mobility of actresses, clearly conspire here—the disavowed quality of the comedy in Special Drama makes the comic scene between Dancer and Buffoon a particularly good place to begin analyzing both the mundane and the fantastic in the organization of socio-spatial paradigms in Tamil society.

The discourse of vulgarity that has swirled around these performances since their appearance in the early twentieth century has succeeded in effectively precluding serious scholarly consideration of what I shall suggest here are actually quite masterful comedic negotiations of the mores of Tamil social life. These negotiations employ parody, irony, and verbal wit as well as the broad physical comedy of exaggerated gesture, mockery, and extreme characterization. Rather than shy away from the coarser elements of such theatrical display, I aim to look directly at the most highly disdained and vehemently dismissed comic scene of all in this already disavowed and disparaged theatrical genre, the opening scene of every Special Drama referred to simply as the Buffoon-Dance Duet.

On Unspoken Stories

Special Drama performances last roughly eight hours, beginning at ten P.M. and concluding at dawn. As outdoor theatrical events, they are generally performed as the entertainment component of a Hindu temple festival in honor of a local deity.[4] The first two hours are a comic warm-up that takes the form of two standard scenes: the Buffoon's opening monologue, and next the Buffoon-Dance Duet that I examine here. Both of these comic scenes are ostensibly not connected in any way to the ensuing six hours of drama subsequently staged. The mythological narrative for which any given drama event is named takes place fully within these later hours; "Vaḷḷi's Wedding," for example, is the story of the marriage of Vaḷḷi and Murukaṉ. The myths presented in the overtly narrative portions of Special Dramas dramatize the valor of male kings, heroes, and deities, as well as the beauty, chastity, and moral uprightness of female queens and goddesses. The dramatic portions of Special Drama are generally performed using formal (or written) Tamil, rather than the colloquial "spoken Tamil" of the comedy scenes.

By all local accounts the comic scenes and the dramatic scenes in Special Drama are completely unrelated. Comedy scenes are said to have no narrative value of any kind. Whenever I asked any question in which I tried to get a sense of what was narratively at stake in the comedy duet—beginning with such simple queries as "Why is she dancing in the middle of the road?" or "What is the story of this duet?"—I was invariably informed, in no uncertain terms, that there simply was no story (*katai*) there. This was "simply comedy" (*kāmaṭi tāṉ*), performers and audience members alike assured me, as though drama and comedy themselves were antithetical terms. "Pure comedy" was opposed to a story, which belonged to a realm of higher, better, more acceptable art—a realm to which comedy seemingly had no access.

A. K. Ramanujan has written of the difference between domestic tales and mythologies in South India as a difference between interior and exterior stylistic forms (*akam* and *puṟam*), respectively. Ramanujan recognizes a continuum of Indian folk genres, ranging from the interior domestic tale to the exterior public performance of theater (1986, pp. 46, 49). I would argue that certain theatrical genres employ the entire spectrum of such continua, since within the night-long theatrical event of Special Drama itself, presentational styles range widely between interior and exterior modes. Ramanujan's understanding of Tamil folktales as bespeaking a particular kind of interior space, and partaking of a particular kind of "taleworld" and "taletime," strikes me as highly relevant to distinctions made within Special Drama between comedy and drama.

Like the folktale, comedy plays on assumed meanings. It offers potent and ambivalent messages and images that are often verbally slippery. Ramanujan writes:

> Tales speak of what cannot usually be spoken. Ordinary decencies are violated. Incest, cannibalism, pitiless revenge are explicit motifs in this fantasy world, which helps us face ourselves, envisage shameless wish fulfillments, and sometimes 'by indirection find direction out' (1989, p. 258).

Any inability to convert the meanings of such artfully indirect artistic forms into "other words" is itself telling.

My attempts to answer my own questions about the narrative burden of the Buffoon-Dance Duet eventually took the form of a videotape that I edited to highlight the highly directed moves that recurred repeatedly in an otherwise seemingly indirect genre. Having seen such comedy scenes performed many times by many different artists, I recognized a very clear and particular story in these duets, or at least, I saw that they were structured by story elements and by a progression of ideas that made the Buffoon-Dance Duet cohere in the first place. It is not that I was determined to find narrative linearity and plot everywhere I looked, but rather that there was here a narrative that somehow escaped recognition as such. It was indeed considered so common, so unremarkable, that no one had words to remark on what seemed to me its remarkable consistencies. Instead they were the given, assumed grounds of popular comedy. In splicing together the recurring story elements from nine different performances of the Buffoon-Dance Duet, I found myself using the very visual material that had prompted me to ask such questions in the first place to prove to myself that the structure I had perceived did indeed exist.

The fact that what gets performed in this scene is not elevated to the level of "story" is a silence that bespeaks its own cultural logic. The silence about comedy maintains it as allied with vulgarity, as well as with all things not publicly "told" but instead banished from the more high-minded domains of Tamil religious mythopoetics into which "stories" properly fit. Both, of course, are true: the story I recognize exists (especially for outsiders like me), and its general nonrecognition as a story also exists. These occur simultaneously each time the narrative of the Buffoon-Dance Duet, in its enactment, appears to me but disappears into the common socio-spatial paradigms of a world into which it seamlessly fits. While the paradigms of that world continue to be foreign to me, the Buffoon-Dance Duet stands out as a foreign thing; but for those for whom the paradigms of this world are familiar, it disappears.

My assertion throughout this essay, then, that an analogic relationship pertains between the comic and dramatic scenes in Special Drama as well as between the comic scenes and everyday life, must be understood as growing out of my own attempt to answer a set of questions that grew and expanded over the course of my two years of fieldwork. These questions stemmed from my own perceptions, intimately bound up with the perceptions of those around me, and particularly with my confusion over how the local audience spoke—and specifically in this case, how they chose not to speak—about what was being staged in the comedy duet. Why were people (audience and performers alike) so reluctant to admit in conversation that they enjoyed these comedy scenes? As these scenes inevitably drew and held the largest crowds, why would no one ever speak of them as having any lasting value or meaning? Why did these same scenes "work" over and over again; indeed, what made them enduringly funny, and funny enough to inaugurate every drama?

The lack of any overt discussion of these matters eventually prompted me to pay close attention to the nonverbal covert features structuring the communicative arena of these staged duets. Such features include the organization and use of stage space, and in particular the very regular division of that space into areas coded by specific qualities of gendered interaction.

Once I recognized the systematicity of the use of stage space in the comic duet, I soon realized that patterns established here were maintained throughout the dramatic scenes to follow. Moreover, not only did common themes literally shape the use of space in both the comic and dramatic scenes, but the kinds of social spaces that were created and deployed in these scenes clearly had much in common with the organization and use of social space offstage, in everyday Tamil practice. Stage space in the comedic duet, I now saw, was an analogue of other socio-spatial paradigms that primarily went unnoticed in daily life. Particularly in relation to conventions of interaction with persons of the opposite sex, I began to understand what took place onstage as literally situating—(re)placing and (re)presenting—relations that otherwise were difficult to articulate. In Ramanujan's terms, I saw that these duets "speak of what cannot usually be spoken."

This insight was forcefully brought home by the one comedic moment in a Buffoon-Dance Duet I had recorded that had *not* worked. This performative failure was a moment of rupture, a moment where a female performer had to step out of the standard frame of the stage and stop the performance. The very possibility of such a rupture finally revealed best of all the extent to which the Buffoon-Dance Duet normally plays out taken-for-granted conventions of social engagement—or socio-spatial stories, if you will.

I hope here to show not simply that the comedy scene has a story so familiar it escapes remark, but that the plot of this story inscribes the entire stage with a spatial organization that is also socially familiar. The socio-spatial paradigms emplotted in the Buffoon-Dance Duet are analogous with those of the entire performative event. Throughout, the plight of actresses represents the potential plight of all women burdened by what is, I will suggest, a suspicious ideology of safely separate spheres. I will return to this question of women's safety after introducing and orienting the reader to the fields of play out of which it arises.

The Buffoon-Dance Duet

What exactly occurs in the Buffoon-Dance Duet? Its conceit is this: a young girl of sixteen is dancing in the road. A young man (of no specific age) comes by and bumps into her. They argue about who bumped whom, and the meaning of a bump between a man and a woman ("bumping" here having definite sexual connotations). They decide to have a contest to see who is the more skilled at song and dance, ending in mutual appreciation. They find out each other's name and birthplace, and decide to "do love" (elope). Through all this, they sing hit cinema songs from the latest popular films, not replicating the choreography of the original cinema numbers so much as quoting filmic conventions of song, dance, and attitude, with all of which they and their audiences alike are already familiar.

In performance, the narrative progression of this Duet develops around five standard bits in a set sequence. These are essentially the five structuring moments in an otherwise improvised scene. They are: (1) the Dancer's entrance; (2) the bumpy meeting between Buffoon and Dancer; (3) their discussion of the meaning of a bump between man and woman; (4) a contest of skills wherein the Buffoon and Dancer are representatives of their sex; and (5) mutual admiration and "love marriage."

In my video editing experiment, I juxtaposed clips of just these five segments as they were enacted by nine different pairs of performers in nine different performances. Immediately, the common use of stage space that all nine pairs of performers shared became apparent: certain actions occurred only in certain places on stage. These places thus resonate with a certain character and quality of their own, by virtue of the repeated practice of performers performing specific kinds of activities there. There are five primary stage areas where such different uses are articulated: the four corners and center stage. The more I watched, the more I saw how each of these areas is quality-encoded. Thus, what had originally seemed an empty stage now appears to me a highly articulated social space.

In lieu of sharing with the reader my compilation of performance clips, I trust here in the older, tried-but-true technology of thick written description to communicate how different qualities of interaction, in the course of the Buffoon-Dance Duet, occur in different areas of the stage. Before beginning such an account, however, it may be useful to the reader to have a preliminary visual diagram of the Special Drama stage (Fig. 1). Subsequent diagrams (Figs. 2 and 3) aim at charting the resultant patterns of spatial use on the stage, as discussed below.

Configuring the Stage

Special Drama is performed outdoors on a proscenium stage. The rectangular stage floor is either dirt, raised wood, or concrete. Thatched walls (made of braided palm fronds) provide a back, ceiling, and sides to the performance space. Special Drama stages are temporary structures erected by the townsfolk or villagers specifically for the event. The audience sits on the dirt ground in front of the stage. The sites of such events are generally public commons, a public road or thoroughfare, or temple grounds.

With a remarkable degree of consistency at each venue I attended, audiences for Special Drama arrange themselves in sex-segregated spheres. Young children and old men sit closest to the front of the stage. Other men and boys sit behind them to one side, and women and girls to the other. An aisle (or sometimes a rope) separates these two sex-segregated sides of

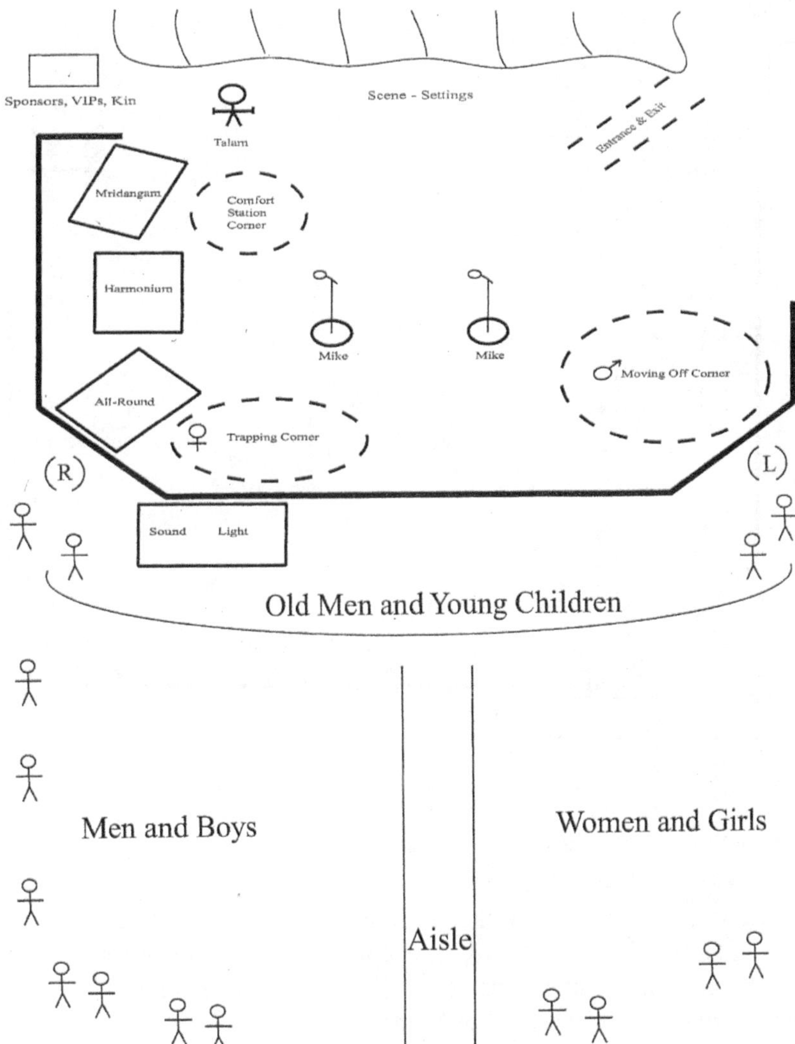

Figure 10.1 The Special Drama stage and its audience context.

the audience. Especially during the comic portions of the event, a wide ring of younger men (bachelors) encircles this entire audience viewing arrangement by standing along the perimeter of the audience on all sides and at the back (represented by stick figures in Fig. 1). During these portions, approximately three-quarters of the audience is male and one-quarter female, though this ratio does change throughout the night as many of the young bachelors leave after the opening comedy scenes

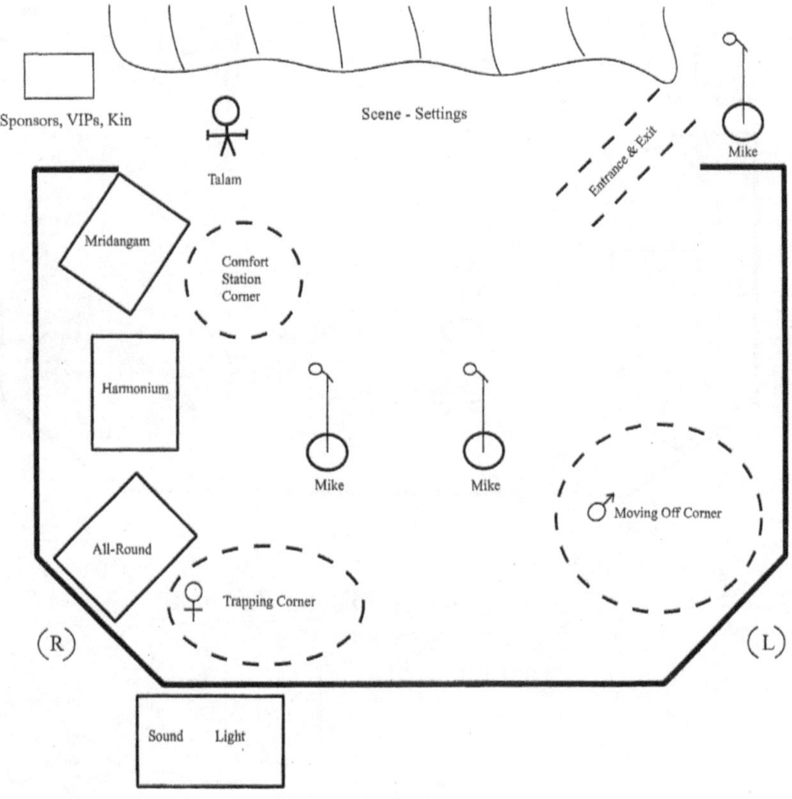

Figure 10.2 Spatial organization of the Special Drama stage.

while women tend to stay the entire night to watch the later dramatic scenes (which, being less lewd, are deemed more appropriate for women).

On stage, four musicians sit stage right: a harmonium player, two drummers (a *miruṭaṅkam* player and an "all-round" or special effects drummer), and a brass cymbal player who keeps rhythm (*tāḷam*). Both drummers sit atop tables with their instruments, while the harmonium player sits on a chair. The *tāḷam* player stands, furthest upstage.

A strict demarcation between backstage and onstage is noted through artists' use of the terms "inside" (*uḷḷē*) and "outside" (*veḷiyē*), respectively. The demarcation is realized by ceiling-to-floor-length painted canvases—referred to with the English words "scene-settings"—that divide backstage from onstage throughout the night. This demarcation between inside as the artists' space and outside as the audience's space reverses the otherwise prevailing everyday identities for the participants

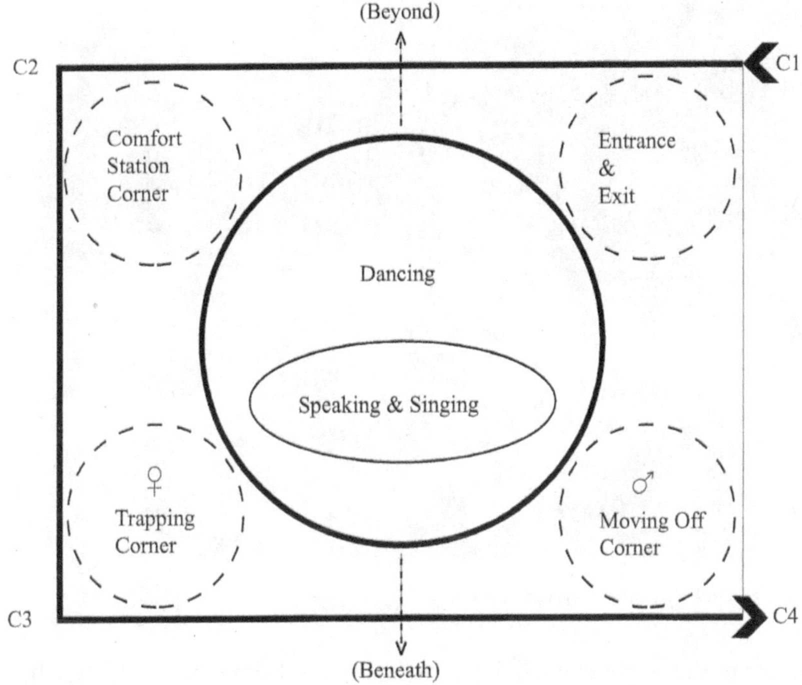

Figure 10.3 Schematic diagram of the use-areas on stage.

in a Special Drama event: it distinguishes *the performers* as inside and insiders (while they are otherwise quintessential outsiders) and utilizes the term "outside" to denote the sphere of the local audience (who are otherwise insiders). This represents a fleeting reversal of dominant relational dynamics between village locals and itinerant performers, and momentarily puts performers in control of a desirable space of controlled and limited access.

It is in this context that performers grant certain local men a partial "insider status" among them at drama events. A privileged position of trafficking between the two realms of inside and outside during the performance is afforded specifically to local VIPs, local drama sponsors, the drama agent (who facilitates the hiring process, acting as a mediary between sponsors and performers), and friends and relatives of performers, who sometimes accompany them to the venue. These men often watch the drama from the upstage right corner of the stage itself (Fig. 4). There they sit or stand beside the musicians, by the far right edge of the painted scene-settings. From this vantage point, they are afforded a

Figure 10.4 "Comfort Station Corner."

much closer experience of the performance and simultaneously they figure into that performance as a sort of paradigm audience, whose every reaction is visible to those on the ground. The contiguity of this privileged audience to the four musicians helps establish the effect of a representative, paradigmatic male audience, a role that the musicians themselves play throughout the night.

In their frequent instrumental and verbal responses to the actors in performance, the musicians serve as a sort of chorus of everymen. This relationship is definitively established in the scene preceding the Buffoon-Dance Duet, the Buffoon's monologue.[5] In these scenes, Buffoons frequently tell stories involving a young man's fantasies about meeting a young woman in public. In telling these stories, the Buffoon uses two different linguistic footings:[6] in the first, he addresses moralizing comments directly to the audience, while in the second, he turns to the musicians and addresses to them any more questionable or vulgar details of his story. It is thus into a space already rhetorically configured as a male domain for discussing women that the Dancer enters the Buffoon-Dance Duet. The Duet, however, is the first fully *enacted* scene of the night. It builds onto an already established use of stage right as a male space, modeling performer-audience relations and mapping larger patterns of stage use by both men and women across the entire onstage space.

Finally, some introduction is due the painted backdrops that mark scene changes throughout the night. These canvases stretch unbroken all the way across the rear of the stage. Special use of the upstage space behind or directly in front of the canvas backdrops themselves is occasionally made for brief and miraculous appearances from gods: visions, voices, and otherworldly advice emanate from just behind these backdrops, while, in "Vaḷḷi's Wedding," upstage center is where Lord Murukaṉ first appears, standing still as a temple icon, giving *darshan* to his audience. This is the "on high" position: directly upstage and behind all the mortal action unfolding onstage, the backdrops are both a touch of realist stage decor and a suggestive space of their own that intimates a "beyond" to the central antics of the drama.

The pictures painted on these canvases create the tone for each scene. The painted road that sets the scene for the Buffoon-Dance Duet bears an interesting relation to this established use of scene settings for otherworldly purposes. Through their exaggerated use of an infinitely receding depth of perspective, the road scene also communicates an atmosphere that suggests that the doings onstage extend past themselves to the point of awe. Further complicating this suggestion is the common knowledge that behind this canvas is a veritable other world, that of the artists and their community, a theatrical *demimonde* known as "the drama world" (*nāṭaka ulakam*). It is onto a stage thus configured that the actress, playing the role of Dancer, makes her first entrance.

The Duet in Performance

Figures 2 and 3 diagram the stage space, highlighting the direction and quality of its use in performance. Both diagrams present the stage's major use-areas and the qualities situated and displayed in each. In the ensuing discussion I begin, as do Special Drama performances, in the upstage left corner, and progress counterclockwise around the stage.

Story Element 1: The Dancer's Entrance

The upstage left corner is the entrance and exit corner for all actors throughout the night. It is the main channel of supply between inside and outside. This corner is strategically *opposite* the orchestra, so that actors can make eye contact with musicians prior to their stage entrance, allowing unrehearsed entrances to be coordinated with the music. A microphone located in this corner, behind the wing, facilitates the singing entrance used primarily for dramatic scenes, in which actors begin singing to musical accompaniment prior to their visible entrance onto the stage (see Fig. 5).

The Duet begins energetically, the Dancer entering the stage to fast-paced instrumental accompaniment. She runs out from the upstage left corner and circles the entire stage counterclockwise. Some Dancers perform this opening entrance as a wide, embracing circle, while others contract the circling quality so narrowly that they essentially spin in place. Whatever its initial diameter, the flurry of the Dancers' opening movements always culminate in a spin, which itself finishes in a flourish and a formal greeting to the musicians: her palms meet before her sternum in the polite gesture of ritualized greeting that is both a common everyday gesture in Hindu Tamilnadu and a formalized tradition of classical South Indian dance (Bhārata nāṭyam). As a ritualized dance gesture opening classical dance performances, this greeting signals humility and respect for the instruments and the players with whom the performer shares the stage. Some Dancers touch their hands in greeting to each of the musical instruments in turn, formally acknowledging the musicians and marking the fact that their performance together is thereby begun.

Figure 3 indicates with an arrow the direction of the Dancer's defining introductory circuit around the stage space. This arrow simultaneously indicates the progression by which the various qualitative use-areas on stage will be introduced in the Duet as a whole. The Dancer's entrance has taken her from corner one, the entrance corner, around the stage in a counterclockwise direction ending at corner two, the comfort corner, where she greets the musicians.

I call this upstage right corner "the comfort corner," as it is often used as a kind of safe place for actors while they are working onstage. It is, as discussed above, the most populated place on the stage; actors join others (family, friends, and people with some degree of local prestige) here to take a break, using this corner as a kind of comfort station for "cooling off" during long stretches onstage. In the midst of a long scene, actors may repair here while another waxes poetic center-stage, and have sodas or drinks of water, wipe sweat off their faces with towels, or readjust slipping costumes. Unlike corner one, this corner is not so much an energized channel between outside and inside as it is a piece of the inside—a familiar community space in which to recharge—situated outside.

Figure 10.5 "Entrance and Exit."

Perhaps most important, this corner allows actors to drop momentarily out of character and into a net of real-life relations in which they can assume a different persona. These relations are both with members of their own *known* community ("drama people"), and with the set of locally prestigious people whose support makes any given performance possible. Dropping into this safety net while onstage thus provides actors a chance to stand apart for a moment from the characters they play, and perhaps enact here a rather idealized instantiation of ease and belonging among a group comprising both local and acting community men—that is, of outsiders and insiders together—such as actors rarely encounter in real life.

As a whole, the right side of the stage that the musicians occupy provides a space for the familiar and known. In Special Drama, musicians and actors are often kin. The community comprises persons of many differing caste, regional, religious, and ethnic backgrounds who have built their own kin network through intermarriage. Even if they are meeting for the first time only that night, musicians and performers nevertheless generally think of themselves as members of the same stigmatized community and tend to address each other with fictive kin terms—older brother or sister, younger brother or sister, uncle, or aunt, as the case may be.

Returning to the Dancer's opening performance in the Duet, we see that she has inaugurated what will prove to be canonical usages of both upstage corners in her very first movements onstage, entering from the left, and respectfully greeting her community on the right upstage corners respectively. Next, she moves from upstage right into center stage, approaching one of the two microphones that stand there. She sings one or two popular film songs, dancing all the while in a style Special Drama performers call "Oriental dance" (the English phrase is used), a chameleon-like rubric under which a wide variety of dance styles have fallen over the course of remaking dance in colonial and postcolonial India (see Erdman, 1996). In Special Drama, Oriental dance is basically Bhārata nāṭyam with simpler hand gestures (*mudrās*) and dance steps, lots of added hip thrusts and shoulder shakes, and a constant megawatt cinema smile. Again, the Dancer in no way attempts to replicate the choreography that accompanied the song in its original film context; live staged performances that aim at reproducing cinema choreography as closely as possible belong to a separate genre of contemporary Tamil popular stage performance, known as "record dance." Rather, here the actress invents her own steps in a loosely interpretive cover of the popular song.

What the Dancer's singing and dancing inaugurates here, in terms of the valence of center stage that will carry over into subsequent acts and scenes, is a kind of "hotting up" of things generally. Center stage is where the fiery debates, impassioned speeches, and punny monologues that constitute the verbal core of Special Drama performances are situated. The many strategic forms of verbal, postural, and gestural address deployed center stage create a constant tension in their performance between arousing the audience and holding them at bay. I think the metaphor that best captures the relations that center stage bears to its periphery is that of a centrifuge: activity heats up in the center, then spins off into a particular edge or corner, each of which is encoded with its own qualitatively different valence.

Over the course of her song and dance numbers centerstage, the Dancer literally warms up the crowd. In one performance I recorded on videotape, a Dancer's exaggerated, slow hip rotation, arms up and body rhythmically circling, received prolonged whistles and hoots from the male audience, one of whom stood at the very lip of the stage snapping still photographs, his intent body posture looming in my camera lens in silhouette before the brightly lit glittering figure of the curvaceous Dancer onstage.

For the Dancer's role in the Duet, actresses wear a glamorized version of a young girl's daily costume, the *tāvaṇi* (demi-shawl) and skirt set traditionally worn by unmarried but postpubescent Tamil women. Here, this consists of a short, tight blouse and matching long skirt decorated with sparkling detail (sometimes fully sequined) and three yards of a separate diaphanous fabric draped over one shoulder (the *tāvaṇi*) and across the chest, then tucked in at the waist. By wearing a *tāvaṇi* and skirt as opposed to a sari, the Dancer here signals that she is young and unmarried. In reality, the contrast between the actress and the young role she plays can be arresting: several of the Dancers I have seen perform in this role were in their late thirties and early forties. What makes the disjuncture arresting is that no women other than actresses in the line of work seem to dare to alter the strict one-to-one relation that pertains in Tamilnadu between code of dress and a woman's life stage. Thus, immediately upon her first appearance, the notion that actresses transgress a wide range of strict behavioral norms adhered to by the majority of Tamil women is visually reinscribed, as is the resultant stigma on actresses that they seem to invite wherever they go.

Story Element 2: The Bumpy Meeting

As the Dancer ends her final song, suddenly the Buffoon hurtles out of the upstage left corner and bumps right into her. Their hips collide. The drummers emphasize their collision with an instrumental thud and clang. Most actors play this opening hip-bump between Buffoon and Dancer as highly exaggerated physical comedy. No attempt is made to hide the artifice of the meeting or to pretend that neither performers, musicians, or audience haven't fully expected just this "unexpected" occurrence. Such stagey timing finds its echo in the bump's spatial logic: it takes place just at the upstage pinnacle of center stage, simultaneously knocking the Dancer offcenter and out of center stage while bringing the Buffoon forward. Sometimes he passes right by her after dislodging her from center, continuing on his entrance trajectory across stage, pulling up to greet the musicians just short of hurtling into them. Other times the Buffoon allows the bump to change the direction of his course so that, while it pushes the Dancer upstage, the Buffoon winds up centerstage at the mike.

The Buffoon's costume communicates an entirely different message from that of the Dancer's; the clothes he wears may be worn by Tamil males of any age, married or unmarried. He wears for this scene the comfort clothes Tamil men wear around the house: an old sleeveless cotton undershirt or cotton T-shirt and a *lungi,* three yards of fabric wrapped around his waist, hanging down to his knees or calves. Over one shoulder he sports a small multipurpose towel, used equally by men to wrap their heads or swat away flies. These items of clothing are supremely ordinary, well-worn, and wrinkled. By his costume alone, the Buffoon embodies a Tamil Everyman.

In contrast to the Dancer's earlier ritualized dance greeting, the Buffoon's greeting to the musicians is casual and colloquial, verbal as well as gestural. It takes place either stage right or center stage at the mike. He banters easily with these men, a continuation of the repartee style established during his monologue scene. Greetings accomplished all around, the Buffoon turns his attention to the Dancer. Their first interchange is immediately argumentative: "Why did you bump me?" he asks, to which, offended, she counters, "Me bump you? You bumped me!" and the main action of the Duet is begun.

Often the Dancer volunteers a defense of her right to mind her own business: "I was simply dancing by myself here on the road, and you came crashing into me!" This defense is more damning, in context, than not saying anything at all: what would a good Tamil girl ever be doing dancing by herself on a public road? This is the second clue to the fact that the Dancer must be viewed as unusual and unusually transgressive.

Indeed, in Tamilnadu dancing itself is a rather extraordinary affair. Professional classical dancers or same-sex groups of male or female dancers at religious events (such as women dancing *kummi,* a folksong genre, in a circle on temple grounds) are the only persons for whom dancing is not seen as degrading activity. Others who dance with impunity are those possessed by deities, including groups of men on religious pilgrimages who dance en route with religious fervor, where a perceived loss of control is excused by the presence of the divine. Otherwise, the norm in Tamilnadu is to strictly control all extraneous physical movement, and dancing without a formal reason is considered vulgar. The fact that she dances in public is perhaps the most stigmatizing aspect of the stage actress's profession, a point to which I shall return.

For now, note simply that the dancing girl's defense of her reputation is no rational defense at all. When I asked actors and non-actors alike about the unusual behavior of the girl in these Duets, the response I received by way of explanation for her highly nonnormative actions always included the word *cummā,* perhaps the best English gloss for which is "just because!" "Why is she dancing in the road?" "*Cummā*!" would come the reply, as though this were quite natural.

Such a response was part and parcel of an overarching attitude I encountered toward these Duets, as mentioned above: the notion that they simply could not be analyzed, since they were "merely comedy." The notion of a girl dancing in the road "just because" further inscribes the taken-for-grantedness of this whole mise-en-scéne for its audience: it is the fantasy flipside to the normative reality that good Tamil girls don't do such things. The unspoken possibility, of course, is that some girls just might.

It is into this fantasy of a protected private space of autonomy for women in the very midst of the public sphere that the bump intrudes and explodes. The bump is a crash with reality; in one exchange I recorded, Padma, a Dancer from the town of Karaikkudi, and Udaiyappa, a Buffoon from the city of Pudukkottai, said it quite succinctly:

B: "Who are you?"

D: "Yo! I am a woman, and I am dancing here in this road, and now you've come along and spoiled it!"

Story Element 3: The Meaning of a Bump between Men and Women

Such initial verbal exchanges quickly lead to more protracted discussions of the *meaning* of a bump between man and woman. These discussions take place between Buffoon and Dancer while standing at the mikes, center stage. The two Tamil words repeated over and over here are *āṇpiḷḷai* (man) and *poṇpiḷḷai* (woman). The "bump" seems to have sprung open a highly productive space of interactive social anxiety necessitating fundamental reiterations of a distinction between genders. The bump jolts the Dancer out of what Lacan might term a prelinguistic imaginary and propels her into the recognition of herself as a signifier in a symbolic, phallic world. Their bump propels Buffoon and Dancer headlong into the world of logos, carving out a new, specific space on stage in the process. Morals and mores tumble out with every utterance emitted from that oblong hot spot on stage containing the two microphones (Fig. 3). First and foremost, these children must establish the difference between them on which the impropriety of the bump rests:

B: Who are you?
D: I'm a woman.
B: And who am I?
D: You're a man!
B: Right.
D: Right! You're a man! I'm a woman! And for a man to bump a woman is wrong!

By reiterating such fundamental moral tenets of gendered interaction, the Dancer makes her onstage persona a mouthpiece for just the kind of social censure so often aimed at the actress herself offstage. The Dancer thus introduces a certain discursive reality into what was a purely imagistic fantasy thus far, and yet it seems to only up the ante of the scenario's seductive social appeal: clearly she (the female character and, by extension, the actress who animates her) knows that what she is doing is wrong, but she (the actress herself now, as a real-life dancing girl) is doing it anyway. Introducing moral discourse by embedding it in an enactment of its transgression simultaneously cracks the primary fantasy of the imaginary and brings it to a heightened, linguistically self-conscious metalevel, as Buffoon and Dancer stand centerstage, flirting by yelling prohibitions at each other!

Once this flow of self-censuring words begins, it often quickly becomes contentious, as though argument might hammer some way out of the self-consciousness in which both players are now trapped, longing for a return to a less problematic imaginary.[7] Much banter already assumes a permanent state of challenge between men and women, as in this impish performance by a Madurai Dancer named Silk:

I'm a woman. If I want to, I can bear a child. You are a man. So you think I need you; you think that without you I can't do it, isn't that what you think? But I tell you, all that is just your fantasy. That's all the past, man! History! These are modern times. Nowadays, for 4,000 rupees I can simply get an injection and give birth to a kid all on my own. There's no need for you, so "get out!" (*in English*) [*Turns to look at audience*] At least, that's what I learned from my foreign friend!
[*points and smiles at me*]

Silk's playful appropriation of modern science here proves that virtually anything can be cunningly harnessed to serve locally enduring purposes. The bump is productively overdetermined: clearly sexual and scandalously immoral in public, its public performance raises a tension between stated, repressive norms of proper gender behavior and the unstated, irrepressible figments of fantasy. The couple promptly determines to resolve this tension in a contest that pits man and woman against each other as adamantly gendered subjects with all the attendant verbal and nonverbal social skills.

Story Element 4: The Contest between Men and Women

The contest begins with a challenge. Meeting it dramatically expands the core logocentric focus of center stage, turning it into an active centrifuge of interacting desires, both conscious and unconscious. The conceit of the contest itself is fantastical: a woman dancing alone on the road agrees to engage in a contest of skills with an unknown man, attempting to outstrip him in everything he does. She is the perfect feisty mate, a woman magically undeterred by norms she has just made us quite aware that she knows.

Buffoon Kannan and Dancer Kasturi, both from Pudukkottai, make this representative player quality overt in their use of the Tamil exclusive first-person plural pronoun (*nāṅkaḷ*) to challenge each other. The exclusive "we" used here gives a strong sense of two opposing teams of exclusively gendered subjects:

B: Can you[8] do anything we (*nāṅkaḷ*) do?
D: We'll do it!
B: We'll drive cars.
D: We'll also drive cars!

B: We'll drive buses.
D: We'll also drive buses!
B: We'll drive lorries.
D: We'll also drive lorries!
B: We'll drive you who drive everything!
D: Only if we give it can you drive it; otherwise, there's nothing you can do!
B: No, that's not how it is, woman! All you've got is the "steering" [*gestures with both hands as if holding a steering wheel in front of his chest*], while we have the "gear box!" [*gestures with one arm in front of his hip*]

As the small children in the audience join in the howling laughter that greets this barely coded symbolic display of sexuality, the Dancer turns directly to address the audience closest to her, a group of young boys sitting among the children up front, and asks them pointedly, "Hey, what is it with you kids? You're laughing, are you? You think you know anything about all this?!" The Buffoon comes to the rescue of the boys, picking one out in particular, and saying, "Though he's just a little guy he is one of our sex (*varkkam*). Like a calf, it may be just a small calf but its horns are big!" The Buffoon has here made the two terms officially overt, both through his choice of image and of word: the term *varkkam* distinguishes everything from a class, a race, and a sex, to a species (here, little boys with big horns).

The feistiness of the Dancer's role here seems to have emboldened the actress herself, blurring the boundaries of self and role; who exactly is chastising the little boys, a character in a comedy? Or the actress who plays her? It is already hard to distinguish the actress from the role of the dancing girl she plays, for who in this society *but* an actress on an outdoor stage comes closest to the fantasy of a woman dancing in public? Tamil films specialize in encouraging fantasies of women dancing outdoors; no Tamil film seems complete without a song and dance sequence set amid waterfalls in rolling hills, temple ruins, or high Himalayan peaks and valleys. The antics of such celluloid dream maidens surely contribute to the audacity with which stage actresses now inhabit their roles as Dancers. Nevertheless, in the flesh, traveling from stage to stage on very real roads in the company of very real publics, this actress essentially *is* the dancing girl she plays—and the young children up front are learning all about it.[9]

Having established the nature of their play through such verbal sparring, Buffoon and Dancer now step back from the mikes to begin enacting the physical dimension of their contest. The musicians strike up a common fast-paced folk tune in a musical genre named for its sing-song chorus, *taṇaṇaṇaṉē*. The actors dive into a dance of thrusting hips, approaching each other and retreating, contracting and expanding the circle of center stage and defining it with strong, wide, voracious steps. In effect, the Buffoon has joined the circle the Dancer first traced with her entrance. Together, they spin in a heated whirl.

They mirror each other's steps in a highly attuned improvisation. In unison, they gradually draw together into a tense, close stance, only their hips moving, bumping together rhythmically. Thus what began with a hip-bump, then spread out, over loudspeakers, in words and songs only to eat up the entire stage in hungry dance, has finally come full circle back to the hips where it began, the bodily center (as Western dancers say) and center stage. For a moment Dancer and Buffoon move together like a single pulse. But this tension quickly proves too much for the man, and he overtakes her, overzealously thrusting his hips at her, practically jumping onto her in such a way that she starts to back away, trying to escape him. His excited over-eagerness ruins the moment.

This turn of events always ends with the Dancer backing up into the downstage right corner of the stage. The couple's deceleration out of their charged, whirling circle of big movement culminates with the Dancer positioned between the Buffoon and the musicians, caught between men both before and behind her. As she backs up to escape the Buffoon, there is nowhere to go but closer to the musicians (Fig. 6).

I have characterized this downstage right corner as the place on a Special Drama stage where women routinely find themselves, and are seen being trapped by men (Figs. 1–3). The corner is structurally walled off from egress into the audience by the musicians' tables, and particularly the table furthest downstage upon which the all-round drummer sits. His wooden table, his own body, and his array of drums effectively create a wall that separates this downstage corner from the offstage space beyond it. Just below and abutted to the lip of the stage in this same corner is another table where the electrical sound and light system and the men who run it sit (drawn into Figs. 1 and 2). These two tiers of men seated at their instruments create a vertical wall of enclosure that extends both above and below the actors. A woman who is backed into this space cannot go beyond it; it is a corner from which there is no escape. It is to this corner that male actors invariably head when they are trying to physically overpower a woman, maintaining eye contact with the musicians, while her back is to them.

Figure 10.6 "Woman-trapping Corner."

At this point in the Duet, the Buffoon corners the Dancer and she literally has to push him away, most often putting her two hands against his chest and giving him a shove. This in and of itself is somewhat humiliating to her, in that she has had to resort to physically touching a man onstage. Public touching itself taints a woman, as the following exchange between Dancer Jothi Stri and Buffoon Ravi Kanth, both of Madurai, overtly reveals:

D: Hey, don't touch me, man! There are lots of people watching. How am I going to get married, who's going to marry me, if they see me up here getting touched by you?
B: Oh, are there, are there people watching?
D: Yes, indeed, there are lots of them watching, and they care about that!

This exchange took place center stage, when the Buffoon tapped the Dancer on the shoulder while talking. Her overt comment here lays bare a normative condition that pertains throughout the Duet: a woman's reputation is negatively affected when a man touches her in public. She loses her reputation in the eyes of the larger society and can no longer be properly married off. Such commentary really constitutes a kind of metacommentary in that it exposes the subtext of danger infusing the whole enterprise of the Buffoon-Dance Duet: a girl-woman dancing with a man, in public, has placed herself conspicuously in the path of all the potential taints on a woman that may be wrought through her sexualized presence in the male public sphere. Equally, when she must resort to physically defending herself in the downstage right corner, it should be clear that a woman is put in a no-win situation, forced to choose between being physically overpowered and having her reputation as a woman who touches men in public confirmed.

In contrast to the security and status provided actresses amid the mix of community in the upstage right corner, the downstage right corner is a site of women's humiliation. Whereas upstage right she may be seen to interact cordially with important and known men on an equal footing of respect, downstage right she is pushed as far as possible into the gaze of strangers: unknown men in the village audience.

Usually, her retreat into this downstage corner, coupled with her retaliating push on his chest, is enough to discourage the Buffoon from literally jumping the Dancer and the action folds back into another round of dancing or verbal sparring. I did, however, witness one particular Buffoon-Dance Duet in which a Buffoon's overzealousness at this point in the act definitively crossed an already blurred line between acting and real life, literally stopping the show. As the wide, hip-thrusting dance circle narrowed into a sexual pulse, instead of merely gesturing at overwhelming the Dancer and driving her into the downstage right corner, Buffoon Udaiyappa went particularly wild in aiming exceedingly high and hostile jumps at Dancer Padma. The first time this happened, she adroitly fended him off with her arms, and managed to steer them both back into the dance. But when it happened a second time, Padma took the radical step of literally stepping out of the normal playing space of the stage. Her step out taught me that there *is* a normal playing space, and that it does have definite boundaries. In this moment, Padma moved into a portion of the stage I had never seen before, and have never since seen any performer occupy. Physically, she moved onto the furthermost downstage lip of the stage, downstage of the center-stage mikes. Symbolically, this downstage step broke the charmed circle of the act. Once there, Padma stood still, glaring at Udaiyappa, her back to the audience. She shook her head no; she put out her hand and shook it no, too. He immediately began chattering nervously, trying to cajole her back into the play; he tried coaxing words, such as "Come, *mā,* come back. What are you going to do out there? Come!" But Padma wasn't playing anymore. She held fast her uncommon ground, making it perfectly clear that unless he stopped his overzealous and sexually aggressive behavior, she would not return to the circle of play.

The moment passed with Udaiyappa seemingly chastised, and they resumed their Duet. But each time he veered again toward an overzealous sexual display, she stepped back onto the dangerous front lip with a look that was a visibly conscious reminder of the precariousness of their agreement, at which point he quickly backed down.

There was a heightened edginess and danger to her standing between him and the actual audience instead of between him and the musicians, the fictive "stand-in" audience. Padma is a particularly bold performer, and the markedness of her unusual move away from the given confines of known men and toward the risks inherent in putting herself nearer to the unknown men in the audience stopped Udaiyappa cold. I felt as though she had broken out of a prevailing, complicit dynamic similar to that of domestic abuse, her own indignation leading her to forge into open unknown territory. While moral indignation is an all-too-common stance for women in India—women as the bearers of the nation's morality and all that this familiar trope implies[10]—in this case it was not simply part of the play but rather caused a frame break. The overwhelming duality of the Dancer's role struck me again: Padma the actress and the nameless Dancer character she plays in this Duet inseparably merged in performing this all-too-real act of moral indignation. Her move punctured the comic frame of the Buffoon-Dance Duet, revealing the ways in which their actions on stage chart very real gender relations under a very thin guise of comedy.

The final space on stage that the dance contest opens up is that of the downstage left corner. This corner, like the others, has recurring standard uses throughout the night. Whenever male actors look for an escape from the action on stage, they do so downstage left. In one Duet, Dancer Kasturi ducked under Buffoon Kannan's legs to escape his advances, only to find, when she stood up, that he had practically disappeared stage left. She had to run after him, grab his hand, and pull him back so as not to lose her partner. Similarly, when Dancer Amutha spunkily attempted to use a thrusting hip move to force her partner Mani to back up (as Buffoons often do in guiding Dancers to the downstage right corner), the ploy headed in the opposite direction, and Mani nearly fell off the stage on its open side, stage left. Here again the Dancer had to grab his hand and pull him back to center to continue their play.

Figure 10.7: "Man-moving-off Corner."

The openness of the downstage left corner is dramatically different, as well as spatially diametrically opposed, to the trapped quality of the downstage right (see Fig. 7). These two downstage corners reflect a strict gender division in use: downstage left is used exclusively by male actors, while, as we have seen, the right is where women are so often confined. In moving downstage left, the Buffoon straddles a kind of semi-on/semi-offstage position. It is here that he embodies the ever-present possibility that exists for Tamil men of moving easily off and out into the public sphere; such a possibility does not exist in the same way for women. The architectural openness of the left side of the stage supports this contrast. Sometimes, late in the night, a Buffoon will dismount the stage to venture out into a sleepy audience with a pail of water to splash, rouse, and startle sleepers; it is always from the downstage left corner that he descends with his pail.

Both downstage corners, then, house a certain threat to the continuity of the contest of skills between Buffoon and Dancer, and keep the tension of their play alive: the energy generated from their dancing center stage spikes out, now to one side, now to the other. Such energy spikes take separate directions for separate genders, as women end up trapped downstage right (fighting a losing battle not to lose face), while men escape any prospect of losing place or face downstage left. In the end, both corners present gender separation, while center stage remains the locus of the push-me-pull-you dance that is the centerpiece of the contest phase of the Buffoon-Dance Duet.

Story Element 5: Mutual Admiration and "Love Marriage"

The contest segment ends when Buffoon and Dancer each seem to suddenly realize that the other has performed admirably. Back from the scare of either side of the stage, they turn to each other with an admiring gaze and renewed interest. Their tone of voice and comportment completely shifts. Sometimes the Dancer begins, in a high-pitched singsong voice, to praise the Buffoon, exclaiming, "Oh! You sing so well! You dance so well! Stay right here, don't go anywhere! I want to bring you home." Equally often, the Buffoon begins by turning to the Dancer and saying, "You sing well. You dance well. What is your name?" followed promptly by the English phrase, "I love you."

This saccharine turn of the Duet is offset by the parodic flair with which it is performed. For example, my camera captured Dancer Jeeva enacting a send-up of the supposed sincerity of this shift by employing a Freudian pseudo-slip: she says, "I'll bite only you!" (*uṉṉai tāṉ nāṉ kaṭikkiṟēṉ*!) instead of "I'll marry only you!" (*uṉṉai tāṉ nāṉ kaṭṭikkiṟēṉ*!). Similarly, when Dancer Sundari flatters insincerely, saying, "Oh! Sir! You are so high up! You have gone, oh, so far somewhere!" her praise simultaneously comments precisely on that evasive prerogative men often exercise, as we have seen. Likewise, when Dancer Jothi exclaims, "I want to marry you right away; we are so well suited!" there is a hint of sarcasm in her choice of words, in their suggestion that the reality of that highly sought-after ideal of a suitable marriage could take the form of a courtship such as we just witnessed, filled with fear, anger, and aggression.

But perhaps the hardest hitting irony of all those couched in the "mutual admiration phase" of the Duet is that displayed by the Buffoon. In the very instant after professing his love for the Dancer, a Buffoon will often turn to a man in the audience and signal to him, through hand and head gestures, to meet the Buffoon backstage after the act if he is interested in the woman. He gestures like a classic pimp, "You want her? You'll pay? Meet me in the back as soon as this is over!" Here, at the expense of his partner's reputation, the Buffoon takes this opportunity to consolidate his same-sex bonds with the men in the audience. He distances himself from her just at the height of the narrative moment in which they ostensibly come together "in love," thus undercutting any narrative realism with parodic cynicism.

His move also most certainly undercuts the moral ground his partner has attempted to stake out for herself as a woman on stage. The Buffoon's actions ensure that stage actresses will never entirely escape their reputation as prostitutes: even a man who has just publicly demonstrated his love for a Dancer and his willingness to view her as a marriageable woman will turn around and pimp her the next instant. With this gesture, the Buffoon reinscribes several extant stereotypes about drama people and the drama world, including the idea that actresses deserve their spoiled reputation. Actresses' own attempts to escape that reputation by enacting a shared moral stance with "good Tamil women" are foiled, then, by the very men with whom they must share the stage.

During such moments, the Dancer does not acknowledge the Buffoon's gesture. The two continue to exchange vows of love and sing a romantic song together, during which they clasp each other in an embrace centerstage. They smile and coo at each other, hold hands, and decide to elope and perform "love marriage." "Love marriage" is the English term used in Tamilnadu to refer to a decision on the part of bride and groom to marry out of love, rather than accept a marriage arranged by their families, the foreign-inflected, risqué ending to a scenario already traditionally tinged with scandal, that of strangers of the opposite sex meeting, mixing, and matching on a public road.

Their decision to "do love" notwithstanding, there remains a certain tension between the couple center stage. The tautly sprung quality at the center of this scene persists. From this point, there are two possible directions this energy may take in ending the Duet. First, the couple completes their song and runs together offstage, exiting through the upstage left corner. This ending was used in roughly half the Buffoon-Dance Duets I watched. The second possibility is that the Dancer does actually manage to give the guy the slip: at a certain point during the song, she spies her "uncle" coming toward them. She looks out in the distance and calls out, "Uncle!" While politely smiling and greeting this imaginary apparition, she extricates herself from the Buffoon's embrace, holds her hands together in formal farewell, and as the Buffoon turns to follow her gaze out into the audience, she quickly backs away and exits upstage left while his back is turned. The Buffoon is left standing alone to finish the song, and the scene, by himself.

While this second ending would seem to offer the Dancer the last laugh, the Buffoon doesn't always go quietly into his cuckolding. Rather, he may take the opportunity of being abandoned onstage to comment on the Dancer in much the same way his prior pimping suggested. I watched an older, well-regarded Buffoon, Arumukam of Ponamaravathy, speak the following lines after Dancer Padma left him in the lurch with just such a ruse, distancing himself definitively from all that he had just enacted in the Duet, drawing a sharp line between his real self and the character he played:

> Blessed woman! She's someone's daughter . . . may you be well! Liking all this is wrong. It is said, "There is only one woman for one man." And who is that one woman? The one who submits herself to the measure of turmeric cord [i.e., the wife], she's the one. I am not alone in asserting this. The Christian Bible, the Muslim Koran, and the Hindu *Kuṟaḷ* all say this same thing: "There is only one woman for one man." All these others [*pointing after Padma*] will disappear.

In this moralizing footing of direct address to the audience at the end of the Duet, note that Arumukam makes his claim for a distinction between his real self (the actor) and his character (the Buffoon) at the Dancer's expense. His ability to rise above the character he played just seconds ago turns on his dismissal of *women such as her,* an attitude that continues to view actresses and their Dancer characters as collapsed into the single entity, "bad woman." It is she who is always worthy of disdain.[11]

Such a use of direct audience address in a moralizing footing at the culmination of the Duet also creates a tidy frame for the act as a whole. It returns to a footing employed throughout the Buffoon's monologue scene that precedes the Duet, so that Buffoons who choose to end the Duet as Arumukam did close this story in the same way it was begun: a Buffoon, alone onstage with his male cohort, offers a moralizing metacommentary on modern relations between Tamil men and women that portrays moral antimony as their natural state.

Analogic Relations

In Special Drama, verbal debates, circumstantial encounters, and physical contests between men and women figure repeatedly in both the comedic and the dramatic scenes that unfold throughout the night. Two separate sets of coupled artists play the lead roles in these scenes: the male Hero and female Heroine in the dramatic scenes, the male Buffoon and the female Dancer in the comedic scenes. For both couples, their interactions always center around marriage, and generally they are cast as unmarried men and women for whom the potential to be drawn, through mutual attraction, into "love marriage" is strong.

In "Vaḷḷi's Wedding" (again, the most popular of all Special Dramas), the play turns on a plot wherein Lord Murukaṉ (the Tamil god of youth and beauty) disguises himself as a hunter for the purpose of convincing the young, beautiful, and spunky Vaḷḷi, daughter of the hunter tribe's chief, to marry him. He surprises her while she is busy guarding her father's millet fields (she is outside, just as the Dancer is in the Buffoon-Dance Duet). His divine identity unknown to her, the girl refuses Murukaṉ's advances. Instead, she argues with him, questioning his propriety in addressing her at all (just as the Dancer did when the Buffoon bumped her). They proceed to debate the morality of arranged marriage versus love marriage in a contest of wits, and he finally uses a supernatural trick to frighten her into submission. Hero and Heroine eventually tie the knot and their "love marriage" ends the drama.

The similarity of this story's structure to that of the Buffoon-Dance Duet is obvious, with the latter essentially a comedic adumbration of the dramatic scenes to follow. "Vaḷḷi's Wedding" and the Buffoon-Dance Duet are awash in the same design elements. As I see it, the opening comedy scene serves as an orienting figuration, a disavowed lesser half that nevertheless provides a diagram to the theatrics that follow. The parallelism between these two scenes is perhaps most vivid at the level of spatial blocking. Throughout, center stage and each of the four corners maintain continuous standard resonances and index the specific paradigms of gendered social relations in Tamilnadu that I have described above. But there is yet another level on which this same parallelism operates. Just as the narrative texts themselves are organized around interactions between unknown women and men, so too is the contextualizing event, that of the performance itself, for audience and performers alike.

First, actors and actresses are themselves often unknown to each other, coming from different towns to perform together for one night on a village stage; the "special nature" of the Special Drama genre, as we have seen, largely inheres in the uniqueness of each performance event: each artist comes to each performance "specially." Thus, the potential of the unknown meeting is scripted into the "real" lives of the actors and actresses who play these roles, as they are, in reality, meeting each other as unknown persons on a public road.

Second, a primary intrigue for viewers lies in watching multiple, intertextual layers of meetings unfold between unknown men and women: (1) Buffoon and Dancer, (2) hunter-god Hero and hunted-girl Heroine, and (3) actor and actress as real people. The audience is offered the possibility of entering a common fantasy of "love" from any and all of these domains, all of which, conveniently, share the same stage.

Finally, at an event like Special Drama, the members of the audience are themselves interacting with people they have never met before, as well as others whom they know quite well, all in the heightened space of the outdoor village commons. On these simultaneous multiple levels, the spatial use of the Special Drama stage reflects and troubles a frequently invoked common-sense Tamil distinction between "known people" and "unknown people."

Known people (*terintavarkaḷ*) are preferable to unknown people (*teriyātavarkaḷ*) in almost every type of interaction, as markedly in affairs of the heart as of the purse. Any interaction with an unknown person is potentially the first step on a path toward increased connectedness with a foreign element, and could lead to who knows what. In Tamilnadu generally, new and unknown alliances are guarded against, and tremendous emphasis is put on strengthening the connectedness of kin networks. Women are enjoined to regard known men as their protectors. The idea is that even distant kin look out for each other, and that one's physical safety as well as moral reputation are ensured by limiting outside interaction.

The norm of endogamous marriage in Tamilnadu reinforces these connections. Here, the ideal-typical marriage is that of parallel cross-cousins. Such marriageable cousins—the sons and daughters of brothers and sisters—are in fact addressed from childhood by the terms "customary bride" and "customary groom" (*muṟaippeṇ, muṟai māppiḷḷai*). The paradigm of cross-cousin marriage is encoded into the language itself, where the kin term *attāṉ* is used equally by a woman to refer to her marriageable male cousin (son of her maternal uncle) as to her husband. In short, the husband *should be* the parallel male cross-cousin (and if he is not, he is called that anyway, a good strategy for incorporating foreign difference).

By contrast, a girl who marries outside her kin network is considered to have moved outside of proper customary relations. Such a woman courts disorder. The word *muṟai* covers the English semantic fields of "custom," "order," and "kin"; the acting community, notably, are proverbially known as "people without *muṟai* (*muṟai illātavarkaḷ*). This is because they so openly engage in interactions with a wide public and also because they are known to frequently marry across caste, both of which are seen as uncustomary and disorderly practices. Coupled with a general suspicion of mimesis as a potentially disordering endeavor, as noted above, the notion of a lack of *muṟai* is at the heart of the stigma encountered by the acting community.

Let us return to the picture of the stage as structured by differently encoded use areas to see how these distinctions between known and unknown persons play out there. I suggested earlier that the two stage-right corners, upstage and downstage, might be seen as complementary spaces, the former a place to enact in a real-life mode the prestige of the known, the latter to encounter in a fictive vein the fear of the unknown. However, the whole of stage right may also be seen as a continuum of known and semi-known men. Here any attempt to neatly separate the spheres of safe versus unsafe, or known versus unknown, is necessarily complicated by the very multidimensionality of the drama community itself. This community transgresses caste, religious, and regional boundaries by replacing them with a fictive kin network of "drama people."

Actors employ a strategy of fictive kin terms of address as they travel through the real world together, just as they do on stage. Everywhere they go, they call each other *aṇṇaṉ* and *taṅkaici,* big brother and little sister, or *tampi* and *akkā,* younger brother and older sister, or uncle, or aunt, or cousin. Though in many ways a brilliant strategy for fending off any outsiders' impressions that a lot of mixing with unknown people goes on in the drama world, the use of fictive kin terms among themselves onstage never quite manages to remove the taint on actresses: for an actress, even the "known" corner is widely recognized to be a broad collection of unrelated men and women moving freely together in ways that for most Tamilians are the definition of the deep unknown. Furthermore, this rather tenuous performance of the known (controlled, respectful) in the upstage right corner shares certain other, more unsettling features with the tense relations enacted in the downstage right corner.

Clearly, this corner is where men enact sexual aggression. But are these men entirely different from those who populate the upstage corner? If the upstage corner serves the drama community and its well-wishers as a source of protection, nevertheless, downstage we find a confusion of protection and danger within the drama community itself.

The mixed message of this continuous zone stage right resonates in disturbing ways with other Tamil social spaces. The men positioned behind the actress, the musicians, simultaneously keep her in and block her escape. They are her community. And yet, what is their role within the comedic performance, in which an unknown man is chasing an unknown woman? Suddenly the musicians are simply male bystanders: do they offer her any of the protection she might otherwise expect from kin? Instead they often ally themselves with the Buffoon, her adversary, greeting him jocularly, and laughing with him as he makes jokes at her expense.[12] Swept up in the performance, they too suddenly become an unknown quantity. The ease of their switch from known to unknown highlights the very fictive nature of their alliance with her in the first place, as we become increasingly aware of the fact that the musicians are equally his community and his kin, and that he too calls them big brother, little brother, uncle.

I wonder if it might not be that because the male actor (the Buffoon) manages to establish a distinction between his real self and his fictive character, he is more able, as his real self (a moral man), to establish same-sex bonds of rapport with the musicians that are inevitably stronger than those the Dancer is able to forge with them. After all, it is a war of the sexes being enacted here over and again. The Dancer never quite seems able to get either the audience or the musicians really on her side, as the overly intertwined figures of her real life as an actress and her fictive persona as a Dancer remain inseparable and as such leave her grappling with stigma, and the lower hand, from beginning to end.

It is often to shore up his moments of direct moralizing address to the audience that the Buffoon interpellates the musicians as his moral support and same-sex peer group, the latter a notoriously strong male bond in Tamilnadu. I find an unresolvable tension in the musicians' presence here: can they really simultaneously egg him on and protect the Dancer? Moreover, in their role as paradigm audience, modeling for the real audience a kind of engaged but distanced spectatorship, what does their ambivalent relation to the Dancer communicate to the men and women in the audience? What can any Tamil woman really expect of the men with whom she interacts, with whom she even shares her home?

Everyone present at an actual Special Drama event knows that being backed up into *this* group of men is safer for the actress than being backed up into an audience of males who are complete strangers. But an ambivalence remains: is this corner home, or street? This downstage right corner houses the predominantly unspoken but nevertheless always underlying possibilities of domestic violence and incest that trouble any easy separation of "home and world" into truly separate domestic and public spheres.

Finally, it should come as no surprise that it is in this same corner that the turning point of "Vaḷḷi's Wedding" is invariably staged: after hours of arguing in a contest of wits center stage, the hunter traps Vaḷḷi downstage right. In this corner, he physically grabs her. She screams out for her brother to come running out to save her. But when her brother finally arrives, and she describes to him all the hunter's disrespectful actions toward her, instead of helping her get away from this lecherous old man (Murukaṉ's guise in this scene), her brother concludes that such trickster-like behavior could only be the antics of a god, and that this hunter must surely therefore be Lord Murukaṉ in disguise, and that, indeed, Vaḷḷi must immediately submit to his will and desires, and marry him forthwith. The marriage of Vaḷḷi to Murukaṉ promptly follows: her brother "gives her away" by supplying the marriage garlands.

Conclusion

My goal in this essay has been to highlight the analogic relations between staged spatial paradigms and everyday offstage social landscapes. The spatial, narrative, and structural continuities between the Buffoon-Dance Duet and the dramatic scenes that follow it in a night of Special Drama are one set of analogous relations. Another broader analogic relation also exists, I have suggested, between the socio-spatial paradigms embodied onstage and those lived in the daily gendered world of Tamil social life. It is in establishing these continuities that theater creates itself as a space for social commentary. My premise has been that spatial use onstage indexes the organization of spatial domains offstage, both on the ground and in the social imagination. As microcosms of Tamil cultural production, the recreations of the drama world address some of the largely unstated organizing principles of Tamil social life.

I have suggested that standardization of the structuring elements in Special Drama—the ordering of scenes, the use of repertory characters and of established musical and rhetorical styles, and the constancy of spatial blocking—makes the unique organization of this genre possible. On any stage, with any combination of known or unknown performers, Special Drama actors rely, in place of rehearsal or direction, on the continuity of these socio-spatial features, all of which are established to quite a remarkable extent in the Duet. Further, I have argued that the staging of the Buffoon-Dance duet, in both its verbal and nonverbal dimensions, not only anticipates and foreshadows the dramatic Vaḷḷi story, but also reflects ongoing tensions in the everyday conventional use and organization of Tamil social space. These offstage analogies bear repeating.

Specifically, what I have termed the performers' "entrance and exit corner" recalls the frequent traffic in Tamil social life between a known community and an unknown public other. What I have termed the "comfort station corner" captures the quality of what is accepted as a dominant pleasure in Tamil life, the existence of a safe space among kin, which then extends protection out into the larger, public world. Center stage provides the analog for the sparring quality attendant on the relations between the sexes in Tamilnadu. And finally, in the two downstage corners, what I have called the "men's moving-off corner" refers to an assumed male freedom that leads men to wander and disappear, while the "women's trapping corner" downstage right speaks to the ambivalent qualities of the domestic sphere for women: Is it desirable and safe? Is it desirable and unsafe? Or is it a trap one would rather escape?

The humor apparent in these performances reveals and questions, but also potentially reinscribes, all these existing tensions in offstage life. It exposes a series of hinges between the staged world and life offstage. The spatial blocking hammered out in these performances is simultaneously a theatrical stage convention and a map of certain broader conventions of socio-spatial life in Tamilnadu. While often cast in a comedic mode on stage, the relations between bodies on the ground and bodies on stage play into locally familiar shaping of *space* into highly codified, qualified, and gendered social *place*.

Notes

All photos by Susan Seizer. Film clips of Special Drama performances can be viewed at http:www.stigmasofthe tamilstage.com.

1. Dell Hymes usefully defines competence in performance as "the knowledge and ability to speak in socially appropriate and interpretable ways" (1971, p. 58).
2. For an extended discussion of actress' strategies for securing a modicum of respect as "good women," see Seizer, 2000.
3. Performances of "Vaḷḷi's Wedding" comprised 65% of all Special Drama plays performed during the 1991–1993 drama seasons in Tamilnadu's Madurai District.

4. Special Dramas are also performed for Christian festivals, though the sheer number of these is far fewer than the number of Hindu festivals celebrated in Tamilnadu.
5. For a fuller explanation of how the everyman chorus is established during the Buffoon's monologue, see Seizer 1997.
6. I have taken this term from Goffman, who uses the term "footing" to refer to the alignment of speaker to hearers. Shifts in footing frequently involve code switching and changes in tone and pitch, as well as literal changes in stance that include postural repositionings of the speaker's "projected self" (1979, pp. 4–5). The Buffoon makes use of all these shifts during his monologue.
7. The Duet lends itself to Lacanian psychological interpretations in interesting ways, as it seems to enact the whole range of dynamics that Lacan's writings on the mirror stage suggest: that it is a state of longing for the lost world of the imaginary, such that these two seem to hold on to some primary dreams, like cranky children stuck in an adult world of logos. A bit later in the Duet, when Buffoon and Dancer exchange love vows, they use baby-talk voices.
8. This is the only singular usage of the second person in this exchange. After use of the exclusive "we" is established, all other uses of "you" also switch to the matching plural, e.g., "only if we give it can you [*plural*] drive it."
9. I witnessed another Buffoon-Dance Duet where a similar lesson was pointedly addressed to the kids sitting in the audience up front. Shridhar, a Buffoon from Madurai, prepared to embark on the contest segment of his Duet with Dancer Silk by first establishing that this young audience knew all that was at stake by asking them:

   > Who are we? We are men! We are heroes! Yes! And in what does the heroism of men consist? *This* [*physically erecting the head of the microphone*] is the heroism of men!

   The Duet is a crash course in iconicity as well as sex ed.
10. For a full account of the history of this role for women in India, see Partha Chatterjee's influential essay, "Women and the Nation," in *The Nation and its Fragments,* 1993.
11. Arumukam enacts this philosophy in real life in ways that have painful repercussions for actresses interacting with him there, too. Now in his sixties, Arumukam married a non-actress. Their son Kannan is now also a popular Special Drama Buffoon. Kannan wants to marry Kasturi, the Dancer with whom he has been working for several years (Kannan and Kasturi are one of the few Buffoon-Dance teams in Special Drama—that is, they are hired as a team—and they are by far the most popular of these). Arumukam is adamantly opposed to his son's plan to marry an actress. He told me that he does not think that a Dancer makes an appropriate wife, and has blocked his son's marriage for years.
12. In a separate comedic duet between the Buffoon and Dancer that occurs much later in a night of Special Drama, known as the *Aṭipiṭi* Scene [the thrashing scene], during an act of overt domestic abuse the musicians clearly side with the husband/Buffoon, egging him on as he kicks and pummels his wife, played by the Dancer (Seizer, 2001).

Bibliography

Primary Sources (Texts and Translations)

Aiṅkuṟunūṟu Mūlamum Paḻaiyavuraiyum. U. Vē. Cāminātaiyar, ed. 6th ed. Chennai: Doctor U. Vē. Cāminātaiyar Nūl Nilaiyam, 1980.

Akanāṉūṟu. Madras: Kaḻakam, 1971.

Annankaracaryar, P. B. *Tivyārttatipikai: Gloss [urai] of Mutaltiruvantāti, Iraṇṭāntiruvantāti, Mūṉṟāntiruvantāti.* Madras: M. R. Govindasami Nayadu, Model Press, 1928, 1929.

Āryaśūra. *The Jatakamala.* J. S. Speyer, tr. Delhi: Motilal Banarsidass, 1982.

Aśokāvadāna. The Legend of King Aśoka: A Study and Translation of the Aśokāvadāna. J. S. Strong, tr. Princeton: Princeton University Press, 1983.

Aśvaghoṣa. *The Buddhacarita: Or, Acts of the Buddha.* Parts I & II. E. H. Johnston, ed. and tr. Calcutta: Baptist Mission Press, 1935, 1936.

Bhagavad-gītā. The Bhagavad-gītā: With a Commentary Based on the Original Sources. R. C. Zaehner, ed. and tr. Oxford: Clarendon Press, 1969.

Bhāgavata-purāṇa. Śrīmad Bhāgavata: The Holy Book of God. 4 vols. Swami Tapasyananda, tr. Madras: Sri Ramakrishna Math, 1980–82.

Cāminātaiyar, U. Vē. *The Story of My Life.* S. K. Guruswamy, tr. A. R. Iyer, ed. Chennai: Doctor U. Vē. Cāminātaiyar Nūl Nilaiyam, 1980.

———. *Eṉ Carittiram.* 2nd ed. Chennai: Doctor U. Vē. Cāminātaiyar Nūl Nilaiyam, 1982.

Cāttaṉār. *Cittalai-c-cāttaṉār iyaṟṟiya Maṇimēkalai.* Tirunelveli and Madras: Kaḻakam, 1964.

Cēkkiḻār. *Periya Purāṇam.* Srivaikuntam: Sri Kumarakuruparan Cankam, 1964.

Ciṉṉamakipaṉ Kuḷuva Nāṭakam. A. N. Perumal, ed. Madras: International Institute of Tamil Studies, 1980.

Epigraphia Indica. Vols. 9 (1907–08), 11 (1911–12), 15 (1919–20), 22 (1933–34), 25 (1938–39).

Hsuan-tsang. *Si-Yu-Ki: Buddhist Records of the Western World (Translated from the Chinese of Hiuen Tsiang [A.D. 629]).* Samuel Beal, tr. London: Kegan Paul, Trench, Trubner, and Co. Ltd., n.d.

Hymns for the Drowning: Poems for Viṣṇu by Nammāḻvār. A. K. Ramanujan, tr. Princeton: Princeton University Press, 1981.

Iḷaṅkōvaṭikaḷ. *Cilappatikāram.* Madras: Kaḻakam, 1977.

Kauṭilīya Arthaśāstra. R. P. Kangle, ed. and tr. 3 vols. Delhi: Motilal Banarsidass, 1988.

Kavirāyar, Ti. Rā. *Kuṟṟāla-k-kuṟavañci*. Pu. Ci. Punnaivananata Mutaliyar, ed. Madras, 1980.

Kuṟuntokai. Po. Vē. Cōmacuntaraṉār, ed. Chennai: Kaḻakam, 1978.

———. U. Vē. Cāminātaiyar, ed. Annamalainagar: Annamalai University, 1983.

———. *The Interior Landscape: Love Poems from a Classical Tamil Anthology*. A. K. Ramanujan, tr. Bloomington: Indiana University Press, 1967.

———. *An Anthology of Classical Love Poetry*. M. Shanmugam Pillai and D. Ludden, tr. Madurai: Koodal Publishers, 1976.

Mahābhārata. 3 vols. J. A. B. van Buitenen, ed. and tr. Chicago: University of Chicago Press, 1973, 1975, 1978.

———. *The Mahābhārata of Krishna-Dwaipayana Vyasa*. K. M. Ganguli, tr. Vols. 4 and 10. Delhi: Munshiram Manoharlal Publishers, 1982, 1991.

Mahāvaṃśa. *The Mahāvaṃśa or the Great Chronicle of Ceylon*. W. Geiger, tr. London: Pali Text Society, 1912.

Mahendra. *Mattavilāsa Prahasana of Mahendravikramavarman*. N. P. Unni, ed. and tr. Trivandrum: College Book House, 1974.

———. *Mattavilāsa Prahasana ('The Farce of Drunken Sport')*. M. Lockwood and A. Vishnu Bhat, ed. and tr. Madras: The Christian Literature Society, 1981.

"*Maturai Mīnāṭciyammai Kuṟam* of Kumarakuruparar." In *Śrī Kumarakurupara Cuvāmikaḷ Pirapanta-t-tiraṭṭu*. Madras, 1939: 529–541.

Mayamata. B. Dagens, tr. Delhi: Sitaram Bharatiya Institute of Scientific Research, 1985.

Mayamatam: A Treatise of Housing, Architecture and Iconography. B. Dagens, ed. and tr. Delhi: Motilal Banarsidass, 1994.

Memoirs of the Archeological Survey of India, no. 79, 1984.

Mukkūṭaṟpaḷḷu. Mu. Arunacalam, ed. Madras, 1940.

Mysore Archaeological Reports, 1925.

Naṟṟiṇai Nāṉūṟu. A. Nārāyaṇacāmi Aiyar and Po. Vē. Cōmacuntaraṉār, comms. 3rd ed. (reprint). Chennai: Kaḻakam, 1976.

Nagaswamy, R. *Thiruttani and Velanjeri Copper Plates*. Madras: State Department of Archaeology, 1979.

Paṉṉiruppāṭṭiyal. K. R. Kōvintarāca Mutaliyār, comm. Tirunelveli: Kaḻakam, 1963.

Paramasaṃhitā. S. Krishnaswami Aiyangar, ed. and tr. Baroda: Oriental Institute, 1940.

Pattuppāṭṭu. U. Vē. Cāminātaiyar, ed. Tanjavur: Kaḻakam, 1961.

———. *Six Long Poems from Sangam Tamil*. N. Raghunathan, tr. Madras: Vighneswara Publishing House, 1978.

Poems of Love and War: From the Eight Anthologies and the Ten Long Poems of Classical Tamil. A. K. Ramanujan, tr. New York: Columbia University Press, 1985.

Poets of the Tamil Anthologies: Ancient Poems of Love and War. G. L. Hart, tr. Princeton: Princeton University Press, 1979.

Poykai. *Mutaltiruvantāti*. In *Iyaṟpa Āyirattiṉ Mutal Sampuṭam: P. B. Aṇṇaṅkarācāriyār iyaṟṟiya Tivyārttatīpikai Urai-y-uṭaṉ*. 4th ed. Kanchipuram: P. B. Annangarachariar Granthamala Office, 1960: 1–80.

Puṟanāṉūṟu. U. Vē. Cāminātaiyar, ed. 6th ed. (reprint). Tanjavur: Kaḻakam, 1985.

The Śatapatha-Brāhmaṇa According to the Text of the Mādhyandina School. J. Eggeling, tr. In 5 parts. *Sacred Books of the East*, M. Mueller, ed. Vols. 12, 26, 41, 43, and 49. Oxford: Clarendon Press, 1882–1900.

Saptarṣi. *Mohini Vilāsa Kuṟavañci.* Tanjavur, 1985.

Sāstriyār, Vē. *Pettalēm (Bethlehem) Kuṟavañci.* Tanjavur, 1800.

Serfoji Rajah. *Devendra Koravañji: A Drama in Marathi Giving the Geography of the World in Songs.* T. L. Thyagaraja Jatavallabhar. Kumbakonam: Tanjore Saraswati Mahal Series No. 18, 1950.

South Indian Inscriptions. E. Hultzsch, ed. 3 vols. Reprint. New Delhi: Navrang, 1987 [1892], 1983 [1892], and 1984 [1895–1913].

Tañcai Veḷḷaippiḷḷaiyār Kuṟavañci. V. Chockalingam, ed. Tanjavur, 1965.

Tēcikar, Ko. Ci. *Carapēntira Pūpāla Kuṟavañci.* Tanjavur, 1940.

Tirukkōvaiyār: Paḻaiya Uraiyum Putiya Viḷakkamum. P. V. Cōmacuntaraṉār, ed. Chennai: Kaḻakam, 1970.

Tirumangai [Kalikaṉṟi]. *Periyatirumōḻi.* P. B. Annankaravariyar, comm. In 4 parts. Kanchipuram: Granthamala Office, 1956–1970.

———. Uttamur T. Virarakavacariyan, comm. Vol. 5. Madras: The Visishtadvaita Pracharini Sabha, 1970.

Tiyakēcar Kuṟavañci. V. Premalatha, ed. Tanjavur, 1970.

Tolkāppiyam. Eḻuttatikāram. Naccinārkkiṉiyar, comm. K. Subramaniyam Pillai, ed. Madras: Kaḻakam, 1944, 1972.

———. *The Earliest Extant Tamil Grammar: Text in Tamil and Roman Scripts with a Critical Commentary in English.* P. S. Subrahmanya Sastri, tr. and comm. Parts 1–3, "*Poruḷatikāram:* Tamil Poetics." Madras: Kuppuswami Sastri Research Institute, 1952, 1956, and 1959.

———. *In English with Critical Studies.* S. Ilakkuvanar, tr. Madurai: Kural Neri Publishing House, 1963.

———. *Poruḷatikāram.* 3 vols. Nacciṉārkkiṉiyar and Pērāciriyar, comms. Ku. Cuntaramūrtti, ed. Annamalainagar: Annamalai University, 1985–86.

———. *Poruḷatikāram.* 3 vols. Iḷampūraṇar, comm. Chennai: Kaḻakam, 1986.

Travancore Archaeological Series. Vol. 3, 1922–23.

Upaniṣads. The Early Upaniṣads: Annotated Text and Translation. J. P. Olivelle, ed. and tr. New York: Oxford University Press, 1998.

Vālmīki. *Rāmāyaṇa.* In 3 parts. 4th ed. Gorakhpur: Gita Press, 1995.

Viṣṇu Purāṇa. H. H. Wilson, ed. and tr. Reprint. Delhi: Nag Publishers, 1980 [1840].

Secondary Sources

Ali, D. S. "Royal Eulogy as World History: Rethinking Copper-plate Inscriptions in Cōḻa India." In *Querying the Medieval: The History of Practice in South Asia.* R. Inden, ed. New York: Oxford University Press, 2000: 165–229.

Ali, S. M. *The Geography of the Purāṇas.* Bombay: Peoples Publishing House, 1966.

Anderson, K. and F. Gale, eds. *Inventing Places: Studies in Cultural Geography.* Melbourne: Longman Cheshire, 1992.

Appadurai, A. *Worship and Conflict Under Colonial Rule.* Cambridge: Cambridge University Press, 1981.

———. "Is Homo Hierarchicus?" In *American Ethnologist* 13/4 (1986): 745–761.

———. "Putting Hierarchy in Its Place." In *Rereading Cultural Anthropology.* G. E. Marcus, ed. Durham: Duke University Press, 1992.

———. "Number in the Colonial Imagination." In *Orientalism and the Postcolonial Predicament: Perspectives on South Asia.* C. A. Breckenridge and P. van der Veer, eds. Philadelphia: University of Pennsylvania Press, 1993: 314–339.

———and C. Breckenridge. "The South Indian Temple: Authority, Honor and Redistribution." In *Contributions to Indian Sociology* 10/2 (1976): 187–211.

Archer, Mildred. *Company Drawings in the India Office Library.* London: H. M. Stationery Office, 1972.

———. *Company Paintings.* London: Victoria and Albert Museum, 1992.

Arunachalam, M. *Tamiḻ Ilakkiya Varalāṟu, Tamiḻ Pulavar Varalāṟu: Patimūṉṟām Nūṟṟāṇṭu.* Tirucchitrambalam: Gandhi Vidyalayam, 1970.

Assayag, J. *La Colére de la Déesse Decapitée: Traditions, Cultes et Pouvoir dans le Sud de l'Inde.* Paris: CNRS Editions, 1992.

Athreya, V., G. Böklin, G. Djurfeldt, and S. Lindberg. "Identification of Agrarian Classes: A Methodological Essay with Empirical Material from South India." In *Journal of Peasant Studies* 14/2 (1987): 147–190.

Austin, J. *How to Do Things with Words.* Cambridge: Harvard University Press, 1962.

Babb, L. A. *The Divine Hierarchy: Popular Hinduism in Central India.* New York: Columbia University Press, 1975.

Bachelard, G. *The Poetics of Space.* M. Jolas, tr. Boston: Beacon Press, 1969 [1958].

Balasubrahmanyam, S. R. *Middle Chola Temples (A.D. 985–1070).* Faridabad: Thomson, 1975.

———. *Four Chola Temples.* Bombay: N. M. Tripathi, 1963.

Balslev, A. N. *A Study of Time in Indian Philosophy.* Weisbaden: Harrassowitz, 1983.

Bäumer, B., ed. *Kālatattvakośa: A Lexicon of Fundamental Concepts of the Indian Arts: Concepts of Time and Space.* 2 vols. Delhi: Motilal Banarsidass, 1992.

Beal, S. *The Life of Hiuen-Tsiang by the Shaman Hwui Li (with an Introduction Containing an Account of the Works of I-Tsing).* London: Kegan Paul, Trench, Trubner and Co., 1914.

Beck, B. E. F. "Colour and Heat in South Indian Ritual." In *Man* 4 (1969): 553–572.

———. "Body Imagery in the Tamil Proverbs of South India." In *Western Folklore* 38/1 (1979): 21–41.

———. "The Goddess and the Demon: A Local South Indian Festival and its Wider Contexts." (In *Autour de la Déesse Hindoue.* M. Biardeau, ed.) *Puruṣārtha* 5 (1981): 85–136.

———. *Peasant Society in Konku: A Study of Right and Left Subcastes in South India.* Vancouver: University of British Columbia Press, 1972.

———. "The Symbolic Merger of Body, Space and Cosmos in Hindu Tamil Nadu." In *Contributions to Indian Sociology* 10/2 (1976): 213–243.

Benveniste, E. *Problems in General Linguistics.* Coral Gables: University of Miami Press, 1971 [1966].

Béteille, A. *Studies in Agrarian Social Structure.* Delhi: Oxford University Press, 1974.

———. "Social Organization of Temples in a Tanjore Village." *History of Religions* 5/1 (1965): 74–92.

———. *Caste, Class and Power.* Berkeley: University of California Press, 1965.

Bharathi, B. S. "Spirit Possession and Healing Practices in a South Indian Fishing Community." In *Man in India* 73/4 (1993): 343–352.

Bhatia, P. *The Paramāras.* Delhi: Munshiram Manoharlal, 1970.

Biardeau, M. "La Décapitation de Renukā dans le Mythe de Paraśurāma." In *Pratidānam: Indian, Iranian and Indo-European Studies Presented to Franciscus Bernardus Jacobus Kuiper on his Sixtieth Birthday.* J. C. Heesterman, G. H. Schokker, and V. I. Subramoniam, eds. The Hague: Mouton, 1968.

———. *Histoires de Poteaux: Variations Védiques autour de la Déesse Hindoue.* Paris: École Française d'Extrême-Orient 154, 1989.

Blackburn, S. H. *Singing of Birth and Death: Texts in Performance.* Philadelphia: University of Pennsylvania Press, 1988.

Bloch, M. *Feudal Society.* Vol. 1. London: Routledge, 1982.

Boddy, J. "Spirit Possession Revisited: Beyond Instrumentality." In *Annual Review of Anthropology* 23 (1994): 407–434.

Bourdieu, P. *Outline of a Theory of Practice.* R. Nice, tr. Cambridge: Cambridge University Press, 1977.

———. *Distinction.* R. Nice, tr. Cambridge: Harvard University Press, 1984.

Brow, J. "Class Formation and Ideological Practice: A Case from Sri Lanka." In *The Journal of Asian Studies* 40/4 (1981): 703–718.

Caldwell, R. "Religion of the Shanars." In *Genealogy of the South-Indian Gods.* B. Ziegenbalg, ed. New Delhi: Unity Book Service, 1984: 156–176.

Caplan, L. *Class and Culture in Urban India: Fundamentalism in a Christian Community.* Oxford: Clarendon Press, 1987.

———. *Religion and Power: Essays on the Christian Community of Madras.* Madras: The Christian Literature Society, 1989.

Caplan, P. *Class and Gender in India: Women and their Organizations in a South Indian City.* London: Tavistock Publications, 1985.

Carter, P. *The Road to Botany Bay: An Exploration in Landscape and History.* Chicago: University of Chicago Press, 1987.

Chakrabarty, D. "Open Space/Public Place: Garbage, Modernity and India." In *South Asia* 14/1 (1991): 15–31.

Chakravarti, A. *Jain Literature in Tamil.* Rev. ed. Arrah: Jaina Siddhanta Bhavana, 1974 [1944].

Chatterjee, P. *The Nation and its Fragments: Colonial and Postcolonial Histories.* Princeton: Princeton University Press, 1993.

Childers, H. "Banjara." In *Pastoralists and Nomads in South Asia.* G. Sontheimer and L. Leshnik, eds. Weisbaden: Harrassowitz, 1975: 247–265.

Clifford, J. *The Predicament of Culture.* Cambridge: Harvard University Press, 1988.

Cohn, B. S. *An Anthropologist Among the Historians and Other Essays.* Delhi: Oxford University Press, 1987.

Cole, S. L. *The Absent One: Mourning Ritual, Tragedy, and the Performance of Ambivalence.* University Park: Pennsylvania State University Press, 1985.

Crane, R. I., ed. *Regions and Regionalism in South Asian Studies; An Exploratory Study.* Duke University Program in Comparative Studies in Southern Asia, Monographs and Occasional Papers 5, 1967.

Csordas, T. J. "Imaginal Performance and Memory in Ritual Healing." In *The Performance of Healing.* C. Laderman and M. Roseman, eds. New York: Routledge 1996: 91–113.

Cutler, N. *Songs of Experience: The Poetics of Tamil Devotion.* Bloomington: Indiana University Press, 1987.

Dagens, B. *Architecture in the Ajitāgama and the Rauravāgama.* Delhi: Sitaram Bharatiya Institute of Scientific Research, 1984.

Dallapiccola, A. L. and S. Z. Lallemant. *Vijayanagara: City and Empire: New Currents of Research.* 2 vols. Stuttgart: Franz Steiner, 1985.

Daniel, E. V. *Fluid Signs: Being a Person the Tamil Way.* Berkeley: University of California Press, 1984.

———. *Charred Lullabies: Chapters in an Anthropography of Violence.* Princeton: Princeton University Press, 1996.

Davis, R. *Ritual in an Oscillating Universe: Worshiping Śiva in Medieval India.* Princeton: Princeton University Press, 1991.

de Certeau, M. *The Practice of Everyday Life.* Berkeley: University of California Press, 1984.

de Heusch, L. *Why Marry Her? Society and Symbolic Structures.* J. Lloyd, tr. Cambridge/Paris: Cambridge University Press and Éditions de la Maison de Sciences de l'Homme, 1981.

Derné, S. "Hindu Men Talk about Controlling Women: Cultural Ideas as a Tool of the Powerful." In *Sociological Perspectives* 37/2 (1994): 203–227.

Desai, P. B. *Jainism in South India and Some Jaina Epigraphs.* Sholapur: Jain Samskrti Samrakshaka Sangha, 1957.

Dharmapal, G. *La Religion des Malabars: Tessier de Quérlay et la Contribution des Missionaires Européens à la Naissance de l'Indianisme.* Immensée, Switzerland: Nouvelle Revue de Science Missionaire, 1982.

Dhere, R. C. and T. Bhavalkar. *Mahāmāyā.* Pune: Ajinkya, 1975.

Dickey, Sara. "Anjali's Prospects: Class Mobility in Urban India." In *Everyday Life in South Asia.* D. Mines and S. Lamb, eds. Bloomington: Indiana University Press, 2002.

———. "Mutual Exclusions: Domestic Workers and Employers on Labor, Class and Character in South India." In *Home and Hegemony: Domestic Service and Identity Politics in South and Southeast Asia.* S. Dickey and K. M. Adams, eds. Ann Arbor: University of Michigan Press, 2000: 31–62.

———. *Cinema and the Urban Poor in South India.* Cambridge: Cambridge University Press, 1993a.

———. "The Politics of Adulation: Cinema and the Production of Politicians in South India." In *The Journal of Asian Studies* 52/2 (1993b): 340–372.

Di Leonardo, M. "The Female World of Cards and Holidays: Women, Families, and the Work of Kinship." In *Signs* 12/3 (1987): 440–453.

Dirks, N. *The Hollow Crown: Ethnohistory of an Indian Kingdom.* Cambridge: Cambridge University Press, 1987.

———. "The Pasts of a *Pālaiyakārar:* The Ethnohistory of a South Indian Little King." In *The Journal of Asian Studies* 41/4 (1982): 655–683.

Doniger, W. *Hindu Myths.* Ed. and tr, Penguin, 1975.

———. *Asceticism and Eroticism in the Mythology of Śiva.* Oxford: Oxford University Press, 1973.

———. *The Origins of Evil in Hindu Mythology.* Delhi: Motilal Banarsidass, 1976.

———. *Women, Androgynes, and Other Mythical Beasts.* Chicago: University of Chicago Press, 1980.

Douglas, M. *Purity and Danger: An Analysis of the Concepts of Pollution and Taboo.* London: Routledge and Kegan Paul, 1966.

Dumont, L. *A South Indian Subcaste: Social Organization and Religions of the Pramalai Kallar.* Delhi: Oxford University Press, 1986 [1957].

———. *Homo Hierarchicus: The Caste System and its Implications.* Chicago: University of Chicago Press, 1970.

———and D. F. Pocock. "Possession and Priesthood." In *Contributions to Indian Sociology* 3 (1959): 55–75.

Duncan, J. and D. Ley, eds. *Place/Culture/Representation.* London: Routledge, 1993.

Dutt, N. *Buddhist Sects in India.* Calcutta: Firma KLM, 1977 [1970].

Dyczkowski, M. S. G. *The Canon of the Śaivāgama and the Kubjikā Tantras of the Western Kaula Tradition.* Albany: State University of New York Press, 1988.

Edney, M. *Mapping an Empire: The Geographical Construction of British India, 1765–1843.* Chicago: University of Chicago Press, 1997.

Elmore, W. T. *Dravidian Gods in Modern Hinduism.* New Delhi: Asian Educational Services, 1984 [1913].

Encyclopaedia of Indian Temple Architecture. M. W. Meister, ed. In 2 parts. New Delhi and Philadelphia: American Institute of Indian Studies/University of Pennsylvania Press, 1983, 1986.

Erdman, J. L. "Dance Discourses: Rethinking the History of the 'Oriental Dance.'" In *Moving Words: Rethinking Dance.* G. Morris, ed. London: Routledge, 1996: 288–305.

Feld, S. and K. K. Basso, eds. *Senses of Place.* Santa Fe: School of American Research Press, 1996.

Ferguson, H. *The Science of Pleasure: Cosmos and Psyche in the Bourgeois World View.* London: Routledge, 1990.

Filliozat, J. "Gopura 'Porte de Ville'." In *Journal Asiatique* 247 (1959): 250–275.

Foucault, M. *Power/Knowledge: Selected Interviews and Other Writings.* C. Gordon, ed. New York: Pantheon Books, 1980.

Foulkes, T. "Grant of the Pallava King Nandi Varma." In *Indian Antiquary* 8 (1879): 167–173.

Freed, S. A. and R. S. Freed. "Spirit Possession as Illness in a North Indian Village." In *Ethnology* 3/2 (1964): 152–171.

———. *Ghosts: Life and Death in North India.* Anthropological Papers of the American Museum of Natural History, 72. Seattle: University of Washington Press, 1993.

Fuller, C. *The Camphor Flame.* Princeton: Princeton University Press, 1992.

———. "The Hindu Pantheon and the Legitimation of Hierarchy." In *Man* 23 (1987): 19–39.

Gandhi, M. *On the Mythology of Indian Plants.* Calcutta: Rupa, 1989.

Geertz, C. "Afterword." In *Senses of Place.* S. Feld and K. K. Basso, eds. Santa Fe: School of American Research Press, 1996: 260–262.

———. "Anti Anti-Relativism." In *American Anthropologist* 86 (1984): 263–278.

Genette, G. *Narrative Discourse: An Essay in Method.* J. E. Lewin, tr. Ithaca: Cornell University Press, 1980.

Godelier, M. *The Mental and the Material: Thought, Economy and Society.* M. Thom, tr. New York: Verso, 1984.

Goetz, H. *The Art of India: Five Thousand Years of Indian Art.* New York: McGraw-Hill, 1959.

Goffman, Erving, "Footing." In *Semiotica* 5/1–2 (1979): 1–29.

———. *Stigma: Notes on the Management of Spoiled Identity.* Englewood Cliffs: Prentice-Hall, 1963.

Gole, S. *Indian Maps and Plans.* New Delhi: Manohar, 1989.

Good, Anthony. "The Annual Goddess Festival in a South Indian Village." In *South Asian Social Scientist* 1/2 (1985): 119–167.

Gopalan, L. V. *Sri Vaishnava Divya Desams (108 Tiruppathis Sung by Azhwars); Along With a Selected List of Some Abhimana Sthalams in India.* Madras: Sri Visishtadvaitha Pracharini Sabha, 1972.

Gopalan, R. *History of the Pallavas of Kanchi.* S. Krishnaswamy Aiyangar, ed. Madras: University of Madras, 1928.

Gopinatha Rao, T. A. *Travancore Archaeological Series.* Vol. 1. Madras: Methodist Publishing House, 1910–13.

Government of India. Census of India 1991, Series 23, Tamil Nadu, Provisional Population Totals, Supplement to Paper-1 of 1991. Delhi.

Gurney, I. *Poems of Ivor Gurney.* London: Chatto and Windus, 1973.

Hanchett, S. *Colored Rice: Symbolization in Hindu Family Festivals.* Delhi: Hindustan Publishing Corp., 1988.

Hansen, K. T. "Domestic Trials: Power and Autonomy in Domestic Service in Zambia." In *American Ethnologist* 17/2 (1990): 360–375.

Harle, J. C. *Temple Gateways in South India.* Oxford: Cassirer, 1963.

Harper, E. "A Hindu Village Pantheon." In *Southwestern Journal of Anthropology* 15 (1959): 227–234.

Harper, E. B. "Spirit Possession and Social Structure." In *Anthropology on the March.* B. Ratnam, ed. Madras: The Book Centre, 1963.

Hart, G. L. *The Poems of Ancient Tamil: Their Milieu and their Sanskrit Counterparts.* Berkeley: University of California Press, 1975.

Hatch, H. J. *The Land Pirates of India.* London: Seeley, 1928.

Heitzman, J. *Gifts of Power: Lordship in an Early Indian State.* Delhi: Oxford University Press, 1997.

Heston, A. "Poverty in India: Some Recent Policies." In *India Briefing: 1990.* M. M. Bouton and P. Oldenburg, eds. Boulder: Westview Press, 1990.

Hiltebeitel, A. *Criminal Gods and Demon Devotees: Essays on the Guardians of Popular Hinduism.* Albany: State University of New York Press, 1989.

———. *The Cult of Draupadī.* 2 vols. Chicago: University of Chicago Press, 1988, 1991.

Hirsch, E. and M. O'Hanlon, eds. *The Anthropology of Landscape: Perspectives on Place and Space.* Oxford: Clarendon Press, 1995.

Holmström, M. *Industry and Inequality: The Social Anthropology of Indian Labour.* Cambridge: Cambridge University Press, 1984.

Hudson, D. D. "Kanchipuram." In *Temple Towns of Tamil Nadu.* G. Michell, ed. Bombay: Marg Publications, 1993a: 18–39.

———. "Krishna's Mandala and the *Bhagavad-gītā.*" *Journal of Vaiṣṇava Studies* 1/1 (2002): 81–130.

———. "Vāsudeva Kṛṣṇa in Theology and Architecture: A Background to Śrīvaiṣṇavism." *Journal of Vaiṣṇava Studies* 2/1 (1993b): 139–170.

———. "Vraja Among the Tamils: A Study of the Bhāgavatas in Early South India." In *Journal of Vaiṣṇava Studies* 3/1 (1994): 113–140.

———. "The *Śrimad Bhāgavata Purāṇa* in Stone: The Text as an Eighth-century Temple and its Implications." *Journal of Vaiṣṇava Studies* 3/3 (1995): 137–182.

———. "The Courtesan and her Bowl: An Esoteric Reading of the *Maṇimēkalai.*" In *A Buddhist Woman's Path to Enlightenment.* P. Schalk, ed. *Historia Religionum* 13. Uppsala: Acta Universitatis Upsaliensis (1997): 151–190.

———. "Pallavamalla's Bhāgavata Rites in Kalikaṉṟi's Poems." In *The Body of God: An Emperor's Palace for Krishna in Eighth-century Kanchipuram* (forthcoming).

Huntington, S. *The Art of Ancient India.* New York: Weatherhill, 1985.

Hymes, D. "Sociolinguistics and the Ethnography of Speaking." In *Social Anthropology and Language.* E. Ardener, ed. London: Tavistock Publications, 1971: 47–93.

Inden, R. "The Temple and the Hindu Chain of Being." In *Puruṣārtha* 8 (1985): 53–73.

———. *Imagining India.* London: Blackwell Press, 1990.

———. "Lordship and Caste in Hindu Discourse." In *Indian Religion.* A. Cantile and R. Burghart, eds. London: Curzon Press, 1985.

Inglis, S. "Possession and Pottery: Serving the Divine in a South Indian Community." In *Gods of Flesh, Gods of Stone: The Embodiment of Divinity in India.* J. Waghorne and N. Cutler, eds. Chambersburg: Anima, 1985: 89–101.

Irschick, E. F. *Politics and Social Conflict in South India: The Non-brahman Movement and Tamil Separatism 1916–1929.* Berkeley: University of California Press, 1969.

Irwin, J. "'Aśokan' Pillars: A Reassessment of the Evidence-IV: Symbolism." In *Burlington* 118 (1976): 734–752.

Jagor, F. "Berichte über verschiedene Völkerstämme in Vorderindien." In *Zeitschrift für Ethnologie* 26 (1894): 61–93.

Jaiswal, S. *The Origin and Development of Vaiṣṇavism.* Delhi: Munshiram Manoharlal, 1967.

Jouveau-Dubrueil, G. *Archaeologie du Sud de l'Inde.* Paris: P. Geuthner, 1917.

Kailasapathy, K. *Tamil Heroic Poetry.* Oxford: Oxford University Press, 1968.

Kakar, S. *Shamans, Mystics, and Doctors: A Psychological Inquiry into India and its Healing Traditions.* New York: Knopf, 1982.

Kalpagam, U. "Cartography in Colonial India." *Economic and Political Weekly* 30/30 (1995) PE87-PE98.

Kanakasabhai, V. *The Tamils Eighteen Hundred Years Ago.* New Delhi: Asian Educational Services, 1979 [1904].

Kapadia, K. *Siva and her Sisters: Gender, Caste and Class in Rural South India.* Boulder: Westview Press, 1995.

Kapferer, B. *A Celebration of Demons.* Bloomington: Indiana University Press, 1991 [1983].

Kersenboom-Story, S. C. "Viṟali." In *Journal of Tamil Studies* 19 (1981): 19–41.

Koyré, A. *From Closed World to the Infinite Universe.* Baltimore: Johns Hopkins University Press, 1957.

Kramrisch, S. *The Hindu Temple.* Calcutta: University of Calcutta, 1946.

Kumar, D. "Private Property in Asia? The Case of Medieval South India." In *Comparative Studies in Society and History* 27/2 (1985): 340–366.

Kumar, N. *The Artisans of Banaras: Popular Culture and Identity, 1880–1986.* Princeton: Princeton University Press, 1988.

———. "Work and Leisure in the Formation of Identity: Muslim Weavers in a Hindu

City." In *Culture and Power in Benares: Community, Performance and Environment 1800–1980.* S. B. Freitag, ed. Delhi: Oxford University Press, 1989: 147–170.

Larson, G. *Classical Sāṃkhya: An Interpretation of its History and Meaning.* Delhi: Motilal Banarsidass, 1979.

Lee, S. *A History of Far Eastern Art.* New York: Abrams, 1982.

Lewis, I. M. "Spirit Possession and Deprivation Cults." In *Man* 1/3 (1966): 307–329.

———. *Ecstatic Religion: An Anthropological Study of Spirit Possession and Shamanism.* Harmondsworth: Penguin Books, 1971.

———. *Religion in Context: Cults and Charisma.* Cambridge: Cambridge University Press, 1986.

Lockwood, M. *Māmallapuram and the Pallavas.* Madras: The Christian Literature Society, 1982.

Lovejoy, A. O. *The Great Chain of Being: A Study in the History of an Idea.* Cambridge: Harvard University Press, 1966.

Ludden, D. *Peasant History in South India.* Princeton: Princeton University Press, 1985.

Mahalingam, T. V. "The Pullur Plates of Nandivarman II Pallavamalla—Year 33." *Epigraphia Indica* 36 (1959): 144–163.

———. *Kancipuram in Early South Indian History.* Bombay: Asia Publishing House, 1969.

———. *Readings in South Indian History.* Delhi: R. R. Publishing Corp., 1977.

Majumdar, R. C. *History of Ancient Bengal.* Calcutta: G. Bharadwaj, 1971.

Malten, T. "Von Dschakaljägern, Akrobaten, und Fahrenden Händlern." *Forschung: Zeitschrift der DFG* (1989).

Mandal, K. K. *A Comparative Study of the Concepts of Space and Time in Indian Thought.* Varanasi: Chowkhamba Publications, 1968.

Marr, J. R. *The Eight Anthologies: A Study in Early Tamil Literature.* Madras: Institute of Asian Studies, 1985.

Marriott, M. "Caste Ranking and Food Transactions: A Matrix Analysis." In *Structure and Change in Indian Society.* M. Singer and B. S. Cohn, eds. Chicago: Aldine Publishing, 1968: 133–171.

———, ed. *India Through Hindu Categories.* Delhi: Sage Publications, 1990.

———and R. Inden. "Toward an Ethnosociology of South Asian Caste Systems." In *The New Wind.* K. David, ed. The Hague: Mouton, 1977: 227–238.

Marx, K. "On the Jewish Question." In *Collected Works.* Vol. 3. New York: International Publishers, 1975.

———. *Capital.* D. Fernback, tr. Vol. 3. Harmondsworth: Penguin, 1981.

———. *Grundrisse.* M. Nicolaus, tr. Harmondsworth: Penguin, 1973.

Masilamani-Meyer, E. *Aṅkāḷaparamēcuvari: A Goddess of Tamilnadu: Her Myths and Cult.* Stuttgart: Franz Steiner Verlag, 1986.

Masselos, J. "Appropriating Urban Space: Social Constructs of Bombay in the Time of the Raj." In *South Asia* 14/1 (1991): 33–63.

McKnight, J. M., Jr. "Kingship and Religion in India's Gupta Age: An Analysis of the Role of Vaiṣṇavism in the Lives and Ideology of the Gupta Kings." In *Journal of the American Academy of Religion* 45/2 (supplement, 1977): 677–701.

Michell, G. *The Hindu Temple.* Chicago: University of Chicago Press, 1977.

Mines, D. P. "Hindu Nationalism, Untouchable Reform, and the Ritual Making of a

South Indian Village." In *American Ethnologist* 29/1 (2002): 58–85.
———. *Making and Remaking the Village: The Pragmatics of Social Life in Rural Tamilnadu.* Ph.D. dissertation, University of Chicago, 1995.
Mines, M. *Public Faces, Private Voices: Community and Individuality in South India.* Berkeley: University of California Press, 1994.
Moffatt, M. *An Untouchable Community of South India: Structure and Consensus.* Princeton: Princeton University Press, 1979.
Mōkaṉ, M. and N. *Kuṟavañci.* Madurai: Muttu, 1977.
Mōkaṉ, N. *Kuṟavañci Ilakkiyam.* Madurai, 1985.
Monier-Williams, M. *A Sanskrit-English Dictionary.* Oxford: Clarendon Press, 1964 [1899].
Moore, M. "The Kerala House as a Hindu Cosmos." In *India Through Hindu Categories.* M. Marriott, ed. New Delhi: Sage Publications, 1990: 169–202.
Moran, M. H. "Civilized Servants: Child Fosterage and Training for Status among the Glebo of Liberia." In *African Encounters with Domesticity.* K. T. Hansen, ed. New Brunswick: Rutgers University Press, 1992: 98–115.
Moreno, M. "God's Forceful Call: Possession as a Divine Strategy." In *Gods of Flesh, Gods of Stone: The Embodiment of Divinity in India.* J. Waghorne and N. Cutler, eds. Chambersburg: Anima, 1985: 103–120.
Mosse, D. *Caste, Christianity and Hinduism: A Study of Social Organization and Religion in Rural Ramnad.* Thesis, Oxford University, 1986.
———. "Catholic Saints and the Hindu Village Pantheon in Rural Tamil Nadu, India." In *Man* 29/2 (1994): 301–332.
Muilwijk, M. *The Divine Kuṟa Tribe: Kuṟavañci and Tamil Prabandhas.* Groningen: Egbert Forsten, 1996.
Nabokov, I. "When the Dead become Brides, Gods, and Gold: Marriage Symbolism in a Tamil Household Ritual." In *Journal of Ritual Studies* 10/1 (1996): 113–133.
———. *"Who Are You?" Spirit Discourse in a Tamil World.* Ph.D. dissertation, University of California-Berkeley, 1995.
Nagaswamy, R. *The Kailasanatha Temple (A Guide).* State Department of Archaeology, Government of Tamilnadu, 1969.
Narain, A. K. "Religious Policy and Toleration in Ancient India with Particular Reference to the Gupta Age." In *Essays on Gupta Culture.* B. L. Smith, ed. Delhi: Motilal Banarsidass, 1983: 17–52.
Nilakanta Sastri, K. A. *A History of South India.* Delhi: Oxford University Press, 1992.
———. *The Culture and History of the Tamils.* Calcutta: Firma K. L. Mukhopadhay, 1964.
———. *The Cōḷas.* Madras: University of Madras, 1955.
Obeyesekere, G. "The Ritual Drama of the *Sanni* Demons: Collective Representations of Disease in Ceylon." In *Comparative Studies in Society and History* 11 (1969): 175–216.
———. "The Idiom of Demonic Possession: A Case Study." In *Social Science and Medicine* 4 (1970): 97–111.
———. "Psychocultural Exegesis of a Case of Spirit Possession in Sri Lanka." In *Case Studies in Spirit Possession.* V. Crapanzano and V. Garrison, eds. New York: John Wiley, 1977: 235–294.
———. *Medusa's Hair: An Essay on Personal Symbols and Religious Experience.* Chi-

cago: University of Chicago Press, 1981.

Oppert, G. *On the Original Inhabitants of Bhāratavarṣa or India.* Westminster: Constable, 1893.

Ortner, S. L. "Reading America: Preliminary Notes on Class and Culture." In *Recapturing Anthropology: Working in the Present.* R. G. Fox, ed. Santa Fe: School of American Research Press, 1991: 163–189.

Paramasivam, K. "Relative Chronology of *Tolkāppiyam* and Early Sangam." In *Studies in Dravidian Linguistics* 10/1. S. Vaidyanatham and J. S. Sidhu, eds. Patiala: Panjabi University, 1980. Offprint.

Parish, S. *Hierarchy and its Discontents.* Philadelphia: University of Pennsylvania Press, 1996.

Parker, S. *Makers of Meaning.* Ph.D. dissertation, University of Chicago, 1989.

———. "Contemporary Temple Construction in South India: The Srirangam Rajagopuram." In *Res* 21 (1992): 110–123.

Pāskaratttoṇṭaimāṉ, T. M. *Vēṅkaṭam Mutal Kumari Varai.* 4 vols. Tirunelveli: S. R. Subramaniya Pillai, 1967.

Pate, H. R. *Tinnevelly District Gazetteer.* Madras: Government Press, 1917.

Peabody, N. "In Whose Turban does the Lord Reside?: The Objectification of Charisma and the Fetishism of Objects in the Hindu Kingdom of Kota." In *Comparative Studies in Society and History* 33/4 (1991): 726–754.

Peiper, J. "The Spatial Structure of Suchindram." In *Ritual Spaces in India.* J. Peiper, ed. London: AARP 1980: 65–80.

Peterson, I. V. *Poems to Śiva: The Hymns of the Tamil Saints.* Princeton: Princeton University Press, 1989.

———. "The Evolution of the Kuṟavañci Dance Drama in Tamilnadu: Negotiating the 'Folk' and the 'Classical' in the Bharata Natyam Canon." In *South Asia Research* 18/1 (1998): 39–72.

———. "The Cabinet of King Serfoji of Tanjore: A European Collection in Early Nineteenth-century India." In *Journal of the History of Collections* 11/1 (1999a): 71–93.

———. "Science in the Tranquebar Mission Curriculum: Natural Theology and Indian Responses." In *Missionberichte aus Indien im 18. Jahrhundert: Ihre Bedeutung für die Europäische Geistesgeschicte und ihr Wissenschaftlicher Quellenwert für die Indienkunde.* M. Bergunder, ed. Vol. 1. Halle: Verlag der Franckeschen Stiftungen, 1999b: 175–219.

Poulet, G. "Criticism and the Experience of Interiority." In *Reader-Response Criticism: From Formalism to Structuralism.* J. P. Tompkins, ed. Baltimore: Johns Hopkins University Press, 1980: 41–49.

Pramar, V. S. "Sociology of the North Gujarat Urban House." In *Contributions to Indian Sociology* 21/2 (1987): 331–345.

Purnalingam Pillai, M. S. *Tamil India.* Madras: Kaḻakam, 1927–1963.

Raheja, G. G. *The Poison in the Gift: Ritual, Prestation, and the Dominant Caste in a North Indian Village.* Chicago: University of Chicago Press, 1988.

———and A. G. Gold. *Listen to the Heron's Words: Reimagining Gender and Kinship in North India.* Berkeley: University of California Press, 1994.

Raju, S. and D. Bagchi, eds. *Women and Work in South Asia: Regional Patterns and Per-*

spectives. London: Routledge, 1993.

Ram, K. *Mukkuvar Women: Gender, Hegemony and Capitalist Transformation in a South Indian Fishing Community.* Delhi: Kali for Women, 1991.

Raman, B. V. *Astrology for Beginners.* Bangalore: IBH Prakashana, 1976.

Raman, K. V. "Archaeological Excavations in Kanchipuram." In *Tamil Civilization* 5/1–2 (n.d.): 61–72.

———. *Sri Varadarājaswāmi Temple—Kanchi: A Study of its History, Art and Architecture.* Delhi: Abhinav Publications, 1975.

Ramanujan, A. K. "Classics Lost and Found." In *Contemporary Indian Tradition: Voices on Culture, Nature, and the Challenge of Change.* C. M. Borden, ed. Washington, D.C.: Smithsonian Institution Press, 1989: 131–146.

———. "Three Hundred *Rāmāyaṇas.*" In *Many Rāmāyaṇas: The Diversity of a Narrative Tradition.* P. Richman, ed. Berkeley: University of California Press, 1991: 22–49.

———. "Two Realms of Kannada Folklore." In *Another Harmony: New Essays on the Folklore of India.* S. H. Blackburn and A. K. Ramanujan, eds. Berkeley: University of California Press, 1986: 41–75.

———. "Telling Tales." In *Daedalus: Journal of the American Academy of Arts and Sciences* 118/4 (1989): 239–262.

Ramaswamy, S. *Passions of the Tongue: Language Devotion in Tamil India, 1891–1970.* Berkeley: University of California Press, 1997.

———. "Catastrophic Cartographies: Mapping the Lost Continent of Lemuria." In *Representations* 67 (1999): 66–103.

Ranade, H. G. *Brahmatva-Manjari: Role of the Brahman Priest in the Vedic Ritual.* Poona, 1984.

Rao, M. S. A. "Some Conceptual Issues in the Study of Caste, Class, Ethnicity and Dominance." In *Dominance and State Power in Modern India.* F. R. Frankel and M. S. A. Rao, eds. Delhi: Oxford University Press, 1989: 21–45.

Rao, V. N., D. Shulman, and S. Subrahmanyam, eds. *Symbols of Substance: Court and State in Nāyaka Period Tamilnadu.* Delhi: Oxford University Press, 1992.

Reiniche, M. *Les Dieux et les Hommes: Études des Cultes d'un Village du Tirunelveli Inde du Sud.* Paris: Mouton, 1979.

———. "Les Démons et leurs Cultes dans la Structure du Panthéon d'un Village du Tirunelveli." In *Puruṣārtha* 2 (1975): 173–203.

Richman, P., ed. *Many Rāmāyaṇas: The Diversity of a Narrative Tradition in South Asia.* Berkeley: University of California Press, 1991.

———. *Women, Branch Stories, and Religious Rhetoric in a Tamil Buddhist Text.* Syracuse: Maxwell School of Citizenship and Public Affairs, Syracuse University, 1988.

Rowland, B. *The Art and Architecture of India.* Harmondsworth: Penguin, 1967.

Sax, W. *Mountain Goddess: Gender and Politics in a Himalayan Pilgrimage.* New York: Oxford University Press, 1991.

Schwartzberg, J. "South Asian Cartography." In *Cartography in the Traditional Islamic and South Asian Societies.* J. B. Harley and D. Woodward, eds. Chicago: University of Chicago Press, 1992.

Scott, D. "The Cultural Politics of Eyesight in Sri Lanka: Composure, Vulnerability, and the Sinhala Concept of Ditiya." In *Dialectal Anthropology* 16 (1991): 85–102.

———. *Formations of Ritual: Colonial and Anthropological Discourses on the Sinhala*

Yaktovil. Minneapolis: University of Minnesota Press, 1994.

Scott, J. *Domination and the Arts of Resistance: Hidden Transcripts.* New Haven: Yale University Press, 1990.

Seizer, S. "Hurt 'til It Laughs: Domestic Violence on the Tamil Popular Stage." Paper presented at the Conference on Visual Media, Mass Communication, and Violence in South Asia, Center for Asian Studies, University of Texas at Austin, April 2001.

———. "Jokes, Gender, and Discursive Distance on the Tamil Popular Stage." In *American Ethnologist* 24/1 (1997): 62–90.

———. "Roadwork: Offstage with Special Drama Actresses in Tamilnadu, South India." In *Cultural Anthropology* 15/2 (2000): 217–259.

Sen, S. "The Colonial Mapping of India: A Study in the History of Cartography." Unpublished manuscript, n.d.

Shulman, D. *Tamil Temple Myths: Sacrifice and Divine Marriage in the South Indian Śaiva Tradition.* Princeton: Princeton University Press, 1980.

———. *The King and the Clown in South Indian Myth and Poetry.* Princeton: Princeton University Press, 1985.

Silpi. *Tirunelveli District in Pictures.* Madurai: T.V.S., n.d.

Sircar, D. C. *Cosmography and Geography in Early Indian Literature.* Calcutta: Indian Studies Past and Present, 1967.

———. *Studies in the Geography of Ancient and Medieval India.* Delhi: Motilal Banarsidass, 1971.

Sivathamby, K. *Literary History in Tamil.* Tanjavur: Tamil University, 1986.

Skultans, V. "The Management of Mental Illness among Maharashtrian Families: A Case Study of a Mahanubhav Healing Temple." In *Man* 22 (1987): 661–679.

Skura, M. A. *The Literary Use of the Psychoanalytic Process.* New Haven: Yale University Press, 1981.

Smith, B. K. *Classifying the Universe: The Ancient Indian Varṇa System and the Origins of Caste.* New York: Oxford University Press, 1994.

Smith, H. D. *A Descriptive Bibliography of the Printed Texts of the Pāñcarātrāgama.* 2 vols. Baroda: Oriental Institute, 1975, 1980.

Sopher, D. E. "Place and Landscape in Indian Tradition." In *Landscape* 29/2 (1986): 1–9.

Spencer, G. "The Sacred Geography of the Tamil Shaivite Hymns." In *Numen* 17 (1970): 232–244.

———. *The Politics of Expansion: The Chola Conquest of Sri Lanka and Sri Vijaya.* Madras: New Era Publications, 1983.

Srinivas, M. N. *Religion and Society among the Coorgs of South India.* Oxford: Clarendon Press, 1952.

Srinivasan, C. K. *Maratha Rule in the Carnatic.* Annamalainagar: Annamalai University, 1944.

Srinivasan, C. R. *Kanchipuram Through the Ages.* Delhi: Agam Kala Prakashan, 1979.

Srinivasan, K. R. *Cave-Temples of the Pallavas.* Delhi: Archaeological Survey of India, 1964.

———. "Monuments and Sculpture A.D. 600 to 1000: South India." In *Jaina Art and Architecture: Published on the Occasion of the 2500th Nirvana Anniversary of Tirthamkara Mahāvira.* A. Ghosh, ed. Vol. 2. Delhi: Bharatiya Jnanpith, 1975: 207–238.

———. "Andhras, Ikṣvākus, and Literary Sources." In *Encyclopedia of Indian Temple*

Architecture: South India: Lower Drāvidadeśa. M. Meister, ed. Philadelphia: University of Pennsylvania Press, 1983: 3–21.

Srinivasa Varma, G. *Vaagri Boli: An Indo-Aryan Language.* Department of Linguistics Publication 21. Annamalainagar: Annamalai University, 1970.

Steedley, M. *Hanging Without a Rope.* Princeton: Princeton University Press, 1994.

Stein, B. *Peasant, State and Society in Medieval South India.* Delhi: Oxford University Press, 1980.

Stirrat, R. L. "Demonic Possession in Roman Catholic Sri Lanka." In *Journal of Anthropological Research* 33/2 (1977): 133–157.

———. *Power and Religiosity in a Post-Colonial Setting: Sinhala Catholics in Contemporary Sri Lanka.* Cambridge: Cambridge University Press, 1992.

Subrahmanian, N. *Pre-Pallavan Tamil Index.* Madras: University of Madras, 1966.

Takahashi, T. *Tamil Love Poetry and Poetics.* Leiden: Brill, 1995.

Tamil Lexicon. 6 vols. Madras: University of Madras, 1982 [1935].

Taṇṭapāṇi Tēcikar, C. *Tirukkōvaiyār Uṇmai Viḷakkam.* Tiruvāvaṭuturai: Tiruvāvaṭuturai Ātiṉam, 1965.

Targa, S. "The Pāla Kingdom: Rethinking Lordship in Early Medieval Northeastern India." M.Phil. Dissertation, School of Oriental and African Studies, London, 1997.

Taylor, C., et al. *Multiculturalism: Examining the Politics of Recognition.* Princeton: Princeton University Press, 1994.

Thomas, I. J. "Cultural Developments in Tamil Nadu during the Vijayanagara Period." In *Vijayanagara—City and Empire: New Currents in Research.* A. L. Dallapiccola, ed. 2 vols. Stuttgart: Franz Steiner, 1985: 5–40.

Thurston, E. *Castes and Tribes of Southern India.* 7 vols. Madras, 1909.

Tilley, C. *Reading Material Culture.* Oxford: Blackwell, 1990.

Tolen, R. "Transfers of Knowledge and Privileged Spheres of Practice: Servants and Employers in a Madras Railway Colony." In *Home and Hegemony: Domestic Service and Identity Politics in South and Southeast Asia.* K. M. Adams and S. Dickey, eds. Ann Arbor: University of Michigan Press, 2000: 63–86.

Trawick, M. "Wandering Lost: A Landless Laborer's Sense of Place and Self." In *Gender, Genre and Power in South Asian Expressive Traditions.* A. Appadurai, F. Korom, and M. Mills, eds. Philadelphia: University of Pennsylvania Press, 1991: 224–266.

———. "The Changed Mother, or What the Smallpox Goddess Did When There Was No More Smallpox." In *South Asian Systems of Healing.* E. V. Daniel and J. F. Pugh, eds. *Contributions to Asian Studies* 18. Leiden: Brill, 1984: 24–45.

———. *Notes on Love in a Tamil Family.* Berkeley: University of California Press, 1992.

———. "The Guru in the Garden: Ambiguity in the Oral Exegesis of a Sacred Text." In *Cultural Anthropology* 3/3 (1988): 316–351.

Turner, V. W. *The Forest of Symbols.* Ithaca: Cornell University Press, 1967.

Vatsyayan, K., ed. *Concepts of Space, Ancient and Modern.* Delhi: Abhinav, 1991.

Veluthat, K. *The Political Structure of Early Medieval South India.* Delhi: Orient Longman, 1993.

Venkataraman, K. R. *Devī Kāmākshi in Kanchi (A Short Historical Study).* Madras: R. A. Sattanathan, 1968.

Wadley, S. S. *Struggling with Destiny in Karimpur, 1925–1984.* Berkeley: University of California Press, 1994.

Washbrook, D. A. "Caste, Class and Dominance in Modern Tamil Nadu: Non-Brahmanism, Dravidianism and Tamil Nationalism." In *Dominance and State Power in Modern India.* F. R. Frankel and M. S. A. Rao, eds. Delhi: Oxford University Press, 1989: 204–264.

Watters, T. *On Yuan Chwang's Travels in India (A. D. 629–645).* T. W. Rhys Davids and S. W. Bushell, eds. 2 vols. Delhi: Munshiram Manoharlal, 1961 [1904–05].

Werth, L. *Von Götinnen und Ihre Menschen: Die Vagri, Vaganten Südindiens.* Berlin: Das Arabische Buch, 1996.

Williams, H. L. "The Criminal and Wandering Tribes of India." In *Journal of the Gypsy-Lore Society,* New Series 6 (1912–13): 34–58, 110–135.

Wolpert, S. *A New History of India.* New York: Oxford University Press, 2000.

Yadava, B. N. S. "Immobility and the Subjection of Indian Peasantry in Early Medieval Complex." In *Indian Historical Review* 1/1 (1974): 18–28.

Yocum, G. E. "Shrines, Shamanism, and Love Poetry: Elements in the Emergence of Popular Tamil Bhakti." In *Journal of the American Academy of Religion* 41/1 (1973): 3–17.

Ziegenbalg, B. *Genealogy of the South-Indian Gods.* G. J. Metzger, tr. Delhi: Unity Book Service, 1984 [1867].

Zimmer, H. *The Art of Indian Asia.* Princeton: Princeton University Press, 1955.

Zvelebil, K. *Companion Studies to the History of Tamil Literature.* Leiden: Brill, 1992.

———. *Tamil Literature.* Leiden: Brill, 1975.

———. *Tamil Literature.* In *A History of Indian Literature* vol. 10, fasc. 1. Wiesbaden: Harrassowitz, 1974.

———. *The Smile of Murugan on Tamil Literature of South India.* Leiden: Brill, 1973.

Contributors

Daud Ali lectures in early Indian history at the School of Oriental and African Studies, London. He is editor of *Invoking the Past* (Oxford, 1999) and co-authored (with Ronald Inden and Jonathan Walters) *Querying the Medieval: Texts and the History of Practice in South Asia* (Oxford, 2000). His new book is *Courtly Culture and Political Life in Early Medieval India* (Cambridge, 2004).

Isabelle Clark-Decès is Associate Professor of Anthropology at Princeton University. She is the author (as Isabelle Nabokov) of *Religion Against the Self: An Ethnography of Tamil Rituals* (New York: Oxford University Press, 2000). Her new book is *No One Cries for the Dead: Tamil Dirges, Rowdy Songs, and Graveyard Petitions* (California, 2005).

Norman J. Cutler was Associate Professor of Tamil at the University of Chicago until his death in 2002. He authored *Songs of Experience: The Poetics of Tamil Devotion* (Indiana, 1987) as well as articles that address topics pertinent to Tamil religious and literary culture. His article, "Three Moments in the Genealogy of Tamil Literary Culture," was published posthumously in *Literary Cultures in History: Reconstructions from South Asia,* edited by Sheldon Pollock (California, 2003).

Sara Dickey is Professor of Anthropology at Bowdoin College. She is author of *Cinema and the Urban Poor in South India* (Cambridge, 1993) and co-editor (with Kathleen M. Adams) of *Home and Hegemony: Domestic Service and Identity Politics in South and Southeast Asia* (Michigan 2000). She has recently received major grants from the National Endowment for the Humanities, the Social Science Research Council, and the American Institute of Indian Studies.

D. Dennis Hudson was World Religions Professor Emeritus at Smith College at the time of his death in late 2006. He specialized in the religious history of Tamil-speaking peoples. He authored *Protestant Origins in India: Tamil Evangelical Christians 1706–1835* (Eerdmans, 2000). His study of an eighth-century imperial Viṣṇu-house in Kāñcīpuram, the Vaikuṇṭha Perumāḷ Temple, will be published posthumously as *The Body of God*.

Diane P. Mines is Associate Professor of Anthropology at Appalachian State University in Boone, North Carolina. She has authored several articles on ritual, caste, and politics in rural Tamilnadu, and co-edited (with Sarah Lamb) *Everyday Life in South Asia* (Indiana, 2002). Her new book is *Fierce Gods: Inequality, Ritual, and the Politics of Dignity in a South Indian Village* (Indiana, 2005).

Samuel K. Parker is Associate Professor of Cultural Anthropology and Director of Graduate Study in an innovative Interdisciplinary Arts and Sciences Program developed for the University of Washington's Tacoma campus. He has done fieldwork on contemporary Hindu temple construction in South India and Bali, and has published a number of articles adopting an ethnographic perspective on the subject. His essay, "Unfinished Work at Mamallapuram, or What is an Indian Art Object?," appeared in *Artibus Asiae* in 2001.

Indira Viswanathan Peterson, David B. Truman Professor of Asian Studies at Mount Holyoke College, is the author of *Poems to Śiva: The Hymns of the Tamil Saints* (Princeton, 1989) and *Design and Rhetoric in a Sanskrit Court Epic: The Kirātārjunīya of Bhāravi* (SUNY, 2003) and editor, Indian Literature, *The Norton Anthology of World Literature* (Norton, 2001). She is editor, with Davesh Soneji, of *Performing Pasts: Reinventing the Arts in Modern South India* (Oxford, 2008), and is currently completing a monograph on Tamil Kuṟavañci dramas and a biography of King Serfoji II of Thanjavur. Peterson is a recent recipient of the Rockefeller Foundation's Bellagio residency.

Martha Ann Selby is Associate Professor of South Asian Studies at the University of Texas at Austin. She is author of *Grow Long, Blessed Night: Love Poems from Classical India* (Oxford, 2000) and *The Circle of Six Seasons: Poems from Sanskrit, Prākrit, and Old Tamil* (Penguin, 2003). She is a recent recipient of grants from the John Simon Guggenheim Memorial Foundation and the National Endowment for the Arts, and was recently Walter Jackson Bate Fellow at the Radcliffe Institute for Advanced Study, Harvard University.

Susan Seizer is Associate Professor in the Department of Communication and Culture at Indiana University. Her book, *Stigmas of the Tamil Stage: An Ethnography of Special Drama Artists of South India* (Duke, 2005), was awarded the Anand Kentish Coomaraswamy Book Prize for 2006 by the South Asia Council of the Association for Asian Studies for the best English-language work in South Asian Studies.

Index

Page numbers in **bold** refer to illustrations

www.ingramcontent.com/pod-product-compliance
Lightning Source LLC
LaVergne TN
LVHW040200080826
844660LV00001B/52

* 9 7 8 0 7 9 1 4 7 2 4 5 3 *